THE
BIG HORN

WOOD PELLET GRILL

AND SMOKER

COOKBOOK FOR

BEGINNERS

600 EASY AND TASTY BBQ RECIPES TO MASTER YOUR BIG HORN WOOD PELLET GRILL AND SMOKER

JOSEPH KAHN

CONTENTS

INTRODUCTION 11
How the BIG HORN Wood Pellet Grill Works.. 11
The Benefits of Choosing the BIG HORN Wood Pellet Grill 12
Hints on Using Your BIG HORN Wood Pellet Grill 13
Cleaning Methods for the BIG HORN Wood Pellet Grill 14

BAKING RECIPES 15
Eyeball Cookies 15
Baked Bourbon Monkey Bread 15
Baked Pumpkin Pie 15
Cinnamon Pull-aparts 15
Donut Bread Pudding 16
Baked Potatoes & Celery Root Au Gratin 16
Irish Soda Bread 16
Mint Butter Chocolate Chip Cookies 17
Baked Bourbon Maple Pumpkin Pie 17
Strawberry Basil Daiquiri 18
Beer Bread 18
Baked Chocolate Brownie Cookies With Egg Nog 19
Smoked, Salted Caramel Apple Pie 19
Caramel Bourbon Bacon Brownies 19
Focaccia 20
Chicken Pot Pie 20
Anzac Coconut Biscuits 20
Chili Cheese Fries 21
Spiced Carrot Cake 21
Sweet Cheese Muffins..21
Cornbread Chicken Stuffing 22
Smoked Sweet Beer Bread 22
Smoky Apple Crepes 22
Baked Chocolate Coconut Brownies 23
Smoked Cheesy Alfredo Sauce...........................23
Rosemary Cranberry Apple Sage Stuffing 24
Double Vanilla Chocolate Cake 24
Cherry Ice Cream Cobbler 24
Chicken Pizza On The Grill 24
Blueberry Bread Pudding 25
Spiced Lemon Cherry Pie 25
Pumpkin Bread..26

Smoked Vanilla Apple Pie 26
Italian Herb & Parmesan Scones........................26
Baked Cheesy Parmesan Grits............................27
Vanilla Chocolate Chip Cookies 27
Zucchini Bread 27
Old Fashioned Cornbread 28
Traeger Baked Focaccia 28
Carrot Cake 28
Sourdough Pizza 29
Caramelized Bourbon Baked Pears 29
Blueberry Sour Cream Muffins 29
Chocolate Lava Cake With Smoked Whipped Cream 30
Smoky Pimento Cheese Cornbread 30
Grilled Apple Pie 30
Garlic Cheese Pull Apart Bread..........................31
Basil Margherita Pizza..31
Grilled Bourbon Pecan Pie 31
Baked Pear Tarte Tatin 31
Smoker Wheat Bread..32
Lemon Strawberry Rhubarb Pie 32
Eggs Ham Benedict...33
Quick Baked Dinner Rolls...................................33
Sopapilla Cheesecake By Doug Scheiding...................33
The Dan Patrick Show Pull-apart Pesto Bread...........34
Crescent Rolls 34
Vanilla Chocolate Bacon Cupcakes 34
Maple Syrup Pancake Casserole 34
Lemon Chicken, Broccoli, String Beans Foil Packs.....35
Blueberry Pancakes 35
Ultimate Baked Garlic Bread..............................35
Cake With Smoked Berry Sauce 35
Garlic Lemon Pepper Chicken Wings 36

Cast Iron Pineapple Upside Down Cake 36
Chocolate Peanut Cookies 37
Pull-apart Dinner Rolls 37
Crème Brûlée 37
Baked Peach Cobbler Cupcakes...............................38
Baked Cast Iron Berry Cobbler 38
Smokin' Lemon Bars..38
Green Bean Casserole Circa 1955 39
Smoked Blackberry Pie 39
Baked Molten Chocolate Cake 39
Baked Buttermilk Biscuits 40
Sweet And Spicy Baked Pork Beans 40
Smoked Lemon Cheesecake.....................................40
S'mores Dip Skillet..41

Vanilla Cheesecake Skillet Brownie...........................41
Pineapple Cake 41
Baked Green Chile Mac & Cheese By Doug
Scheiding...42
Onion Cheese Nachos 42
Butternut Squash Macaroni And Cheese 42
Dark Chocolate Brownies With Bacon-salted Caramel43
Savory Cheesecake With Bourbon Pecan Topping......43
Skillet Buttermilk Cornbread 43
Traeger Baked Protein Bars.....................................44
Marbled Brownies With Amaretto & Ricotta............44
Pizza Bites 44
Pretzel Rolls 45

PORK RECIPES..**46**

Beer-braised Cabbage With Bacon...........................46
Spiced Grilled Pork Chops 46
Smoked Pork Tomato Tamales.................................46
Simple Smoked Ribs 47
Hickory Smoked Pork Shoulder 47
Spiced Orange Ribs 47
Everything Pigs In A Blanket 48
Rub-injected Pork Shoulder 48
Beer Braised Garlic Bbq Pork Butt 48
Spicy Bacon Wrapped Grilled Chicken Skewers..........49
Egg Sausage Casserole 49
Smoked Rack Of Pork 49
Cider Glazed Baked Holiday Ham 50
Bbq Pork Belly Burnt Ends 50
Double Smoked Apple Spiral Ham 51
Delicious Smoked Bone-in Pork Chops 51
Smoked Chili Con Queso By Doug Scheiding............51
Onion Pork Shoulder 52
Traeger Pulled Pork Sandwiches..............................52
Hanging St. Louis-style Grilled Ribs........................53
Bourbon Chile Glazed Ham 53
Bbq Pulled Pork Grilled Cheese Sandwich...................53
Smoked Porchetta 54
3-2-1 Bbq Baby Back Ribs.......................................54
Grilled Pork Belly..55
Bacon Wrapped Pickles...55
St. Louis–style Pork Steaks 55

Bbq 3-2-1 St. Louis Ribs...56
Grilled Pork Loin 56
Grilled Raspberry Chipotle Pork Ribs......................56
Smoked Apple Pork Belly 57
Smoked Baby Back Ribs 57
Maple Baked Ham 57
Fast Bbq Spare Ribs...57
Smoke-roasted Beer-braised Brats............................58
Wet-rubbed St. Louis Ribs 58
Smoked Bologna 58
Grilled Pork Tacos Al Pastor....................................59
Spicy Ribs 59
Bbq Pork Short Ribs..59
Holiday Smoked Cheese Log 60
Bbq Pork Shoulder Roast With Sugar Lips Glaze 60
Honey Glazed Pork Chops.......................................60
Pork Loin Porchetta 61
Baked Honey Glazed Ham.......................................61
Korean Pulled Pork Lettuce Wraps 61
3-2-1 Spare Ribs..62
Jalapeno Cheddar Smoked Sausages........................62
Jalapeño-bacon Pork Tenderloin 62
Bacon Stuffed Smoked Pork Loin 63
Grilled Dr. Pepper Ribs 63
Lip-smackin' Pork Loin 63
Maple-smoked Pork Chops......................................64
Bbq Pulled Pork With Sweet & Heat Bbq Sauce 64

Crown Roast Of Pork 64
Chinese Alcoholic Bbq Pork Tenderloin 65
Bbq Pork Belly 65
Cuban Onion Pork Sandwich 65
Pulled Pork Corn Tortillas 66
Leftover Pulled Pork With Eggs...............................66
Delicious Pulled Pork Poutine 66
Bacon Weave Smoked Country Sausage......................67
Home-cured Hickory-smoked Bacon 67
Dry Rub Grilled Ribs 68
The Dan Patrick Show Chorizo Armadillo Eggs 68
Pig On A Stick With Buffalo Glaze 68
Smoked Stuffed Avocado Recipe 69
Smoky Pork Tenderloin 69
Triple Threat Pork Fattywith Stuffed Jalapeños 69
Classic Pulled Pork...70
Whole Hog 70
Lynchburg Bacon 70
Grilled Bacon Dog 71

Bbq Pulled Pork Hash 71
Baked Maple And Brown Sugar Bacon......................71
Barbecued Tenderloin...71
Pickle Brined Grilled Pork Chops 71
Sweet Bacon 72
Championship Ribs With Kansas City Style 72
Baby Back Ribs With Mustard Slather 72
Apple Cider Maple Glazed Ham 73
Pulled Pork Shoulder And Chicken 73
Grilled German Sausage With A Smoky Traeger
Twist 73
Cajun Double-smoked Ham 74
Savory Pork Belly Banh Mi 74
Smoked Blt Sandwich..74
Sweet And Spicy Pork Roast 75
Pork & Pepperoni Burgers..75
Amazing Bacon Cheese Fries 75
Orange & Maple Baked Ham 75

SEAFOOD RECIPES 77

Grilled Garlic Shrimp With Cajun Dip......................77
Grilled Albacore Tuna With Potato-tomato Casserole 77
Simple Glazed Salmon Fillets 77
Honey-soy Garlic Salmon 77
Garlic Blackened Catfish...78
Pacific Northwest Salmon 78
Grilled Salmon 78
Alder Smoked Scallops With Citrus & Garlic Butter
Sauce..78
Oysters Margarita 79
Barbecued Scallops 79
Baked Whole Fish In Sea Salt 79
Grilled Mussels With Lemon Butter 80
Smoked Honey Salmon...80
Moules Marinières With Garlic Butter Sauce 80
Traeger Crab Legs 81
Mezcal Shrimp With Salsa De Molcajete....................81
Baked Steelhead 81
Tequila & Lime Shrimp With Smoked Tomato
Sauce..82
Lemon Shrimp Scampi 82
Sweet Smoked Salmon Jerky.....................................82

Grilled Whole Steelhead Fillet 83
Whole Vermillion Red Snapper 83
Salmon Cakes With Homemade Tartar Sauce 83
Garlic Grilled Shrimp Skewers...................................83
Smoked Mango Shrimp...84
Grilled Crab Legs With Herb Butter 84
Teriyaki Smoked Honey Tilapia.................................84
Cider Hot-smoked Salmon 85
Shrimp Cabbage Tacos With Lime Cream..................85
Delicious Smoked Trout..85
Flavour Fire Spiced Shrimp 86
Spicy Crab Poppers...86
Seared Bluefin Tuna Steaks.......................................86
Bacon Wrapped Shrimp 87
Cajun Catfish..87
Kimi's Simple Grilled Fresh Fish 87
Bacon Wrapped Scallops 87
Grilled Lobster Tails With Smoked Paprika Butter 88
Lemon Herb Grilled Salmon.....................................88
Grilled Shrimp Brochette 88
Florentine Shrimp Al Cartoccio 89
Prosciutto-wrapped Scallops.....................................89

Traeger Smoked Salmon 89
Traeger Baked Rainbow Trout 90
Swordfish With Sicilian Olive Oil Sauce................90
Lemon Lobster Rolls..................................90
Smoked Crab Legs 91
Grilled Pepper Lobster Tails 91
Barbecued Shrimp 91
Lobster Tail 91
Vodka Brined Smoked Wild Salmon..........................91
Mexican Mahi Mahi With Baja Cabbage Slaw 92
Cedar Smoked Garlic Salmon............................92
Spicy Shrimp Skewers 93
Bbq Oysters 93
Smoked Lobster Scampi.................................93
Smoky Crab Dip 93
Planked Trout With Fennel, Bacon & Orange 94
Smoked Salt Cured Lox 94
Garlic Bacon Wrapped Shrimp.........................95
Roasted Halibut With Spring Vegetables...................95
Oysters In The Shell 95
Charleston Crab Cakes With Remoulade...................95
Wood-fired Halibut 96
Smoked Sugar Halibut 96
Grilled Maple Syrup Salmon 96

Coconut Shrimp Jalapeño Poppers............................97
Honey Balsamic Salmon 97
Grilled Fresh Fish 97
Citrus-smoked Trout 97
Lemon Scallops Wrapped In Bacon 98
Grilled Lemon Lobster Tails 98
Thai-style Swordfish Steaks With Peanut Sauce 98
Smoke-roasted Halibut With Mixed Herb
Vinaigrette 99
Grilled Lemon Salmon 99
Garlic Blackened Salmon 99
Grilled Artichoke Cheese Salmon 99
Grilled Oysters With Mignonette 100
Grilled Lemon Shrimp Scampi 101
Peper Fish Tacos......................................101
Summer Paella 101
Seared Ahi Tuna Steak With Soy Sauce 102
Spicy Lime Shrimp 102
Grilled Salmon Steaks With Dill Sauce 102
Cajun-blackened Shrimp 103
Spiced Smoked Swordfish 103
Grilled Salmon Gravlax 103
Mango Rice Wine Thai Shrimp...........................104
Grilled Blackened Saskatchewan Salmon 104

POULTRY RECIPES **105**

Grilled Hand Pulled Chicken 105
Spiced Smoked Chicken Quarters 105
Smoked Deviled Eggs 105
Crispy Spiced Chicken Wings 106
Smoked Boneless Chicken Thighs.....................106
Glazed Bbq Half Chicken 106
Smoked Airline Chicken...............................107
Easy Rapid-fire Roast Chicken 107
Smoked Drumsticks 107
Chicken Tenders 107
Smoked Avocado Turkey Tamale Pie.....................108
Smo-fried Chicken 108
The Grilled Chicken Challenge 108
Jalapeno Chicken Sliders.............................109
Smoked Chicken Leg & Thigh Quarters 109
Peanut Butter Chicken Wings.........................109
Smoked Spatchcocked Cornish Game Hens 110

Spatchcocked Chicken With White Barbecue Sauce. 110
Wild West Wings 110
Jamaican Jerk Chicken Quarters......................111
Roasted Honey Bourbon Glazed Turkey 111
Smoked Turkey Breast.................................111
Lemon Cajun Chicken Carbonara 111
Jalapeño- & Cheese-stuffed Chicken 112
Loaded Chicken Fries.................................112
Savory-sweet Turkey Legs 112
Bacon Wrapped Turkey Legs...........................113
Green Chile Chicken Enchiladas 113
Sweet And Spicy Smoked Wings 113
Smoked Turkey Legs 114
Bell Pepper Chicken Sliders 114
Kansas City Hot Fried Chicken 114
Chicken Egg Rolls With Buffalo Sauce 114
Bbq Cheese Chicken Stuffed Bell Peppers................115

Savory Smoked Turkey Legs....................................115
Roasted Christmas Goose....................................115
Easy Bbq Chicken Wings....................................116
Cheese Buffalo Chicken Wings....................................116
Smoked Turkey Wings....................................116
Big Game Roast Chicken....................................116
Juicy Jerk Chicken Kebabs....................................117
Onion Turkey Burger Sliders....................................117
Applewood-smoked Whole Turkey....................................117
Smoked Cheesy Chicken Quesadilla....................................118
Roasted Beer Can Chicken....................................118
Chicken Cordon Bleu Rollups....................................118
Bbq Game Day Chicken Wings And Thighs....................119
Grilled Beantown Chicken Wings....................................119
Gen's Old-fashioned Barbecued Chicken....................................119
Bbq Chicken Breasts....................................119
Lemon Chicken Breast....................................120
Smoked Quarters....................................120
Yucatán-spiced Chicken Thighs....................................120
Grilled Parmesan Chicken Wings....................................121
Buffalo Wings....................................121
Marinated Grilled Honey Chicken Wings....................121
Smoked Turkey....................................121
Cheesy Buffalo Chicken Pinwheels....................................122
Apricot Glazed Ham....................................122
Whole Smoked Honey Chicken....................................122
Smoked Thanksgiving Turkey....................................123
Cider-brined Turkey....................................123

Spiced Bbq Turkey....................................123
Green Goddess Chicken Legs....................................124
Roasted Prosciutto Stuffed Chicken....................................124
Bbq Pulled Turkey Sandwiches....................................124
Easy Grilled Chicken Shawarma....................................125
Fried Chicken Sliders....................................125
Smoked Chicken Fajita Quesadillas....................................125
Smoked Bourbon & Orange Brined Turkey....................126
Lemon Parmesan Chicken Wings....................................126
Bbq Smoked Turkey Jerky....................................126
Garlic Sriracha Buffalo Chicken Wings....................................127
Traeger Mandarin Wings....................................127
Grilled Honey Chicken Kabobs....................................127
Asian Chicken Sliders....................................127
Spatchcocked Turkey....................................128
Bbq Chicken Tostada....................................128
Asian Bbq Chicken....................................128
County Fair Turkey Legs....................................129
Injected Drunken Smoked Turkey Legs....................................129
Smoked Whole Chicken....................................129
Smoked Ditch Chicken....................................130
Cranberry Turkey Breast....................................130
Smoked Whiskey Peach Pulled Chicken....................................131
Bbq Turkey Drumsticks....................................131
Cornish Game Hens....................................131
Bbq Chicken Drumsticks....................................131
Smoked Chicken With Apricot Bbq Glaze....................132
Wood-fired Chicken Breasts....................................132

VEGETABLES RECIPES....................................133

Roasted Hasselback Potatoes By Doug Scheiding......133
Roasted Mashed Potatoes....................................133
Broccoli-cauliflower Salad....................................133
Roasted Potato Poutine....................................133
Salt Crusted Baked Potatoes....................................134
Grilled Street Corn....................................134
Roasted Asparagus....................................134
Twice-smoked Potatoes....................................134
Bacon Wrapped Corn On The Cob....................................135
Grilled Asparagus And Hollandaise Sauce....................135
Traeger Smoked Coleslaw....................................135
Grilled Corn On The Cob With Parmesan And
Garlic....................................136

Smoked Asparagus Soup....................................136
Smoked Pico De Gallo....................................136
Traeger Baked Potato Torte....................................136
Smoked Macaroni Salad....................................137
Roasted Pumpkin Seeds....................................137
Stuffed Jalapenos....................................137
Roasted Olives....................................138
Grilled Asparagus And Spinach Salad....................................138
Red Potato Grilled Lollipops....................................138
Baked Breakfast Mini Quiches....................................138
Butternut Squash....................................139
Steak Fries With Horseradish Creme....................................139
Baked Winter Squash Au Gratin....................................139

Parmesan Roasted Cauliflower..........................139
Smoked Parmesan Herb Popcorn 140
Baked Heirloom Tomato Tart 140
Grilled Ratatouille Salad 140
Roasted Artichokes With Garlic Butter.....................141
Chef Curtis' Famous Chimichurri Sauce 141
Roasted Garlic Herb Fries.................................141
Grilled Zucchini Squash Spears 141
Potluck Salad With Smoked Cornbread 142
Smoked Pickled Green Beans 142
Sweet Potato Marshmallow Casserole 142
Roasted Sheet Pan Vegetables..........................143
Roasted Sweet Potato Steak Fries 143
Baked Loaded Tater Tots 143
Smoked Mushrooms.......................................144
Roasted New Potatoes.....................................144
Grilled Asparagus & Honey-glazed Carrots.............144
Baked Bacon Green Bean Casserole 144
Baked Sweet Potatoes.....................................145
Mashed Red Potatoes......................................145
Smoked Jalapeño Poppers 145
Roasted Vegetable Napoleon 145
Portobello Marinated Mushroom 146
Roasted Jalapeño Poppers 146
Roasted Green Beans With Bacon......................146
Double-smoked Cheese Potatoes.......................146
Whole Roasted Cauliflower With Garlic Parmesan
Butter...147
Roasted Jalapeno Cheddar Deviled Eggs...................147
Roasted Beet & Bacon Salad.............................148
Grilled Fingerling Potato Salad 148
Butter Braised Green Beans 148
Roasted Pickled Beets 148

Traeger Grilled Whole Corn 149
Baked Sweet Potato Casserole With Marshmallow
Fluff... 149
Tater Tot Bake... 149
Smoked & Loaded Baked Potato 150
Roasted Tomatoes 150
Braised Creamed Green Beans 150
Blt Pasta Salad 151
Grilled Chili-lime Corn................................... 151
Smoked Beet-pickled Eggs 151
Smoked Mashed Potatoes................................ 151
Carolina Baked Beans 152
Baked Garlic Duchess Potatoes 152
Roasted Fall Vegetables 152
Skillet Potato Cake 153
Baked Artichoke Parmesan Mushrooms 153
Grilled Broccoli Rabe 153
Baked Sweet And Savory Yams By Bennie Kendrick. 153
Spicy Asian Brussels Sprouts 154
Grilled Beer Cabbage...................................... 154
Baked Stuffed Avocados 154
Roasted New Potatoes With Compound Butter........ 154
Green Bean Casserole 155
Sicilian Stuffed Mushrooms 155
Roasted Tomatoes With Hot Pepper Sauce.............. 155
Christmas Brussel Sprouts 156
Smoked Bbq Onion Brussels Sprout 156
Grilled Cabbage Steaks With Warm Bacon
Vinaigrette 156
Baked Kale Chips 157
Cast Iron Potatoes 157
Roasted Red Pepper White Bean Dip...................... 157
Roasted Do-ahead Mashed Potatoes........................ 157

APPETIZERS AND SNACKS

APPETIZERS AND SNACKS..159
Chicken Wings With Teriyaki Glaze 159
Bacon-wrapped Jalapeño Poppers 159
Bacon Pork Pinwheels (kansas Lollipops).................159
Bayou Wings With Cajun Rémoulade......................160
Pulled Pork Loaded Nachos..............................160
Citrus-infused Marinated Olives........................161
Chorizo Queso Fundido...................................161
Grilled Guacamole 161

Pigs In A Blanket.. 162
Simple Cream Cheese Sausage Balls 162
Deviled Eggs With Smoked Paprika 162
Smoked Cashews 163
Pig Pops (sweet-hot Bacon On A Stick) 163
Chuckwagon Beef Jerky.................................... 163
Smoked Cheese... 164
Roasted Red Pepper Dip 164

Delicious Deviled Crab Appetizer 165
Smoked Turkey Sandwich.......................................165
Sriracha & Maple Cashews 165

COCKTAILS RECIPES 167

Smoked Berry Cocktail 167
Smoking Gun Cocktail 167
Traeger Smoked Daiquiri 167
In Traeger Fashion Cocktail 167
Smoked Apple Cider..168
Grilled Blood Orange Mimosa 168
Sunset Margarita 168
Ryes And Shine Cocktail 168
Grilled Peach Sour Cocktail......................................169
Zombie Cocktail Recipe 169
Smoked Hot Buttered Rum 169
Strawberry Mule Cocktail 169
Garden Gimlet Cocktail..170
Grilled Hawaiian Sour 170
Smoked Pomegranate Lemonade Cocktail.................170
Smoked Mulled Wine 171
Batter Up Cocktail 171
Smoked Ice Mojito Slurpee 171
Grilled Frozen Strawberry Lemonade 171
Smoked Sangria..172
Smoked Pumpkin Spice Latte 172
Fig Slider Cocktail 172
Bacon Old-fashioned Cocktail...................................172
Smoked Salted Caramel White Russian 173
Smoky Scotch & Ginger Cocktail...............................173

A Smoking Classic Cocktail 173
Cran-apple Tequila Punch With Smoked Oranges ... 174
Smoked Cold Brew Coffee 174
Smoked Hibiscus Sparkler 174
Smoked Jacobsen Salt Margarita 175
Smoked Barnburner Cocktail 175
Smoked Pineapple Hotel Nacional Cocktail 175
Dublin Delight Cocktail 176
Grilled Peach Mint Julep...176
Smoked Irish Coffee 176
Smoked Texas Ranch Water 176
Traeger Old Fashioned 177
Traeger Boulevardier Cocktail 177
Grilled Rabbit Tail Cocktail 177
Traeger Paloma Cocktail 178
Smoked Grape Lime Rickey 178
Honey Glazed Grapefruit Shandy Cocktail 178
Smoked Plum And Thyme Fizz Cocktail 178
Grilled Peach Smash Cocktail 179
Smoked Eggnog..179
Traeger Gin & Tonic...179
Smoke And Bubz Cocktail 180
Smoked Raspberry Bubbler Cocktail.........................180
Smoky Mountain Bramble Cocktail 180

BEEF LAMB AND GAME RECIPES 181

Bbq Burnt End Sandwich 181
Wagyu Corned Beef Hash 181
Breakfast Brisket Hash Recipe 181
Brined Smoked Brisket 182
Bbq Brisket Tacos 182
Duck Fat Fries (confit)..182
Citrus Grilled Lamb Chops 183
Rosemary Prime Rib 183
Savory Chili Mac And Cheese 183
Herb Grilled Venison Stew 184
Lime Carne Asada Tacos 184
Smoked Pheasant 184

Jalapeño Poppers With Chipotle Sour Cream............165
Cold-smoked Cheese..166

Savory Teriyaki Smoked Steak Bites 185
Bacon Burger 185
Italian Beef Pinwheels...186
Philly Cheese Onion Steaks......................................186
Baked Venison Tater Tot Casserole 186
Flavour Bbq Brisket Burnt Ends 186
Sirloin Steak..187
Smoked Black Pepper Beef Ribs...............................187
Smoked Brisket 187
Naked Juicy Lucy Burgers With Special Sauce 188
Smoked Moink Burger By Scott Thomas 188
The Perfect T-bones 188

Santa Maria Tri-tip With Pico De Gallo 188
Cheese Onion Steak Sandwiches 189
Smoked Garlic Meatloaf...189
Cheddar Bacon Beef Burgers 190
Braised Onion Chuck Roast Beef Sandwiches............190
Flavour Memphis Bbq Beef Brisket 190
Teriyaki Deer Jerky 191
Bbq Brisket Breakfast Tacos 191
Reverse-seared Tri-tip...191
Smoked Prime Rib 191
Smoked Peppered Beef Tenderloin...........................192
Smoked Spiced Beef Pot Roast 192
Savory Reverse Seared Ny Steak 192
Grilled Bell Pepper Flank Steak Fajitas 193
Flavour Texas Twinkies 193
Delicious Reverse Seared Picanha Steak 193
Beginner's Smoked Beef Brisket 194
Roasted Prime Rib 194
Flank Steak Breakfast Potato Burrito........................194
Garlic Pigs In A Blanket 195
Delicious Barbecue Beef Brisket 195
Reverse-seared Steaks 196
Kansas City Cheese Brisket Burger...........................196
Easy Breakfast Cheeseburger 196
Salt & Pepper Dinosaur Bones 196
Spiced Smoked Kielbasa Dogs 197
Savory Bacon Wrapped Hot Dogs.............................197
Pastrami...198
Smoked Chicken Steak Sandwiches..........................198
Beer Chili Bratwurst..198

Chuck Roast Burnt Ends..199
Spiced Cowboy Steak 199
Bbq Sweet Pepper Meatloaf 200
Grilled Brisket Burger..200
Garlic Cheese Bacon Burger.....................................200
Bistro Steaks With Avocado Relish............................200
Sweetheart Steak...201
Savory Smoked Brisket 201
Bistecca Alla Fiorentina With Mushroom Ragout.....201
Smoked Garlic Prime Rib Roast................................202
Smoked Bourbon Jerky 202
Green Bell Pepper Cheese Steak Burger 203
Roasted Venison Steaks By The Bowmars.................203
Diva Q's Herb-crusted Prime Rib 203
Spicy Smoked Chili Beef Jerky.................................204
Smoked Beer Brisket..204
Succulent Lamb Chops...204
Cheesy French Dip Sliders 205
Slow Smoked And Roasted Prime Rib.......................205
Garlic Prime Rib Roast...205
Cheesy Nachos..206
Smoked Tomato Brisket Chili....................................206
Zucchini Onion Meatloaf..206
Slow Smoked Rib-eye Roast......................................207
Smoked Sirloin Roast Beef 207
Burnt Beer Beef Brisket..207
Smoked Bacon Brisket Flat 208
Pulled Beef..208
Texas Style Smoked Beer Brisket 208

RECIPE INDEX...**209**

INTRODUCTION

How the BIG HORN Wood Pellet Grill Works

Because pellet grills can perform so many cooking functions and require little to no monitoring, you might expect them to operate using complicated technology. In reality, wood pellet smokers are simple, straightforward cooking tools that are easy and safe to operate.

The following parts of a pellet grill work together to help you achieve a delicious, evenly cooked meal:

1. **Wood Pellets:** Pellets are small cylindrical food-grade wood that act as fuel for a pellet grill. Some wood pellets come from flavored woods, like apple or hickory, which add layers of flavor to food.

2. **Hopper:** The hopper is the vessel that holds the pellets, keeping them dry until they are ready for use.

3. **Auger:** Once you start the grill, the auger moves wood pellets from the hopper onto the firepot.

4. **Firepot:** The firepot is exactly what you expect — the place where the fire ignites, using the wood pellets for fuel.

5. **Induction fan:** The induction fan keeps the fire going and circulates the heat and smoke throughout your pellet grill and into your food.

6. **Controller:** The controller is on the outside of the pellet grill, and it is where you set and monitor the cooking temperature and pellet grill heating. Every smoker is different, so keep in mind some models may offer more precise control than others.

7. **Drip tray:** You'll find the drip tray between the cooking grates and the grill's inner workings. This tray collects any grease or food drippings, so they don't fall into the fire, and keeps food safe from direct heat.

To use a pellet grill, you fill the hopper with wood pellets marked safe for pellet grills. Follow manufacturer guidelines and be careful not to overfill or underfill your smoker. Once the pellets are in the hopper, use the digital controller to set your desired temperature. The induction fan will keep the fire going while your pellets move through the auger into the firepot. As the wood pellets ignite, the hot smoke circulates back through the grill to create a flavorful cooking chamber.

The Benefits of Choosing the BIG HORN Wood Pellet Grill

1. Amazing Versatility

One of the best features of having a pellet grill is its versatility.

A traditional charcoal grill or gas grill simply doesn't compare when cooking with pellets, as with this grill you are also able to smoke, braise, bake, roast, and sear your food.

This means you can have the chance to cook a lot more varieties of food and try out different recipes and cooking styles, including smoked meat which totally eliminates the need for a separate smoker.

The temperature is also a benefit of using a pellet grill as they mostly feature precision temperature control systems which can range from around 180 degrees to 500 degrees.

2. ADDS GREAT FLAVOR

If you haven't already heard, one of the main benefits of having a pellet grill is the quality and flavor food that you can prepare when using it.

Sometimes, when using more traditional grills, they can tend to leave quite a smoky or chemical taste on the meat after it's been smoked. With pellet grills, however, the addition of smoking with pellets can make a big difference to the final flavor.

This is because the wood pellets used really help to flavor the meat, a whole lot better than when cooking over gas and charcoal.

Wood pellets also come in various different flavors, such as apple, peach, mesquite, pecan, oak, cherry, maple and hickory, which can all really make a difference to your meals.

These pellets can also be mixed and matched as you like, allowing you to discover the perfect flavor for your taste buds.

In fact, many professional chefs opt for wood when cooking as it provides the best flavor possible. Therefore, if it is top flavor you are after, a pellet grill is your best option.

3. EASY TO USE

When it comes to cooking with a pellet grill, there are more advantages yet again.

Although some people may at first seem intimidated by their versatile design, they are actually not difficult to operate at all and in fact very easy to use.

Quite a few of the more recent grill styles have integrated one button start up controls, which means they will be super easy to get working.

As previously mentioned, the temperature control systems on a pellet grill is a lot better than more traditional ones.

These grills will be able to control the temperature throughout the entire cooking process, meaning all you will have to do is place the meat down and let the grill do its job.

They work similar to a convection oven, in that you won't need to fear your food ever being cooked uneven. This definitely helps to give the BBQ chef complete peace of mind!

Most pellet grills also feature flare prevention, which can stop any troubling flare-ups from occurring.

Hints on Using Your BIG HORN Wood Pellet Grill

1.   Allow yourself some time to get acquainted with your new grill/smoker.

Allow yourself some time to get acquainted with your new grill/smoker. We know you'll be anxious to try it out, but don't be overly ambitious. Instead of a whole brisket, which could take 15 hours or more, or a budget-busting prime rib roast, start with chicken (parts, such as breasts or wings, or a whole bird), pork loin tenderloin, or blade (shoulder) steaks, Cornish hens, salmon steaks or fillets, or other relatively inexpensive cuts that can be completed in 2 hours or less.

2.   Identify any hot spots—most grills have them.

Identify any hot spots—most grills have them. Preheat your grill to medium-high as directed by the owner's manual, then lay slices of cheap white bread shoulder to shoulder across the grate. Watch carefully, then flip after a few minutes. Take a photo of the results. The darkest bread will indicate where the temperature might be hotter. (Print the photo out and add it to your owner's manual for reference.)

3.   Don't let your meat come to room temperature before cooking.

Whatever meat you select, put it on the preheated grill/smoker straight from the refrigerator. Do not, as many recipes suggest, allow it to come to room temperature before cooking.

As Steven often notes, high-end steak houses do not leave their meats out at room temperature. (The danger area is 40 to 140 degrees.) The heat of the grill is sufficient to raise the internal temperature of the meat by those few degrees.

4.   Invest in a good meat thermometer.

A laser-type thermometer such as this one will give you a more accurate temperature reading at grill level than a built-in dome thermometer. Determine the temperature range of your grill model from lowest to highest (180 degrees to 500+, for example).

5.   Take advantage of your pellet grill's searing capabilities.

Many pellet grills feature searing capabilities, meaning they can reach temperatures over 500 degrees. Again, check your owner's manual for information

Cleaning Methods for the BIG HORN Wood Pellet Grill

A clean grill is a safe appliance that makes delicious food as a bonus. Before you begin your search for kitchen items to clean your grill, you should know some general grill cleaning tips.

1. Clean and scrape grates while they're still warm: Warm residue is easier to clean than dry, stuck-on grease. If you go with this method, be extra careful while handling your grill grates. Use protective gloves and be sure the DIY grill cleaner you're using isn't flammable if you're working with a warm grill.

2. Give it a quick clean after every use: You don't need to do a deep clean every time you grill out. But a once-over scrub after using it can save you from painstaking scraping later.

3. Do deep cleans depending on your usage: In general, you should do a deep clean every couple of months. If you use your grill more often, consider a deep clean once a month. If you hardly use your grill — but let's be real, we're using it all the time — every few months will suffice.

4. Deep clean a cool grill: If you have to get deep into your grill to clean it, make sure it's had a chance to cool. If you're cleaning up charcoal or pellet ash, be sure the material isn't still warm before taking a shop vacuum to it.

Along with those grill cleaning tips, some preventive measures can save you from dealing with a gunked-up grill. Be sure to:
- Cover surfaces with aluminum foil.
- Use a grill pan or basket.
- Use cooking oil, either on the grates or the food itself.
- Clean out ashes from pellets or charcoal.
- Use a grill cover when you aren't cooking.

BAKING RECIPES

Eyeball Cookies

Servings: 20
Cooking Time: 35 Minutes

Ingredients:
- 2 Packages Candy Eyeballs
- Green, Blue And Purple Food Coloring
- 1 Box Of Yellow Gluten Free Cake Mix
- 1/2 Cup (Optional) Granulated Sugar
- 2 Large Eggs
- 1/3 Cup Powdered Sugar
- 1 Teaspoon Pure Vanilla Extract
- 6 Tablespoon Melted Vegan Butter (Unsalted)

Directions:
1. Supply your smoker with wood pellets and follow the start-up procedure. Preheat the grill, with the lid closed, to 350° F.
2. Line two large baking sheets with parchment paper. In a large bowl, combine cake mix, melted butter, eggs (or egg substitute), powdered sugar, sugar (optional), and vanilla and stir until combined. (substitute 2 flax eggs for Vegan – 1 tbsp flax seed meal and 5 tbsp water per egg).
3. Divide dough between 3 bowls and dye each bowl a different color.(We used green, blue and purple).
4. Roll dough into tablespoon-sized balls.
5. Place about 2" apart on the baking sheet and grill until tops have cracked and the tops look set, 8 to 10 minutes. – Turn half way through baking, after 4-5 minutes.
6. Immediately, while the cookies are still warm, stick candy eyeballs all over the cookies.
7. Let cool completely before serving.

Baked Bourbon Monkey Bread

Servings: 6
Cooking Time: 40 Minutes

Ingredients:
- 3 Can Pillsbury Grands Buttermilk Biscuits
- 1 Cup sugar
- 3 Teaspoon ground cinnamon
- 1 Cup Butter, unsalted
- 1 Cup dark brown sugar
- Tablespoon bourbon

Directions:
1. Supply your smoker with wood pellets and follow the start-up procedure. Preheat the grill, with the lid closed, to 350° F.
2. Cut each biscuit into quarters. In a Ziploc bag, combine sugar and cinnamon and add quartered biscuits. Toss to coat in cinnamon sugar.
3. Dump coated biscuit dough into a bundt pan coated with non-stick spray.
4. In a small saucepan, combine the brown sugar, butter, and bourbon. Cook over medium heat until the sugar has dissolved.
5. Pour the butter mixture over the biscuits in the bundt pan.
6. Place in the center of the grill and cook for 40 minutes or until dark golden brown.
7. Let cool on the counter for 5-10 minutes, then flip out onto a serving plate. Enjoy!

Baked Pumpkin Pie

Servings: 6
Cooking Time: 50 Minutes

Ingredients:
- 4 Ounce cream cheese
- 15 Ounce pumpkin puree
- 1/3 Cup Cream, whipping
- 1/2 Cup brown sugar
- 1 Teaspoon pumpkin pie spice
- 3 Large eggs
- 1 frozen pie crust, thawed

Directions:
1. Supply your smoker with wood pellets and follow the start-up procedure. Preheat the grill, with the lid closed, to 325° F.
2. Mix cream cheese, puree, milk, sugar, and spice. One at a time, incorporate an egg to the mixture. Pour mixture into pie shell.
3. Bake for 50 minutes, edges should be golden and pie should be firm around edges with slight movement in middle. Let cool before whip cream is applied. Serve and enjoy! Grill: 325 °F

Cinnamon Pull-aparts

Servings: 6
Cooking Time: 20 Minutes

Ingredients:
- 16.3 Ounce Biscuits, Homestyle, Canned
- 1 Cup packed brown sugar
- 1/2 Cup butter
- 1/4 Cup water
- 1 Teaspoon ground cinnamon
- 1/2 Cup Nuts (optional)

Directions:

1. Cut each biscuit into 4 pieces and peel each piece in half; set aside.

2. Combine brown sugar, butter and water in a large saucepan and bring to a boil; reduce heat and simmer for 1 minute. Stir in cinnamon and nuts; add biscuit quarters and mix to coat. Pour into greased 13 by 9 inch casserole dish and spread evenly in the dish.

3. Supply your smoker with wood pellets and follow the start-up procedure. Preheat the grill, with the lid closed, to 350° F.

4. Place the casserole dish on the grill; close lid and cook for 20 to 25 minutes or until the biscuits are done. Grill: 350 ˚F

5. Remove from the grill and transfer to a serving platter making sure to get all the gooey syrup onto the biscuits. Serve warm. Enjoy!

Donut Bread Pudding

Servings: 8
Cooking Time: 40 Minutes

Ingredients:
- 16 Cake Donuts
- 1/2 Cup Raisins, seedless
- 5 eggs
- 3/4 Cup sugar
- 2 Cup heavy cream
- 2 Teaspoon vanilla extract
- 1 Teaspoon ground cinnamon
- 3/4 Cup Butter, melted, cooled slightly
- Ice Cream

Directions:
1. Lightly butter a 9- by 13-inch baking pan. Layer the donuts in an even thickness in the pan. Distribute the raisins over the top, if using. Drizzle evenly with the butter.

2. Make the custard: In a medium bowl, whisk together the sugar, eggs, cream, vanilla, and cinnamon. Whisk in the butter. Pour over the donuts. Let sit for 10 to 15 minutes, periodically pushing the donuts down into the custard. Cover with foil.

3. Supply your smoker with wood pellets and follow the start-up procedure. Preheat the grill, with the lid closed, to 350° F.

4. Bake the bread pudding for 30 to 40 minutes, or until the custard is set. Remove the foil and continue to bake for 10 additional minutes to lightly brown the top. Grill: 350 ˚F

5. Let cool slightly before cutting into squares. Drizzle with melted ice cream, if desired. Enjoy!

Baked Potatoes & Celery Root Au Gratin

Servings: 2
Cooking Time: 60 Minutes

Ingredients:
- 5 Tablespoon butter, softened
- 2 Large leeks, white parts only, cleaned and sliced into half moons
- kosher salt
- freshly ground black pepper
- 5 Small Yukon Gold potatoes, sliced 1/4 inch thick
- 2 Whole celery root, peeled and sliced 1/4 inch thick
- 2 Cup cream
- 1 Tablespoon minced sage
- 1 Cup shredded Gruyere or other hearty Swiss cheese, divided

Directions:
1. Supply your smoker with wood pellets and follow the start-up procedure. Preheat the grill, with the lid closed, to 400° F.

2. Butter a 9x13 baking dish with 1 tablespoon of the softened butter. In a medium frying pan over medium heat, melt the remaining butter. Add the leeks and a generous pinch of salt and pepper and cook, stirring often until softened, about 5 minutes.

3. Remove from the heat and allow to cool. Place the potato and celery root slices into a large mixing bowl. Add the cream, leek mixture, minced sage, 1 teaspoon salt, 1/2 teaspoon pepper and 1 cup cheese. Stir gently to coat.

4. Arrange a layer of potato and celery root slices so they're slightly overlapping in the prepared baking dish. Repeat two more times so there are three layers of potatoes. Pour remaining cream from the bowl over the gratin, then sprinkle the top with the remaining cup of cheese.

5. Cover the dish loosely with foil and bake on the grill for 45 minutes. Remove the foil and continue baking until the top is golden and bubbly and the potatoes are tender when pierced, about 30 to 45 minutes longer. Let stand for 10 minutes before serving. Enjoy!

Irish Soda Bread

Servings: 8-12
Cooking Time: 45 Minutes

Ingredients:
- As Needed Cornmeal
- 3 1/2 Cup all-purpose flour
- 1 1/2 Teaspoon sugar
- 1 1/4 Teaspoon baking soda
- 1 Teaspoon salt
- 1 Cup buttermilk
- To Taste butter

Directions:
1. When ready to cook, set the temperature to 400F (205 C) and preheat, lid closed, for 10 to 15 minutes.

2. Lightly dust the bottom of an 8-inch (20-cm) round cake pan with cornmeal and set aside.

3. Tear off a large sheet of wax paper and lay it on your work surface.

4. Combine the flour, sugar, soda, and salt in a large sifter and sift onto the wax paper. Carefully lift up the sides of the wax paper and tip the flour mixture back into the sifter. Re-sift into a large mixing bowl.

5. Lightly flour your work surface. Make a well in the middle of the flour mixture in the bowl and pour in 1 cup (240 mL) of buttermilk. Stir with a wooden spoon. Work quickly and gently as the carbon dioxide bubbles formed when the buttermilk hits the dry ingredients will deflate, the dough will look somewhat shaggy. If the dough seems dryish, add a little more buttermilk.

6. Turn out onto the floured surface, and with floured hands, knead gently for 10 to 20 seconds - just long enough to bring the dough bits together. (It will look more like biscuit dough than bread dough.)

7. Form into a flattish round and transfer to the prepared pan. Flour a sharp knife, and deeply cut a cross in the top of the loaf all the way to the edge of the bread. Quickly get it in to bake, if it sits too long, it will deflate.

8. Bake the bread for 45 to 50 minutes, or until it is browned and the bottom of the loaf sounds hollow when rapped with your knuckles.

9. Remove the bread from the baking pan and cool on a cooling rack. Just be-fore serving, cut the loaf in half and then slice each half into thin slices.

10. Serve with butter. Wrap leftovers tightly in plastic wrap or foil. This bread makes great toast. Enjoy!

Mint Butter Chocolate Chip Cookies

Servings: 24
Cooking Time: 12 Minutes

Ingredients:
- 1/2 Cup Butter, Melted
- 1 Package Chocolate Chip Cookie Mix
- 8-10 Drop Food Coloring
- 1/2 Tsp Mint, Extract

Directions:
1. Supply your smoker with wood pellets and follow the start-up procedure. Preheat the grill, with the lid closed, to 350° F.

2. Follow the directions on the back of the Chocolate Chip Cookie mix and also add the mint extract and green food coloring. Mix until combined.

3. On a baking sheet lined with parchment paper, drop balls of dough about 2 tbsp in size onto the pan.

4. Place in your Grill and bake for 10-12 minutes. Let cool for a couple minutes before removing from the pan. Enjoy!

Baked Bourbon Maple Pumpkin Pie

Servings: 6-8
Cooking Time: 60 Minutes

Ingredients:
- 1/4 Cup Cocoa Powder, Unsweetened
- 1 Tablespoon Cocoa Powder, Unsweetened
- 3 1/2 Tablespoon sugar
- 1 Teaspoon salt
- 1 1/4 Cup all-purpose flour
- 1 Tablespoon all-purpose flour
- 6 Tablespoon butter
- 2 Tablespoon vegetable oil
- 1 Large Egg Yolk
- 1/2 Teaspoon apple cider vinegar
- 1/4 Cup ice water
- 1 Large egg, beaten
- 15 Ounce Pumpkin, canned
- 1/4 Cup sour cream
- 2 Tablespoon bourbon
- 1 Teaspoon ground cinnamon
- 1/2 Teaspoon salt
- 1/4 Teaspoon ground ginger
- 1/4 Teaspoon ground nutmeg
- 1/8 Teaspoon Allspice, ground
- 1/8 Teaspoon Mace, ground
- 3 Large eggs
- 3/4 Cup maple syrup
- 2 Tablespoon sugar
- 1/2 Vanilla Bean, halved
- 1 Cup heavy cream

Directions:
1. For the Chocolate Pie Dough: Pulse cocoa powder, granulated sugar, salt, and 1-1/4 cups plus 1 Tbsp flour in a food processor to combine. Add butter and shortening and pulse until mixture resembles coarse meal with a few pea-sized pieces of butter remaining. Transfer to a large bowl.

2. Whisk together the egg yolk, vinegar, and 1/4 cup ice water in a small bowl. Drizzle half of the egg mixture over flour mixture and, using a fork, mix gently just until combined. Add remaining egg mixture and mix until the dough just comes together (you will have some unincorporated pieces).

3. Turn out dough onto a lightly floured surface, flatten slightly, and cut into quarters. Stack pieces on top of one another. Placing unincorporated dry pieces of dough between layers, and press down to combine. Repeat process twice more (all pieces of dough should be incorporated at this point). Form dough into a 1" thick disk. Wrap in plastic; chill at least 1 hour.

4. Roll out a disk of dough on a lightly floured surface into a 14" round. Transfer to a 9" pie dish. Lift up the edge and allow the

dough to slump down into the dish. Trim. Leaving about 1" overhang. Fold overhang under and crimp edge. Chill in freezer 15 minutes.

5. When ready to cook, set the smoker to 350℉ and preheat, lid closed for 15 minutes.

6. Line pie with parchment paper or heavy-duty foil, leaving a 1-1/2" overhang. Fill with pie weights or dried beans. Bake until crust is dry around the edge, about 20 minutes.

7. Remove paper and weights and bake until surface of the crust looks dry, 5-10 minutes.

8. Brush bottom and sides of crust with 1 beaten egg. Return to grill and bake until dry and set, about 3 minutes longer.

9. For the Pumpkin Maple Filling: Whisk together pumpkin puree, sour cream, bourbon, cinnamon, salt, ginger, nutmeg, allspice, mace (optional) and remaining 3 eggs in a large bowl; set aside.

10. Pour maple syrup and 2 tbsp sugar in a small saucepan. Scrape in the seeds from vanilla bean (reserve pod for another use) or add vanilla extract and bring syrup to a boil. Reduce heat to medium-high and simmer, stirring occasionally, until mixture is thickened and small puffs of steam start to release about 3 minutes.

11. Remove from heat and add cream in 3 additions, stirring with a wooden spoon after each addition until smooth. Gradually whisk hot maple cream into pumpkin mixture.

12. Place pie dish on a rimmed baking sheet and pour in pumpkin filling. Bake pie, rotating halfway through, until set around edge but center barely jiggles 50-60 minutes.

13. Transfer pie dish to a wire rack and let the pie cool. Slice and serve. Enjoy!

Strawberry Basil Daiquiri

Servings: 2
Cooking Time: 20 Minutes

Ingredients:
- 4 strawberries, stemmed
- 6 Tablespoon granulated sugar, divided
- 6 basil leaves
- 3 Ounce white rum
- 2 Ounce lime juice
- 1 Ounce Smoked Simple Syrup
- 2 fresh basil leaves, for garnish
- 2 lime slice, for garnish

Directions:
1. Supply your smoker with wood pellets and follow the start-up procedure. Preheat the grill, with the lid closed, to 375° F.

2. Cut strawberries in half and coat in 2 tablespoons granulated sugar. Place directly on grill grate and cook for 15 to 20 minutes. Remove from heat and cool. Grill: 375 ℉

3. Add 1 tablespoon granulated sugar and basil leaves to shaking tin and lightly muddle. Add strawberries and muddle again.

4. Pour in white rum, lime juice and Smoked Simple Syrup. Shake with ice.

5. Strain contents into a chilled glass and garnish with large fresh basil leaf and sliced lime. Enjoy!

Beer Bread

Servings: 4
Cooking Time: 60 Minutes

Ingredients:
- 400 g all-purpose flour
- 2 Tablespoon sugar
- 1 Tablespoon baking powder
- 1 Teaspoon salt
- 12 Ounce beer
- 2 Tablespoon honey
- 6 Tablespoon butter, melted

Directions:
1. Supply your smoker with wood pellets and follow the start-up procedure. Preheat the grill, with the lid closed, to 350° F.

2. Spray a loaf pan (9x5x3 inches) (55x12x20 cm) with nonstick cooking spray and set aside.

3. Put the flour, sugar, baking powder, and salt in a large mixing bowl. Whisk with a wire whisk to combine and aerate. Add the beer and honey and stir with a wooden spoon until the batter is just mixed. (Do not overmix.) If desired, gently stir in one or more of the optional add-ins.

4. Pour half of the melted butter in the prepared loaf pan and spoon in the batter. Pour the remainder of the butter over the top of the loaf.

5. Put the loaf pan directly on the grill grate and bake until a wooden skewer or toothpick inserted in the center of the loaf comes out clean, 50 to 60 minutes, and the bread is golden-brown. (Note: If using a glass loaf pan, the baking time might be shorter.)

6. Let the loaf cool slightly in the pan before removing from the pan. Leftovers make great toast.

7. Optional Add-ins: Bacon, cooked and crumbled, 1 cup (100 g) Grated Cheese, Red Bell Pepper and Onion, diced and sauted in Butter (1/4 cup each), Green Onions, minced, Dried Herbs such as Dill, Rosemary, Mixed Italian Herbs, etc,.Cracked Black Pepper, Your favorite Barbecue Rub, such as Traeger's Pork and Poultry Shake, Ground Cinnamon, Dry Ranch Dressing Mix, Coarse-grained Mustard.

Baked Chocolate Brownie Cookies With Egg Nog

Servings: 6
Cooking Time: 12 Minutes

Ingredients:

- 16 Ounce Bar bittersweet chocolate, finely chopped
- 4 Tablespoon unsalted butter, room temperature
- 4 eggs
- 1 1/3 Cup granulated sugar
- 1 Teaspoon vanilla extract
- 1 1/2 Cup all-purpose flour
- 1/2 Teaspoon baking powder
- 1 Cup semisweet chocolate chips

Directions:

1. Supply your smoker with wood pellets and follow the start-up procedure. Preheat the grill, with the lid closed, to 350° F.
2. Line two baking sheets with parchment paper.
3. Put the finely chopped chocolate and butter in a heatproof bowl and set over a saucepan of barely simmering water; stir occasionally until chocolate is completely melted and smooth. Set aside and allow to cool to room temperature.
4. Whisk together eggs, sugar and vanilla extract in a medium bowl. Set aside.
5. Sift together the flour and baking powder in a small bowl. Add the melted chocolate mixture to the egg mixture and stir with a rubber spatula until completely combined.
6. Add the flour mixture in three batches, folding gently into the batter with a spatula. Once all of the flour has been incorporated, stir in the chocolate chips.
7. Scoop 1-1/2 tablespoons of dough onto prepared baking sheets. Bake for 10 to 12 minutes or until they are firm on the outside. Do not over bake. Grill:350° F
8. Leave to cool completely on the baking sheets. Enjoy!

Smoked, Salted Caramel Apple Pie

Servings: 4
Cooking Time: 60 Minutes

Ingredients:

- 1 Cup cream
- 1 Cup brown sugar
- 3/4 Cup Light Corn Syrup
- 6 Tablespoon butter
- 1 Teaspoon sea salt
- 1 Pastry for Double-Crust Pie
- 6 Granny Smith Apples, Cut Into Wedges

Directions:

1. Supply your smoker with wood pellets and follow the start-up procedure. Preheat the grill, with the lid closed, to 180° F.
2. Fill a large pan with ice and water. Pour the cream into a smaller, shallow pan. Place the pan with the cream in the ice bath and place them both on the Traeger to smoke for 15-20 minutes. Grill: 180 °F
3. To make the caramel, combine the sugar and corn syrup in a saucepan and cook over medium heat, stirring constantly until it coats the back of your spoon and starts to turn a copper color, then stir in butter, salt, and smoked cream.
4. To assemble the pie, gather the pie crust, salted caramel, and apples. Place one of the pie crusts into the pie plate and fill with apple slices. Pour caramel over the apples. Lay the top crust over the filling, then crimp the top and bottom crusts together.
5. Make slits in the top crust to release the steam and finish by brushing with egg or cream. Sprinkle with raw sugar and sea salt.
6. When ready to bake, set the Traeger to 375°F and preheat, lid closed for 15 minutes.
7. Place the pie on the grill and bake for 20 minutes. Grill: 375 °F
8. Reduce heat to 325°F and cook for 25 more minutes. When ready, the crust should be golden brown and the filling, bubbly. Grill: 325 °F
9. Remove the pie from the grill and let cool. Serve with vanilla ice cream. Enjoy!

Caramel Bourbon Bacon Brownies

Servings: 16
Cooking Time: 60 Minutes

Ingredients:

- 2 Cup All-Purpose Flour
- 1/4 Cup Bourbon
- 1 Cup Brown Sugar
- 1 Cup Canola Oil
- Caramel Sauce
- 1.5 Cup Cocoa Powder
- 1 Tablespoon Hickory Honey Sea Salt
- 2 Tablespoon Instant Coffee
- 6 Large Eggs
- 1/2 Teaspoon Smoked Infused Hickory Honey Sea Salt
- 1 Cup Powdered Sugar
- 6 Slices Bacon, Raw
- 4 Tablespoons Water
- 3 Cups White Sugar

Directions:

1. Supply your smoker with wood pellets and follow the start-up procedure. Preheat the grill, with the lid closed, to 400° F.
2. In a large mixing bowl, whisk together the cocoa, powdered sugar, white sugar, instant coffee and flour.
3. To the flour mixture, add the eggs, oil and water until just combined.

4. Spray the 9 x 13 pan well with cooking spray.

5. Pour half the batter in the pan, drizzle with caramel.

6. Pour other half of batter on top and drizzle with caramel again and add candied bacon to the top.

7. Bake the brownies in the smoker for 1 hour, or until a toothpick inserted in the center of the pan comes out clean.

8. Remove from the smoker and allow to cool before slicing.

Focaccia

Servings: 6
Cooking Time: 40 Minutes

Ingredients:

- 1 Cup warm water (110°F to 115°F)
- 1/2 Ounce Yeast, active
- 1 Teaspoon sugar
- 2 1/2 Cup flour
- 1 Teaspoon salt
- 1/4 Cup extra-virgin olive oil
- 1 1/2 Teaspoon Italian herbs, dried
- 1/8 Teaspoon red pepper flakes
- As Needed coarse sea salt

Directions:

1. Measure the water in a glass-measuring cup. Stir in the yeast and sugar. Let rest for in a warm place. After 5 to 10 minutes, the mixture should be foamy, indicating the yeast is "alive." If it does not foam, discard it and start again.

2. Pour the water/yeast mixture in the bowl of a food processor. Add 1 cup of the flour as well as the salt and 1/4 cup of olive oil. Pulse several times to blend. Add the remaining flour, Italian herbs, and hot pepper flakes.

3. Process the dough until it's smooth and elastic and pulls away from the sides of the bowl, adding small amounts of flour or water through the feed tube if the dough is respectively too wet or too dry.

4. Let the dough rise in the covered food processor bowl in a warm place until doubled in bulk, about 1 hour5. Remove the dough from the food processor (it will deflate) and turn onto a lightly floured surface.

5. Oil two 8- to 9-inch round cake pans generously with olive oil. (Just pour a couple of glugs in and tilt the pan to spread the oil.) Divide the dough into two equal pieces, shape into disks, and put one in each prepared cake pan.

6. Oil the top of each disk with olive oil and dimple the dough with your fingertips. Sprinkle lightly with coarse salt, and if desired, additional dried Italian herbs.

7. Cover the focaccia dough with plastic wrap and let the dough rise in a warm place, about 45 minutes to an hour.

8. When ready to cook, start the smoker grill and set the temperature to 400F and preheat, lid closed, for 10 to 15 minutes.

9. Put the pans with the focaccia dough directly on the grill grate. Bake until the focaccia breads are light golden in color and baked through, 35 to 40 minutes, rotating the pans halfway through the baking time.

10. Let cool slightly before removing from the pans. Cut into wedges for serving.

Chicken Pot Pie

Servings: 6
Cooking Time: 60 Minutes

Ingredients:

- 2 Chicken, Boneless/Skinless
- 1 Cream Of Chicken Soup, Can
- 1 Tsp Curry Powder
- 1/2 Cup Mayo
- 1 1/2 Cups Mixed Frozen Vegetables
- 1 Onion, Sliced
- 2 Frozen Pie Shell, Deep
- 1/2 Cup Sour Cream

Directions:

1. Supply your smoker with wood pellets and follow the start-up procedure. Preheat the grill, with the lid closed, to 425° F.

2. Cut the onion in half and place on the grates of the grill. If you"re using fresh chicken breasts, barbecue the chicken at the same time as the onions. The chicken is fully cooked when the internal temperature reached 170F. While the onion and chicken are cooking, prepare the pie crust by putting one crust in a pie plate. When the chicken and onions are done, shred chicken and chop onion into small pieces and place in the prepared pie plate along with the mixed vegetables.

3. Combine cream of chicken soup, mayo, sour cream, and curry powder in a bowl. Pour into the pie crust with the chicken and mix to combine. Wet the sides of the bottom crust with a small amount of water and top with the second pie crust. Push gently along the sides of the crust to seal the two pie crusts together.

4. Place in the and bake for 40 minutes, or until the crust is golden brown. Serve hot.

Anzac Coconut Biscuits

Servings: 4
Cooking Time: 30 Minutes

Ingredients:

- This recipe makes a dozen biscuits.
- 1 cup rolled oats
- 3/4 cup raw sugar
- 3/4 cup desiccated coconut
- 1 cup plain flour, sifted
- 125 g butter, melted
- 2 tablespoons Golden Syrup
- 1/2 tsp bicarb soda

- 3 tablespoons boiling water

Directions:

1. Combine and mix thoroughly sifted flour, oats, sugar and coconut in a large bowl.

2. Melt the butter and Golden Syrup over low heat.

3. Add boiling water to the bicarb soda, once dissolved add into the butter/syrup mix, it will bubble/fizz up a bit.

4. Add the liquid into the dry ingredients and mix throughly.

5. Rolls the mix into golf ball size balls and layout on grease proof paper on baking tray and flatten the tops just slightly.

6. Space the balls with about 3 fingers between each ball as they will flatten to about triple the diameter as they cook.

7. Supply your smoker with wood pellets and follow the start-up procedure. Preheat the grill, with the lid closed, to 350° F. Cook for 25-30 minutes until golden brown.

8. Rest on cooling rack until at room temperature then store in air-tight container.

Chili Cheese Fries

Servings: 6
Cooking Time: 10 Minutes

Ingredients:

- 1 Cup Cheddar Cheese, Shredded
- 1 Cup Chili Con Carne, Prepared
- 1 Bag French Fries
- 1 Tablespoon Olive Oil
- 1 Tablespoon Sweet Heat Rub

Directions:

1. Supply your smoker with wood pellets and follow the start-up procedure. Preheat the grill, with the lid closed, to 350° F. If you're using charcoal or gas, set it up for medium high heat.

2. Bake the fries according to manufacturer's instructions. Once the fries are done, place them in a large bowl and add the olive oil and Sweet Heat Rub. Toss the fries to coat. Once everything is well coated with the oil and seasoning, spread the fries on a baking sheet.

3. Top the fries with the chili and the shredded cheddar cheese. Place the baking sheet on the grill and grill for 7-10 minutes, or until the cheese is melted and bubbly, and the chili is warm all the way through.

4. Remove the baking sheet from the grill and serve the fries immediately.

Spiced Carrot Cake

Servings: 10
Cooking Time: 35 Minutes

Ingredients:

- 1/2 Cup Apple Sauce, Unsweetened
- 2 Tsp Baking Powder
- 1 Tsp Baking Soda
- 1 1/2 Cups Brown Sugar
- 1/2 Cup Butter, Room Temp
- 3/4 Cup Canola Oil
- 3 Cups Carrot, Grated
- 1 1/2 Tsp Cinnamon, Ground
- 2 (8-Ounce) Packages Cream Cheese, Room Temperature
- 4 Egg
- 2 Cups Flour, All-Purpose
- 1/2 Tsp Ginger, Ground
- 1/4 Tsp Nutmeg, Ground
- 1/2 Tsp Salt
- 1/2 Cup Sugar
- 3 Cups Sugar, Icing

Directions:

1. Supply your smoker with wood pellets and follow the start-up procedure. Preheat the grill, with the lid closed, to 350° F.

2. Line the bottom of 2 9-inch cake pans with parchment paper and spray the sides with cooking spray. Set aside.

3. In a large bowl, combine flour, baking powder and soda, spices and salt.

4. In a smaller bowl, combine oil, eggs, sugars, and applesauce and whisk together. Add carrots and stir until well combined.

5. Pour the wet ingredients into the dry. Stir until combined but take care not to over mix. Pour the batter evenly between the two cake pans. Bake for about 35 minutes in your Grill, rotating the cake pans halfway between the cook. Remove once a toothpick is inserted in the middle of the cake and comes out clean.

6. While the cake is cooling, prepare the frosting. Beat the cream cheese until smooth with a hand mixer. Add the butter and icing sugar and mix until fully combined.

7. On a clean plate or cake stand, place one half of the cake and top with a good layer of cream cheese frosting. Place the second half on top and cover with the remaining frosting. Icing tip: try not to lift your knife while icing. Instead make long, smooth strokes. Lifting the knife often make cause crumbs to get into your icing. Top with pecans if desired.

Sweet Cheese Muffins

Servings: 3
Cooking Time: 15 Minutes

Ingredients:

- 1 package butter cake mix
- 1 package Jiffy Corn Muffin Mix
- 1 cup self-rising or cake flour
- 12 tablespoons (1½ sticks) unsalted butter, softened, plus 8 tablespoons (1 stick) melted
- 3½ cups shredded Cheddar cheese

- 2 eggs, beaten, at room temperature
- 2¼ cups buttermilk
- Nonstick cooking spray or butter, for greasing
- ¼ cup packed brown sugar

Directions:

1. Supply your smoker with wood pellets and follow the start-up procedure. Preheat, with the lid closed, to 375°F.
2. In a large mixing bowl, combine the cake mix, corn muffin mix, and flour.
3. Slice the 1½ sticks of softened butter into pieces and cut into the dry ingredients. Add the cheese and mix thoroughly.
4. In a medium bowl, combine the eggs and buttermilk, then add to the dry ingredients, stirring until well blended.
5. Coat three 12-cup mini muffin pans with cooking spray and spoon ¼ cup of batter into each cup.
6. Transfer the pans to the grill, close the lid, and smoke, monitoring closely, for 12 to 15 minutes, or until the muffins are lightly browned.
7. While the muffins are cooking, make the topping: In a small bowl, stir together the remaining 1 stick of melted butter and the brown sugar until well combined.
8. Remove the muffins from the grill. Brush the tops with the sweet butter and serve warm.

Cornbread Chicken Stuffing

Servings: 6 - 8
Cooking Time: 95 Minutes

Ingredients:

- 2 Tbsp Butter
- 1 Cup Chicken Stock
- 6 Cups Cornbread, Cubed
- ½ Cup Dried Cranberries
- 1 Egg
- ½ Cup Heavy Whipping Cream
- 1 Lb. Italian Sausage
- 1 Diced Onion
- 1 ½ Tsp Pulled Pork Rub
- 2 Tbsp Sage, Fresh
- ½ Tsp Fresh Thyme

Directions:

1. Supply your smoker with wood pellets and follow the start-up procedure. Preheat the grill, with the lid closed, to 250° F. If using a gas or charcoal grill, set the temp to low heat.
2. Portion sausage into quarter-size pieces and place on mesh grate. Place grate on the grill and cook for 1 hour. Sausage pieces will have a smoky deep brown color. Move the mesh tray of sausage to the side of the grill with indirect heat.
3. Open the Flame Broiler Plate and increase the temperature to 350°F. Place a large cast iron skillet on the grill, over direct flame. Add butter and onions and cook until the onions caramelize lightly, stirring often. Add the sage and thyme and stir to combine.
4. Gently fold in the dried cranberries and cubed cornbread, then add sausage directly from mesh grate.
5. In a small mixing bowl, whisk together the heavy cream, chicken stock, egg, and Pulled Pork Rub. Pour mixture over the cornbread stuffing mix.
6. Cover grill and cook 30 minutes or until heated through and crispy on top.

Smoked Sweet Beer Bread

Servings: 6
Cooking Time: 60 Minutes

Ingredients:

- 3 cups all-purpose flour, sifted
- 2 tbsp. sugar
- 1 tbsp. baking powder
- 1 tsp. salt
- 1 (12 oz) can or bottle beer (not too dark or bitter)
- 2 tbsp. honey or agave, warmed
- 6 tbsp. butter, melted

Directions:

1. Supply your smoker with wood pellets and follow the start-up procedure. Preheat the grill, with the lid closed, to 350° F.
2. Lightly grease a 9 ×5 inch loaf pan.
3. In a large mixing bowl, put in the flour, sugar, baking powder, and salt. Whisk to combine and aerate, using a wire whisk. Add the beer and honey and stir with a wooden spoon until the batter is properly mixed (Do not over-mix).
4. Pour half of the melted butter into the prepared loaf pan and pour in the batter. Pour the remaining butter over the top of the loaf.
5. Place the loaf pan on the grill grate and bake for 50 to 60 minutes or until the bread is golden brown.
6. Allow the loaf to cool slightly in the pan before removing it from the pan. Leftovers make great toast.

Smoky Apple Crepes

Servings: 6
Cooking Time: 60 Minutes

Ingredients:

- 1/2 Cup Apple Juice
- 2 Lbs Apples
- 2 Tbsp Brown Sugar
- 5 Tbsp Butter
- 3 Tbsp Butter, Melted
- Tt Caramel

- 3/4 Tsp Cinnamon, Ground
- Tt Cinnamon-Sugar
- 3/4 Tsp Cornstarch
- 2 Eggs
- 1 Cup Flour
- 2 Tsp Lemon Juice
- Tennessee Apple Butter Seasoning
- 1/2 Cup Water
- 3/4 Cup Milk

Directions:

1. Supply your smoker with wood pellets and follow the start-up procedure. Preheat the grill, with the lid closed, to 225° F. If using a gas or charcoal grill, set it up for low, indirect heat.
2. Peel, halve, and core apples.
3. Season apples with Tennessee Apple Butter then place directly on the grill grate, and smoke for 1 hour.
4. Meanwhile, prepare crêpe batter: combine eggs, milk, water, flour, and 3 tbsp of melted butter in a blender, and blend until smooth.
5. Refrigerate for 30 minutes.
6. Remove apples from grill, cool slightly, then slice thin.
7. Place a cast iron skillet on the grill and melt 3 tbsp butter with brown sugar, cinnamon, cornstarch, apple and lemon juices. Cook for 5 minutes until thick.
8. Add apples and cook for another 3 to 5 minutes, stirring to coat apples in sauce.
9. Remove from grill and set aside.
10. Preheat griddle to medium-low. If using a standard grill, preheat a cast iron skillet on medium-low heat.
11. Melt 1 teaspoon of butter on the griddle.
12. Then add ½ cup of batter, and spread with the bottom of a metal spatula, working quickly, as the batter cooks fast.
13. Cook one minute per side, until edges begin to brown. Remove from griddle, set aside, and repeat with remaining batter.
14. Spoon ¼ cup of apple filling into the center of each crêpe, then quarter-fold into a triangle.
15. Serve warm with additional apple filling, drizzle of warm caramel, and a dusting of cinnamon-sugar.

Baked Chocolate Coconut Brownies

Servings: 4
Cooking Time: 25 Minutes

Ingredients:

- 1/2 Cup gluten-free or all-purpose flour, such as Bob's Red Mill
- 1/4 Cup unsweetened alkalized cocoa powder
- 1/2 Teaspoon sea salt
- 4 Ounce semisweet chocolate, coarsely chopped
- 3/4 Cup unrefined coconut oil
- 1 Cup raw cane sugar
- 4 eggs
- 1 Teaspoon vanilla extract
- 4 Ounce semisweet chocolate chips, optional

Directions:

1. Supply your smoker with wood pellets and follow the start-up procedure. Preheat the grill, with the lid closed, to 350° F.
2. Grease a 9x9 inch baking pan and line with parchment paper.
3. Combine the flour, cocoa powder and salt in a medium bowl. Set aside.
4. In a double boiler or microwave, melt the chopped chocolate and coconut oil. Let cool slightly.
5. Add the sugar, eggs and vanilla. Whisking until well combined.
6. Whisk in the flour mixture and fold in the chocolate chips. Pour into the prepared pan.
7. Place on the grill and bake until a toothpick inserted in the center of the brownies comes out clean, about 20 to 25 minutes. This will yield a somewhat gooey brownie. Continue to bake for 5 to 10 minutes if you prefer a drier brownie. Grill: 350 °F
8. Let the brownies cool completely, then cut into squares. Store in an airtight container at room temperature for up to 3 days. Enjoy!

Smoked Cheesy Alfredo Sauce

Servings: 2
Cooking Time: 40 Minutes

Ingredients:

- 1 Cup heavy cream
- 1 Stick butter
- 1 block Parmesan cheese
- 1 Sprig fresh sage
- 2 Pinch Nutmeg

Directions:

1. Supply your smoker with wood pellets and follow the start-up procedure. Preheat the grill, with the lid closed, to 180° F.
2. Pour the cream into a saucepan along with the butter and place on the Traeger grill grate to smoke along with the parmesan cheese.
3. Smoke for 30 minutes to 1 hour, depending on how much smoke flavor you want. Turn the heat on the Traeger up to 300°F. Grill: 180 °F
4. Shred the parmesan cheese and add it and the sage sprig into the pan with the cream and butter.
5. Whisk until the cheese has all melted and season to taste with the salt and pepper and a pinch or two of the ground nutmeg.
6. While warm, pour this sauce on anything. Enjoy!

Rosemary Cranberry Apple Sage Stuffing

Servings: 7
Cooking Time: 45 Minutes

Ingredients:
- 10 Cups Day Old Diced Bread, Sliced Loaf
- 2 1/2 Cups Broth, Chicken
- 1 Cup Butter, Unsalted
- 1 Cup Diced Celery, Cut
- 1 1/2 Cups Fresh Cranberries
- 1 Beaten Egg
- 1 Medium Granny Smith Apple, Peel, Core And Dice
- 2 Tbsp Minced Parsley, Fresh
- 1 Tbsp Minced Rosemary, Fresh
- 2 Tbsp Roughly Chopped Sage
- Salt And Pepper
- 1 Tbsp Minced Thyme
- 2 Cups Diced Yellow Onion, Sliced

Directions:
1. Supply your smoker with wood pellets and follow the start-up procedure. Preheat the grill, with the lid closed, to 350° F.
2. Melt butter over medium heat. Add onions then celery and cook until onions start to become translucent.
3. In a large bowl, mix together bread, apples, cranberries, cooked onion and celery mixture, and fresh herbs.
4. Add half of the chicken broth to the mixture and stir.
5. Beat together eggs and the rest of the chicken broth in a small bowl. Pour into the bread mixture and stir until completely combined.
6. Add salt and pepper to taste.
7. Pour stuffing into a cast iron pan or baking dish. Cover with foil and bake on the grill for 30 minutes. Remove the foil and cook for an additional 15 minutes.
8. Serve immediately and enjoy!

Double Vanilla Chocolate Cake

Servings: 12
Cooking Time: 40 Minutes

Ingredients:
- 1 1/2 Tsp Baking Soda
- 1/2 Cup Butter, Melted
- 1 Cup Buttermilk, Low Fat
- 1 Jar Chocolate Icing, Prepared
- 3/4 Cup Cocoa, Powder
- 1 Cup Coffee, Hot
- 2 Large Egg
- 1 3/4 Cups Flour, All-Purpose
- 3/4 Tsp Salt
- 2 Cups Sugar
- 1 Tbsp Vanilla

Directions:
1. Supply your smoker with wood pellets and follow the start-up procedure. Preheat the grill, with the lid closed, to 350° F.
2. Stir together flour, sugar, cocoa, baking soda and salt in a large bowl. Combine eggs, buttermilk, butter and coffee and mix until smooth. Add in hot coffee and stir until combined and the dough is runny.
3. Pour the batter into two prepared baking pans and bake on the top rack of your for 40 minutes, turning the pans 180 degrees halfway through.
4. Allow to cool and then frost with chocolate icing.

Cherry Ice Cream Cobbler

Servings: 8
Cooking Time: 45 Minutes

Ingredients:
- 1 Tsp Baking Powder
- 3 Tbsp Butter, Melted
- 1 Cup Flour
- Ice Cream, Prepared
- 1/4 Tsp Salt
- 3/4 Cup Sugar
- 1/2 Cup Milk

Directions:
1. Supply your smoker with wood pellets and follow the start-up procedure. Preheat the grill, with the lid closed, to 350° F.
2. In a bowl, combine flour, sugar, baking powder, salt and mix to incorporate. Stir in butter and milk and mix until combined. In a cast iron pan, dump in cherry pie filling and pile on the prepared topping to cover.
3. Place in your Grill and bake for about 45 minutes, or until the topping is golden brown.
4. Let cool for a couple minutes and serve with ice cream.

Chicken Pizza On The Grill

Servings: 4
Cooking Time: 10 Minutes

Ingredients:
- 3 Boneless, Skinless Chicken Breast
- 5 Cups Flour, Strong
- 3 Cups Georgia Style Bbq Sauce
- 3 Cups Mozzarella Cheese, Shredded
- 1 Tsp Olive Oil
- 3 Cups Georgia Style BBQ Sauce
- 1 1/2 Cups Red Bell Peppers, Diced
- 1 1/2 Cups Red Onion, Diced

- 1 Tsp Sugar
- 1/2 Cup Water, Hot
- 1 1/4 Cup Water, Warm
- 2 Tsb Active Yeast, Instant

Directions:

1. Roll your pizza dough so it forms a base about a 1/2 inch thick. To impress your friends and family, you'll want to aim for a nice, pizza like shape. HINT: use a sprinkle of cornmeal on the countertop to aid in moving the dough.

2. Now for the toppings! Start by spreading 1 cup of Georgia Style BBQ sauce onto each base. Make sure to leave a small portion for the crust! Next, load up with sliced, cooked chicken breasts, diced red onions and red bell peppers before finishing off with a two cups of shredded mozzarella cheese.

3. Supply your smoker with wood pellets and follow the start-up procedure. Preheat the grill, with the lid closed, to 500° F. Place the pizza stone in your grill. Pick up your pizza using a flat surface like a chopping board and slide the pizza carefully onto the hot stone. Close the lid and let your homemade wood-fired pizza bake for 10 - 12 minutes. Remove once your pizza has a golden crust and the cheese is bubbling. Cut and serve for pizza you'll hardly want to share.

Blueberry Bread Pudding

Servings: 4

Cooking Time: 60 Minutes

Ingredients:

- 5 eggs
- 3 Cup sugar
- 2 1/2 Cup milk
- 1 1/2 Teaspoon vanilla
- 1 Teaspoon cinnamon
- 1 Pinch salt
- 5 Cup Bread
- 3 Cup blueberries

Directions:

1. Beat the eggs in a large mixing bowl. Whisk in the sugar, milk, vanilla, cinnamon, and salt.

2. In another large bowl, combine the bread and 2 cups (200 g) of the blueberries.

3. Pour the egg mixture over the bread-blueberry mixture and let sit for 30 minutes. Meanwhile, place muffin liners in a muffin tin.

4. Supply your smoker with wood pellets and follow the start-up procedure. Preheat the grill, with the lid open.

5. Spoon the bread-blueberry mixture into the prepared cups; evenly top each with the remaining cup of blueberries, pressing them gently into the pudding with the back of a spoon.

6. Dust the top with sugar.

7. Arrange the pan directly on the grill grate and smoke for 30 minutes. Grill:180°F

8. Increase the temperature to 350F (180 C), and bake until the pudding is set and golden brown on top, about 25 minutes. Grill:350°F

9. Let cool slightly, then sift powdered sugar on top. Serve warm with sweetened whipped cream or vanilla ice cream, if desired.

Spiced Lemon Cherry Pie

Servings: 6-8

Cooking Time: 60 Minutes

Ingredients:

- 1/2 Teaspoon Cinnamon, Ground
- 1/2 Teaspoon Cloves, Ground
- 1/2 Cup Cornstarch
- 1 Pound Frozen Sweet Dark Cherries, Thawed
- 1 Teaspoon Water (Beaten With Egg) 1 Egg
- 1 Lemon, Juice
- 1 Lemon, Zest
- 2 Prepared Store Bought Or Homemade Pie Crust
- 1 Teaspoon Hickory Honey Sea Salt Seasoning
- 1 Cup Sugar, Granulated
- 1 Teaspoon Vanilla Extract

Directions:

1. In a large bowl, mix together the thawed cherries and their juices, sugar, cornstarch, lemon zest, lemon juice, cinnamon, clove, vanilla extract and Hickory Honey Sea Salt. Allow to sit for 30 minutes.

2. Flour a work surface and roll out one of the prepared pie crusts so that it fits a 9 inch pie tin. Fill with the cherry pie filling and refrigerate. When the pie is chilled, roll out the second pie crust, brush the edge of the first pie crust with the egg mixture, top with the second pie crust, crimp the edge with a fork, and chill. Alternatively, cut the second pie crust into strips and form a lattice pattern, attaching the strips with the egg mixture. Chill the pie for 15-30 minutes, or until the dough is very cold and firm. Brush the top of the pie with the remaining egg mixture.

3. Supply your smoker with wood pellets and follow the start-up procedure. Preheat the grill, with the lid closed, to 350° F and grill for 45 minutes to 1 hour, or until the pie crust is golden and firm and the filling is bubbly. Remove from the grill and allow to cool at room temperature for at least 4 hours to set the filling, then serve and enjoy!

Pumpkin Bread

Servings: 6
Cooking Time: 60 Minutes

Ingredients:

- 1 Cup Pumpkin, canned
- 2 eggs
- 2/3 Cup vegetable oil
- 1/2 Cup sour cream
- 1 Teaspoon vanilla extract
- 2 1/2 Cup flour
- 1 1/2 Teaspoon baking soda
- 1 Teaspoon salt
- 1/2 Teaspoon ground cinnamon
- 1/4 Teaspoon ground nutmeg
- 1/4 Teaspoon ground cloves
- 1/4 Teaspoon ground ginger
- As Needed butter

Directions:

1. In a large mixing bowl, combine the pumpkin, eggs, vegetable oil, sour cream, and vanilla and whisk to blend.
2. In a separate bowl, combine the flour, baking soda, salt, cinnamon, nutmeg, cloves, and ginger. Add the dry ingredients to the wet ingredients and stir to combine. Do not overmix.
3. If desired, stir in one or more of the optional ingredients (walnuts, dried cranberries, raisins, or chocolate chips). Butter the interiors of two loaf pans.
4. Sprinkle with flour to coat the buttered surfaces, and tap out any excess. Divide the batter evenly between the two pans.
5. When ready to cook, set the smoker to 350°F and preheat, lid closed for 15 minutes.
6. Arrange the loaf pans directly on the grill grate. Bake for 45 to 50 minutes, or until a skewer or toothpick inserted in the center comes out clean. Also, the top of the loaf should spring back when pressed gently with a finger.
7. Transfer the loaf pans to a cooling rack and let cool for 10 minutes before carefully turning out the pumpkin bread. Let the loaves cool thoroughly before slicing. Wrap in aluminum foil or plastic wrap if not eating right away. Serve and enjoy!

Smoked Vanilla Apple Pie

Servings: 6
Cooking Time: 45 Minutes

Ingredients:

- 1 1/2 cups of self-raising flour
- 3/4 cup of sugar
- 0.3 lbs of butter melted
- 1 tsp of vanilla extract
- 1 egg
- 0.9-lb tin of pie apples
- sugar & cinnamon for dusting

Directions:

1. Supply your smoker with wood pellets and follow the start-up procedure. Preheat the grill, with the lid closed, to 350° F.
2. Combine the self-raising flour, sugar, melted butter, vanilla, and egg in a large bowl until a golden dough texture is formed.
3. Spread half the mixture in a pie dish and press the bottoms and up the sides of the dish.
4. Pour pie apple tin into the pie and spread out evenly.
5. Sprinkle the remaining mixture over the top of the apple evenly and place in the smoker.
6. Leave for 45 minutes or until the golden crust forms on the top.
7. Dust with cinnamon and a little sugar if desired.
8. Serve warm with custard, ice cream, or both.

Italian Herb & Parmesan Scones

Servings: 8
Cooking Time: 20 Minutes

Ingredients:

- 2 1/2 Cup all-purpose flour
- 2 Teaspoon baking powder
- 1 Teaspoon baking soda
- 1/2 Teaspoon garlic salt
- 1 Tablespoon Italian Seasoning
- 1 Cup Parmesan cheese, grated
- 2 Large eggs
- 1 1/2 Cup buttermilk
- 1/4 Cup olive oil

Directions:

1. In a large mixing bowl, combine flour, baking powder, baking powder, soda, garlic salt, Italian seasoning, and 1/2 cup of the cheese. Make a well in the center.
2. In a smaller bowl, whisk together eggs, buttermilk, and olive oil.
3. Pour into the well in the dry ingredients, and stir batter just until it's combined. It will appear lumpy.
4. Oil 12 muffin cups, spray with cooking spray, or line with disposable paper liners.
5. Divide the batter evenly between the cups. Sprinkle the tops of the muffins with the remaining Parmesan cheese.
6. Supply your smoker with wood pellets and follow the start-up procedure. Preheat the grill, with the lid closed, to 400° F.
7. Arrange the muffin tin directly on the grill grate and bake the muffins for 20 to 25 minutes, or until a toothpick inserted in the center of the muffin comes out clean.
8. Cool for several minutes before removing from the muffin tin. Serve warm with butter or olive oil. Enjoy!

Baked Cheesy Parmesan Grits

Servings: 4
Cooking Time: 60 Minutes

Ingredients:
- 4 Cup chicken stock
- 3 Tablespoon butter
- 3/4 Teaspoon salt
- 1 Cup quick grits
- 1 Cup shredded cheddar cheese
- pepper
- 1/2 Cup Monterey Jack cheese, shredded
- 1/2 Cup whole milk
- 2 Large eggs

Directions:
1. Supply your smoker with wood pellets and follow the start-up procedure. Preheat the grill, with the lid closed, to 350° F.
2. Butter an 8" baking dish or a 10" cast iron pan.
3. Bring the chicken stock, butter, and salt to boil in medium saucepan. Gradually whisk in grits.
4. Reduce heat to medium and cook until mixture thickens slightly, stirring often about 8 minutes. Remove from heat.
5. Add cheeses and stir until melted. Season with pepper and salt to taste.
6. Whisk together milk and eggs in small bowl. Gradually whisk mixture into grits.
7. Pour the cheese grits into the buttered cast iron pan. Bake until grits feel firm to touch, about 1 hour. Grill: 350 °F
8. Remove from grill and let stand 10 minutes before serving. Enjoy!

Vanilla Chocolate Chip Cookies

Servings: 12
Cooking Time: 20 Minutes

Ingredients:
- 3/4 cup brown sugar
- 3/4 cup white sugar
- 1 stick butter, room temp
- 2 eggs
- 1 tsp vanilla
- 2 1/2 cups flour
- 1/2 tsp salt
- 1 tsp baking soda
- 1 cup Chocolate Chips

Directions:
1. Cream your butter and sugar together in a mixing bowl using a hand mixer or stand mixer on medium speed for about 4-5 minutes.
2. Once the butter is creamed, add the eggs and vanilla. Continue mixing for an additional minute.
3. Put flour, salt, and baking soda in a sifter. Sift it into your creamed butter mixture.
4. Scrape the sides of your mixing bowl with a rubber spatula, and then turn your mixer on to low speed.
5. Let it mix a little, and then scrape the sides again. Stop mixing when there are one or two streaks of flour left in the cookie dough.
6. Scrape the sides of your bowl and pour in a cup of chocolate chips, and turn the mixer to low again to mix the chocolate. It should take just a few turns for the chocolate pieces to be well incorporated.
7. Line a large baking sheet with parchment paper. Using a medium cookie scoop (about 1.5 tbsp), drop evenly spaced dollops of cookie dough onto the cookie sheet.
8. Supply your smoker with wood pellets and follow the start-up procedure. Preheat the grill, with the lid closed, to 350° F. Place the cookie sheet in your smoker, and let them cook for about 12 minutes.
9. Let them sit on a cooling rack while you continue to cook the additional cookies.
10. Cool for a few minutes to let cookies set.
11. Enjoy!

Zucchini Bread

Servings: 6
Cooking Time: 50 Minutes

Ingredients:
- 1 Cup Walnuts, Chopped
- 2 Large zucchini
- 1 Teaspoon salt
- 1 Teaspoon ground cinnamon
- 1/4 Teaspoon ground cloves
- 1/4 Teaspoon baking powder
- 3 Cup all-purpose flour
- 1 eggs
- 2 Cup sugar
- 1/2 Cup vegetable oil
- 1/2 Cup Yogurt
- 1 1/2 Teaspoon vanilla extract

Directions:
1. Grease and flour two 9- by 5-inch bread pans, preferably nonstick.
2. When ready to cook, set the temperature to 350°F and preheat, lid closed for 15 minutes.
3. Spread the walnuts on a pie plate and toast for 10 minutes, stirring once. Let cool, then coarsely chop. Set aside.
4. Trim the ends off the zucchini, then coarsely grate into a colander set over the sink on a box grater (or use the shredding disk on a food processor). You'll need 2 cups.

5.   Sprinkle with the salt and let drain for 30 minutes. Press on the zucchini with paper towels to expel excess water.

6.   Sift the flour, baking powder, cinnamon, and cloves in a mixing bowl or on a large sheet of parchment or wax paper.

7.   Combine the eggs, sugar, oil, yogurt, and vanilla in a large mixing bowl and mix on medium speed. (You can mix the batter by hand, if desired.) Add half the dry ingredients and mix on low speed; add the remaining dry ingredients and mix until just combined.

8.   Stir in the walnuts and zucchini by hand.

9.   Divide the batter between the prepared baking pans.

10.   Arrange the pans directly on the grill grate and bake for 50 minutes, or until a bamboo skewer inserted in the center of the breads comes out clean.

11.   Transfer to a wire rack and let cool for 10 minutes, then remove the breads from the pans. For best results, let the breads cool completely before slicing.

Old Fashioned Cornbread

Servings: 4
Cooking Time: 25 Minutes

Ingredients:
- 1 Cup all-purpose flour
- 1 Cup Cornmeal
- 1 Tablespoon sugar
- 2 Teaspoon baking powder
- 1/2 Teaspoon salt
- 3 Tablespoon butter
- 1 Cup milk
- 1 Whole egg, lightly beaten

Directions:
1.   In a mixing bowl, combine the flour, cornmeal, sugar, baking powder, and salt.

2.   Melt the butter in a small saucepan. Remove from the heat, and stir in the milk and the egg. (Make sure the mixture isn't hot or the egg will curdle.)

3.   Add the milk-egg mixture to the dry ingredients and stir to combine. Do not overmix.

4.   Spread the batter evenly in a greased 8 or 9-inch square baking pan or pie plate.

5.   Supply your smoker with wood pellets and follow the start-up procedure. Preheat the grill, with the lid closed, to 375° F.

6.   Bake the cornbread until it begins to pull away from the sides of the pan and the top is beginning to brown, 25 to 35 minutes. Cut into squares (or wedges, if you used a pie plate) for serving. Grill: 375 °F

Traeger Baked Focaccia

Servings: 4
Cooking Time: 40 Minutes

Ingredients:
- 2 1/2 Cup all-purpose flour
- 1 Cup warm water (110°F to 115°F)
- 1 Tablespoon instant yeast
- 1 Teaspoon sugar
- 1 Teaspoon salt
- 3 Tablespoon olive oil, plus more as needed
- 1 Tablespoon fresh herbs such as thyme, rosemary and sage
- 2 Tablespoon freshly grated Parmesan, optional
- flaky sea salt

Directions:
1.   Place the flour, water, yeast, sugar, salt and oil in the bowl of a stand mixer and mix for 60 seconds. You may also use a food processor by adding the flour, sugar, salt and yeast to the bowl and process while streaming in the warm water followed by the olive oil. Process until combined and a ball forms.

2.   Gently form the sticky dough into a ball, if needed, and place in a well-oiled 12 inch cast iron skillet. Drizzle the top of the dough with more olive oil. Cover with plastic wrap and a kitchen towel and let rise in a warm spot for 45 to 60 minutes.

3.   After the dough has risen, press the dough to the edges of the pan and cover it again. Let rise for 15 minutes.

4.   Supply your smoker with wood pellets and follow the start-up procedure. Preheat the grill, with the lid closed, to 375° F.

5.   Uncover the dough and press it again to the edges of the pan using your fingertips to create divots.

6.   Drizzle with olive oil, then sprinkle with herbs, Parmesan and flaky salt.

7.   Bake it on the Traeger for 30 to 40 minutes, or until golden brown and cooked through. Allow it to cool slightly before removing from cast iron and slicing. Enjoy! Grill: 375 °F

Carrot Cake

Servings: 4-6
Cooking Time: 60 Minutes

Ingredients:
- 8 carrots, peeled and grated
- 4 eggs, at room temperature
- 1 cup vegetable oil
- ½ cup milk
- 1 teaspoon vanilla extract
- 2 cups sugar
- 2 cups self-rising or cake flour
- 2 teaspoons baking soda
- 1 teaspoon salt
- 1 cup finely chopped pecans
- Nonstick cooking spray or butter, for greasing
- 8 ounces cream cheese
- 1 cup confectioners' sugar
- 8 tablespoons (1 stick) unsalted butter, at room temperature

- 1 teaspoon vanilla extract
- ½ teaspoon salt
- 2 tablespoons to ¼ cup milk

Directions:

1. For the cake:
2. Supply your smoker with wood pellets and follow the start-up procedure. Preheat, with the lid closed, to 350°F.
3. In a food processor or blender, combine the grated carrots, eggs, oil, milk, and vanilla, and process until the carrots are finely minced.
4. In a large mixing bowl, combine the sugar, flour, baking soda, and salt.
5. Add the carrot mixture to the flour mixture and stir until well incorporated. Fold in the chopped pecans.
6. Coat a 9-by-13-inch baking pan with cooking spray.
7. Pour the batter into prepared pan and place on the grill grate. Close the lid and smoke for about 1 hour, or until a toothpick inserted in the center comes out clean.
8. Remove the cake from the grill and let cool completely.
9. For the frosting:
10. Using an electric mixer on low speed, beat the cream cheese, confectioners' sugar, butter, vanilla, and salt, adding 2 tablespoons to ¼ cup of milk to thin the frosting as needed.
11. Frost the cooled cake and slice to serve.

Sourdough Pizza

Servings: 4
Cooking Time: 12 Minutes

Ingredients:

- 1 1/2 Cup Fresh Sourdough Starter
- 1 Tablespoon olive oil
- 1 Teaspoon Jacobsen Salt Co. Pure Kosher Sea Salt
- 1 1/4 Cup all-purpose flour

Directions:

1. Supply your smoker with wood pellets and follow the start-up procedure. Preheat the grill, with the lid closed, to 450° F.
2. Mix together the fresh sourdough starter, one tablespoon of oil, Jacobsen salt and 1-1/4 cups of flour. Add more flour, a little at a time, as needed to form a pizza dough consistency.
3. Allow the dough to rest for 30 minutes, to allow for easier rolling. Roll the dough out into a circle, using a small amount of flour to prevent sticking.
4. Place on a pizza stone. Bake the crust for approximately 7 minutes Grill: 450 °F
5. Remove the crust from the grill; brush on remaining oil to prevent toppings from soaking into the crust. Add the desired toppings and return pizza to grill; bake until the crust browns and the cheese melts.

Caramelized Bourbon Baked Pears

Servings: 4
Cooking Time: 30 Minutes

Ingredients:

- 3 Whole Pears, fresh
- 1/4 Cup brown sugar
- 1/4 Cup bourbon
- 2 Tablespoon butter, melted
- 1 Teaspoon vanilla extract
- 1/2 Teaspoon salt

Directions:

1. Supply your smoker with wood pellets and follow the start-up procedure. Preheat the grill, with the lid closed, to 325° F.
2. Peel and core the pears. Arrange them in a buttered baking dish.
3. In a small bowl, combine the brown sugar, bourbon, butter, vanilla, cinnamon and salt. Pour the bourbon mixture over the pears.
4. Place the baking dish on the grill grate, close the lid and bake for 30-35 minutes or until the pears are fork tender. Grill: 325 °F
5. Transfer to a serving plate and spoon the caramelized bourbon mixture over the pears.
6. Serve warm over vanilla ice cream. Enjoy!

Blueberry Sour Cream Muffins

Servings: 8
Cooking Time: 25 Minutes

Ingredients:

- 2 Cup flour
- 1/2 Teaspoon salt
- 1/2 Teaspoon baking soda
- 1/2 Cup butter
- 3/4 Cup sugar, plus more for muffin tops
- 2 Large eggs
- 3/4 Cup sour cream
- 1 1/2 Teaspoon vanilla extract
- 1 1/2 Cup blueberries, fresh or thawed

Directions:

1. In a small mixing bowl, whisk together the flour, salt and baking soda.
2. In another bowl, using a wooden spoon or a mixer, beat the butter and sugar until light-colored and fluffy. Beat in the eggs, one at a time. Stir in sour cream and vanilla.
3. Add the flour mixture gradually and mix just until incorporated. Using a rubber spatula, gently fold in the blueberries.
4. Line a 12-cup muffin tin with the cupcake liners. Using an ice cream scoop or spoon, fill each muffin cup two-thirds full with the batter. Sprinkle sugar evenly over the top of each muffin.

5.   Supply your smoker with wood pellets and follow the start-up procedure. Preheat the grill, with the lid closed, to 375° F.

6.   Bake the muffins 25 to 30 minutes, or until a toothpick inserted comes out clean. Served warm and with butter. Grill: 375 °F

Chocolate Lava Cake With Smoked Whipped Cream

Servings: 4
Cooking Time: 45 Minutes

Ingredients:
- 1 Pint heavy whipping cream
- 9 Tablespoon Butter
- 220 G Semisweet Chocolate
- 1 1/4 Cup powdered sugar
- 2 Large eggs
- 2 egg yolk
- 6 Tablespoon flour
- 1 Tablespoon Bourbon Vanilla
- Powdered Sugar
- cocoa powder

Directions:
1.   Supply your smoker with wood pellets and follow the start-up procedure. Preheat the grill, with the lid closed, to 180° F.

2.   For the Smoked Whipped Cream: Add cream to a shallow, aluminum baking pan. Place the pan on the grill and smoke for 30 minutes.

3.   Pour the smoked cream into a large mixing bowl and refrigerate for later use. Grill: 180 °F

4.   Increase the grill temperature to 375°F and preheat. Grill: 375 °F

5.   Brush 4 small soufflé cups with 1 tablespoon melted butter.

6.   Melt the chocolate and remaining butter in a heatproof bowl over simmering water, stir until smooth.

7.   Stir in powdered sugar. Add eggs and egg yolks, stirring continuously. Whisk in flour until blended completely.

8.   Pour batter into the prepared soufflé cups. Place them on the Traeger and bake for 13-14 minutes, or until the sides are set. Grill: 375 °F

9.   For the Whipped Cream: Remove the chilled smoked cream from the refrigerator, add the bourbon vanilla and whip until airy.

10.   Add confectioners sugar and continue whipping until whipped cream forms stiff peaks.

11.   Dust lava cakes with confectioners sugar and cocoa, top with a dollop of smoke-infused whipped cream. Enjoy!

Smoky Pimento Cheese Cornbread

Servings: 4

Cooking Time: 30 Minutes

Ingredients:
- 2 Tsp Baking Powder
- 2 Cups Buttermilk, Low Fat
- 1/2 Cup Cornmeal, Yellow
- 2 Egg
- 1 1/2 Cups Flour, All-Purpose
- 16 Oz Pimento Cheese Spread
- 2 Tbsp Bacon Cheddar Seasoning
- 1/4 Cup Sugar

Directions:
1.   Supply your smoker with wood pellets and follow the start-up procedure. Preheat the grill, with the lid closed, to 350° F. Place a cast iron skillet in the grill to preheat.

2.   In a bowl, mix together the eggs, buttermilk, Bacon Cheddar Seasoning, and pimento cheese spread. Add in the sugar, baking powder, cornmeal and flour. Mix until well combined.

3.   With cooking gloves, carefully remove the cast iron skillet from the grill, grease it, and add the cornbread batter.

4.   Grill for 25-30 minutes, or until the cornbread is golden and pulling away from the edges of the skillet.

Grilled Apple Pie

Servings: 4
Cooking Time: 40 Minutes

Ingredients:
- 5 Whole Apples
- 1/4 Cup sugar
- 1 Tablespoon cornstarch
- 1 Whole refrigerated pie crust
- 1/4 Cup Peach, preserves

Directions:
1.   Supply your smoker with wood pellets and follow the start-up procedure. Preheat the grill, with the lid closed, to 375° F.In a medium bowl, mix the apples, sugar, and cornstarch; set aside.

2.   Unroll pie crust. Place in ungreased pie pan. With the back of a spoon, spread preserves evenly on crust. Arrange the apple slices in an even layer in the pie pan. Slightly fold crust over filling.

3.   Place a baking sheet upside down on the grill grate to make an elevated surface. Put the pan with pie on top so it is elevated off grill. (This will help prevent the bottom from overcooking.) Cook the pie for 30 to 40 minutes or until crust is golden brown, the filling is bubbly. Grill: 375 °F

4.   Remove from grill; cool 10 minutes before serving. Enjoy!
*Cook times will vary depending on set and ambient temperatures.

Garlic Cheese Pull Apart Bread

Servings: 2
Cooking Time: 20 Minutes

Ingredients:

- 1 Loaf Bread, Sourdough Round
- 2 1/2 Tbsp Butter, Salted
- 8 Oz Fontina Cheese
- 1 Grated Garlic, Roasted
- 1/4 Cup Parsley, Minced Fresh
- 1 Tsp Red Flakes Pepper
- 1 Pinch Salt

Directions:

1. Start your Grill on "smoke" with the lid open until a fire is established in the burn pot (3-7 minutes). Supply your smoker with wood pellets and follow the start-up procedure. Preheat the grill, with the lid closed, to 300° F.

2. In a small bowl, add the soft butter, grated garlic, red pepper flakes, sea salt, and ¼ cup of the chopped parsley, and whisk together. With a bread serrated knife, cut 1-inch slices into the bread, not cutting all the way through the bottom of the load. With a butter knife, spread a thin layer of the butter mixture on each slice of the bread. Take the serrated knife again, and cut across the loaf to form 1 inch squares. Next, slice the cheese into small thin slices, then stuff one slice into each bread opening. Place the bread on a baking sheet, and cover tightly with aluminum foil. Place on the grill for about 10 minutes, remove the foil, and grill for a few more minutes until the top is nicely golden and the cheese is oozing. Remove from the grill, sprinkle with fresh parsley leaves, then serve.

Basil Margherita Pizza

Servings: 6
Cooking Time: 25 Minutes

Ingredients:

- Basil, Chopped
- 2 Cups Flour, All-Purpose
- Mozzarella Cheese, Sliced Rounds
- 1 Cup Pizza Sauce
- 1 Teaspoon Salt
- 1 Teaspoon Sugar
- 1 Tomato, Sliced
- 1 Cup Water, Warm
- 1 Teaspoon Yeast, Instant

Directions:

1. Combine the water, yeast, and sugar in a small bowl and let sit for about 5 minutes.

2. In a large bowl, stir together the flour and salt. Pour in the yeast mixture and mix until a soft dough forms. Knead for about 2 minutes. Place in an oiled bowl and cover with a cloth. Let the dough sit and rise for about 45 minutes or until the dough has doubled in size.

3. Roll out on a flat, floured surface (or on a pizza stone) until you"ve reached your desired shape and thickness.

4. Supply your smoker with wood pellets and follow the start-up procedure. Preheat the grill, with the lid closed, to 350° F.

5. On the rolled out dough, pour on the pizza sauce, cheese, and then tomatoes and basil. Place in your Grill and bake for about 25 minutes, or until the cheese is melted and slightly golden brown.

Grilled Bourbon Pecan Pie

Servings: 6
Cooking Time: 45 Minutes

Ingredients:

- 2 Tbsp Bourbon
- 1/2 Cup Brown Sugar
- 1/3 Cup Unsalted Butter, Melted
- 1/2 Cup Light, 1/2 Cup Dark Corn Syrup
- 3 Egg
- 1/4 Tsp Hickory Honey Smoked Salt
- Decoration Pecan
- 1 1/4 Cup Chopped Pecans, Coarsely Broken
- 1 Prepared Or Homemade Pie Shell, Deep
- 1/2 Cup Sugar
- 1 Tsp Vanilla Extract

Directions:

1. Supply your smoker with wood pellets and follow the start-up procedure. Preheat the grill, with the lid closed, to 375° F. Meanwhile, prepare your pie crust in a 9 cast iron skillet or heat proof pie plate.

2. In a large bowl, beat the eggs until smooth. Add the brown sugar and white sugar and mix until smooth. Add the light corn syrup, dark corn syrup, vanilla, bourbon, melted butter, and Hickory Honey Salt. Mix until smooth. Stir in your chopped pecans and pour into the pie crust. Top with the whole pecans, if desired.

3. Grill covered for 35-45 minutes, until the pie is just set around the edges but still has a slight jiggle in the center.

4. Allow the pie to cool completely before slicing. Enjoy!

Baked Pear Tarte Tatin

Servings: 6
Cooking Time: 45 Minutes

Ingredients:

- 2 1/2 Cup all-purpose flour
- 2 Tablespoon sugar
- butter chilled
- 8 Tablespoon cold water

- 1/4 Cup granulated sugar
- 1/4 Cup butter
- 8 Whole Bartlett Pear

Directions:

1. Supply your smoker with wood pellets and follow the start-up procedure. Preheat the grill, with the lid closed, to 350° F.

2. For the crust: Place flour and sugar in a food processor and pulse to mix. Add butter a little at a time while pulsing. Once it starts to looks like cornmeal, add the water until dough start to come together.

3. Form a round with the dough, wrap in plastic and let it cool in the refrigerator.

4. While dough cools, make the caramel sauce. In a sauce pan, add 1/4 cup granulated sugar and 1/4 cup butter. Cook butter and sugar until it becomes a dark caramel, a couple minutes.

5. Pour caramel in the bottom of 10 inch deep cake pan. While the caramel is still hot, arrange pear wedges in a fan formation covering the caramel.

6. Roll the chilled pie dough into a circle big enough to cover the pan. Prick the pie dough with a fork and cover the pan with the pie dough. Trim the crust leaving room for shrinkage.

7. Place on the grill and bake for 45 minutes or until pears are soft. The pears will be soft and most of the juice will evaporate and thicken.

8. Let sit for 3 minutes. While pan is still hot, place a plate over pie and flip over. Slowly lift the plate.

9. Serve warm, topped with vanilla ice cream or whipped cream. Enjoy!

Smoker Wheat Bread

Servings: 6
Cooking Time: 60 Minutes

Ingredients:

- As Needed extra-virgin olive oil
- 2 Cup all-purpose flour
- 1 Cup whole wheat flour
- 1 1/4 Ounce Packet, Active Dry Yeast
- 1 1/4 Teaspoon salt
- 1 1/2 Cup water
- As Needed Cornmeal

Directions:

1. Oil a large mixing bowl and set aside. In a second mixing bowl, combine the flours, yeast, and salt.

2. Push your sleeve up to your elbow and form your fingers into a claw. Mix the dry ingredients until well-combined.

3. Add the water and mix until blended. The dough will be wet, shaggy, and somewhat stringy.

4. Tip the dough into the oiled mixing bowl and cover with plastic wrap.

5. Allow the dough to rise at room temperature-- about 70 degrees-- for 2 hours, or until the surface is bubbled.

6. Turn the dough out onto a lightly floured work surface and lightly flour the top. With floured hands, fold the dough over on itself twice. Cover loosely with plastic wrap and allow the dough to rest for 15 minutes.

7. Dust a clean lint-free cotton towel with cornmeal, wheat bran, or flour. With floured hands, gently form the dough into a ball and place it, seam side down, on the towel.

8. Dust the top of the ball with cornmeal, wheat bran, or flour, and cover the dough with a second towel. Let the dough rise until doubled in size; the dough will not spring back when poked with a finger.

9. In the meantime, start the smoker grill and set temperature to 450 F. Preheat, lid closed, for 10-15 minutes.

10. Put a lidded 6- to 8-quart cast iron Dutch oven - preferably one coated with enamel, on the grill grate.

11. When the dough has risen, remove the top towel, slide your hand under the bottom towel to support the dough, then carefully tip the dough, seam side up, into the preheated pot.

12. Remove the towel. Shake the pot a couple of times if the dough looks lopsided: It will straighten out as it bakes.

13. Cover the pot with the lid and bake the bread for 30 minutes. Remove the lid and continue to bake the bread for 15 to 30 minutes more, or until it is nicely browned and sounds hollow when rapped with your knuckles.

14. Turn onto a wire rack to cool. Slice with a serrated knife. Enjoy!

Lemon Strawberry Rhubarb Pie

Servings: 8
Cooking Time: 30 Minutes

Ingredients:

- 1/3 Cup Flour
- 1 Tbsp Lemon, Zest
- 1 Prepard Pie Shell, Deep
- 3 Stalks Rhubarb
- 2 1/2 Cups Strawberry
- 1 Cup Sugar

Directions:

1. Summer baking never has to stop when you can use your Wood Pellet Grill to bake anything from cookies to pie! In this recipe, we will show you how to bake a delicious barbecued strawberry rhubarb pie without turning your kitchen into an oven.

2. Supply your smoker with wood pellets and follow the start-up procedure. Preheat the grill, with the lid closed, to 400° F.

3. Slice rhubarb and strawberries into bite sized pieces. Combine sugar, flour and lemon zest with rhubarb and strawberries. Pour into prepared pie crust. Cover with top crust.

4. Bake in Grill for 1 hour or until crust is crispy.

5. Serve hot.

Eggs Ham Benedict

Servings: 6
Cooking Time: 15 Minutes

Ingredients:
- 1 Biscuit Dough, Tube
- 6 Egg
- 16 Ham, Sliced
- 1 Packet Hollandaise Sauce, Package

Directions:
1. Supply your smoker with wood pellets and follow the start-up procedure. Preheat the grill, with the lid closed, to 350° F.
2. Grease a muffin tin and crack an egg in each cup. Place on the grate of the for about 10 minutes or until the whites are fully cooked.
3. At the same time, place your biscuit dough on a greased pan. Follow the directions on the packaging but bake on the . Place 2 slices of ham per biscuit on the pan as well.
4. While the ham, eggs, and biscuits are cooking, prepare the Hollandaise Sauce according to the directions on the packet.
5. When everything is fully cooked, cut a biscuit in half, and stack one or two slices of ham, 1 egg and a dollop of Hollandaise sauce. Repeat for each half biscuit. Serve with fresh fruit.

Quick Baked Dinner Rolls

Servings: 8
Cooking Time: 30 Minutes

Ingredients:
- 2 Tablespoon quick-rise yeast
- 1 Teaspoon salt
- 1/4 Cup sugar
- 3 1/3 Cup flour
- 1/4 Cup unsalted butter, softened
- 1 egg
- cooking spray
- 1 egg, for egg wash

Directions:
1. Combine yeast and warm water in a small bowl to activate the yeast. Let sit until foamy, about 5-10 minutes.
2. Combine salt, sugar, and flour in the bowl of a stand mixer fitted with the dough hook. Pour water and yeast into the dry ingredients with the machine running on low.
3. Add butter and egg and mix for 10 minutes gradually increasing the speed from low to high.
4. Form the dough into a ball and place in a buttered bowl. Cover with a cloth and let the dough rise for approximately 40 minutes.
5. Transfer the risen dough to a lightly floured surface and divide into 8 pieces forming a ball with each.

6. Lightly spray a cast iron pan with cooking spray and arrange balls in the pan. Cover with a cloth and let rise 20 minutes.
7. Supply your smoker with wood pellets and follow the start-up procedure. Preheat the grill, with the lid closed, to 375° F.
8. Brush rolls with egg wash and then bake for 30 minutes until lightly browned. Serve hot. Enjoy! Grill: 375 °F

Sopapilla Cheesecake By Doug Scheiding

Servings: 8
Cooking Time: 45 Minutes

Ingredients:
- 2 Tablespoon softened butter
- 24 Ounce cream cheese
- 2 Cup granulated sugar, divided
- 2 Teaspoon vanilla
- 2 Can Pillsbury Butter Flake Crescent Rolls
- 1/2 Cup butter, melted
- cinnamon

Directions:
1. Coat a 9x13 inch baking dish with 2 tablespoons softened butter and set aside.
2. Supply your smoker with wood pellets and follow the start-up procedure. Preheat the grill, with the lid closed, to 350° F.
3. In a mixer, combine cream cheese, 1 to 1-1/2 cups of sugar and vanilla. Mix for 60 to 90 seconds on high with paddle attachment.
4. Take crescents out of the refrigerator. Open one can and place into the buttered 9x13 inch rectangular metal pan or glass dish. Make sure to fill in the gaps in this bottom layer of crescents.
5. Put the cream cheese mixture on the top of the crescent layer using a spatula to make it level.
6. Open the second can of crescents and put on top of the cream cheese layer, again filling in the gaps in the crescents to cover middle.
7. Pour 1/2 cup of melted butter on the top of the last layer of crescent. Start on sides first then middle.
8. Then sprinkle 1/4 cup to 1/2 cup of sugar over the entire pan followed by a light, even dusting of cinnamon.
9. Place pan directly on the grill grate and bake for 40 to 50 minutes until top is brown and starting to get crusty. Grill: 350 °F
10. Remove from grill and let cool 5 to 10 minutes. This allows the cheesecake to set which makes portioning easier. This dessert can be served warm or cold. Enjoy!

The Dan Patrick Show Pull-apart Pesto Bread

Servings: 8
Cooking Time: 25 Minutes

Ingredients:
- 1 Sourdough Bread, loaf
- 1/2 Cup butter, melted
- 1 Cup Pesto Sauce
- 1 1/2 Cup Italian Cheese Blend

Directions:
1.   Supply your smoker with wood pellets and follow the start-up procedure. Preheat the grill, with the lid closed, to 350° F.
2.   Using a serrated knife, make 1" diagonal cuts through the bread leaving the bottom crust intact. Turn the bread and make diagonal cuts in the opposite direction, creating diamonds.
3.   Place the bread on a sheet of foil large enough to wrap around the entire loaf. Pour the melted butter into the cracks in the bread. Using a spoon spread the pesto into the cracks then follow with the cheese stuffing it down into each crack.
4.   Fold up the edges of the foil to wrap up the loaf and transfer to a baking sheet. Place the baking sheet directly on the grill grate.
5.   Bake for 15 minutes then unwrap the foil and cook for an additional 10 minutes. Remove from the grill and serve. Enjoy! Grill: 350 °F
6.   Follow along as we give you a recipe each day this week from The Dan Patrick Show Game Day Recipes eBook.

Crescent Rolls

Servings: 8
Cooking Time: 12 Minutes

Ingredients:
- 1 Crescent Dough, Can

Directions:
1.   Supply your smoker with wood pellets and follow the start-up procedure. Preheat the grill, with the lid closed, to 375° F.
2.   Unroll the dough and separate into triangles. Roll up the triangles and place on an ungreased nonstick cookie sheet. Bake for 10 -12 minutes on your Grill. You will know that they are finished when the rolls are golden brown.

Vanilla Chocolate Bacon Cupcakes

Servings: 12
Cooking Time: 120 Minutes

Ingredients:
- 1 Lb Bacon
- 1 1/2 Tsp Baking Powder
- 1 1/2 Tsp Baking Soda
- 1 Cup Cocoa, Powder
- 2 Egg
- 1 3/4 Cups Flour
- 1 Cup Milk, Whole
- 1/2 Cup Oil
- 1 Tsp Salt
- 2 Cups Sugar
- 2 Tsp Vanilla

Directions:
1.   Supply your smoker with wood pellets and follow the start-up procedure. Preheat the grill, with the lid closed, to 250° F.
2.   Once your grill is preheated, place bacon strips on the grates. Smoke for 1hr-1 ½ hours or until desired crispiness is achieved.
3.   Remove the bacon from the grill and set aside.
4.   Increase set the temperature to 350°F and preheat.
5.   Mix the rest of the ingredients in a bowl with an electric mixer until it is nice and smooth.
6.   Pour the mixture into a cupcake tin.
7.   Transfer the tin to your grill and bake for about 20 - 25 minutes.
8.   Allow the cupcakes to cool on a wire rack. Once cooled, top with your favorite premade icing and a half of strip of the bacon. Serve and enjoy!

Maple Syrup Pancake Casserole

Servings: 6
Cooking Time: 60 Minutes

Ingredients:
- 2 Tbsp Butter
- 1/2 Cup Chocolate Chips
- 4 Egg
- Maple Syrup
- 12 - 14 Pancakes
- Powdered Sugar
- 1/4 Cup Sugar, Granulated
- 1 Tsp Vanilla Extract
- 1 1/2 Cup Whole Milk

Directions:
1.   In a mixing bowl, whisk together flour, baking powder, sugar, and salt. Then pour in the milk, egg and melted butter; mix until smooth.
2.   Supply your smoker with wood pellets and follow the start-up procedure. Preheat the grill, with the lid closed, to medium-low heat. If using a gas or charcoal grill, preheat a large cast iron skillet over medium-low heat.
3.   Lightly oil the griddle, then scoop the batter onto the griddle, using approximately ¼ cup for each pancake. Cook 1 to 2 minutes per side, until golden brown. Set aside to cool for 15 minutes, then assemble the casserole.

Lemon Chicken, Broccoli, String Beans Foil Packs

Servings: 4
Cooking Time: 20 Minutes

Ingredients:

- 2 Cups Broccoli
- 3 Tbsp Butter, Melted
- 4 Chicken, Boneless/Skinless
- 1 Garlic, Minced
- 1 1/2 Tsp Italian Seasoning, Dried
- 1 Lemon, Sliced
- Pepper
- Salt
- 1 Cup String Beans

Directions:

1. Supply your smoker with wood pellets and follow the start-up procedure. Preheat the grill, with the lid closed, to 450° F.
2. Lay four 12 x 12 inch pieces of foil out on a flat surface, then place one chicken breast in the middle of each foil.
3. Divide the broccoli and string beans between the four foil packs. Thinly slice the lemon, split them between each foil pack, and place the slices on, in and around the chicken and vegetables.
4. Mix the butter, garlic, juice of the remaining lemon, and Italian seasoning together, and then brush over the chicken and vegetables. Sprinkle with salt and pepper to taste.
5. Fold the foil over the chicken and vegetables to close the pack, and pinch the ends together so the pack will remain closed.
6. Grill for 7-9 minutes on each side. Turn off grill, remove the foil packets, and serve immediately.

Blueberry Pancakes

Servings: 4
Cooking Time: 10 Minutes

Ingredients:

- 2 Cups Blueberries, Fresh
- 1 Cup Pancake Mix
- 1/2 Cup Sugar
- 3/4 Cup Water, Warm

Directions:

1. Supply your smoker with wood pellets and follow the start-up procedure. Preheat the grill, with the lid closed, to 350° F.
2. Place the cast iron griddle on the grates of your grill.
3. In a large bowl, pour water, pancake mix and 1/2 cup of the blueberries and mix until combined.
4. Pour the batter onto the griddle in 4 equal parts. Cook with the lid closed for about 6 minutes, or until the edges of the pancakes are slightly cooked. Flip each pancake and continue cooking for another 4 minutes.
5. Pour the hot blueberry sauce over your freshly cooked pancakes and enjoy!

Ultimate Baked Garlic Bread

Servings: 4
Cooking Time: 20 Minutes

Ingredients:

- 1 baguette
- 1/2 Cup softened butter
- 1/2 Cup mayonnaise
- 4 Tablespoon chopped Italian parsley
- 6 Clove garlic, minced
- salt
- chile flakes
- 1 Cup mozzarella cheese
- 1/2 Cup Parmesan cheese

Directions:

1. Supply your smoker with wood pellets and follow the start-up procedure. Preheat the grill, with the lid closed, to 375° F.
2. Lay baguette on a cutting board and cut it in half lengthwise.
3. In a bowl, add butter, mayonnaise, parsley, garlic, salt and chile flakes. Mix well.
4. Spread butter mixture on baguette halves and top with mozzarella and Parmesan cheese.
5. Place baguette on the grill (if you like the bread crisp, do not use foil and if you like it soft, wrap with foil). Grill for approximately 15 to 25 minutes. Serve warm. Enjoy! Grill: 375 °F

Cake With Smoked Berry Sauce

Servings: 12
Cooking Time: 90 Minutes

Ingredients:

- 12 Oz Blackberries
- 18 Oz Blueberries, Fresh
- 1/4 Cup Brown Sugar
- 2 Tsp Cinnamon, Ground
- 4 Eggs
- 2 Tbsp Flour
- 1 3/4 Cup Granulated Sugar
- 1 Lemon, Juice & Zest
- 1/2 Cup Unsalted Butter
- 3.4 Ounce Box Vanilla Instant Pudding Mix
- 3/4 Cup Vegetable Oil
- 3/4 Cup Water
- 1 Cup White Wine
- 1 Box Yellow Cake Mix

Directions:

1. Fire up your Grill and set to Smoke mode. If using a gas or charcoal grill, set it up for low, indirect heat. Supply your smoker with wood pellets and follow the start-up procedure. Preheat the grill, with the lid closed, to 450° F.

2. Place blueberries and blackberries on a sheet tray, then transfer to upper shelf of smoking cabinet. Make sure that the sear slide and side dampers are open, then preheat the grill, with the lid closed, to 375° F, to ensure the cabinet maintains temperature between 225° F and 250° F. Smoke for 30 to 45 minutes.

3. Place cast iron skillet on grill grate. Add sugar, lemon juice and zest, and wine to skillet. Stir with a wooden spoon until sugar dissolves, then add berries from smoking cabinet.

4. Simmer berries for 15 minutes, then remove sauce from grill to cool.

5. While berries are smoking, prepare cake pans and batter. Grease and flour 2 - 9-inch round cake pans. Set aside.

6. In a large mixing bowl, combine cake mix, brown sugar, granulated sugar, pudding mix, cinnamon, eggs, water, oil, and white wine. Using a hand mixer, mix on low speed for 1 minute, then slowly increase mixing speed to high, and beat an additional 2 to 3 minutes, or until batter is smooth.

7. Evenly distribute batter among cake pans, then place pans on grill shelf and bake at 350° F, for 25 to 30 minutes, or until a toothpick inserted comes out clean. Remove from grill and set aside to cool slightly.

8. While cake is cooling, prepare glaze. Melt butter with sugar in a sauce pot on the grill. Stir for 3 minutes, then add wine. Remove from grill and set aside.

9. Turn out cake onto a sheet tray lined with parchment. Use a toothpick to poke holes in the cake, then slowly pour hot glaze over cake.

10. Spread half of smoked berry sauce on top of one layer, then place second cake layer on top. Pour additional sauce on top of cake and dust with powdered sugar, if desired. Serve warm, or room temperature.

Garlic Lemon Pepper Chicken Wings

Servings: 4
Cooking Time: 30 Minutes

Ingredients:
- 1/4 Cup Black Peppercorns, Ground
- 4 Pounds Chicken, Wing
- 2 Tsp Coriander, Ground
- 2 Tsp Garlic Powder
- 2-3 Tbsp Lemon, Zest
- 1 Tsp Salt, Kosher
- 3 Tsp Dried Thyme, Fresh Sprigs

Directions:

1. Supply your smoker with wood pellets and follow the start-up procedure. Preheat the grill, with the lid closed, to 400° F.

2. In a bowl, begin to mix the ground pepper and zest of the lemon together, then add the rest of the ingredients.

3. Place the wings in a bowl and toss with a little olive oil, add a few tablespoons of the seasoning, toss with your hands, then repeat until the wings are well seasoned to your liking.

4. Place the wings on the grill, and cook them for about 15 minutes, then flip and grill for another 15 minutes.

5. Continue to flip the wings, until they are done and crispy. Remove the wings from the grill, and serve.

Cast Iron Pineapple Upside Down Cake

Servings: 6
Cooking Time: 40 Minutes

Ingredients:
- 1/4 Cup butter, melted
- 1 Cup brown sugar
- 20 Ounce Pineapple, sliced
- 6 Ounce maraschino cherries
- 1 Whole Yellow Cake Mix, Boxed
- vegetable oil
- eggs

Directions:

1. Supply your smoker with wood pellets and follow the start-up procedure. Preheat the grill, with the lid closed, to 350° F.

2. Pour melted butter into a 12-inch cast iron pan. Sprinkle brown sugar on top of the butter. Arrange pineapple slices on brown sugar, squeezing in as many slices as possible. Place a cherry in center of each pineapple slice; press gently into brown sugar.

3. Make cake batter as directed on box, substituting pineapple juice mixture for as much of the water as possible, and adding in required oil and eggs. Pour batter into cast iron dish, over pineapple and cherries.

4. Place the cast iron pan on the grill grate and cook for 20 minutes. Rotate the pan a half turn to ensure it cooks evenly. Cook for an additional 20 minutes, or until toothpick inserted in center comes out clean.

5. Immediately run knife around side of pan to loosen cake. Place heatproof serving plate upside down onto pan; turn plate and pan over.

6. Leave pan over cake 5 minutes so brown sugar topping can drizzle over cake. Cool 30 minutes. Enjoy!

Chocolate Peanut Cookies

Servings: 4
Cooking Time: 12 Minutes

Ingredients:

- 1/2 Tsp Baking Soda
- 1/2 Cup Brown Sugar
- 1/2 Cup + 1 Tbsp Butter, Unsalted
- 1/3 Cup Cocoa Powder, Dark And Unsweetened
- 2 Eggs, Beaten
- 1 1/2 Cups Flour, All-Purpose
- 1/3 Cup Miniature Chocolate Chips
- 2 Cups Peanut Butter Chips, Divided
- 1/4 Tsp Sea Salt
- 1/2 Cup Sugar, Granulated
- 1 Tsp Vanilla Extract

Directions:

1. Supply your smoker with wood pellets and follow the start-up procedure. Preheat the grill, with the lid closed, to medium-low heat. If using a gas or charcoal grill, preheat a cast iron skillet.
2. In a mixing bowl, whisk together the flour, cocoa powder, baking soda, and salt. Set aside.
3. Set a metal saucepan on the griddle, then add ½ cup of butter to melt. Whisk in the sugars and vanilla extract and cook for 2 minutes. Remove the pan from the griddle, and transfer contents to a large mixing bowl.
4. Slowly pour the beaten eggs into the sugar mixture, whisking constantly to temper the eggs.
5. Add the dry mixture to the wet ingredients until just combined. Fold in 1 cup of peanut butter chips and chocolate chips. Refrigerate mixture for 15 to 30 minutes.
6. Remove the dough from the refrigerator, then add an additional cup of peanut butter chips.
7. Portion dough into 16 to 18 cookie balls.
8. Melt 1 tablespoon of butter on the griddle, then transfer the cookie balls to the griddle. Press down gently on the cookies, then cook for 10 to 12 minutes, flipping halfway.
9. Transfer cookies to a cooling rack for 5 minutes before enjoying.

Pull-apart Dinner Rolls

Servings: 8
Cooking Time: 10 Minutes

Ingredients:

- 1/4 Cup warm water (110°F to 115°F)
- 1/3 Cup vegetable oil
- 2 Tablespoon active dry yeast
- 1/4 Cup sugar
- 1/2 Teaspoon salt
- 1 egg
- 3 1/2 Cup all-purpose flour
- cooking spray

Directions:

1. Supply your smoker with wood pellets and follow the start-up procedure. Preheat the grill, with the lid closed, to 400° F.
2. In the bowl of a stand mixer, combine warm water, oil, yeast and sugar. Let mixture rest for 5 to 10 minutes, or until frothy and bubbly.
3. With a dough hook, mix in salt, egg and 2 cups of flour until combined. Add remaining flour 1/2 cup at a time (dough will be sticky).
4. Prepare a cast iron pan with cooking spray and set aside.
5. Spray your hands with cooking spray and shape the dough into 12 balls.
6. After shaped, place in the prepared cast iron pan and let rest for 10 minutes. Bake in Traeger for about 10 to 12 minutes, or until tops are lightly golden. Enjoy! Grill: 400 °F

Crème Brûlée

Servings: 2
Cooking Time: 45minutes

Ingredients:

- 1 Quart heavy whipping cream
- 1 Pieces Vanilla Bean, split and scraped
- 6 Large egg yolk
- 1 Cup sugar

Directions:

1. Supply your smoker with wood pellets and follow the start-up procedure. Preheat the grill, with the lid closed, to 325° F.
2. Pour the cream into a saucepan over medium-high heat, add the vanilla bean and the scraped seeds. Bring to a boil. Remove from the heat and allow to steep (about 15 minutes). Remove the vanilla bean from saucepan and discard.
3. In a bowl, whisk together egg yolks and 1/2 cup (100 g) of the sugar until the mix starts to lighten in color. Add the cream a little at a time, stirring continually.
4. Pour the mixture into 6 (8 oz) ramekins and place the ramekins into a large roasting pan. Pour hot water into the pan so that it comes halfway up the sides of the ramekins.
5. Place water bath pan on the grill and bake until the Crème Brûlées still jiggle in the center, about 40 to 45 minutes. Grill: 325 °F
6. Remove the ramekins from the roasting pan and refrigerate for at least 2 hours and up to 2 days.
7. To serve, let the Crème Brûlée come to temperature (about 20 minutes) before torching the tops.

8.   Sprinkle the remaining 1/2 cup (100 g) sugar equally on top of each ramekin. Using a torch in a circular motion, melt the sugar until it caramelizes and forms a crispy top.

9.   Allow the Crème Brûlée to sit for a few minutes before serving. Enjoy!

Baked Peach Cobbler Cupcakes

Servings: 8
Cooking Time: 30 Minutes

Ingredients:

- 2 Large Peaches, fresh
- 3/4 Cup sugar
- 2 Teaspoon lemon juice
- 1/2 Teaspoon ground cinnamon
- Yellow Cake Mix, Boxed
- 1 Can vanilla icing

Directions:

1.   Bring a pot of water to a boil. Turn peaches upside down and cut a small shallow X across the bottom. Put peaches in boiling water and boil for 1 minute to help loosen the skin.

2.   Drain the peaches into a colander and rinse off with cold water. Peel skin off peaches.

3.   Filling: Dice peaches and place into a large pan. Cook peaches over medium heat. As it starts to sizzle, add sugar, lemon and cinnamon. Cook mixture on medium heat for 10-15 minutes until a majority of the juice from the peaches evaporates leaving a thick syrup.

4.   Transfer to a bowl to cool.

5.   Supply your smoker with wood pellets and follow the start-up procedure. Preheat the grill, with the lid closed, to 350° F.

6.   Cupcakes: Follow the directions on box cake mix and put the mixture into cupcake pan with liners.

7.   When grill has preheated, bake cupcakes for 13-16 minutes, until a light golden brown. Grill: 350 ˚F

8.   When cupcakes have cooled, use a piping bag to pipe the peach cobbler mixture into the middle of the cupcake.

9.   Ice with your favorite vanilla icing. Enjoy!

Baked Cast Iron Berry Cobbler

Servings: 6
Cooking Time: 35 Minutes

Ingredients:

- 4 Cup Berries
- 12 Tablespoon sugar
- Cup orange juice
- 2/3 Cup Flour
- 3/4 Teaspoon baking powder
- 1 Pinch salt

- 1/2 Cup butter
- 1 Tablespoon Sugar, raw

Directions:

1.   Supply your smoker with wood pellets and follow the start-up procedure. Preheat the grill, with the lid closed, to 350° F.

2.   In a 10-inch (25-cm) cast iron or other baking pan, mix together the berries, 4 Tbsp sugar and the orange juice.

3.   In a small bowl, mix together the flour, baking powder and salt. Set aside.

4.   In a separate bowl, cream together the butter and granulated sugar. Add the egg and vanilla extract and mix to combine. Gradually fold in the flour mixture.

5.   Spoon the batter on top of the berries and sprinkle raw sugar on top.

6.   Bake the cobbler for approximately 35-45 minutes. Cool slightly and serve with whipped cream. Enjoy! Grill: 350 ˚F

Smokin' Lemon Bars

Servings: 8-12
Cooking Time: 60 Minutes

Ingredients:

- 3/4 Cup lemon juice
- 1 1/2 Cup sugar
- 2 eggs
- 3 Egg Yolk
- 1 1/2 Teaspoon cornstarch
- Pinch sea salt
- 4 Tablespoon unsalted butter
- 1/4 Cup olive oil
- 1/2 Tablespoon lemon zest
- 1 1/4 Cup flour
- 1/4 Cup granulated sugar
- 3 Tablespoon Confectioner's Sugar
- 1 Teaspoon lemon zest
- 1/4 Teaspoon Sea Salt, Fine
- 10 Tablespoon Unsalted Butter, Cut Into Cubes

Directions:

1.   When ready to cook, set grill temperature to 180˚F and preheat, lid closed for 15 minutes.

2.   In a small mixing bowl, whisk together lemon juice, sugar, eggs and yolks, cornstarch and fine sea salt. Pour into a sheet tray or cake pan and place on grill. Smoke for 30 minutes whisking mixture halfway through smoking. Remove from grill and set aside.

3.   Pour mixture into a small saucepan. Place on stove top set to medium heat until boiling. Once boiling, boil for 60 seconds. Remove from heat and strain through a mesh strainer into a bowl. Whisk in cold butter, olive oil, and lemon zest.

4.   To make a crust, pulse together the flour, granulated sugar, confectioners' sugar, lemon zest and salt in a food processor. Add

butter and pulse until just mixed into a crumbly dough. Press dough into a prepared 9" by 9" baking dish lined with parchment paper that is long enough to hang over 2 of the sides.

5.   When ready to cook, set the smoker to 350℉ and preheat, lid closed for 15 minutes.

6.   Bake until crust is very lightly golden brown, about 30 to 35 minutes.

7.   Remove from grill and pour the lemon filling over the crust. Return to grill and continue to bake until filling is just set about 15 to 20 minutes.

8.   Allow to cool at room temperature, then refrigerate until chilled before slicing into bars. Sprinkle with confectioners' sugar and flaky sea salt right before serving. Enjoy!

Green Bean Casserole Circa 1955

Servings: 6
Cooking Time: 30 Minutes

Ingredients:
- 1 1/2 Pound Green Beans, fresh
- 1 Can cream of mushroom soup
- 1/2 Cup milk
- 2 Teaspoon soy sauce
- 1/2 Teaspoon Worcestershire sauce
- 1/2 Teaspoon black pepper
- 1.334 Cup French's Original Crispy Fried Onions
- 1/4 Cup red bell pepper, diced

Directions:
1.   In a mixing bowl, combine the beans (trimmed and cooked until tender, or may use 2 16 oz. cans), soup, milk, soy sauce, Worcestershire sauce, black pepper, 2/3 cup of the onion rings, and red pepper, if using. Transfer to a 1-1/2 quart casserole dish.

2.   Supply your smoker with wood pellets and follow the start-up procedure. Preheat the grill, with the lid closed, to 375° F.

3.   Cook the casserole until the filling is hot and bubbling, 25 to 30 minutes. Top with the remaining onions and cook for 5 to 10 minutes more, or until the onions are crisp and beginning to brown. Grill: 375 ℉

Smoked Blackberry Pie

Servings: 4-6
Cooking Time: 25 Minutes

Ingredients:
- Nonstick cooking spray or butter, for greasing
- 1 box (2 sheets) refrigerated piecrusts
- 8 tablespoons (1 stick) unsalted butter, melted, plus 8 tablespoons (1 stick) cut into pieces
- ½ cup all-purpose flour
- 2 cups sugar, divided
- 2 pints blackberries
- ½ cup milk
- Vanilla ice cream, for serving

Directions:
1.   Supply your smoker with wood pellets and follow the start-up procedure. Preheat, with the lid closed, to 375°F.

2.   Coat a cast iron skillet with cooking spray.

3.   Unroll 1 refrigerated piecrust and place in the bottom and up the side of the skillet. Using a fork, poke holes in the crust in several places.

4.   Set the skillet on the grill grate, close the lid, and smoke for 5 minutes, or until lightly browned. Remove from the grill and set aside.

5.   In a large bowl, combine the stick of melted butter with the flour and 1½ cups of sugar.

6.   Add the blackberries to the flour-sugar mixture and toss until well coated.

7.   Spread the berry mixture evenly in the skillet and sprinkle the milk on top. Scatter half of the cut pieces of butter randomly over the mixture.

8.   Unroll the remaining piecrust and place it over the top of skillet or slice the dough into even strips and weave it into a lattice. Scatter the remaining pieces of butter along the top of the crust.

9.   Sprinkle the remaining ½ cup of sugar on top of the crust and return the skillet to the smoker.

10.   Close the lid and smoke for 15 to 20 minutes, or until bubbly and brown on top. It may be necessary to use some aluminum foil around the edges near the end of the cooking time to prevent the crust from burning.

11.   Serve the pie hot with vanilla ice cream.

Baked Molten Chocolate Cake

Servings: 4
Cooking Time: 20 Minutes

Ingredients:
- all-purpose flour
- butter
- 4 Ounce butter
- 6 Ounce Chocolate, Bittersweet
- 2 eggs
- 2 egg yolk
- 1/2 Cup sugar
- 1 Pinch salt

Directions:
1.   Supply your smoker with wood pellets and follow the start-up procedure. Preheat the grill, with the lid closed, to 450° F.

2.   Butter and flour four (6oz) ramekins. Tap out excess flour. Place ramekins on a baking sheet and reserve.

3. Melt butter and chocolate in a double boiler over simmering water. In a medium bowl, beat eggs and yolks with sugar and salt on high until thick and pale.

4. Whisk in chocolate until smooth and quickly fold into the egg mixture along with flour.

5. Spoon the batter into prepared ramekins and bake for 20 minutes or until sides are firm but centers are soft. Grill: 450 °F

6. Let cool for 1 minute, then cover each with an inverted dessert plate. Carefully turn each over, let stand 10 seconds, then unmold.

7. Serve immediately with Maple Ice Cream with Candied Bacon. Enjoy!

Baked Buttermilk Biscuits

Servings: 4
Cooking Time: 15 Minutes

Ingredients:
- 2 Cup all-purpose flour
- 1/4 Cup butter
- 3/4 Cup buttermilk

Directions:
1. Supply your smoker with wood pellets and follow the start-up procedure. Preheat the grill, with the lid closed, to High heat. Spoon the flour into a measuring cup and level with a knife.

2. Put the flour into a mixing bowl. Using a pastry blender, cut the butter into the flour until the mixture resembles coarse crumbs.

3. With a fork, gently stir in just enough of the buttermilk so the dough leaves the sides of the bowl. (You may not need all the buttermilk.) For the most tender biscuits, do not overmix.

4. Lightly flour a work surface as well as your hands. Tip the dough onto the floured surface and gently bring together using your fingertips. (Re-flour your hands or the board if the dough is too sticky.) Knead two or three times, just to bring the dough together.

5. With a floured rolling pin, lightly and quickly roll the dough out to a thickness of about 1/2". Using a 1-1/2" floured cutter, cut out as many biscuits as you can. (Do not twist the cutter; push it straight down.) You can reroll the scraps if desired, but the "second string" biscuits will be tougher.

6. Transfer the biscuits to an ungreased baking sheet. Using a pastry brush, brush the tops with melted butter. Bake until golden brown, 10 to 15 minutes. Enjoy! Grill: 500 °F

Sweet And Spicy Baked Pork Beans

Servings: 20
Cooking Time: 120 Minutes

Ingredients:
- 1 - 21 Oz Apple Pie Filling, Can

- 1 Gallon Baked Beans
- 1 Tbs Chilli, Powder
- 1 Green Bell Pepper, Diced
- 1 10 Oz Drained Jalapeno, Can Diced
- 1 Cup Maple Syrup
- 1 Onion, Diced
- 1 Lb Pork, Pulled

Directions:
1. Supply your smoker with wood pellets and follow the start-up procedure. Preheat the grill, with the lid closed, to 350° F.
2. Place all ingredients in mixing bowl and mix well.
3. Pour bean mixture into foil pans.
4. Bake in grill till bubbling throughout – about 2 hours.
5. Rest at least 15 minutes before serving.

Smoked Lemon Cheesecake

Servings: 16
Cooking Time: 130 Minutes

Ingredients:
- For the crust
- Vegetable oil, for oiling the pan
- 12 ounces gingersnaps (about 36) or chocolate icebox cookies (about 36)
- 3 tablespoons light brown sugar
- 8 tablespoons (1 stick) unsalted butter, melted
- For the filling
- 4 packages (8 ounces each) cream cheese, at room temperature
- 1 cup firmly packed light brown sugar
- 2 teaspoons pure vanilla extract
- 2 teaspoons finely grated lemon zest
- 1 tablespoon fresh lemon juice
- 2 tablespoons (1/4 stick) unsalted butter, melted
- 5 large eggs
- Burnt Sugar Sauce (recipes follows, optional)

Directions:
1. Supply your smoker with wood pellets and follow the start-up procedure. Preheat the grill, with the lid closed, to 400° F. Lightly oil the springform pan with vegetable oil and wrap a sheet of aluminum foil around the outside.

2. Make the crust: Break the cookies into pieces and grind with the brown sugar to a fine powder in a food processor. You'll want about 1 3/4 cups of crumbs. Add the melted butter and run the processor in short bursts to obtain a crumbly dough. Press the mixture evenly across the bottom and halfway up the sides of the springform pan. Indirect-grill or bake the crust until lightly browned, 5 to 8 minutes. Transfer the pan to a wire rack and let cool.

3.   Make the filling: Wipe out the food processor bowl. Add the cream cheese, brown sugar, vanilla, lemon zest, lemon juice, and butter, and process until smooth. Work in the eggs one by one, processing until smooth after each addition. (You can also use a stand mixer, beating the cream cheese mixture until smooth and beating in the eggs one at a time.) Pour the filling into the crust. Gently tap the pan on the countertop a few times to knock out any air bubbles.

4.   Supply your smoker with wood pellets and follow the start-up procedure. Preheat the grill, with the lid closed, to 225 °F-250 °F.

5.   Place the cheesecake in the smoker. Smoke until the top is bronzed with smoke and the filling is set, 1 1/2 to 2 hours. To test for doneness, gently poke the side of the pan—the filling will jiggle, not ripple. Alternatively, insert a slender metal skewer in the center of the cake; it should come out clean.

6.   Transfer the cheesecake in its pan to a wire rack to cool to room temperature. Refrigerate until serving; the cheesecake can be made up to 8 hours ahead. Run a slender knife around the inside of the springform pan. Unclasp and remove the ring. (You'll serve the cheesecake off the bottom of the pan.) Let the cheesecake warm slightly at room temperature before serving.

7.   If serving with the sauce, pour some of it over the cheesecake and the rest into a pitcher. Cut into wedges and pass the remaining sauce.

S'mores Dip Skillet

Servings: 4-6
Cooking Time: 8 Minutes

Ingredients:
- 2 tablespoons salted butter, melted
- ¼ cup milk
- 12 ounces semisweet chocolate chips
- 16 ounces Jet-Puffed marshmallows
- Graham crackers and apple wedges, for serving

Directions:
1.   Supply your smoker with wood pellets and follow the start-up procedure. Preheat, with the lid closed, to 450°F.

2.   Place a cast iron skillet on the preheated grill grate and pour in the melted butter and milk, stirring for about 1 minute.

3.   Once the mixture starts to heat, top with the chocolate chips in an even layer and arrange the marshmallows standing up to cover all of the chocolate.

4.   Close the lid and smoke for 5 to 7 minutes, or until the marshmallows are lightly toasted.

5.   Remove from the heat and serve immediately with graham crackers and apple wedges for dipping.

Vanilla Cheesecake Skillet Brownie

Servings: 2

Cooking Time: 30 Minutes

Ingredients:
- 1 Box Brownie Mix
- 1 Package Cream Cheese
- 2 Egg
- 1/2 Cup Oil
- 1 Can Pie Filling, Blueberry
- 1/2 Cup Sugar
- 1 Tsp Vanilla
- 1/4 Cup Water, Warm

Directions:
1.   Combine all brownie ingredients and mix. In a separate bowl, combine cream cheese, sugar, egg and vanilla and mix until smooth. Grease skillets and pour in brownie batter. Top with cheesecake and cherry pie filling, using a knife to blend to give it that marbled look.

2.   Supply your smoker with wood pellets and follow the start-up procedure. Preheat the grill, with the lid closed, to 350°F and bake for about 30 minutes.

3.   Let cool for about 10 minutes and enjoy!

Pineapple Cake

Servings: 4
Cooking Time: 30 Minutes

Ingredients:
- 2/3 cup of vegetable oil (olive oil works great, not virgin)
- 3 eggs
- 1/3 cup brown sugar (not too sweet)
- 3/4 cup self raising plain flour
- 1/4 cup wholemeal self raising flour
- 1/3 cup saltanas
- 1/3 cup diced canned pineapple (drained)
- 1/3 cup diced raw walnuts
- 2 large carrots grated
- Icing Ingredients
- 250 grams cream cheese
- 35 grams icing sugar (not too sweet)
- Whole lemon or orange zest

Directions:
1.   Mix all ingredients in a large bowl.

2.   Place into 6″ greased baking tray or un-greased silicone tray.

3.   Supply your smoker with wood pellets and follow the start-up procedure. Preheat the grill, with the lid closed, to 190 °F. Cook for 25-30min until golden brown and no dough when probed.

4.   Let cool on rack (not directly on plate or board) then apply icing.

5.   Whip icing ingredients and place in fridge until ready to coat the cake.

Baked Green Chile Mac & Cheese By Doug Scheiding

Servings: 8
Cooking Time: 120 Minutes

Ingredients:

- 24 Ounce shredded cheddar cheese, divided
- 8 Ounce mozzarella cheese, shredded
- 6 Tablespoon unsalted butter
- 16 Ounce large dry elbow macaroni noodles
- 2 1/2 Cup half-and-half
- 2 Cup heavy whipping cream
- 8 Ounce cream cheese
- 16 Ounce 505 Southwestern Hatch Valley Flame Roasted Green Chile
- 2 Tablespoon Prime Rib Rub

Directions:

1.   Supply your smoker with wood pellets and follow the start-up procedure. Preheat the grill, with the lid closed, to 165° F.

2.   Place 16 ounces of the shredded cheddar and the 8 ounces of shredded mozzarella cheese into a shallow pan or cookie sheet and place the pan directly on the grill grate. Smoke for 30 to 40 minutes. Remove from grill and set aside. Grill: 165 °F

3.   Increase the grill temperature to 300°F and place a large disposable aluminum half pan in the Traeger with the butter. Remove the pan from the grill after the butter has fully melted. Grill: 300 °F

4.   Add the noodles to the pan, along with half-and-half, heavy whipping cream, 16 ounces of the cold smoked cheddar, all of the smoked mozzarella cheese and cream cheese broken into small pieces. Add the green chiles to taste (12 ounces for mild and 16 ounces for spicy) and stir to combine.

5.   Place the pan in the grill and bake for 2 hours, stirring every 20 minutes. If macaroni and cheese looks like it is getting dry, add a little more half-and-half and stir to combine. Grill: 300 °F

6.   During the last 20 minutes of cooking, sprinkle the remaining (unsmoked) cheddar cheese on top and add a light dusting of Traeger Prime Rib Rub. Serve hot. Enjoy!

Onion Cheese Nachos

Servings: 6
Cooking Time: 10 Minutes

Ingredients:

- 1 Pound Beef, Ground
- 3 Cups Cheddar Cheese, Shredded
- 1 Green Bell Pepper, Diced
- 1/2 Cup Green Onion
- 1/2 Cup Red Onion, Diced
- 1 Large Bag Tortilla Chip

Directions:

1.   Supply your smoker with wood pellets and follow the start-up procedure. Preheat the grill, with the lid closed, to 350° F.

2.   While you're waiting, empty a large bag of nacho chips evenly onto a cast iron pan. Start loading up with toppings - cooked ground beef, red onion, red pepper, cheese, green onions. These are just the toppings we had on hand, so feel free to add anything you like! Make sure you do a couple layers of chips so everyone gets a good serving of nachos. And don't be skimpy with the cheese - lay it on heavy!

3.   Place your loaded nachos on the grill and let the hot smoke melt your toppings into one cheesy creation. Heat at 350°F for 10 minutes or until the cheese has fully melted. Remove and serve with sour-cream and salsa.

Butternut Squash Macaroni And Cheese

Servings: 2
Cooking Time: 50 Minutes

Ingredients:

- 1 Medium butternut squash
- 2 Cup macaroni, uncooked
- 1 Small yellow onion
- 1/2 Cup chicken broth
- 1 Cup milk
- salt
- pepper
- 1 Cup cheese, grated

Directions:

1.   Supply your smoker with wood pellets and follow the start-up procedure. Preheat the grill, with the lid closed, to 225° F.

2.   Puncture butternut squash with a fork several times and place on grill grate. Cook until tender, about 40 minutes to an hour. When cooked, scoop out meat and discard seeds. Grill: 225 °F

3.   Cook elbow macaroni according to package instructions. Drain and set aside.

4.   In a medium skillet, sauté chopped onion until fragrant and golden. Add broth, milk, salt, onions and butternut squash to a food processor. Puree until smooth and creamy. Add salt and pepper to taste.

5.   Pour pureed sauce over cooked noodles and add the shredded cheese. Stir to melt the cheese and add milk to reach desired consistency. Serve warm. Enjoy!

Dark Chocolate Brownies With Bacon-salted Caramel

Servings: 8
Cooking Time: 40 Minutes

Ingredients:
- 8 Strips bacon
- 1/2 Cup kosher salt
- 1 Whole Brownie Mix
- 1 Jar caramel sauce

Directions:
1. For the bacon salt: Cook a few strips of bacon (6 to 8) until very crisp: 350 degrees for about 25 minutes should do it. Let cool, then pulse in a food processor until finely chopped. Mix with 1/2 cup kosher salt. Store in the refrigerator until ready to use.
2. Supply your smoker with wood pellets and follow the start-up procedure. Preheat the grill, with the lid closed, to 350° F.
3. Mix the brownies according to package directions and pour into a greased pan. Drizzle approximately 2 tablespoons of the caramel sauce over the brownie batter. Sprinkle with approximately 1 teaspoon of the bacon salt. Place directly on the grill grate of your preheated Traeger.
4. Bake the brownies for 20-25 minutes, until the batter has started to set up. Remove from the grill and drizzle with 2 more tablespoons of caramel sauce and sprinkle with more bacon salt. Return to the grill for 20-25 more minutes, or until a toothpick inserted in the middle of the brownies comes out clean.
5. If you like extra caramel, drizzle another layer of caramel on the hot brownies and sprinkle with a final bit of bacon salt. Allow the brownies to cool completely before cutting them into squares. Clean your knife in between each slice to prevent the brownies from sticking to the knife. Enjoy!

Savory Cheesecake With Bourbon Pecan Topping

Servings: 6
Cooking Time: 75 Minutes

Ingredients:
- Crust
- 12 ounce Oreos
- 6 ounce melted butter
- Filling
- 24 ounces cream cheese - room temperature
- 1 cup granulated sugar
- 3 tbs cornstarch
- 2 large eggs
- 2/3 cup heavy cream
- 1 tbs vanilla
- 1 1/2 tbs bourbon
- Topping
- 3 large eggs beaten
- 1/3 cup granulated sugar
- 1/3 cup brown sugar
- 8 tbsp corn syrup dark corn syrup recommended
- 2 tbsp bourbon
- 1/2 tbsp vanilla
- 1/8 tbsp salt
- 3/4 cup rough chopped pecans (smoked pecans recommended)

Directions:
1. Supply your smoker with wood pellets and follow the start-up procedure. Preheat the grill, with the lid closed, to 350 °F.
2. Wrap foil on the bottom and up the sides of a 9" spring-form pan (outside of pan).
3. Butter the bottom & insides of the pan.
4. Crust
5. Throw ingredients in a food processor until they are finely ground.
6. Spread in 9" cheesecake pan on bottom & about ½ way upsides.
7. Filling
8. Place 8 oz of cream cheese in mixer bowl with 1/3 of sugar & cornstarch.Mix until smooth andcreamy.
9. Add another 8 oz cream cheese andbeat until smooth, then add remaining cream cheese,beating until smooth.
10. Then mix in the rest of the sugar, bourbon & vanilla.
11. Add eggs one at a time beating well after each one.
12. Add the heavy cream and mix just until smooth. Reminder: Do not over mix.
13. Pour batter into the prepared crust.
14. Topping
15. Mix all together except pecans.
16. Sprinkle pecans on top of cheesecake batter.
17. Pour topping over cheesecake batter.
18. Place in a pan big enough to hold a spring-form pan. Pour boiling water in the roasting pan to come up about ½ way up the spring-form pan.
19. Bake at 350 °F for 75 minutes until the top just barely jiggles. Carefully take the pan out of water-bath and put on cooling rack.
20. Let cool for 2 hours in pan. After 2 hours put in fridge until totally chilled then serve.

Skillet Buttermilk Cornbread

Servings: 6
Cooking Time: 25 Minutes

Ingredients:
- 1 Cup Cornmeal

- 1 Cup all-purpose flour
- 1/3 Cup granulated sugar
- 1 Teaspoon salt
- 1 Teaspoon baking powder
- 1 1/2 Cup buttermilk
- 2 Whole eggs
- 8 Tablespoon butter, melted

Directions:

1. Grease a cast iron skillet or 9-inch square baking pan with bacon fat. Put a 10-inch well-seasoned cast iron skillet on the grill grate. If using a regular baking pan, do not preheat.

2. Supply your smoker with wood pellets and follow the start-up procedure. Preheat the grill, with the lid closed, to 400° F.

3. In a large mixing bowl, combine the cornmeal, flour, sugar, salt, and baking powder and whisk to mix thoroughly. Make a well in the center of the dry ingredients.

4. In a separate mixing bowl, whisk together the buttermilk and eggs until well-combined. Add the melted butter. Pour into the dry ingredients and mix until the batter is fairly smooth. Do not overmix.

5. Carefully pour the batter into the preheated skillet. Bake for 20 to 25 minutes, or until the top is firm and a tester inserted in the center of the cornbread comes out clean. Be careful when removing the skillet from the grill as it will be very hot. Let the cornbread cool slightly on a trivet or cooling rack before slicing into wedges or squares.

Traeger Baked Protein Bars

Servings: 6
Cooking Time: 25 Minutes

Ingredients:

- 2 Cup Frozen Sweet Cherries
- 1 Cup Apricots, Frozen
- 1 Scoop Vanilla Protein Powder
- 2 Tablespoon honey
- 1 Teaspoon vanilla extract
- 1 Cup rolled oats

Directions:

1. Supply your smoker with wood pellets and follow the start-up procedure. Preheat the grill, with the lid closed, to 350° F.

2. In the bowl of a food processor, add cherries, apricots (revived in hot water for 5 minutes and drained), vanilla protein powder, honey, and vanilla. Pulse about 10 to 15 times, to break the fruit into smaller pieces and to mix all ingredients.

3. In a separate bowl, fold together oats and fruit mixture. Transfer mixture to a loaf pan or silicone mold and place in grill.

4. Bake for approximately 20 to 25 minutes. Grill: 350 °F

5. Let cool completely and cut into 8 pieces. Enjoy!

Marbled Brownies With Amaretto & Ricotta

Servings: 4
Cooking Time: 30 Minutes

Ingredients:

- 1 Cup Ricotta Cheese
- 1 eggs
- 1 Tablespoon Amaretto Liqueur
- 1/4 Cup sugar
- 2 Teaspoon cornstarch
- 1/2 Teaspoon vanilla extract
- 1 Brownie Mix

Directions:

1. Coat a 9- by 13-inch nonstick baking pan with cooking spray or softened butter and set aside. (If you do not have a nonstick pan, line a regular one with buttered foil or parchment paper.)

2. In a medium bowl, combine the ricotta, egg, amaretto, sugar, cornstarch, and vanilla and whisk together thoroughly. Set aside.

3. Prepare the brownie mix according to the package directions. Spread the brownie batter evenly in the prepared pan. Randomly drop dollops of the ricotta mixture over the batter. Run a plastic knife through the ricotta mixture to give the brownies a marbled look. (A plastic knife is less likely to scratch your pan's nonstick surface.)

4. Supply your smoker with wood pellets and follow the start-up procedure. Preheat the grill, with the lid closed, to 350° F.

5. Put the pan with the brownie mixture directly on the grill grate and bake, about 25 to 30 minutes. Insert a bamboo skewer or toothpick in the center of the brownies to determine if they are done: the batter should not be wet. Grill: 350 °F

6. Transfer the brownies to a wire cooling rack to cool completely. Cut into squares.

Pizza Bites

Servings: 6
Cooking Time: 20 Minutes

Ingredients:

- 4 1/2 Cup Bread Flour
- 1 1/2 Tablespoon sugar
- 2 Teaspoon Instant Yeast
- 2 Teaspoon kosher salt
- 3 Tablespoon extra-virgin olive oil
- 15 Fluid Ounce Water, Lukewarm
- 8 Ounce Pepperoni, sliced
- 1 Cup pizza sauce
- 1 Cup mozzarella cheese
- 1 Whole egg, for egg wash
- 1 As Needed salt

Directions:

1. For the Pizza Dough: Combine flour, sugar, salt, and yeast in food processor. Pulse 3 to 4 times until incorporated evenly. Add olive oil and water. Run food processor until mixture forms ball that rides around the bowl above the blade, about 15 seconds. Continue processing 15 seconds longer.

2. Transfer dough ball to lightly floured surface and knead once or twice by hand until smooth ball is formed. Divide dough into three even parts and place each into a 1 gallon zip top bag. Place in refrigerator and allow to rise at least one day.

3. At least two hours before baking, remove dough from refrigerator and shape into balls by gathering dough towards bottom and pinching shut. Flour well and place each one in a separate medium mixing bowl. Cover tightly with plastic wrap and allow to rise at warm room temperature until roughly doubled in volume.

4. When ready to cook, set the grill temperature to 350°F and preheat, lid closed for 15 minutes.

5. After the first rise remove the dough from the fridge and let come to room temperature. Roll dough on a flat surface. Cut dough into long strips 3" wide by 18" long.

6. Slice pepperoni into strips.

7. In a medium bowl combine the pizza sauce, mozzarella and pepperoni.

8. Spoon 1 TBSP of the pizza filling onto the pizza dough every two inches, about halfway down the length of the dough. Dip a pastry brush into the egg wash and brush around pizza filling. Fold the half side of the dough (without the pizza filling) over the other the half that contains the pizza filling.

9. Press down between each pizza bite slightly with your fingers. With a ravioli or pizza cutter, cut around each filling- creating a rectangle shape and sealing the crust in.

10. Transfer each pizza bite onto a parchment lined cookie sheet. Cover with a kitchen towel and let them rise for 30 minutes.

11. When ready to cook, preheat the grill to 350 °F with the lid closed for 10-15 minutes.

12. Brush the bites with remaining egg wash, sprinkle with salt and place directly on the sheet tray. Bake 10-15 minutes until the exterior is golden brown.

13. Remove from grill and transfer to a serving dish. Serve with extra pizza sauce for dipping and enjoy!

Pretzel Rolls

Servings: 6
Cooking Time: 20 Minutes

Ingredients:

- 2 3/4 Cup Bread Flour
- 1 Quick-Rising Yeast, envelope
- 1 Teaspoon salt
- 1 Teaspoon sugar
- 1/2 Teaspoon celery seed
- 1/2 Teaspoon Caraway Seeds
- 1 Cup hot water
- As Needed Cornmeal
- 8 Cup water
- 1/4 Cup baking soda
- 2 Tablespoon sugar
- 1 Whole Egg White
- Coarse salt

Directions:

1. Combine bread flour, 1 envelope yeast, salt, 1 teaspoon sugar, caraway seeds and celery seeds in food processor or standing mixer with dough hook and blend.

2. With machine running, gradually pour hot water, adding enough water to form smooth elastic dough. Process 1 minute to knead. (You could also knead it by hand for a few minutes.)

3. Grease medium bowl. Add dough to bowl, turning to coat. Cover bowl with plastic wrap, then towel; let dough rise in warm draft-free area until doubled in volume, about 35 minutes.

4. Flour a large baking sheet. Punch dough down and knead on lightly floured surface until smooth. Divide into 8 pieces. Form each dough piece into a ball.

5. Place dough balls on prepared sheet, flattening each slightly. Using serrated knife, cut X in top center of each dough ball. Cover with towel and let dough balls rise until almost doubled in volume, about 20 minutes.

6. When ready to cook, start the smoker on Smoke with the lid open until a fire is established (4-5 minutes). Turn temperature to 375 F (190 C) and preheat, lid closed, for 10 to 15 minutes.

7. Grease another baking sheet and sprinkle with cornmeal. Bring water to boil in large saucepan. Add baking soda and sugar (water will foam up). Add 3 rolls (or however many will fit comfortably in the pot) and cook 30 seconds per side.

8. Using slotted spoon, transfer rolls to prepared sheet, arranging X side up. Repeat with remaining rolls. Brush rolls with egg white glaze. Sprinkle rolls generously with coarse salt.

9. Bake rolls until brown, about 20 to 25 minutes. Transfer to racks and cool 10 minutes. Serve rolls warm or at room temperature. Enjoy!

PORK RECIPES

Beer-braised Cabbage With Bacon

Servings: 4

Cooking Time: 30 Minutes

Ingredients:

- 1/4 Pound Bacon, bulk unsliced
- 1 Cup yellow onion, diced
- 1 Cup Apple, diced small
- 2 Pound Cabbage, green, sliced
- salt
- ground black pepper
- 12 Ounce Beer, light

Directions:

1. Supply your smoker with wood pellets and follow the start-up procedure. Preheat the grill, with the lid closed, to 325° F.

2. On a stovetop, heat a large heavy pot or Dutch oven over medium heat. Add the bacon and cook until crisp (about 5 mins). Transfer to a plate lined with paper towels.

3. Return the pot to medium heat. Add the onion and cook for 5 minutes, or until golden brown. Add the apple, stir, then add the cabbage. Sprinkle generously with salt and a touch of black pepper and stir for 3 minutes.

4. Pour in the beer and bring to a boil over medium-high heat. Cover and move the pot immediately into the Traeger.

5. Cook at 325 degrees F (160 C) for 10 minutes. Remove lid and cook for an additional 10-15 more minutes, or until cabbage is tender and most of the liquid has evaporated. Grill: 325 °F

6. Add the reserved bacon and stir into the cabbage. Enjoy!

Spiced Grilled Pork Chops

Servings: 4

Cooking Time: 30 Minutes

Ingredients:

- 3 Tbsp Black Peppercorns, Ground
- 1 Tbsp Coriander, Seed
- 1/4 Cup Cumin
- 1 - 2 Tsp Dry Rub
- 1 Tsp Olive Oil
- 4 Pork, Chop Bone-In
- 1 1/2 Tsp Salt
- 2 Tbsp Sugar

Directions:

1. Supply your smoker with wood pellets and follow the start-up procedure. Preheat the grill, with the lid open, to 450° F.

2. Combine the cumin seeds, whole black peppercorns, and coriander seeds in a cast iron skillet. Stir over medium heat for about 8 minutes until toasted. Let them cool slightly. Finely grind toasted spices in a blender and transfer to a small bowl, then mix in sugar and salt.

3. Rub the spices into the pork chops on both sides. Place cast iron skillet inside the grill. Once hot, add the olive oil to the skillet and coat the bottom. Sprinkle the pork chops with salt, and then add to the skillet. Make sure that each pork chop has enough space in between one another. Cook the chops for about 30 minutes. Once pork chops are fully cooked, turn off the grill, remove skillet, plate and enjoy!

Smoked Pork Tomato Tamales

Servings: 6-8

Cooking Time: 60 Minutes

Ingredients:

- 1 Boneless, Netted Pork Roast
- 1 Cup, Fresh Cilantro, Chopped
- 3 Cloves Garlic, Peeled
- 20 Dried Cornhusks
- 1 Tbsp Lime Juice
- ¼ Cup Olive Oil
- 1 Onion, Quartered
- 4 - 6 Cups Prepared Masa Harina Tamale Dough
- 3 – 4 Serrano Peppers, Deseeded
- 1 Tbsp Sweet Heat Rub
- 1 Lb. Tomatillos, Husked And Washed

Directions:

1. Began by soaking the corn husks in a pan filled with water. Soak for 2 – 4 hours, or if needed, overnight.

2. Unwrap the tomatillos from their shell and place all of them into a grill basket followed by a few Serranos, deseeded, garlic cloves and 1 onion cut into quarters.

3. Supply your smoker with wood pellets and follow the start-up procedure. Preheat the grill, with the lid open, to 400° F. If you're using a gas or charcoal grill, set it up for medium low heat, and use smoke chips to fill your grill with smoke for 15 minutes. Place the grill basket filled with your vegetables and roast them over an open flame on your smoker until vegetables have become charred.

4. Place tomatillos, peppers, garlic and onions in a bowl, cover with plastic wrap, and let stand until cool enough to handle, 10 to 15 minutes.

5. Season the pork roast generously with Sweet Heat Rub and grill at 350°F for 1 hour until the roast has a nice crust on the outside.

6. While the pork roast is cooking, add a handful of cilantro, charred vegetables, 1 tbsp of Sweet Heat Rub, 1 tbsp lime juice,

and ¼ cup of olive oil to a food processor. Pulse in food processor until mixture is consistent. Set aside

7. After the pork roast has been grilled for an hour, turn heat down to 275°F. Put roast in pan with about a cup of water, cover with aluminum foil and cook for another 4 hours or until the roast can be shredded. Pour chile verde sauce over shredded pork and toss to combine.

8. To being assembling tamales, place a corn husk on a work surface. Place 2-3 tablespoons of tamale dough on larger end of husk and spread into a rectangle, about ¼" thick, leaving a small border along the edge. Place large tablespoon of chili and pork filling on top of dough. Fold over sides of husk so dough surrounds filling, then fold bottom of husk up and secure closed by tying a thin strip of husk around tamale.

9. To cook tamales, place them in a large metal colander over a large stockpot filled with water. Cover and let steam for 1 hour. After the tamales have been steamed, take them off and grill them at 350°F for about 10-20 minutes until corn husks have charred marks.

Simple Smoked Ribs

Servings: 6
Cooking Time: 240 Minutes

Ingredients:
- 3 Rack baby back ribs
- 3/4 Cup Pork & Poultry Rub
- 3/4 Cup 'Que BBQ Sauce

Directions:
1. Peel membrane from the back side of ribs and trim any excess fat.
2. Season both sides of ribs with Traeger Pork & Poultry Rub, about 1/4 cup per rack.
3. Supply your smoker with wood pellets and follow the start-up procedure. Preheat the grill, with the lid closed, to 180° F.
4. Place ribs on the grill and smoke for 3 to 4 hours. Grill: 180 °F Probe: 160 °F
5. When the internal temperature registers between 160°F to 165°F, remove ribs from the grill and increase Traeger temperature to 350°F. Grill: 350 °F
6. Place about 1/4 cup of Traeger 'Que BBQ Sauce on a large sheet of heavy-duty aluminum foil, then place a rack of ribs meat-side down on top and wrap tightly. Repeat with each rack.
7. Place the wrapped ribs back on the grill and cook for 45 minutes, or until internal temperature registers 204°F. Grill: 350 °F Probe: 204 °F
8. Remove from grill and let rest 20 minutes before slicing. Enjoy!

Hickory Smoked Pork Shoulder

Servings: 7
Cooking Time: 420 Minutes

Ingredients:
- 1 Cup Apple Cider Vinegar
- 2 Tbsp   Hickory Bacon Seasoning
- 5 - 6 Lbs Pork Shoulder, Bone In
- 1 Tbsp Sugar

Directions:
1. Supply your smoker with wood pellets and follow the start-up procedure. Preheat the grill, with the lid open, to 225° F. If you're using a gas or charcoal, set up your grill for low, indirect heat.
2. Rinse the pork shoulder (aka pork butt) under cold running water and make sure to pat dry the entire surface, including any small cracks and crevices.
3. Place the pork shoulder in the aluminum pan, fat side up, and sprinkle a liberal amount of   Hickory Bacon seasoning over the top. You want to be very generous with the outer layer of seasoning here, making sure to coat the meat from end to end.
4. In a large bowl, pour the 1 cup of apple cider vinegar, the 2 tablespoons of Hickory Bacon, and 1 tablespoon of sugar. Mix until the sugars are completely dissolved.
5. Fill your marinade injector with the marinade and inject it deep into the meat. For even flavor, inject the marinade all over the pork shoulder at one-inch intervals. Pressing the syringe slowly will help avoid the marinade squirting out.
6. Tightly wrap aluminum foil over the top of the pan, set it on your grill, and close the lid.
7. Smoke the pork shoulder for 6-8 hours, or until the meat is tender and the internal temperature is 195°F to 200°F.
8. Remove from the grill and let it rest on a cutting board for 20-30 minutes with the aluminum foil loosely tented over the top.
9. When you're ready to serve, shred the pork shoulder, discarding any large pieces of fat.

Spiced Orange Ribs

Servings: 4
Cooking Time: 180 Minutes

Ingredients:
- 1 Tablespoon Adobo Sauce
- 2 (2 1⁄2-Pound) Racks Baby Back Rib
- 1⁄3 Cup Firmly Packed Light Brown Sugar
- 1 Tablespoon Chili Powder
- 5 In Adobo Sauce Chipotle Peppers
- 1⁄3 Cup Leaves Cilantro, Fresh
- 1 Teaspoon Ground Cumin
- 1⁄4 Cup Honey
- 1⁄4 Cup Ketchup

* 2 Tablespoons Lime Juice
* 1 Cup Orange Juice, Fresh
* 5 Tablespoons Sweet Heat Rub

Directions:

1. First, make the barbecue sauce. Into the bowl of a blender, add ¾ cup of orange juice, cilantro, honey, ketchup, lime juice, 2 chipotles in adobo, adobo sauce, and 1 tablespoon of the Sweet Heat Rub. Place the lid on the blender and blend until completely smooth. Pour into a bowl, reserve ½ cup and set aside.

2. Prepare the ribs. Using the paper towels, pull the membrane off of the back of the ribs and discard. In the bowl of a blender, add the orange juice, brown sugar, chipotle peppers, chili powder, ground cumin, and Sweet Heat. Place the lid on the blender and blend until smooth. Pour this mixture over the ribs and massage into the meat. Place the ribs in the refrigerator and marinade for 8 hours.

3. Supply your smoker with wood pellets and follow the start-up procedure. Preheat the grill, with the lid open, to 275° F. Place the ribs, meat side up, and grill for 1 ½ hours. Baste the ribs with the reserved barbecue sauce, then BBQ for another 1 ½ hours, or until the ribs are extremely tender. Remove the ribs from the grill and serve with barbecue sauce.

Everything Pigs In A Blanket

Servings: 4
Cooking Time: 15 Minutes

Ingredients:

* 2 Tablespoon poppy seeds
* 1 Tablespoon dried minced onion
* 2 Teaspoon garlic, minced
* 2 Tablespoon sesame seeds
* 1 Teaspoon salt
* 8 Ounce (8 oz) Can Pillsbury Original Crescent Rolls
* 1/4 Cup Dijon mustard
* 1 Large egg, beaten

Directions:

1. Supply your smoker with wood pellets and follow the start-up procedure. Preheat the grill, with the lid closed, to 350° F.

2. Mix together poppy seeds, dried minced onion, dried minced garlic, salt and sesame seeds. Set aside.

3. Cut each triangle of crescent roll dough into thirds lengthwise, making 3 small strips from each roll.

4. Brush the dough strips lightly with Dijon mustard. Put the mini hot dogs on 1 end of the dough and roll up.

5. Arrange them, seam side down, on a greased baking pan. Brush with egg wash and sprinkle with seasoning mixture.

6. Bake in Traeger until golden brown, about 12 to 15 minutes.

7. Serve with mustard or dipping sauce of your choice. Enjoy!

Rub-injected Pork Shoulder

Servings: 8-12
Cooking Time: 1200 Minutes

Ingredients:

* 1 (6- to 8-pound) bone-in pork shoulder
* 2 cups Tea Injectable made with Pork Rub
* 2 tablespoons yellow mustard
* 1 batch Pork Rub

Directions:

1. Supply your smoker with wood pellets and follow the start-up procedure. Preheat the grill, with the lid closed, to 225°F.

2. Inject the pork shoulder throughout with the tea injectable.

3. Coat the pork shoulder all over with mustard and season it with the rub. Using your hands, work the rub into the meat.

4. Place the shoulder directly on the grill grate and smoke until its internal temperature reaches 160°F and a dark bark has formed on the exterior.

5. Pull the shoulder from the grill and wrap it completely in aluminum foil or butcher paper.

6. Increase the grill's temperature to 350°F.

7. Return the pork shoulder to the grill and cook until its internal temperature reaches 195°F.

8. Pull the shoulder from the grill and place it in a cooler. Cover the cooler and let the pork rest for 1 or 2 hours.

9. Remove the pork shoulder from the cooler and unwrap it. Remove the shoulder bone and pull the pork apart using just your fingers. Serve immediately.

Beer Braised Garlic Bbq Pork Butt

Servings: 6-8
Cooking Time: 300 Minutes

Ingredients:

* One 12Oz Bottle Dark Beer
* 1/2 Cup Brown Sugar
* 2 Tablespoons Granulated Garlic
* 4 Tablespoons Honey
* 1 Cup Ketchup
* 1 Tablespoon Olive Oil
* Pulled Pork Rub
* 1 Pork Butt, Boneless
* 2 Tablespoons Worcestershire Sauce
* 4 Tablespoons Yellow Mustard

Directions:

1. Generously season the pork butt with Pulled Pork Rub, making sure to rub the seasoning in on all surfaces of roast. Place the pork onto a roasting rack inside a 9x13 pan.

2. Pour about half a bottle of dark beer into the bottom of the pan and save the remaining amount of beer, you'll need this later.

3. Supply your smoker with wood pellets and follow the start-up procedure. Preheat the grill, with the lid open, to high heat. If you're using a gas or charcoal, set it up for high direct heat. Place the pan in the center of the grill and grill for 30 minutes until the pork roast is dark in color and charred in some spots.

4. Remove the pork from the grill and decrease the temperature of the grill to 325°F. Set aside and began to make the BBQ sauce.

5. In a medium sized bowl, add ketchup, brown sugar, yellow mustard, honey, Worcestershire, granulated garlic, half bottle of dark beer, and finally 1 tbsp of Pulled Pork Rub. Mix together thoroughly.

6. Take the sauce and pour it over the roast, cover with aluminum foil.

7. Cook the roast for 4 - 6 hours or until the meat is falling apart tender and the bone easily comes away from the meat and reaches an internal temperature of 200°F. Remove the pork from the grill and allow it to rest for 10-15 minutes.

8. Shred the pork with meat claws or forks, discarding any fat or gristle. Toss the shredded pork with the barbecue sauce and serve immediately.

Spicy Bacon Wrapped Grilled Chicken Skewers

Servings: 6
Cooking Time: 20 Minutes

Ingredients:

- 1/2 Cup Ranch
- 1/2 Teaspoon garlic powder
- 2 Tablespoon Chile Sauce
- 1/2 Teaspoon dried oregano
- 16 Ounce Chicken Breast, cubed
- 1 Whole red onion, sliced
- 1 Whole green bell peppers, sliced
- 8 Strips Bacon, sliced

Directions:

1. In a large bowl, mix together ranch, garlic powder, oregano, and chile sauce. Add in cubed chicken, tossing to thoroughly coat. Allow the chicken to marinate in fridge for 1 to 3 hours.

2. Supply your smoker with wood pellets and follow the start-up procedure. Preheat the grill, with the lid closed, to High heat.

3. Begin assembling Traeger skewers: slide on a wedge of onion, a pepper, a slice of bacon, and chicken. Continue to alternate bacon and chicken, so the bacon weaves around the chicken pieces. Finish off each skewer with a pepper and onion wedge. Be sure to not overcrowd skewer, to allow faster and even cooking. Repeat with all skewers.

4. Place the skewers on the grill grate, keeping a piece of foil under the end of the skewers to prevent them from burning and to make turning them easier.

5. Cook for approximately 5 minutes per side, doing a quarter-turn each time, for a total of 20 minutes, or until the chicken reaches an internal temperature of 165°F. Remove skewers. Enjoy! Grill: 450°F

Egg Sausage Casserole

Servings: 12
Cooking Time: 60 Minutes

Ingredients:

- 12 sausage links
- 30 oz hash browns, thawed
- 1 1/2 c. marble jack cheese, shredded
- 1/2 tsp pepper
- 12 large eggs
- 1 tsp salt
- 1/2 c. yellow onion, chopped
- 1 c. milk

Directions:

1. Supply your smoker with wood pellets and follow the start-up procedure. Preheat the grill, with the lid closed, to 350° F.

2. Grill sausage links on the preheated grill for 10-15 minutes or until heated through.

3. Remove the sausage links from grill and cut them into 1-inch pieces.

4. Spray a 9" ×13" tin pan with non-stick spray. Spread out hash browns on bottom of pan. Top with sausage pieces.

5. Combine eggs, salt, pepper, 1 c. cheese, onions, and milk in a bowl. Pour the mixture over sausage and hash browns. Then top with the remaining 1/2 c. of cheese.

6. Transfer the tin pan to the grill grate, and grill at 350 °F for 45 minutes or until the middle is set.

Smoked Rack Of Pork

Servings: 6
Cooking Time: 360 Minutes

Ingredients:

- 4 Bay Leaves
- 2 Jalapeno Peppers
- 1 Six Bone Rack Of Pork
- 1 Cup Salt
- Salt & Freshly Ground Black Pepper
- 2 Tbsp Smokey Apple Chipotle Rub
- 10 Thyme, Fresh Sprigs
- 1 Gallon Water

Directions:

1.   To make the rack of pork: Combine the salt, water, bay, thyme and jalapeño in a large stock pot and bring to a boil, let boil for 10 minutes until salt is dissolved.

2.   Remove from heat and let cool completely, add pork to the brine and brine overnight. Remove from the brine and rinse. Pat dry and season with Apple Chipotle seasoning and salt and pepper.

3.   Supply your smoker with wood pellets and follow the start-up procedure. Preheat the grill, with the lid open, to 140° F. Place the rack of pork on the smoker with a probe inserted and cook for about 5 to 6 hours.

4.   Turn the heat up to 450°F and open the heat shield.

5.   Sear the pork on all sides, once seared move to a cutting board and tent with foil, rest for 20 minutes then slice in between each bone and serve.

6.   To make the pickled fennel: Place the fennel in a bowl. In a small saucepan over medium low heat, add the pickling spice and toast for about 2 minutes or until fragrant.

7.   Add the cider vinegar and bring to a boil over high heat. Add the sugar, salt and water and bring to a boil.

8.   Cook for 10 minutes over medium high heat to meld the flavors. Strain over the fennel and set aside to cool. Once cool cover and place in the fridge until ready to use.

9.   To make the caramelized sweet potato puree: In a large pan add the olive oil over high heat until the oil is shimmering, add the sweet potatoes and cook browning on all sides.

10.   Once the sweet potatoes are caramelized add 1 cup of the water and cook until it has evaporated and repeat the process with the remaining water.

11.   In a saucepan add the milk and the cream and warm over low heat. Once the sweet potatoes are tender add them to a blender with the milk mixture and blend until smooth but be careful not to over process and turn the potatoes into glue.

12.   To make the mustard gravy: Add the olive oil to a large pan over medium high heat, once shimmering, add the shallots and cook until translucent but not browned.

13.   Add the bourbon and cooked until almost entirely reduced. Add the heavy cream and the mustard and cook for about 8 to 10 minutes stirring often until the sauce thickens and coats the back of a spoon.

14.   Stir in the parsley and season with salt and pepper.

15.   To make the fried shallots: Place the shallots in a small bowl and cover them with the milk, let soak in the milk for at least 1 hour.

16.   Drain the shallots and transfer them to a large Ziplock bag, add the flour, salt and pepper. Seal the bag and shake well to coat all the shallots in the flour. Remove from the bag shaking off the excess flour.

17.   Heat the oil to 350°F in a deep pot. Fry the shallots until golden brown then remove them to a plate lined with paper towels. Season with salt.

18.   To put it all together and plate: Spread the puree in a circle in the middle of the plate, place a small handful of the pickled fennel on one side of the puree, Place the pork leaning on the fennel, Spoon over the sauce and top with the fried shallots and the micro arugula.

Cider Glazed Baked Holiday Ham

Servings: 6
Cooking Time: 120 Minutes

Ingredients:

- 3 apples, cored and cut into thick slices
- 1 Large ham
- 4 Cup apple cider, divided
- 1/4 Cup bourbon
- 1/4 Cup Dijon mustard
- 1/4 Cup honey or maple syrup
- 1/2 Teaspoon ground cinnamon
- 1/4 Teaspoon ground cloves
- 1 Pinch ground nutmeg or allspice

Directions:

1.   Supply your smoker with wood pellets and follow the start-up procedure. Preheat the grill, with the lid closed, to 325° F.

2.   Line a roasting pan with heavy-duty foil for easier clean-up.

3.   Arrange the apple slices in the bottom of the roasting pan for a natural roasting rack. Place ham on top of the apple slices and pour remaining 1 cup of apple cider around the ham.

4.   Place roasting pan directly on grill grate and bake for 1-1/2 hours. Grill: 325 °F

5.   For the glaze, combine remaining 3 cups of apple cider and bourbon in a small saucepan and bring to a boil over medium-high heat. Simmer until reduced by one-third. Whisk in the mustard, honey, cinnamon, cloves and nutmeg.

6.   Glaze ham with apple cider mixture as needed (use any left over for serving) and continue cooking for another 30 minutes or until a thermometer inserted into the thickest part of the meat reaches an internal temperatures of 140°F. Grill: 325 °F Probe: 140 °F

7.   Remove ham from grill and allow to rest for 20 minutes before serving.

8.   Warm remaining sauce and serve with ham if desired. Enjoy!

Bbq Pork Belly Burnt Ends

Servings: 8
Cooking Time: 240 Minutes

Ingredients:

- 1 (5-7 lb) skinless pork belly, cut into 1 inch cubes
- Meat Church Honey Hog, Honey Hog Hot or The Gospel Rub

- 1 Cup apple juice, for spritzing
- 1 1/2 Cup Apricot BBQ Sauce
- 1/2 Cup clover honey

Directions:

1. Supply your smoker with wood pellets and follow the start-up procedure. Preheat the grill, with the lid closed, to 275° F.

2. Thoroughly coat all sides of the pork belly cubes with your choice of Meat Church Honey Hog, Honey Hog Hot or The Gospel Rub. I prefer a spicier rub because I finish these with a sweet sauce.

3. Allow the rub to adhere on all sides for at least 15 minutes. Place the pork belly in the Traeger fat-side down. I prefer to do this on a wire rack.

4. Cook the pork belly for 3 hours, spritzing with apple juice every 45 minutes or whenever it starts to look dry. Grill: 275 °F

5. Pull the belly when the meat reaches an internal temperature of 190°F to 195°F. Some people pull the belly a lot earlier, but I want it really tender. Grill: 275 °F Probe: 190 °F

6. Place the cubes in the half-size aluminum pan. Season and toss the cubes with more Meat Church rub.

7. Cover the cubes with Traeger Apricot BBQ Sauce. Drizzle clover honey across the top. Finally, toss the cubes thoroughly to ensure they are completely covered.

8. Return the pan (uncovered) to the Traeger and cook for another hour or until all liquid has reduced and caramelized. Grill: 275 °F

9. Allow them to cool for 15 minutes before serving. Enjoy!

Double Smoked Apple Spiral Ham

Servings: 12
Cooking Time: 150 Minutes

Ingredients:

- 1 10 lb ham spiral cut
- 1 cup apple jelly
- 1 cup raspberry chipotle BBQ sauce

Directions:

1. Supply your smoker with wood pellets and follow the start-up procedure. Preheat the grill, with the lid closed, to 275° F.

2. Remove ham from all packaging and transfer to a chicken tray, cut-side-down. Then place on a cooking tray and transfer to the smoker. Close the lid and cook for 2 hours.

3. Heat up saucepan over medium heat. Add apple jelly and stir well, until it reaches a liquid consistency.

4. Add raspberry chipotle. Stir in and bring glaze to a simmer. Leave saucepan on warm heat until ham is ready.

5. After two hours, transfer ham to a shallow aluminum pan. Apply the glaze to ham generously using a basting brush. Make sure all cracks on ham surfaceare glazed.

6. Still in a shallow pan, put ham back in smoker. Close the lid and leave to smoke for over 30 minutes.

7. Remove ham from smoker and transfer to a cutting board. Leave to rest for 10 minutes.

8. Cut along the outer seam of the ham, allowing the slices to fall away.

Delicious Smoked Bone-in Pork Chops

Servings: 4
Cooking Time: 90 Minutes

Ingredients:

- 1/2 Cup Apple Cider Vinegar
- 4 Pork Butt Roast, Bone-In
- 2 Tbsp Salt
- 1 Tbsp Sugar
- 4 Tablespoons Tennessee Apple Butter Seasoning
- 1/4 Cup Vinegar, Red Wine
- 1/4 Cup Water

Directions:

1. Supply your smoker with wood pellets and follow the start-up procedure. Preheat the grill, with the lid closed, to 250° F.

2. In a large mixing bowl, combine the sugar, red wine vinegar, salt, 2 tablespoons of Tennessee Apple Butter and water to create a brine for the pork chops. Whisk the brine well until the sugar, salt and Tennessee Apple Butter have dissolved.

3. Generously rub the pork chops on all sides with olive oil and season on all sides with the Tennessee Apple Butter. Make sure the meat is coated on all sides.

4. Place the pork chops in the smoker, insert a temperature probe into the thickest part of one of the pork chops, and smoke until the internal temperature reaches 145°F, or about 1 hour 30 minutes. The pork chops should have developed a good color and be juicy, but no longer be pink in the center.

5. Remove the pork chops from the smoker and allow them to rest for 5-10 minutes under tented aluminum foil, then slice along the grain and serve.

Smoked Chili Con Queso By Doug Scheiding

Servings: 8
Cooking Time: 45 Minutes

Ingredients:

- 1 Pound hot pork sausage
- 1 (2 lb) block Velveeta cheese
- 1 Pound smoked Gouda cheese

- 1 (10 oz) can RO*TEL Original Diced Tomatoes and Green Chilies
- 1 (10 oz) can RO*TEL Fire Roasted Diced Tomatoes and Green Chilies
- 1 (10 oz) can cream of mushroom soup
- 4 Tablespoon Coffee Rub
- 1/2 Cup chopped cilantro

Directions:

1.   Heat a medium cast iron skillet over medium heat and fully cook pork sausage, breaking into small chunks as you go. Remove the sausage and drain and discard the fat.

2.   Supply your smoker with wood pellets and follow the start-up procedure. Preheat the grill, with the lid closed, to 350° F.

3.   Use a 4 to 5 quart cast iron Dutch oven or other oven safe dish. Divide the block of Velveeta into 5 to 6 large pieces and cut the smoked Gouda into small 1 inch cubes. Add the canned ingredients including the liquid. Add the sausage and Traeger Coffee Rub last. Grill: 350 ˚F

4.   Smoke the queso for 45 minutes on the Traeger, stirring 3 to 4 times. Grill: 350 ˚F

5.   Add most of the cilantro the last 5 minutes of smoking. Sprinkle remaining cilantro on the top before serving. Enjoy!

Onion Pork Shoulder

Servings: 8 - 10
Cooking Time: 240 Minutes

Ingredients:

- Aluminum Foil
- 1 Diced Apple
- 1 Cup Broth, Chicken
- 2 Tbsp Butter, Salted
- 1 Diced Onion
- 1 Pork Shoulder Or Pork Butt Roast
- 1 Box Or Bag Of Stovetop Stuffing Mix
- Champion Chicken Seasoning

Directions:

1.   Prepare the pork shoulder. Place the pork shoulder on the cutting board, and with a sharp knife, trim any very fatty sections of the pork shoulder and remove. Then, butterfly the shoulder. Beginning on one side, carefully cut a slit horizontally into one side of the pork shoulder and carefully continue to slice almost all the way to the right side, rolling the shoulder as you cut, unfolding the meat like a book, until the pork shoulder is one long strip.

2.   Began to make the stuffing by using a medium sized pan and adding 2 tbsp of salted butter to the pan. Add in the onion and apple and let cook for about 5 minutes making sure to stir in between. Add 2 tbsp of Champion Chicken Seasoning. Add the 1 cup of chicken broth followed by a bag of stuffing mix. Let reduce

and mix together very well and remove from heat. Transfer to a bowl and set aside.

3.   Once the pork shoulder is butterflied, place some stuff on the roast making sure to leave enough space to roll and tie the roast as well.

4.   Starting on one end of the pork shoulder, roll the pork shoulder up into a tight spiral, and set onto the cutting board, seam side down. Cut four even lengths of butcher's twine, and wiggle under the pork shoulder, two inches apart from each other. Tie tightly to hold the roast together and place on a sheet pan.

5.   Supply your smoker with wood pellets and follow the start-up procedure. Preheat the grill, with the lid open, to 250° F. If you're using a gas or charcoal grill, set it up for medium low heat. Place the aluminum pan in the center of the grill and cook for 3-4 hours, or until the temperature of the pork shoulder reaches an internal temperature of 180˚F and is very tender.

6.   Remove the pork shoulder from the grill and allow to rest for 15 minutes, then slice and serve.

Traeger Pulled Pork Sandwiches

Servings: 8
Cooking Time: 660 Minutes

Ingredients:

- 1 (5-7 lb) bone-in pork shoulder
- Pork & Poultry Rub
- 2 Cup apple juice, in food-grade spray bottle
- BBQ Sauce
- 10 hamburger buns
- coleslaw, for serving

Directions:

1.   Generously season pork roast on all sides with Traeger Pork & Poultry rub.

2.   Supply your smoker with wood pellets and follow the start-up procedure. Preheat the grill, with the lid closed, to 225° F.

3.   Put the roast on the grill grate, fat-side up and smoke for 3 hours. Spray the roast with apple juice every hour after the first hour. Grill: 225 ˚F

4.   After 3 hours, transfer pork to a disposable aluminum foil pan large enough to hold the roast. Increase the grill temperature to 250˚F, and continue to cook for 6 to 8 additional hours, or until an instant-read meat thermometer inserted in the thickest part, but not touching bone, registers 203˚F. If the pork starts to brown too much, cover it loosely with aluminum foil. Grill: 250 ˚F Probe: 203 ˚F

5.   Carefully transfer the pork roast to a cutting board and let it rest for 20 minutes. Pour the juices from the bottom of the pan into a gravy separator. Discard any fat that has floated to the top.

6.   With your hands (preferably protected from the heat with lined, heavy-duty rubber gloves) pull the pork into chunks.

Discard the bone and any lumps of fat, including the cap. Pull each chunk into shreds and transfer to a large mixing bowl.

7.   Season with additional rub and moisten with the reserved pork juice. Add your favorite Traeger BBQ sauce to the pulled pork and mix well.

8.   Pile the pork mixture on the hamburger buns and serve with coleslaw. Enjoy!

Hanging St. Louis-style Grilled Ribs

Servings: 4
Cooking Time: 270 Minutes

Ingredients:
- 1 1/3 Cup Apple Juice
- 1 2/3 Cup BBQ Sauce, Divided
- Pulled Pork Rub
- 4 Half Racks Spare Ribs, St. Louis Style

Directions:
1.   Supply your smoker with wood pellets and follow the start-up procedure. Preheat the grill, with the lid open, to 250° F. If using a gas or charcoal grill, set it up for low, indirect heat.
2.   Using a sharp knife, remove the back membrane from the rib racks and pat dry with paper towel. Cut rib racks in half, then season generously with Pulled Pork Rub.
3.   Insert a hanging hook under the top rib, then transfer racks to the smoking cabinet. Smoke for 2 ½ hours.
4.   Remove ribs from the smoking cabinet and set on heavy duty foil. Mix together ⅔ cup BBQ sauce and ⅓ cup apple juice, then brush thinned BBQ sauce on both sides of ribs. Pour ¼ cup of apple juice around each of the ribs. Fold over foil, then transfer to the grill, meat side down. Increase temperature to 300° F and continue cooking for an additional 2 hours.
5.   Remove ribs from the grill, baste with BBQ, then return to the grill and cook for another 10 to 15 minutes. Allow to rest for 15 minutes, then slice and serve hot.

Bourbon Chile Glazed Ham

Servings: 8 – 10
Cooking Time: 90 Minutes

Ingredients:
- ¼ Cup Apple Cider Vinegar
- 2 Cups Bourbon
- 1 Cup Brown Sugar
- 2 Canned Chipotle Chiles In Adobo Sauce
- 2 Cups Chicken Stock
- 2 Dried Ancho Chiles
- 1 Dried Arbol Chile
- 2 Dried Guajillo Chiles
- 2 Tbsp Extra Virgin Olive Oil
- 4 Fresh Garlic, Roughly Chopped
- 4 Cloves Roasted Garlic
- Salt
- 2 Shallots, Roughly Chopped
- 1 Spiral Cut Ham

Directions:
1.   Supply your smoker with wood pellets and follow the start-up procedure. Preheat the grill, with the lid open, to 450° F.
2.   In a large, heavy-bottomed skillet, heat the oil over medium-high heat. Add the shallots and cook for 5 minutes, or until softened.
3.   Add the roasted and fresh garlic and cook, stirring occasionally, for 3 to 4 minutes, until the garlic is browned.
4.   Remove the skillet from the heat and add the bourbon.
5.   Return the skillet to medium-high heat, add the vinegar, and cook until the liquid is reduced by one third, about 10 minutes.
6.   Add the ancho, guajillo, árbol, and chipotle chiles and the brown sugar, then add the chicken stock and continue to cook until the mixture reduces by two thirds, about 15 minutes.
7.   Strain the reduction through a fine-mesh strainer into a bowl, then pour it into a small saucepan.
8.   Return to the heat over medium and reduce until the glaze coats the back off a spoon. Taste and add salt if needed.

Bbq Pulled Pork Grilled Cheese Sandwich

Servings: 8
Cooking Time: 540 Minutes

Ingredients:
- 1 Pork Butt, bone-in, 8-10 lbs.
- 2 Tablespoon Pork & Poultry Rub
- 1 1/2 Cup apple juice
- 4 Tablespoon brown sugar
- 1 Tablespoon salt
- Sweet & Heat BBQ Sauce
- 16 Pieces White Bread
- cheddar cheese
- butter, softened

Directions:
1.   Trim pork butt of all excess fat leaving 1/4-inch of the fat cap attached.
2.   Combine 2 Tbsp Traeger Pork & Poultry Rub, apple juice, brown sugar and salt in a small bowl stirring until most of the sugar and salt are dissolved.
3.   Inject the pork butt every square inch or so with the apple juice mixture. Season the exterior of the pork butt with remaining rub.

4.   Supply your smoker with wood pellets and follow the start-up procedure. Preheat the grill, with the lid closed, to 250° F.

5.   Place pork butt directly on the grill grate and cook for about 6 hours or until the internal temperature reaches 160 degrees F. Remove pork butt from grill and wrap in two layers of foil. Pour in 1/2 cup of apple juice. Secure tin foil tightly to contain the apple juice. Grill: 250 ˚F Probe: 160 ˚F

6.   Increase temperature to 275 degrees F and return to grill in a pan large enough to hold the pork butt in case of leaks. Cook an additional 3 hours or until internal temperature reaches 205 degrees F. Grill: 275 ˚F Probe: 205 ˚F

7.   Remove from the grill and discard the bone. Shred the pork removing any excess fat or tendons. Season with additional Traeger Pork & Poultry Rub and salt if needed. Add Traeger Sweet & Heat BBQ Sauce and mix to combine. Set pork aside.

8.   For the grilled cheese sandwiches: Butter two pieces of bread and place one in a pan warmed over medium heat, butter side down. Place a slice of cheddar cheese on top of the bread and top with pulled pork. Place another slice of cheese on top of pork and finish with the other slice of bread, butter side up.

9.   Cook on first side 5-7 minutes until bread is lightly browned. Flip and cook for another 5-7 minutes. Remove from heat and slice in half. Enjoy!

Smoked Porchetta

Servings: 6
Cooking Time: 360 Minutes

Ingredients:
- 1 Tbs Ancho Chili Powder
- 1/2 Cup Brown Sugar
- 3 Tbs Grilling Seasoning
- 1 Tbs Chopped Italian Parsley
- 1/2 Cup Maple Syrup
- 1 Tsp Dry Oregano
- 1 Tbs Chopped Oregano, Leaves
- 1/2 Pork, Belly (Skinless)
- 1 Whole Pork, Tenderloins
- 6 Slices Prosciutto, Sliced
- 1 Tbs Chopped Rosemary, Fresh
- 1 Tbs Chopped Sage, Leaves
- 1/2 Cup Sugar, Cure

Directions:
1.   Sprinkle Sugar Cure on each side and rub in. (You can cure pork belly without using Sodium Nitrite (in the cure mix) but it is much safer if you use it, so I definitely recommend it).

2.   In a small bowl, mix brown sugar, maple syrup, ancho chili powder and oregano, and whisk. Slather on both sides of each pork belly piece.

3.   Place pork bag (if you can find a 2 gallon or larger one) or container and refrigerate Rotate and flip each 24 hours.

4.   After 3 days remove pork belly and rinse each piece thoroughly.

5.   If you do not rinse well the porchetta (or bacon) will be too salty due to the sugar cure.

6.   Lay pork belly skin side down on a large cutting board.

7.   Lightly score the meat side with diamond cuts to allow the seasoning to penetrate.

8.   Lightly sprinkle with grilling seasoning, then coat well with the herb mix.

9.   Lay out the prosciutto, then lay the pork tenderloin on the pork belly.

10.   Lightly sprinkle tenderloin with seasoning, and wrap the pork belly tightly around it.

11.   Use cooking twine to tie up tightly.

12.   Season the exterior of the pork belly lightly but evenly with grilling seasoning.

13.   Supply your smoker with wood pellets and follow the start-up procedure. Preheat the grill, with the lid open, to 250° F.

14.   Smoke for 6 hours, or until internal temperature reaches around 175°F.

15.   Remove and allow to rest for 20 minutes. Once it cools, then slice thinly and sear in a hot skillet.

16.   Let it cool again for about 10 minutes before serving.

3-2-1 Bbq Baby Back Ribs

Servings: 6
Cooking Time: 360 Minutes

Ingredients:
- 2 Rack baby back pork ribs
- 1/3 Cup yellow mustard
- 1/2 Cup apple juice, divided
- 1 Tablespoon Worcestershire sauce
- Pork & Poultry Rub
- 1/2 Cup dark brown sugar
- 1/3 Cup honey, warmed
- 1 Cup 'Que BBQ Sauce

Directions:
1.   If your butcher has not already done so, remove the thin silverskin membrane from the bone-side of the ribs by working the tip of a butter knife or a screwdriver underneath the membrane over a middle bone. Use paper towels to get a firm grip, then tear the membrane off.

2.   In a small bowl, combine the mustard, 1/4 cup of apple juice (reserve the rest) and the Worcestershire sauce. Spread the mixture thinly on both sides of the ribs and season with Traeger Pork & Poultry Rub.

3.   Supply your smoker with wood pellets and follow the start-up procedure. Preheat the grill, with the lid closed, to 180° F.Smoke the ribs, meat-side up for 3 hours.

4.   After the ribs have smoked for 3 hours, transfer them to a rimmed baking sheet and increase the grill temperature to 225°F .

5.   Tear off four long sheets of heavy-duty aluminum foil. Top with a rack of ribs and pull up the sides to keep the liquid enclosed. Sprinkle half the brown sugar on the rack, then top with half the honey and half the remaining apple juice. Use a bit more apple juice if you want more tender ribs. Lay another piece of foil on top and tightly crimp the edges so there is no leakage. Repeat with the remaining rack of ribs.

6.   Return the foiled ribs to the grill and cook for an additional 2 hours.

7.   Carefully remove the foil from the ribs and brush the ribs on both sides with Traeger 'Que Sauce. Discard the foil. Arrange the ribs directly on the grill grate and continue to grill until the sauce tightens, 30 to 60 minutes more.

8.   Let the ribs rest for a few minutes before serving. Enjoy!

Grilled Pork Belly

Servings: 15
Cooking Time: 370 Minutes

Ingredients:
- Peanut Oil
- Mandarin Habanero Spice
- 13 Lbs Pork, Belly (Skin And Fat)
- Salt
- Sweet Barbecue Sauce

Directions:
1.   Supply your smoker with wood pellets and follow the start-up procedure. Preheat the grill, with the lid open, to 250° F.

2.   Place the pork belly on the grates of your preheated , meat side down. Smoke until the internal temperature reaches 195°F (this normally takes about 6 hours).

3.   Open the flame broiler and flip the pork belly so that the meat side is up. Brush on the BBQ Sauce (on meat side). Sear the fat side for about 5 minutes, or until crispy.

4.   Using your grill gloves, remove the pork belly from the grill and wrap in aluminum foil for 15 minutes or until it's cool enough to pull apart with your Meat Claws. Or dice into cubes with a knife. Serve hot.

Bacon Wrapped Pickles

Servings: 6
Cooking Time: 60 Minutes

Ingredients:
- 13 Strips Bacon
- 3 Bratwursts, Raw
- 1/2 Cup Colby Jack Cheese, Shredded
- 4 Oz Cream Cheese
- 13 Large Dill Pickles, Spears
- Hickory Bacon Rub
- 2 Scallion, Sliced Thin
- 1/4 Cup Sour Cream

Directions:
1.   Supply your smoker with wood pellets and follow the start-up procedure. Preheat the grill, with the lid open, to 375° F.

2.   Preheat griddle to medium- low flame.

3.   In a mixing bowl combine cream cheese, sour cream, and scallions.

4.   Use a hand mixer to blend well, then fold in grated cheddar-jack. Set aside.

5.   Cook bratwurst on the griddle. Use a metal spatula to chop up sausage into smaller bits and cook until browned.

6.   Remove from the griddle and set aside on a sheet tray to cool.

7.   Place pickles on a sheet tray. Cut in half, then remove seeds with a small measuring spoon.

8.   Stuff one half of each pickle with cream cheese mixture and top with crumbled bratwurst.

9.   Top with the other pickle half, then wrap in bacon.

10.   Season bacon-wrapped pickles with Hickory Bacon Rub, place in cast iron skillet, then transfer to grill.

11.   Grill pickles for 45 to 55 minutes, until bacon starts to crisp on top. Remove from grill. Serve warm.

St. Louis–style Pork Steaks

Servings: 4
Cooking Time: 120 Minutes

Ingredients:
- 1 cup low-carb barbecue sauce
- ¼ cup low-carb beer or sugar-free dark-colored soda or sugar-free root beer
- 4 bone-in pork shoulder steaks, each about 1lb (450g) and at least 1 inch (2.5cm) thick
- for the rub
- 1 tbsp coarse salt
- 1 tbsp freshly ground black pepper
- 1 tbsp granulated light brown sugar or low-carb substitute
- 1 tbsp sweet or smoked paprika
- 1 tsp granulated garlic or garlic powder
- 1 tsp celery salt

Directions:
1.   Supply your smoker with wood pellets and follow the start-up procedure. Preheat the grill, with the lid closed, to 250° F.

2.   In a small bowl, combine the barbecue sauce and beer. Set aside.

3.   In a small bowl, make the rub by combining the ingredients. Mix well. Season the steaks on both sides with some of the rub.

4. Place the steaks on the grate at an angle to the bars and smoke for 30 minutes. Transfer the steaks to an aluminum foil roasting pan. Pour the barbecue mixture over them. Use tongs to turn the steaks, making sure each is coated well with the sauce.

5. Tightly wrap aluminum foil over the top of the pan and place it on the grate. Braise the steaks until they're fork tender, about 1½ hours. (Protect your hands when lifting a corner of the foil because steam will escape.)

6. Remove the pan from the grill and serve the steaks immediately.

Bbq 3-2-1 St. Louis Ribs

Servings: 6
Cooking Time: 360 Minutes

Ingredients:

- 2 Rack St. Louis-style ribs
- Pork & Poultry Rub
- 1/2 Cup brown sugar, divided
- 1/3 Cup honey, divided
- 1 Cup BBQ Sauce
- BBQ Sauce

Directions:

1. If your butcher has not done so already, remove the thin silverskin membrane from the bone-side of the ribs by working the tip of a butter knife underneath the membrane over a middle bone. Use paper towels to get a firm grip, then tear the membrane off.

2. Season both sides of the ribs generously with Traeger Pork & Poultry Rub.

3. Supply your smoker with wood pellets and follow the start-up procedure. Preheat the grill, with the lid closed, to 180° F.

4. Smoke the ribs, meat-side up for 3 hours. Transfer the ribs to a rimmed baking sheet and increase the grill temperature to 225°F. Preheat the grill with the lid closed. Grill: 225 °F

5. Tear off four long sheets of heavy-duty aluminum foil. Top with a rack of ribs. Sprinkle half the brown sugar on the rack then top with half the honey. Tightly wrap the ribs with the foil to create a leak-proof pouch. Repeat with remaining rack of ribs. Grill: 225 °F

6. Return the foiled ribs to the grill, meat side down and cook for an additional two hours. Grill: 225 °F

7. Carefully remove the foil from the ribs – watch out for hot steam – and brush the ribs on both sides with your favorite Traeger BBQ sauce. Discard the foil. Arrange the ribs directly on the grill grate, bone side down and continue to grill until the sauce tightens, about 30 minutes to 60 minutes more. Let the ribs rest for a few minutes before serving. Enjoy! Grill: 225 °F

Grilled Pork Loin

Servings: 4

Cooking Time: 30 Minutes

Ingredients:

- 2 Tablespoons Balsamic Vinegar
- 2 Cups Fresh Washed And Dried Blackberries
- ¼ Cup Seedless Blackberry Preserve
- ½ Teaspoon Dijon Mustard
- Pinch Of Kosher Salt
- 1 Tablespoon Olive Oil
- 1 Pound Silver Skin And Extra Fat Removed Pork Loin
- 2 Tablespoons Sweet Rib Rub
- 1 Tablespoon Worcestershire Sauce

Directions:

1. Place your pork loin on a flat work surface. Trim the pork loin if necessary. Rub the tenderloin all over with olive oil until it is fully coated. Once the pork loin is completely coated, generously season all over with Sweet Rib Rub until every part of the pork loin is coated. Allow the pork tenderloin to rest at room temperature for 30 minutes.

2. While the pork loin rests, make the blackberry sauce. In a small bowl, place a metal strainer on top combine the fresh blackberries, seedless blackberry preserves, balsamic vinegar, Worcestershire sauce, Dijon mustard, and Sweet Rib Rub. Mix well and set aside.

3. Supply your smoker with wood pellets and follow the start-up procedure. Preheat the grill, with the lid open, to 350° F. If you're using a gas or charcoal grill, set it up for medium heat. Insert a temperature probe into the thickest part of the pork loin and smoke at 225°F for 4-5 hours, flipping once, until the pork loin is golden brown and charred in some spots, and reaches an internal temperature of 145°-165°F. Remove the pork loin from the grill and allow it to rest for 5 minutes.

4. Slice the pork loin thinly and serve with the blackberry sauce.

Grilled Raspberry Chipotle Pork Ribs

Servings: 4
Cooking Time: 180 Minutes

Ingredients:

- Baby Back Rib
- Original Bbq Sauce
- Raspberry Chipotle Spice Rub

Directions:

1. Begin by gently rinsing off your ribs in cool water. Pat dry and remove the flavor blocker (thin membrane on the underside of the ribs) to allow the seasoning to permeate right into the meat.

2. Generously season your ribs with Raspberry Chipotle seasoning and place in the refrigerator for an hour for flavor to set in.

3. Supply your smoker with wood pellets and follow the start-up procedure. Preheat the grill, with the lid open, to 250° F. Place your seasoned rack of ribs on the grill and let cook for 2 hours. Next, lather on a thick coating of Original BBQ Sauce, turn up the grill to 300°F and let your ribs roast for another hour. Remove, cut and serve for a meal that will surely make its way into the weekly rotation.

Smoked Apple Pork Belly

Servings: 12
Cooking Time: 370 Minutes

Ingredients:
- 4 Pounds Slab Pork Belly (Uncured)
- 2 Cups Apple Juice (Divided Use)
- ½ Cup BBQ Sauce
- ¼ Cup Signiture Sweet Rub

Directions:
1. Supply your smoker with wood pellets and follow the start-up procedure. Preheat the grill, with the lid closed, to 250° F.
2. Score the top layer of fat on the pork belly in 1 inch squares. Don't cut too deep, just barely into the muscle. Season liberally with the Sweet Rub on all sides.
3. Place the seasoned pork belly on the grill and smoke until the internal temperature reaches 165 degrees F (about 6 hours). Spritz with the apple juice every hour while it is cooking.
4. Once the belly reaches 165 degrees F, remove from the grill and wrap in heavy duty tinfoil with 1/2 cup of the apple juice. Seal the edges of the foil completely and return to the grill until the internal temperature reaches 200 degrees F.
5. Carefully remove the belly from the foil and drizzle with the apple juices from the foil. Return the pork belly to the grill and brush with BBQ sauce. Cook on the grill for 10 more minutes.
6. Remove the finished pork belly from the grill and let it rest for 10-15 more minutes before serving.

Smoked Baby Back Ribs

Servings: 4
Cooking Time: 180 Minutes

Ingredients:
- 3 Rack baby back ribs
- kosher salt
- cracked black pepper

Directions:
1. Peel membrane from back side of the ribs and season both sides with salt and pepper.
2. Supply your smoker with wood pellets and follow the start-up procedure. Preheat the grill, with the lid closed, to 225° F.

3. Cook meat side up for two hours. Flip ribs so the meat side is down and cook for an additional hour. Enjoy! Grill: 225 °F

Maple Baked Ham

Servings: 8
Cooking Time: 60 Minutes

Ingredients:
- 1 (14-16 lb) ham
- whole cloves
- 1/2 Cup pure maple syrup
- 1/2 Cup brown sugar
- 1/2 Cup apple juice
- 1 Tablespoon brown mustard
- ground cinnamon
- ground ginger

Directions:
1. Supply your smoker with wood pellets and follow the start-up procedure. Preheat the grill, with the lid closed, to 325° F.
2. Score the ham all over in a diamond pattern, cutting to a depth of about 3/4 inch. Insert a clove into each intersection or "X" of the diamond pattern.
3. In a saucepan, stir together the maple syrup, brown sugar, apple juice, brown mustard, cinnamon and ginger and simmer over medium heat until brown sugar has melted. Set aside and keep warm.
4. Place ham in large roasting pan lined with aluminum foil. Place pan on grill and cook for 1-1/2 hours. Grill: 325 °F
5. Open grill and glaze ham with reserved mixture. Continue cooking for another 30 minutes or until a thermometer inserted into the thickest part of the meat reaches an internal temperatures of 135°F. Grill: 325 °F Probe: 135 °F
6. Remove ham from grill and allow to rest covered with foil for 20 minutes before serving. Warm remaining sauce and serve with ham if desired. Enjoy!

Fast Bbq Spare Ribs

Servings: 6
Cooking Time: 180 Minutes

Ingredients:
- 1/2 Tsp Black Pepper
- 1/4 Cup Brown Sugar
- 2 Garlic Cloves, Peeled And Smashed
- 1 Tbsp Honey
- 1/4 Cup Ketchup
- 1 Tsp Kosher Salt
- 1 Tbsp Paprika
- 1 Tbsp Parsley, Chopped
- Pulled Pork Rub

- 2 Red Bell Pepper
- 2 Scallions, Chopped
- 10 Lbs Spare Ribs, Rack
- 2 Tbsp Tamari
- 1 Tbsp Tomato Paste

Directions:

1. Supply your smoker with wood pellets and follow the start-up procedure. Preheat the grill, with the lid open, to 325° F, and pull both the side knobs out to ensure the smoking cabinet maintains a temperature of 200°F.

2. Season ribs on both sides with Pulled Pork Rub, then lay on the racks in the smoking cabinet. Smoke for 2 ½ hours.

3. Meanwhile, prepare the sauce: Brush the bell pepper with oil, season with salt, then place directly on the grill grate.

4. Open the sear slide and char over direct flame for 3 minutes, turning often.

5. Remove from the grill, and set aside to cool, then skin and remove seeds.

6. In a food processor, combine peppers, garlic, ketchup, brown sugar, scallions, tamari, honey, tomato paste, parsley, paprika, salt, and pepper.

7. Process for 3 minutes, scraping down sides once or twice. Transfer to a jar and set aside.

8. Lay out 4 large pieces of aluminum foil on a sheet tray. Remove ribs from the smoking cabinet, then lay each rack on 2 overlapping pieces of foil. Spoon sauce over each rack, then tightly close foil around the ribs.

9. Lower temperature to 275°F. Transfer to the lower grill, then cook ribs another 1 to 1 ½ hours, rotating racks half way through cooking.

10. Carefully open foil, place racks directly on grates, and cook for another 10 minutes.

11. Remove ribs from the grill, then rest for 15 minutes, before slicing. Serve warm.

Smoke-roasted Beer-braised Brats

Servings: 8
Cooking Time: 65 Minutes

Ingredients:

- 8 Wisconsin-style bratwursts
- low-carb beer (enough to cover the brats)
- 2 tbsp unsalted butter
- 2 large sweet onions, peeled and sliced crosswise
- 2 garlic cloves, peeled and smashed with a chef's knife
- 8 brat buns (optional)
- coarse ground mustard or German-style mustard

Directions:

1. Supply your smoker with wood pellets and follow the start-up procedure. Preheat the grill, with the lid closed, to 325° F.

2. Place the brats on the grate at a diagonal to the bars. (Don't pierce the brats or the juices will run out.) Grill until the skin is nicely browned, about 40 to 45 minutes.

3. In a Dutch oven on the stovetop over medium-high heat, bring the beer, butter, onions, and garlic to a boil. Transfer the Dutch oven to the grill.

4. Use tongs to transfer the brats to the Dutch oven and let them steep for at least 20 minutes. The brats will stay at serving temperature—160°F (71°C)—for 1 hour or more.

5. Remove the Dutch oven from the grill and serve the brats on buns (if using) with mustard.

Wet-rubbed St. Louis Ribs

Servings: 2
Cooking Time: 240 Minutes

Ingredients:

- 1/2 Cup brown sugar
- 1 Tablespoon ground cumin
- 1 Tablespoon ancho chile powder
- 1 Tablespoon smoked paprika
- 1 Tablespoon garlic salt
- 3 Tablespoon balsamic vinegar
- 1 Rack St. Louis-style ribs
- 2 Cup apple juice

Directions:

1. In a bowl, combine all ingredients except ribs. Place wet rub on both sides of ribs; let sit for at least 10 minutes.

2. Supply your smoker with wood pellets and follow the start-up procedure. Preheat the grill, with the lid closed, to 180° F.

3. Turn temperature to 250°F; transfer the ribs into a foil pan, or wrap in tinfoil. Pour apple juice in the foil. Place foiled ribs back on grill. Cook for 2 hours. Remove from grill and let rest 10 minutes. Enjoy! Grill: 250 °F

Smoked Bologna

Servings: 4
Cooking Time: 240 Minutes

Ingredients:

- 1 Pound bologna log
- 1/4 Cup brown sugar
- 1 Tablespoon yellow mustard
- 1 Teaspoon soy sauce
- Worcestershire sauce

Directions:

1. Score the bologna log being careful not to cut too deep.

2. Mix brown sugar, mustard, soy sauce and Worcestershire sauce together.

3. Once mixed, rub it all over the bologna.

4. Supply your smoker with wood pellets and follow the start-up procedure. Preheat the grill, with the lid closed, to 225° F.

5. Smoke bologna for 3 to 4 hours. Grill: 225 ℉

6. Remove from grill and let cool.

7. Slice and serve with sandwiches. Enjoy!

Grilled Pork Tacos Al Pastor

Servings: 8
Cooking Time: 15 Minutes

Ingredients:
- 2 Tsp Annatto Powder
- Cilantro, Chopped
- Corn Tortillas
- 2 Tsp Cumin
- 1 Tsp Granulated Garlic
- 2 Tbsp Guajillo Chili Powder
- Jalapeno Pepper, Minced
- Lime, Wedges
- 1 Tsp Oregano, Dried
- 1/2 Tsp Pepper
- 1/2 Cup Pineapple, Juice
- 1/2 Pineapple, Skinned & Cored
- 2 Lbs Pork Shoulder, Boneless, Sliced Thin
- 1 1/2 Tsp Salt
- 2 Tbsp Tomato Paste
- 2 Tbsp Vegetable Oil
- 1/4 Cup White Vinegar
- Yellow Onion, Chopped

Directions:
1. Prepare marinade: In a mixing bowl, whisk together pineapple juice, vinegar, oil, tomato paste, chili powder, annatto, cumin, granulated garlic, oregano, salt, and pepper. Set aside.

2. Slice pork shoulder into thin slices (around ¼" thick), then place in a resealable plastic bag. Pour marinade over pork, seal bag, and turn to coat. Refrigerate overnight.

3. Supply your smoker with wood pellets and follow the start-up procedure. Preheat the grill, with the lid open, to 450° F. If using a gas or charcoal grill, set it up for high heat.

4. Remove the pork from the marinade and set on the grill. Grill over high heat for 3 to 5 minutes, turning frequently. Transfer to a cutting board to rest for 10 minutes, then slice thin.

5. Grill pineapple for 3 minutes, turning once. Set aside on a cutting board, and chop once cooled.

6. Assemble tacos: tortillas, pork, pineapple, jalapeño, onion, and cilantro. Serve warm with fresh lime wedges.

Spicy Ribs

Servings: 4

Cooking Time: 300 Minutes

Ingredients:
- 2 Finely Minced Chipotle In Adobo
- 1 Cup (Any Kind) Barbecue Sauce
- 1/2 Cup Brown Sugar
- 1/4 Cup Honey
- 1/4 Cup Olive Oil
- 1 Rack St. Louis-Style Rib(S)
- 3 Tablespoons Sweet Heat Rub

Directions:
1. Remove the ribs from their packaging, drain, and pat dry. Using a paper towel, grip the membrane on the back of the ribs and pull off. Discard the membrane and paper towel.

2. In a small mixing bowl, combine the brown sugar, olive oil, honey, BBQ sauce, and chiles in adobo. Using a basting brush, brush the front and back of the ribs generously with the BBQ mixture. Save the basting brush for later along with half of the sauce.

3. Generously season the ribs with Sweet Heat rub, making sure to focus especially on the front of the ribs.

4. Supply your smoker with wood pellets and follow the start-up procedure. Preheat the grill, with the lid open, to 225° F. If you're using a gas or charcoal grill, set it up for low heat. Place the ribs on the grill and smoke at 225°F for 4-6 hours making sure to baste in the sauce every 2 hours.

5. Remove from the grill and serve with additional barbecue sauce.

Bbq Pork Short Ribs

Servings: 4
Cooking Time: 360 Minutes

Ingredients:
- 2 Pork Short Rib Racks With At Least 1 1/2-2" of Meat On Bone
- Pork & Poultry Rub

Directions:
1. Clean and trim short ribs. Season generously on all sides with Traeger Pork and Poultry rub.

2. Supply your smoker with wood pellets and follow the start-up procedure. Preheat the grill, with the lid closed, to 250° F.

3. Place ribs directly on the grill grate and cook for 4-6 hours or until the internal temperature reaches 202-204℉ when an instant read thermometer is inserted in the thickest part of meat. Spritz with apple juice every hour if desired. Grill: 250 ℉ Probe: 202 ℉

4. Remove from grill and allow to rest 10 minutes before slicing. Cut into individual ribs and serve with your favorite sides. Enjoy!

Holiday Smoked Cheese Log

Servings: 8
Cooking Time: 60 Minutes

Ingredients:

* 16 Ounce cream cheese
* 3 Cup shredded cheddar cheese
* 1 Tablespoon Worcestershire sauce
* 1 Teaspoon hot sauce
* 8 Slices bacon
* 2 green onion
* 1 Cup coarsely chopped pecans

Directions:

1. In a mixing bowl, using an electric mixer or large spoon, combine the cream cheese (room temperature) and the cheddar cheese.
2. Add in the Worcestershire sauce and hot sauce. Mix again.
3. Add in the cooked and crumbled bacon and chopped green onions. Mix until combined.
4. Cover the bowl with plastic wrap and refrigerate for 4 hours or until the cheese mixture is firm enough to mold. Shape it into a log and layer the outside with the toasted pecans.
5. Cover with plastic wrap. Freeze the cheese log overnight to make sure it doesn't get too soft while it's smoking.
6. The next day supply your smoker with wood pellets and follow the start-up procedure. Preheat the grill, with the lid closed, to 180° F.
7. Take the cheese log out of the freezer and unwrap. Place on a cooking sheet and smoke for 1 hour. Keep an eye on it to make sure it doesn't get too soft. Grill: 180 ˚F
8. Move the cheese log to a serving tray and serve with your favorite crackers. (If the cheese is too soft, throw it in the fridge for an hour or two.)

Bbq Pork Shoulder Roast With Sugar Lips Glaze

Servings: 8
Cooking Time: 540 Minutes

Ingredients:

* 1 (8-10 lb) bone-in pork butt
* 1/4 Cup Pork & Poultry Rub, divided
* 1 1/2 Cup apple juice, divided
* 4 Tablespoon brown sugar
* 1 Tablespoon salt
* 1/2 Cup apple juice
* Sugar Lips Glaze

Directions:

1. Trim pork butt of all excess fat leaving 1/4 inch of the fat cap attached.
2. Combine 2 tablespoons Traeger Pork & Poultry Rub, 1 cup apple juice, brown sugar and salt in a small bowl stirring until most of the sugar and salt are dissolved. Inject the pork butt every square inch or so with the apple juice mixture.
3. Season the exterior of the pork butt with remaining Traeger Pork & Poultry Rub.
4. Supply your smoker with wood pellets and follow the start-up procedure. Preheat the grill, with the lid closed, to 250° F.
5. Place pork butt directly on the grill grate and cook for about 6 hours or until the internal temperature reaches 160°F. Grill: 250 ˚F Probe: 160 ˚F
6. Wrap the pork butt in two layers of foil and pour in 1/2 cup of apple juice. Secure tin foil tightly to contain the apple juice.
7. Increase Traeger temperature to 275°F and return wrapped pork butt to grill in a pan large enough to hold the pork butt in case it leaks. Cook an additional 3 hours or until internal temperature reaches 195°F. Grill: 275 ˚F Probe: 195 ˚F
8. Remove from the grill and allow to rest 10 to 15 minutes. Slice the pork butt around the bone and top with Traeger Sugar Lips BBQ Sauce. Serve with your favorite sides. Enjoy!

Honey Glazed Pork Chops

Servings: 6
Cooking Time: 16 Minutes

Ingredients:

* 4-6 Pork Chop
* 1/2 Cup of Honey
* 4 Tablespoons Soy Sauce
* 2 Tablespoons Olive Oil
* 2 Garlic Cloves, pressed
* Salt & Pepper

Directions:

1. Supply your smoker with wood pellets and follow the start-up procedure. Preheat the grill, with the lid closed, to 350° F.
2. Mix together the honey, soy sauce, and garlic in a small dish.
3. Brush the olive oil over the pork chops and sprinkle with salt and pepper.
4. Place the pork chops on the grill and brush the honey mixture over the top side.
5. When you flip the pork chops over, brush the second side with the honey mixture.
6. Grill for about 8 minutes on each side or until a thermometer inserted reads 170 degrees. Brush a final layer of the honey glaze over the pork chops before serving. Enjoy!

Pork Loin Porchetta

Servings: 8
Cooking Time: 120 Minutes

Ingredients:

- 1 center-cut pork loin roast, about 2½ to 3lb (1.2 to 1.4kg)
- Mustard Caviar
- for the paste
- 4 garlic cloves, peeled and coarsely chopped
- zest and juice of 1 lemon
- ½ cup coarsely chopped fresh curly or flat-leaf parsley
- 2 tbsp coarsely chopped fresh rosemary
- 2 tbsp coarsely chopped fresh sage
- 2 tsp fennel seeds
- 1 tsp coarse salt, plus more
- 1 tsp freshly ground black pepper, plus more
- 1 tsp crushed red pepper flakes
- ¼ cup extra virgin olive oil, plus more

Directions:

1. Supply your smoker with wood pellets and follow the start-up procedure. Preheat the grill, with the lid closed, to 450° F.
2. Use a sharp, slender knife to slice the pork almost in half lengthwise, leaving a 1-inch (5cm) hinge. (This is called "butterflying.") Open like a book and make a similar lengthwise cut on either side of the first cut—stopping when you reach the last 1 inch (2.5cm) of meat.
3. In a food processor, make the seasoning paste by combining the garlic, lemon zest and juice, parsley, rosemary, sage, fennel seeds, salt and pepper, and red pepper flakes. With the machine running, add the olive oil in a thin stream. Thinly spread the paste on the interior surfaces of the pork loin, leaving a 1-inch (2.5cm) border. Starting on a long side, reform the pork loin and tie at 2-inch (5cm) intervals with butcher's twine. Brush the outside surface with olive oil and then season with salt and pepper.
4. Place the pork on the grate and roast for 30 minutes. Lower the temperature to 325°F (163°C) and continue to roast the pork until the internal temperature reaches 145°F (63°C), about 60 to 90 minutes more.
5. Transfer the porchetta to a cutting board and let rest for 10 minutes. Remove the butcher's twine and carve the meat into finger-thick slices. Serve with the mustard caviar or a good-quality aged balsamic vinegar.

Baked Honey Glazed Ham

Servings: 8
Cooking Time: 120 Minutes

Ingredients:

- 1 (6-8 lb) Snake River Farms Kurobuta Half Bone-In Ham
- 20 whole cloves
- 1 Stick butter, softened
- 1/4 Cup dark corn syrup
- 1 Cup honey, room temperature

Directions:

1. Supply your smoker with wood pellets and follow the start-up procedure. Preheat the grill, with the lid closed, to 325° F.
2. Score ham. Smear the entire ham with softened butter and stud with the whole cloves and place ham in foil-lined pan.
3. Combine the dark corn syrup and honey. Warm to combine if needed. Pour 3/4 of the glaze over ham, and bake for 1-1/2 to 2 hours on the grill or until the ham reaches 140°F. Grill: 325 °F Probe: 140 °F
4. Baste ham every 20 minutes with remaining honey glaze. Grill: 325 °F Probe: 140 °F
5. Remove from grill and let rest a few minutes.
6. Slice and serve. Enjoy!

Korean Pulled Pork Lettuce Wraps

Servings: 8
Cooking Time: 480 Minutes

Ingredients:

- 1 bone-in pork shoulder, about 6lb (2.7kg)
- 1 cup low-carb beer or sugar-free light-colored soda
- for the sauce
- 1½ cups low-carb barbecue sauce
- ¼ cup low-carb beer or sugar-free light- or dark-colored soda
- 3 tbsp gochujang
- 3 tbsp light soy sauce
- 1 tbsp rice wine vinegar
- 1 tbsp toasted Asian sesame oil
- 1 tsp gochugaru
- for the rub
- 3 tbsp coarse salt
- 3 tbsp gochugaru
- 3 tbsp granulated light brown sugar or low-carb substitute
- 2 tsp granulated garlic
- 2 tsp onion powder
- 1 tsp ground ginger

Directions:

1. Supply your smoker with wood pellets and follow the start-up procedure. Preheat the grill, with the lid closed, to 250° F.
2. In a small bowl, make the barbecue sauce by whisking together the ingredients. Cover and refrigerate until ready to serve.
3. In a small bowl, make the rub by combining the ingredients. Rinse the meat with cold running water and pat dry with paper towels. Sprinkle the rub evenly over the surface, using your fingertips to pat it on.
4. Place the pork shoulder on the grate and smoke until the internal temperature reaches 165°F (74°C), about 4 to 5 hours.

Transfer the meat to an aluminum foil roasting pan. Add the beer and then cover the pan tightly with heavy-duty aluminum foil. Continue to cook until the internal temperature reaches 200°F (93°C), about 3 hours more. (Keep the probe from touching bone or it will give you a false reading.) When the pork is tender enough to pull, the meat will release easily from the bone.

5.   Transfer the pork shoulder to a cutting board. Drain the accumulated juices into a separate container and reserve. While the pork is still hot, pull out the bone and separate the meat into chunks. Using meat claws, forks, or your fingers, pull the meat into shreds, discarding any lumps of fat or undesirable bits. Return the meat to the pan. Stir in some of the reserved cooking juices if desired. You want the pork to be moist but not soupy.

6.   Wrap the hot pork in lettuce leaves. Top with thinly sliced garlic, thinly sliced crosswise jalapeños, toasted sesame seeds, pickled ginger, and barbecue sauce. You can also serve the pork the American way: piled high on sesame seed buns.

3-2-1 Spare Ribs

Servings: 4
Cooking Time: 180 Minutes

Ingredients:
- 2 racks of St. Louis–cut pork spare ribs, each about 3lb (1.4kg)
- all-purpose barbecue rub
- 3 tbsp unsalted butter, cut into cubes
- 1 cup apple juice or apple cider
- low-carb barbecue sauce

Directions:
1.   Supply your smoker with wood pellets and follow the start-up procedure. Preheat the grill, with the lid closed, to 225° F.
2.   Place the ribs on a rimmed sheet pan and dust with the rub. Place the ribs bone side down on the grate and smoke for 3 hours.
3.   Tear off 2 large sheets of heavy-duty aluminum foil. Place one rack of ribs bone side down on the foil and top with half the butter cubes. Place the second rack of ribs bone side down on the butter cubes and top with the remaining butter cubes.
4.   Bring up all 4 sides of the foil and pour in the apple juice. Crimp the edges of the foil so the ribs are tightly enclosed. Place the foil package on the grate and smoke for 2 hours more.
5.   Transfer the ribs to a workspace and carefully open the foil package. (Be careful of escaping steam.) Discard the foil and any accumulated juices. Brush the ribs on both sides with barbecue sauce. Place the ribs on the grate and smoke for 1 hour more to set the sauce and firm up the bark.
6.   Transfer the ribs to a cutting board. Use a sharp knife to cut the slabs in half or into individual ribs. Serve immediately.

Jalapeno Cheddar Smoked Sausages

Servings: 6
Cooking Time: 180 Minutes

Ingredients:
- hog casings
- 2 Pound ground pork
- 5 Medium jalapeños, seeded and diced small
- 1/2 Cup shredded sharp cheddar cheese
- 1/2 Tablespoon kosher salt
- 1 Teaspoon black pepper
- 1 Teaspoon granulated garlic
- 1 Teaspoon onion powder

Directions:
1.   Soak your hog casings in water according to package directions. While casings are soaking, make your sausage.
2.   Place all ingredients in the bowl of a food processor and pulse to combine. Be careful not to overwork, the meat should be a little tacky and all spices fully incorporated.
3.   Place sausage mixture in your sausage stuffer and proceed to stuff the casing according to manufacturer's directions. Be sure to stuff the length of the casing, then create the links afterwards. Use caution not to overstuff or they will burst when you go to create the links.
4.   Hang the sausages and allow to air dry at room temperature for an hour or so, then transfer to the refrigerator to dry overnight.
5.   Supply your smoker with wood pellets and follow the start-up procedure. Preheat the grill, with the lid closed, to 180° F.
6.   Place the sausages directly on the grill grate and smoke for 2 to 3 hours, or until they reach an internal temperature of 155°F. Enjoy! Grill: 180 °F Probe: 155 °F

Jalapeño-bacon Pork Tenderloin

Servings: 4-6
Cooking Time: 150 Minutes

Ingredients:
- ¼ cup yellow mustard
- 2 (1-pound) pork tenderloins
- ¼ cup Pork Rub
- 8 ounces cream cheese, softened
- 1 cup grated Cheddar cheese
- 1 tablespoon unsalted butter, melted
- 1 tablespoon minced garlic
- 2 jalapeño peppers, seeded and diced
- 1½ pounds bacon

Directions:
1.   Slather the mustard all over the pork tenderloins, then sprinkle generously with the dry rub to coat the meat.

2. Supply your smoker with wood pellets and follow the start-up procedure. Preheat, with the lid closed, to 225°F.

3. Place the tenderloins directly on the grill, close the lid, and smoke for 2 hours.

4. Remove the pork from the grill and increase the temperature to 375°F.

5. In a small bowl, combine the cream cheese, Cheddar cheese, melted butter, garlic, and jalapeños.

6. Starting from the top, slice deeply along the center of each tenderloin end to end, creating a cavity.

7. Spread half of the cream cheese mixture in the cavity of one tenderloin. Repeat with the remaining mixture and the other piece of meat.

8. Securely wrap one tenderloin with half of the bacon. Repeat with the remaining bacon and the other piece of meat.

9. Transfer the bacon-wrapped tenderloins to the grill, close the lid, and smoke for about 30 minutes, or until a meat thermometer inserted in the thickest part of the meat reads 160°F and the bacon is browned and cooked through.

10. Let the tenderloins rest for 5 to 10 minutes before slicing and serving.

Bacon Stuffed Smoked Pork Loin

Servings: 4-6
Cooking Time: 60 Minutes

Ingredients:
- 3 Pound Pork Loin, Butterflied
- As Needed Pork Rub
- 1/4 Cup Walnuts, Chopped
- 1/3 Cup Craisins
- 1 Tablespoon Oregano, fresh
- 1 Tablespoon fresh thyme
- 6 Pieces Asparagus, fresh
- 6 Slices Bacon, sliced
- 1/3 Cup Parmesan cheese, grated
- As Needed Bacon Grease

Directions:
1. Lay down 2 large pieces of butcher's twine on your work surface. Place butterflied pork loin perpendicular to twine.

2. Season the inside of the pork loin with the pork rub.

3. On one end of the loin, layer in a line all of the ingredients, beginning with the chopped walnuts, craisins, oregano, thyme, and asparagus.

4. Add bacon and top with the parmesan cheese.

5. Starting at the end with all of the fillings, carefully roll up the pork loin and secure on both ends with butcher's twine.

6. Roll the pork loin in the reserved bacon grease and season the outside with more Pork Rub.

7. When ready to cook, set temperature to 180°F and preheat, lid closed for 15 minutes. Place stuffed pork loin directly on the grill grate and smoke for 1 hour.

8. Remove the pork loin; increase the temperature to 350°F and allow to preheat.

9. Place the loin back on the smoker and grill for approximately 30 to 45 minutes or until the temperature reads 135°F on an instant-read thermometer.

10. Move the pork loin to a plate and tent it with aluminum foil. Let it rest for 15 minutes before slicing and serving. Enjoy!

Grilled Dr. Pepper Ribs

Servings: 4
Cooking Time: 300 Minutes

Ingredients:
- Aluminum Foil
- 2 Racks Baby Back Ribs
- 1 Cup Bbq Sauce
- 1 Stick Butter, Melted
- 1/2 Cup Dark Brown Sugar
- 12 Oz Dr. Pepper Soda
- 1/4 Cup Sweet Rib Rub
- 1/4 Cup Yellow Mustard

Directions:
1. Supply your smoker with wood pellets and follow the start-up procedure. Preheat the grill, with the lid open, to 225° F. If using a gas or charcoal grill, set it up for low, indirect heat.

2. After the grill comes to temp, place the ribs directly on the grill grates, close the lid, and smoke for 2 hours.

3. In a glass measuring cup, whisk together butter, brown sugar, and 8 ounces of Dr. Pepper.

4. Pour half of the mixture on a foil-lined sheet tray.

5. Place ribs, meat-side down, on top of the mixture, then pour remaining mixture on the bone-side. Tent the sheet tray with foil, then return to the grill for another 2 hours.

6. Remove ribs from liquid and set meat-side up directly on the grill grate.

7. Whisk together BBQ sauce and 4 ounces of Dr. Pepper, then brush half of the sauce all over the ribs.

8. Increase temperature to 275°F and cook an additional 30 to 60 minutes until ribs are tender, and meat pulls away from the bones.

9. Place ribs on a sheet tray, allow to rest for 10 minutes, then slice and serve with remaining BBQ sauce.

Lip-smackin' Pork Loin

Servings: 8
Cooking Time: 180 Minutes

Ingredients:

- ¼ cup finely ground coffee
- ¼ cup paprika
- ¼ cup garlic powder
- 2 tablespoons chili powder
- 1 tablespoon packed light brown sugar
- 1 tablespoon ground allspice
- 1 tablespoon ground coriander
- 1 tablespoon freshly ground black pepper
- 2 teaspoons ground mustard
- 1½ teaspoons celery seeds
- 1 (1½- to 2-pound) pork loin roast

Directions:

1. Supply your smoker with wood pellets and follow the start-up procedure. Preheat, with the lid closed, to 250°F.

2. In a small bowl, combine the ground coffee, paprika, garlic powder, chili powder, brown sugar, allspice, coriander, pepper, mustard, and celery seeds to create a rub, and generously apply it to the pork loin roast.

3. Place the pork loin on the grill, fat-side up, close the lid, and roast for 3 hours, or until a meat thermometer inserted in the thickest part of the meat reads 160°F.

4. Let the pork rest for 5 minutes before slicing and serving.

Maple-smoked Pork Chops

Servings: 4
Cooking Time: 55 Minutes

Ingredients:

- 1 (12-pound) full packer brisket
- 2 tablespoons yellow mustard
- 1 batch Espresso Brisket Rub
- Worcestershire Mop and Spritz, for spritzing

Directions:

1. Supply your smoker with wood pellets and follow the start-up procedure. Preheat the grill, with the lid closed, to 180°F.

2. Season the pork chops on both sides with salt and pepper.

3. Place the chops directly on the grill grate and smoke for 30 minutes.

4. Increase the grill's temperature to 350°F. Continue to cook the chops until their internal temperature reaches 145°F.

5. Remove the pork chops from the grill and let them rest for 5 minutes before serving.

Bbq Pulled Pork With Sweet & Heat Bbq Sauce

Servings: 4
Cooking Time: 540 Minutes

Ingredients:

- 10 Pound Bone-In Pork Butt
- 2 Tablespoon Pork & Poultry Rub
- 1 1/2 Cup apple juice
- 4 Tablespoon brown sugar
- 1 Tablespoon salt
- 1 To Taste salt
- 1 To Taste Pork & Poultry Rub
- 1 As Needed Sweet & Heat BBQ Sauce

Directions:

1. Trim pork butt of all excess fat leaving 1/4" of the fat cap attached. Combine 2 Tbsp Pork and Poultry rub, apple juice, brown sugar, and salt in a small bowl stirring until most of the sugar and salt are dissolved. Inject the pork butt every square inch or so with the apple juice mixture. Season the exterior of the pork butt with remaining rub.

2. Supply your smoker with wood pellets and follow the start-up procedure. Preheat the grill, with the lid closed, to 225° F.

3. Place pork butt directly on the grill grate and cook for about 6 hours or until the internal temperature reaches 160°F. Grill: 225 °F Probe: 160 °F

4. Wrap the pork butt in two layers of foil and pour in 1/2 cup of apple juice. Secure tin foil tightly to contain the apple juice. Increase temperature to 275°F and return to grill in a pan large enough to hold the pork butt in case of leaks. Cook an additional 3 hours or until internal temperature reaches 205°F. Grill: 275 °F Probe: 205 °F

5. Remove from the grill and discard the bone. Shred the pork removing any excess fat or tendons. Season with additional Pork and Poultry Rub and salt if needed.

6. Add Sweet & Heat BBQ sauce and serve. Enjoy!

Crown Roast Of Pork

Servings: 4
Cooking Time: 60 Minutes

Ingredients:

- 1 Whole Crown Roast of Pork, 12-14 ribs
- 1/4 Cup Pork & Poultry Rub
- 1 Cup apple juice
- 1 Cup Apricot BBQ Sauce

Directions:

1. Supply your smoker with wood pellets and follow the start-up procedure. Preheat the grill, with the lid closed, to 375° F.

2. Season the pork roast liberally with Traeger Pork and Poultry Rub. Let sit at room temperature for 30 minutes. Wrap each tip of the crown roast in a small piece of aluminum foil. This will protect the bones during the cook and prevent them from turning black.

3. Place the roast directly on the grill grate and cook for about 90 minutes spraying with apple juice every 30 minutes or so.

4. When the roast reaches an internal temperature of 125 degrees F, remove the aluminum foil from the bones and return to the grill.

5. Spray again with apple juice and continue to cook until the internal temperature reaches 135 degrees F in the thickest part of the roast. In the last ten minutes, baste the roast with the Apricot BBQ Sauce to let the glaze set.

6. Remove from the grill, tent with foil, and let it rest 15-20 minutes before slicing. Enjoy!

Chinese Alcoholic Bbq Pork Tenderloin

Servings: 4
Cooking Time: 30 Minutes

Ingredients:
- 14 Cup Bbq Sauce
- 2 Garlic Cloves, Minced
- 14 Cup Hoisin Sauce
- 2 Lbs Pork Tenderloin, Trimmed With Silver Skins Removed
- 1 Tbsp Sugar, Granulated
- 1 Tsp Sweet Rib Rub Seasoning
- 14 Cup Tamari
- 14 Cup White Wine

Directions:
1. In a glass measuring cup, whisk together the hoisin sauce, tamari, wine, garlic, sugar, and Sweet Rib Rub.
2. Place pork tenderloin in a resealable bag, then pour the marinade over the pork and allow to marinate in the refrigerator for 4 to 6 hours.
3. Supply your smoker with wood pellets and follow the start-up procedure. Preheat the grill, with the lid open, to 400° F. If using a gas or charcoal grill, preheat to medium-high heat.
4. Remove the pork from the marinade, then pour the marinade into a grill-safe pan.
5. Place the marinade on the grill and bring to a boil for 3 minutes. Add the BBQ sauce and simmer for 2 minutes. Remove from the grill, and set aside.
6. Place the pork on the grill and cook for 18 to 20 minutes, until an internal temperature of 145° F. Flip and baste the pork with the sauce every 3 to 5 minutes.
7. Remove the pork from the grill and allow it to rest on a cutting board for 10 minutes, prior to serving warm with additional sauce.

Bbq Pork Belly

Servings: 6
Cooking Time: 180 Minutes

Ingredients:
- 1 (3 lb) pork belly, skin removed
- 4 Tablespoon salt
- 1/2 Teaspoon black pepper
- Pork & Poultry Rub

Directions:
1. Supply your smoker with wood pellets and follow the start-up procedure. Preheat the grill, with the lid closed, to 275° F.
2. Meanwhile, season pork belly on both sides with salt, pepper and Traeger Pork & Poultry Rub. Place pork belly directly on the grill grate and cook for 3 to 3-1/2 hours or until the internal temperature reaches 200°F. Grill: 275 °F Probe: 200 °F
3. Remove from grill and let rest 10 to 15 minutes before slicing.
4. Serve in tacos, mac and cheese, nachos or your favorite dish. Enjoy!

Cuban Onion Pork Sandwich

Servings: 4
Cooking Time: 270 Minutes

Ingredients:
- 1 Tbsp Butter
- 3 Cups Chicken Stock
- 4 Ciabatta Bread Or Torta Rolls, Halved
- 1/4 Cup Dijon Mustard
- 4 Dill Pickle, Slice
- 1 Lb Ham Or Prosciutto
- 1/4 Cup Mayonnaise
- Pulled Pork Rub
- 3 1/2 Lbs Pork Shoulder
- 8 Oz Swiss Cheese, Sliced
- 1 Tbsp Vegetable Oil
- 1 White Onion, Sliced

Directions:
1. Supply your smoker with wood pellets and follow the start-up procedure. Preheat the grill, with the lid open, to 250° F. If using a gas or charcoal grill, set it up for low, indirect heat.
2. Generously season pork shoulder with Pulled Pork Rub, then transfer to the grill grate. Smoke for 1 hour, then flip pork and smoke for an additional hour.
3. Place onion and chicken stock in a deep cast iron skillet, or metal grill pan. Transfer the pork to the skillet, then cover with a shallow cast iron skillet, or aluminum foil. Braise for 2 hours, then increase grill temperature to 300° F, and braise for 1 more hour.
4. Remove the cover then pull pork with tongs while still on the grill. The stock will have reduced, so be sure and toss the pork in the reduced, seasoned stock and onions. Remove from the grill and set aside.
5. Preheat the griddle to medium-low flame. If using a different grill, preheat a clean cast iron skillet on medium low heat.

6. Heat butter and oil on the griddle, then toast rolls, pressing down by hand or with a metal spatula. Combine mustard and mayonnaise, then spread onto both sides of rolls. Set aside.

7. Divide pork into 4 portions, and place on the griddle, along with the sliced ham. Cook for 2 to 3 minutes, rotating ham and pork. Layer pork, ham, cheese, and pickles. Cover for 1 minute to allow cheese to melt. Return rolls to the griddle, cut each portion of filling in half, then stack 2 per prepared rolls. Press each sandwich down with the bottom of a metal spatula. Carefully flip, and press down again.

8. Remove sandwiches from the griddle and serve warm.

Pulled Pork Corn Tortillas

Servings: 4
Cooking Time: 15 Minutes

Ingredients:
- Cilantro
- Cilantro, Chopped
- 8 Corn Tortillas
- Jalepeno, Sliced
- 1 Lime, Wedges
- 2 Cups Pulled Pork
- Radishes, Sliced
- White Onion, Diced

Directions:
1. Supply your smoker with wood pellets and follow the start-up procedure. Preheat the grill, with the lid open, to 350° F. Grill the corn tortillas until they are softened and have charred spots, about 30 seconds.

2. To assemble the carnitas, add the pulled pork to the tortillas, and top with radishes, diced onion, cilantro, jalapeno and a squeeze of lime juice, if desired. Serve and enjoy!

Leftover Pulled Pork With Eggs

Servings: 4
Cooking Time: 20 Minutes

Ingredients:
- 1 Teaspoon Coarse Black Pepper
- 4 Eggs
- 1 Green Bell Pepper, Diced
- 1 Teaspoon Kosher Salt
- 3 Tablespoons Olive Oil
- 1 Small Onion, Diced
- 1 Tablespoon Hickory Bacon Seasoning
- 2 Cups Of Leftover Pulled Pork
- 1 Red Bell Peppers, Diced
- 1 ½ Pounds Red Potatoes, Diced

Directions:

1. Supply your smoker with wood pellets and follow the start-up procedure. Preheat the grill, with the lid open, to 350° F.

2. In a large bowl, toss the potatoes with 2 tablespoons of olive oil and Hickory Bacon seasoning. You want to get the potatoes coated well and evenly with the oil and seasoning.

3. Add the potatoes to the skillet and cook on the grill for 12-15 minutes or until they're cooked all the way through and browned. Remove from the pan and set aside.

4. Add 1 more tablespoon of olive to the pan and cook the peppers and onion for 2-3 minutes or until soft. Remove from the pan and set aside.

5. Add the pork to the pan and cook until warmed through. Because the pork is already cooked this should only be 1-2 minutes so the meat stays moist.

6. Add the potatoes, peppers and onions back to the pan, then give everything in the skillet a quick mix, so the hash is evenly blended.

7. Crack the 4 eggs on top of the hash. Try to space them evenly around. Sprinkle the teaspoons of salt and pepper on top of the eggs, then place the lid on top of the pan and allow the eggs to cook for 5-6 minutes, or until the whites are firm and the yolks are still runny.

8. Remove from the grill and serve immediately.

Delicious Pulled Pork Poutine

Servings: 4
Cooking Time: 240 Minutes

Ingredients:
- 2 Tbsp Apple Cider Vinegar
- 1/2 Cup Bbq Sauce
- 1 1/2 Cups Beef Stock
- 2 Tbsp Butter
- For Assembly, Cheese Curds
- 2 Cups Chicken Stock
- 2 Tbsp Flour
- For Assembly, French Fries
- 3 Garlic Cloves, Minced
- 1 Tbsp Olive Oil
- 2 1/2 Lbs Pork Shoulder Roast, Bone-In
- To Taste, Pulled Pork Rub
- For Assembly, Sliced Scallions
- 1/2 Yellow Onion, Minced
- 1/2 Yellow Onion, Sliced

Directions:
1. Supply your smoker with wood pellets and follow the start-up procedure. Preheat the grill, with the lid open, to 225° F. If using a gas or charcoal grill, set it up for low, indirect heat.

2. Season the pork shoulder with a pork rub, then transfer to the grill grate, fat side up. Smoke the pork shoulder for 2 ½ hours.

3.   Add chicken stock, vinegar, and sliced onion to a Dutch oven. Transfer the smoked pork shoulder to the Dutch oven, then cover and increase the grill temperature to 325° F. Braise the pork shoulder for 1 ½ hours, until tender.

4.   When tender, remove the pork from the grill and rest for 20 minutes, then shred.

5.   While the pork is resting, prepare the gravy: set a cast iron skillet on the grill. Heat the butter and olive oil in the skillet, then sauté the onion and garlic for 2 minutes, stirring often. Stir in the flour and cook for 1 minute. Slowly add the beef stock, and stir until thickened. Add bbq sauce and simmer for 3 minutes. Remove from the grill and set aside for assembly.

6.   Assemble the poutine: spread out a layer of French fries, then layer gravy, pulled pork, cheese curds, additional gravy, and scallions. Serve warm.

Bacon Weave Smoked Country Sausage

Servings: 4
Cooking Time: 120 Minutes

Ingredients:
- Pound Sausage, Uncooked
- Pork & Poultry Rub
- 8 Slices bacon

Directions:
1.   Using your hands, form sausage into a loaf-shape. Season lightly with Traeger Pork and Poultry Shake.

2.   Supply your smoker with wood pellets and follow the start-up procedure. Preheat the grill, with the lid closed, to 180° F.

3.   Put the sausage loaf directly on the grill grate and smoke for 1-1/2 hours.

4.   While sausage is smoking, assemble the bacon weave on a piece of wax paper. First, lay out 4 pieces of bacon so they are touching each other on the wax paper. Next, lay the 5th piece of bacon so it crosses the others. Tuck every other slice under the 5th piece of bacon. Find the two pieces of bacon that were under the 5th piece of bacon and fold them back on top of themselves.

5.   Lay down the 6th piece of bacon and unfold the two that were laid back. Continue folding the bacon back that was most recently under the last piece of bacon, two pieces at a time, laying the next piece of bacon on top until your weave is complete. Set aside. After your sausage has smoked for 1-1/2 hours, take it off the grill and increase the heat of your Traeger, lid closed to 350°F and preheat. Grill: 350 ˚F

6.   While the grill is heating, wrap your sausage loaf in the bacon weave. Lay the middle of the weave directly on top of the sausage loaf and press the bacon all around the sausage.

7.   Flip the sausage and bacon over to finish the weave on the bottom of the sausage. Alternate the bacon ends across the bottom and tuck the ends around each other.

8.   Put your sausage back on the grill and cook for 25-30 minutes until the internal temperature of the sausage reaches 160°F. Enjoy! Probe: 160 ˚F

Home-cured Hickory-smoked Bacon

Servings: 4
Cooking Time: 180 Minutes

Ingredients:
- 1 pork belly, about 5lb (2.3kg) and 1½ inches (3.75cm) thick, rind removed
- for the cure
- ⅓ cup kosher salt
- ⅓ light brown sugar, turbinado sugar, or maple sugar or low-carb substitute
- 3 tbsp freshly ground black pepper
- 3 bay leaves, crumbled
- 2 tsp pink curing salt #1
- 2 tsp granulated garlic

Directions:
1.   Rinse the pork belly under cold running water and pat dry with paper towels. Place in a resealable plastic bag.

2.   In a small bowl, make the cure by combining the ingredients, ensuring to especially distribute the pink curing salt. Sprinkle the rub as evenly as possible on the pork belly and use your hands to thoroughly distribute it. (You might want to wear disposable gloves.) Close the bag and refrigerate for 7 days, turning once a day and occasionally massaging the spices into the meat. Some liquid will appear in the bag and the pork belly will start firming up.

3.   Rinse the pork under cold running water and pat dry with paper towels. Place the pork belly on a wire rack placed on a rimmed sheet pan. Refrigerate uncovered for 48 hours so it has an opportunity to develop a pellicle—a surface that's very amenable to receiving smoke.

4.   Supply your smoker with wood pellets and follow the start-up procedure. Preheat the grill, with the lid closed, to 200° F.

5.   Place the sheet pan on the grate and smoke the pork until the internal temperature reaches 150°F (66°C), about 2 to 3 hours.

6.   Remove the pan from the grill and let the bacon cool. Cover and refrigerate until it's firmed up again. Slice while cold and either grill or fry the first slices of the batch. Wrap the bacon in plastic wrap. Refrigerate for up to 1 week or freeze for up to 3 months.

Dry Rub Grilled Ribs

Servings: 4

Cooking Time: 300 Minutes

Ingredients:

- 1 Rack Baby Back Rib
- 1 Tablespoon Olive Oil
- Sweet Heat Rub

Directions:

1. Supply your smoker with wood pellets and follow the start-up procedure. Preheat the grill, with the lid open, to 225° F.

2. Remove the membrane from the back of the ribs. Rub the ribs down with olive oil, then generously coat both sides with Sweet Heat Rub. For deeper flavor penetration, gently pat the spices into the meat and let sit in the refrigerator for at least an hour.

3. Smoke the ribs for about 5 hours or until the temperature is between 180°F and 195°F, and the meat is dark, glossy and easily tears apart.

4. When the ribs are finished, remove from the grill and let them rest for 5 minutes before serving.

The Dan Patrick Show Chorizo Armadillo Eggs

Servings: 8

Cooking Time: 45 Minutes

Ingredients:

- 2 Pound Ground Pork
- 1/4 Cup Chili Powder
- 4 Tablespoon Paprika
- 3 Tablespoon Oregano
- 2 Teaspoon Ground Cumin
- 2 Teaspoon Salt
- 3 Clove Garlic, Minced
- 4 Ounce Cream Cheese, Softened
- 1/2 Cup Shredded Cheddar Cheese
- 1 Tablespoon Chopped Cilantro
- 6 Large Jalapeños, Halved And Seeded
- 2 Tablespoon Pork & Poultry Rub

Directions:

1. To mix the chorizo, place ground pork, chili powder, paprika, oregano, ground cumin, salt and minced garlic in a small bowl and mix just until combined being careful not to overwork. Set aside.

2. In the bowl of a stand mixer, combine cream cheese, cheddar cheese and cilantro. Mix with the paddle attachment until well combined.

3. Spoon cheese mixture into each jalapeño half then cut in half again. Take 1/4 cup of chorizo and flatten it into a 1/4 inch thick disk. Place the cheese-stuffed jalapeño in the center and wrap the sausage around the jalapeño forming it into an egg shape. Repeat with remaining jalapeños. Season chorizo balls with Traeger Pork & Poultry Rub.

4. Supply your smoker with wood pellets and follow the start-up procedure. Preheat the grill, with the lid closed, to 300° F.

5. Place the chorizo balls directly on the grill grate and cook for 30 minutes until lightly browned and cooked through, turning once.

6. Let cool 5 to 10 minutes before serving. Enjoy!

Pig On A Stick With Buffalo Glaze

Servings: 12

Cooking Time: 75 Minutes

Ingredients:

- 4lb (1.8kg) pork shanks, each about 4 to 6oz (110 to 170g), trimmed and thawed if frozen
- 1½ cups sugar-free dark-colored soda, sugar-free root beer, or no-sugar-added apple juice
- for the brine (optional)
- 1 gallon (3.8 liters) distilled water
- ¾ cup kosher salt
- 5 tsp pink curing salt #1
- for the glaze (optional)
- ½ cup unsalted butter
- 1 cup hot sauce
- 2 tsp granulated garlic
- 1 tsp Worcestershire sauce

Directions:

1. In a stockpot on the stovetop over medium-high heat, make the brine by combining the ingredients and bringing the mixture to a boil. Stir until the salts dissolve. Remove the pot from the stovetop and let the brine cool to room temperature.

2. Add the pork shanks to the brine. Cover and refrigerate for 2 days.

3. Supply your smoker with wood pellets and follow the start-up procedure. Preheat the grill, with the lid closed, to 180° F.

4. Drain the pork shanks and discard the brine. (If you didn't brine the pork shanks, season them on all sides with your favorite barbecue rub.) Place the pork on the grate and smoke for 3 hours. Transfer the shanks to an aluminum roasting pan.

5. Raise the temperature to 275°F (135°C).

6. Add the soda to the pan and cover tightly with aluminum foil. Place the pan on the grate and braise the meat until it's tender but still attached to the bone, about 2 to 3 hours. Be careful when removing the foil because steam will escape. Remove the pan from the grill and set aside.

7. Raise the temperature to 325°F (163°C).

8. In a saucepan on the stovetop over medium heat, make the buffalo glaze by melting the butter. Stir in the remaining

ingredients. Let the sauce simmer for 5 minutes to allow the flavors to blend.

9.   Dip the pork shanks into the glaze and then transfer them to an aluminum foil roasting pan. Cover tightly with aluminum foil. Place the pan on the grate and cook the shanks until hot, about 30 minutes.

10.   Remove the pan from the grill. Serve the pork with plenty of napkins.

Smoked Stuffed Avocado Recipe

Servings: 8
Cooking Time: 30 Minutes

Ingredients:

- 6 Whole avocados
- 3 Cup leftover pulled pork
- 1 1/2 Cup Monterey Jack cheese, shredded
- 1 Cup Salsa, tomato
- 1/4 Cup cilantro, finely chopped
- 8 Whole Quail Eggs

Directions:

1.   Supply your smoker with wood pellets and follow the start-up procedure. Preheat the grill, with the lid closed, to 375° F.

2.   Remove the pits from the avocados, removing some avocado from the center if needed.

3.   In a bowl, mix together pork, cheese, salsa and cilantro. Place pork mixture on top of avocados and place in grill. Cook for 25 minutes.

4.   Take a spoon and make a divot or "nest" for the quail egg. Carefully crack the quail egg into the "nest" and cook for an additional 5 to 8 minutes or until the egg reaches desired doneness.

5.   Remove from the grill and serve. Enjoy!

Smoky Pork Tenderloin

Servings: 4
Cooking Time: 20 Minutes

Ingredients:

- 2 Pork Tenderloins (3-5 Pounds Total), Trimmed of Excess Fat or Silver Skin
- 1 Tablespoon Olive Oil
- 1-2 Tablespoons Fresh Lime Juice
- 1/4 Cup Light Brown Sugar
- 2 Teaspoons Smoked Paprika
- 1 Teaspoon Onion Powder
- 1 Teaspoon Garlic Powder
- 1 Teaspoon Coarse, Kosher Salt
- Pinch of Coarsely Ground Black Pepper

Directions:

1.   Stir together the olive oil, lime juice, brown sugar, paprika, onion powder, garlic powder, salt, and pepper in a small bowl.

2.   Rub the mixture over the pork and place the meat in a shallow dish. You can grill right away, but for more flavor, cover the dish and refrigerate up to 24 hours.

3.   Supply your smoker with wood pellets and follow the start-up procedure. Preheat the grill, with the lid closed, to 375° F.

4.   Grill the pork tenderloin for 10 minutes, flip and continue to cook until internal temperature at the thickest part of the meat registers 145 degrees F on an instant-read thermometer, about 8-10 minutes.

5.   Remove the pork from the grill and cover with aluminum foil for 10-15 minutes before slicing and serving.

Triple Threat Pork Fattywith Stuffed Jalapeños

Servings: 10
Cooking Time: 150 Minutes

Ingredients:

- 16 strips of bacon, about 1¼lb (565g) total, not thick cut
- 1½ tsp Tajin seasoning, plus more
- 8oz (225g) light cream cheese, at room temperature
- 3 large jalapeños, decored, destemmed, and deseeded
- 1lb (450g) seasoned breakfast sausage
- 1lb (450g) ground pork
- 6 to 8oz (170 to 225g) thinly sliced pepper Jack cheese

Directions:

1.   Supply your smoker with wood pellets and follow the start-up procedure. Preheat the grill, with the lid closed, to 275° F.

2.   Moisten a workspace with a damp towel. Place a 15-inch (38cm) rectangle of plastic wrap on the workspace. Place 8 strips of bacon, sides touching, parallel to the edge of the plastic. Fold back the even-numbered strips at the halfway point and place a 9th snugly against the folds (perpendicular to the first 8). Unfold.

3.   Fold back the odd-numbered strips and place a 10th snugly against the folds. Unfold. Repeat until the weave is complete. Place another sheet of plastic over the weave. Use a rolling pin to thin and tighten the weave.

4.   In a small bowl, combine the Tajin and cream cheese. Tightly stuff each jalapeño with the mixture. Reserve any extra filling.

5.   Place the sausage and pork in a large bowl. Wet your hands with cold water and knead the meats to combine. Transfer to a resealable plastic bag. Use a rolling pin to create a rectangle that's smaller than the dimensions of your bacon weave. (For reference, place the weave alongside the bag.) Slit the sides of the bag to release the meat and then position the bag over the weave and remove the remaining plastic.

6.   Cover the meat with the pepper Jack, leaving 1 inch (2.5cm) around the edges. Pipe the reserved cream cheese mixture randomly over the surface. Position the stuffed jalapeños end to end on the long side of the meat. Use the plastic under the weave to tightly roll up the fatty from the side with the jalapeños. Use

bamboo skewers to secure the weave. Lightly season the outside with more Tajin seasoning.

7. Place the fatty seam side down on the grate and smoke until the internal temperature reaches 160°F (71°C), about 2 to 2½ hours.

8. Transfer the fatty to a cutting board and let rest for 10 minutes. Use an electric knife to slice the fatty into 1-inch (2.5cm) rounds before serving.

Classic Pulled Pork

Servings: 8-12
Cooking Time: 1200 Minutes

Ingredients:
- 1 (6- to 8-pound) bone-in pork shoulder
- 2 tablespoons yellow mustard
- 1 batch Pork Rub

Directions:
1. Supply your smoker with wood pellets and follow the start-up procedure. Preheat the grill, with the lid closed, to 225°F.
2. Coat the pork shoulder all over with mustard and season it with the rub. Using your hands, work the rub into the meat.
3. Place the shoulder on the grill grate and smoke until its internal temperature reaches 195°F.
4. Pull the shoulder from the grill and wrap it completely in aluminum foil or butcher paper. Place it in a cooler, cover the cooler, and let it rest for 1 or 2 hours.
5. Remove the pork shoulder from the cooler and unwrap it. Remove the shoulder bone and pull the pork apart using just your fingers. Serve immediately as desired. Leftovers are encouraged.

Whole Hog

Servings: 2
Cooking Time: 420 Minutes

Ingredients:
- 3/8 Cup apple juice
- 1/8 Cup Pork & Poultry Rub, divided
- 2 2/3 Pound whole hog, dressed
- yellow mustard
- canola oil
- apple cider vinegar
- 1/4 Tablespoon salt
- 1/8 Tablespoon hot sauce

Directions:
1. Supply your smoker with wood pellets and follow the start-up procedure. Preheat the grill, with the lid closed, to 225° F.
2. Combine apple juice with 1/2 cup Traeger Pork & Poultry Rub and stir well to dissolve.

3. Inject the apple juice mixture into the hog, focusing on the hams and shoulders.
4. Rub the inside of the cavity with mustard and season generously with remaining rub. Grill: 250 °F
5. Place the hog on the grill skin side up and cook for 2 hours at 225°F. After 2 hours, baste the outside of the hog with the canola oil to help develop a deep mahogany color and crisp the skin. Grill: 225 °F
6. Continue cooking for 5 to 6 hours more until the hog reaches an internal temperature of 203°F when an instant-read thermometer is inserted into the ham and shoulder. Grill: 225 °F Probe: 203 °F
7. Remove the hog from the grill and let rest for 25 minutes.
8. Pull and shred the meat from the hog and transfer to a large serving dish. Combine the ingredients for the sauce in a medium bowl and mix well. Add the sauce to the pulled meat and toss to mix well.
9. Enjoy alone, as sandwiches or in your favorite pulled pork recipes.

Lynchburg Bacon

Servings: 4
Cooking Time: 20 Minutes

Ingredients:
- 1 Pound country-style bacon
- 1 Cup Tennessee whiskey, such as Jack Daniel's or apple juice
- 1 Tablespoon Pork & Poultry Rub
- 3/4 Cup all-purpose flour
- 1/3 Cup brown sugar
- 1 Teaspoon freshly ground black pepper

Directions:
1. Separate the bacon slices and place them into a large resealable bag.
2. Stir the Traeger Pork & Poultry Rub into the whiskey (or apple juice). Pour the whiskey over the bacon, massaging the bag to coat all the slices.
3. Set aside for at least 30 minutes.
4. On a piece of wax paper, sift together the flour, brown sugar and black pepper. Transfer to a second resealable bag.
5. Drain the bacon and add to the flour mixture a few slices at a time.
6. Shake the bag to coat each piece evenly, then arrange in a single layer on a baking pan.
7. Supply your smoker with wood pellets and follow the start-up procedure. Preheat the grill, with the lid closed, to 375° F.
8. Bake the bacon until it is golden brown and crisp, about 20 to 25 minutes. Enjoy! Grill: 375 °F

Grilled Bacon Dog

Servings: 4
Cooking Time: 25 Minutes

Ingredients:
- 16 hot dogs
- 16 Slices Bacon, sliced
- 2 Vidalia onion, sliced
- 16 hot dog buns
- 'Que BBQ Sauce
- Velveeta cheese

Directions:
1.   Supply your smoker with wood pellets and follow the start-up procedure. Preheat the grill, with the lid closed, to 375° F.
2.   Wrap bacon strips around the hot dogs, and grill directly on the grill grate for 10 minutes each side. Grill onions at the same time as the hot dogs, and cook for 10 -15 minutes.
3.   Open hot dog buns and spread Traeger 'Que sauce, the grilled hot dogs, cheese sauce and grilled onions. Top with vegetables. Serve, enjoy!

Bbq Pulled Pork Hash

Servings: 4
Cooking Time: 30 Minutes

Ingredients:
- 1/2 Cup carrots, peeled and cut into 1 inch pieces
- 1/2 Cup beets
- 1/2 Cup small new potatoes
- 1/2 Cup asparagus
- 1 Tablespoon olive oil
- leftover pulled pork
- 3 egg

Directions:
1.   Supply your smoker with wood pellets and follow the start-up procedure. Preheat the grill, with the lid closed, to 375° F.
2.   Chop all vegetables into even pieces, about 1/2 inch cubes. Pre heat a cast iron pan over Medium-High heat.
3.   Add a Tablespoon of olive oil then the carrots, new potatoes, and beets. Season with salt and pepper to taste and sauté stirring every few minutes until vegetables are cooked through (about 8 to 10 minutes).
4.   Add the asparagus and cook an additional 2 minutes. Add a layer of pulled pork over vegetables. Crack 3 eggs over that being careful not to break the yokes.
5.   Place into preheated Traeger and cook for about 10 minutes or until eggs are just set. Remove from grill and serve immediately with your favorite hot sauce. Enjoy! Grill: 375 ˚F

Baked Maple And Brown Sugar Bacon

Servings: 4

Cooking Time: 60 Minutes

Ingredients:
- 1 Pound cold bacon
- 1/2 Cup pure maple syrup, warmed
- 1/2 Cup brown sugar, plus more as needed

Directions:
1.   Supply your smoker with wood pellets and follow the start-up procedure. Preheat the grill, with the lid closed, to 300° F.
2.   Line a rimmed baking sheet with foil and place a wire rack on top. Lay bacon strips in a single layer on the wire rack.
3.   Using a pastry brush, brush each strip of bacon on both sides with the warmed maple syrup, then sprinkle brown sugar evenly on both sides.
4.   Put the baking sheet in the grill and cook bacon for 60-75 minutes, or until bacon browns and appears to be crisping. Grill: 300 ˚F
5.   Allow the bacon to cool slightly before eating. Enjoy!

Barbecued Tenderloin

Servings: 4-6
Cooking Time: 30 Minutes

Ingredients:
- 2 (1-pound) pork tenderloins
- 1 batch Sweet and Spicy Cinnamon Rub

Directions:
1.   Supply your smoker with wood pellets and follow the start-up procedure. Preheat the grill, with the lid closed, to 350°F.
2.   Generously season the tenderloins with the rub. Using your hands, work the rub into the meat.
3.   Place the tenderloins directly on the grill grate and smoke until their internal temperature reaches 145°F.
4.   Remove the tenderloins from the grill and let them rest for 5 to 10 minutes, before thinly slicing and serving.

Pickle Brined Grilled Pork Chops

Servings: 4
Cooking Time: 60 Minutes

Ingredients:
- 4 pork chops
- 3 Cup Dill Pickle Brine, jar
- coarse ground black pepper, divided

Directions:
1.   Put the pork chops and pickle brine in a resealable plastic bag. Refrigerate for at least 4 hours. Drain well and pat dry with paper towels.
2.   Season generously with black pepper.
3.   Supply your smoker with wood pellets and follow the start-up procedure. Preheat the grill, with the lid closed, to 300° F.

4.   Put the chops directly on the grill grate and grill, turning once, for about 1 hour, or until the internal temperature of the chop is at least 145°F. Grill: 300 °F Probe: 145 °F

5.   Let rest for 5 minutes before serving. Enjoy!

Sweet Bacon

Servings: 4
Cooking Time: 60 Minutes

Ingredients:
- 1 Pack Bacon, Thick Cut
- 1/2 Cup Brown Sugar
- 1/2 Cup Maple Syrup
- Mandarin Habanero Seasoning

Directions:

1.   Place the bacon in a deep dish. Add the maple syrup, cover and refrigerate 2 - 3 hours or overnight.

2.   Supply your smoker with wood pellets and follow the start-up procedure. Preheat the grill, with the lid open, to 225° F.

3.   When the grill has preheated, place the bacon directly on the cooking grids and sprinkle with brown sugar and Mandarin Habanero. Check every 15-20. After 30 minutes, flip and rotate bacon and baste with syrup. Allow to hot smoke for another 20 to 30 minutes or until the bacon is done to your desired liking.

4.   Allow to cool on a rack and serve.

5.   Can be refrigerated in an airtight container.

Championship Ribs With Kansas City Style

Servings: 4
Cooking Time: 210 Minutes

Ingredients:
- Apple Juice
- 2 Racks Baby Back Rib
- 2 Cups Brown Sugar
- 24 Oz Dijon Mustard
- 4 Tbsp Sweet Rib Rub
- Spray Bottle

Directions:

1.   Pour Dijon Mustard into a mixing bowl. Mix in brown sugar until mustard taste diminishes and a sweet taste takes over.

2.   Generally, you will use a half bag of brown sugar for 2 bottles and the whole bag for 4 bottles. The key is for the tangy mustard taste to turn sweet.

3.   When this mix is brushed on the ribs the mix of pork flavor and this glaze will produce a sweet and sassy result. The easiest way to mix is with an electric mixer but a whisk will do nicely. This will become very thick and sticky.

4.   Supply your smoker with wood pellets and follow the start-up procedure. Preheat the grill, with the lid open, to 275° F.

5.   Place ribs, back side down, on the cooking grid. Note: If you are doing multiple slabs, I suggest you use a rib rack. Most Rib Racks will hold 6 slabs. This will allow ribs to cook evenly. The rib rack allows for more slabs since ribs will sit in rack on their edge. Try to put meatier side up.

6.   Spray ribs thoroughly with apple juice every 30-40 minutes. Apple Juice not only helps to keep meat moist and juicy while cooking, the acidity also helps to break down the muscles, thus tenderizing as well. I have had people tell me they prefer Pineapple juice or a mixture of apple and pineapple. Personally, I can't tell the difference, but you can experiment for yourself if you want to. The result will be same.

7.   Note: How to tell when ribs are done? It is hard to measure temp of a rib with a meat thermometer due to the meat between the bones being so tight. You can get a false reading if the thermometer is touching a bone. Take your tongs and pick up slab in the middle. If the rib folds over and is limp and the meat just begins to pull away from the bone, they are done.

8.   Remove ribs from grill and place in a pan (long enough for ribs to fit)

9.   Glaze both sides of ribs with a light coat of the sassy glaze. This is a flavor enhancer, not a cover up. Just a light coat is plenty. If you really like the glaze there will generally always be some left over, and you can add to your desire while on the plate.

10.   Wrap ribs in foil and let stand for 15 minutes

11.   Serve (you can serve in slab form and let each guest cut his own or I like to cut ribs and serve as single bones.

12.   Enjoy!

Baby Back Ribs With Mustard Slather

Servings: 4
Cooking Time: 120 Minutes

Ingredients:
- 2 racks of baby back ribs, each about 2lb (1kg)
- all-purpose barbecue rub
- low-carb barbecue sauce (optional)
- for the mustard
- ½ cup yellow or brown mustard
- 2 tbsp dill pickle juice or apple cider vinegar

Directions:

1.   Supply your smoker with wood pellets and follow the start-up procedure. Preheat the grill, with the lid closed, to 325° F.

2.   Remove the thick membrane on the bone side of the ribs. Don't remove the thin membrane on top of the bones because it holds them together. Trim off any odd bits of meat or excess fat. Place the ribs on a rimmed sheet pan.

3.   In a small bowl, make the mustard slather by combining the mustard and pickle juice. Brush the ribs on both sides with the mixture and then season with the barbecue rub.

4.   Place the ribs on the grate and smoke until the ribs are tender, about 1½ to 2 hours. (A toothpick inserted between bones should go in with little resistance. The meat will also have pulled back from the bone about ½ inch [1.25cm].) Brush the ribs with barbecue sauce (if using) during the last 10 minutes of smoking. Place the ribs meat side down on the grate for 5 minutes. Turn and grill for 5 minutes more. This sets the sauce.

5.   Transfer the ribs to a cutting board. Use a sharp knife to cut the slabs in half or into individual ribs. Serve immediately with more barbecue sauce.

Apple Cider Maple Glazed Ham

Servings: 10 - 14
Cooking Time: 190 Minutes

Ingredients:

- 1 1/2 Cups Apple Cider
- 3 Tbsp Apple Cider Vinegar
- 1/2 Cup Packed Light Brown Sugar
- 2 Tbsp Unsalted Butter
- ¼ Tsp Chili Powder
- 2 Tsp Cornstarch
- 3 Tbsp Dijon Mustard
- ½ Tsp Ground Cinnamon
- ¼ Tsp Ground Cloves
- Large Cast Iron Skillet
- 1/2 Cup Pure Maple Syrup
- 2 Tsp Tennessee Apple Butter Rub
- 1 Spiral-Sliced Ham, Bone-In
- ¼ Tsp Thyme, Dried
- 3 Tbsp Yellow Mustard

Directions:

1.   Remove ham from refrigerator and let rest at room temperature for 2-3 hours.

2.   Supply your smoker with wood pellets and follow the start-up procedure. Preheat the grill, with the lid open, to 300° F. If using a gas or charcoal grill, set heat to medium-high heat.

3.   Create a bed of foil in the bottom of a large cast iron pan, making sure to have enough to seal entire ham. Set ham inside foil and add one cup of water to the bottom of pan. Pour some glaze (about ⅓ of mixture) over ham, making sure to coat in between slices. Wrap ham tightly in foil and grill for 2 hours.

4.   Remove ham from grill and increase temperature to 400° F. Carefully unfold foil to expose ham and pour an additional ⅓ of glaze over ham. Leave ham exposed and grill for 30 minutes or until edges are golden brown and caramelized.

5.   Remove ham from grill and carefully remove foil from underneath ham, so that ham is directly sitting on cast iron. Return to grill, brush with more glaze, and grill another 15 minutes. Remove ham from grill, let rest for 15 minutes, then carve and serve with remaining glaze.

Pulled Pork Shoulder And Chicken

Servings: 6 - 8
Cooking Time: 300 Minutes

Ingredients:

- 1/3 Cup Apple Cider Vinegar
- 4 Cups Chicken Broth
- 1/3 Cup Ketchup
- 2 Tbsp Pulled Pork Seasoning
- 4 Lbs. Pork Shoulder, Bone In

Directions:

1.   Supply your smoker with wood pellets and follow the start-up procedure. Preheat the grill, with the lid open, to 350° F. In a bowl, combine the chicken broth, ketchup, apple cider vinegar, and 1 tablespoon of Pulled Pork Seasoning. Whisk well to combine and set aside.

2.   Generously season the pork shoulder with the remaining 3 tablespoons of Pulled Pork Seasoning on all sides of the pork shoulder, then place on the grill and sear on all sides until golden brown, about 10 minutes.

3.   Remove the pork shoulder from the grill and place in the disposable aluminum pan. Pour the chicken broth mixture over the pork shoulder. It should come about 1/3 to ½ way up the side of the pork shoulder. Cover the top of the pan tightly with aluminum foil.

4.   Reduce the temperature of your grill to 250°F. Place the foil pan on the grill and grill for four to five hours, or until the pork is tender and falling off the bone.

5.   Remove the pork from the grill and allow to cool slightly. Drain the liquid from the pan, reserving about a cup, then shred the pork and cover with the reserved liquid. Serve and enjoy!

Grilled German Sausage With A Smoky Traeger Twist

Servings: 8
Cooking Time: 120 Minutes

Ingredients:

- 2 Tablespoon Jacobsen Salt Co. Pure Kosher Sea Salt
- 1 Teaspoon The Sausage Maker Instacure #1
- 1 Tablespoon ground nutmeg
- 2 Teaspoon ground mace
- 1 Teaspoon ground ginger
- 4 Pound ground pork, 80% lean

- 1 Pound ground veal or ground beef
- 2 Large eggs
- 1 Cup nonfat dry milk powder

Directions:

1. Combine salt, Instacure #1, nutmeg, mace and ginger in a large pitcher or small bowl. Add the milk and eggs. Beat until well combined. Pour the egg mixture over the ground meat and mix gently. Using your hands, mix in the milk powder until evenly distributed.

2. Form the meat into sausage links, roughly 4 to 6 inches in length.

3. Supply your smoker with wood pellets and follow the start-up procedure. Preheat the grill, with the lid closed, to 225° F.

4. Smoke for approximately 2 hours, or until the internal temperature reaches 175°F. Serve immediately or refrigerate until ready to serve. Enjoy! Grill: 225 °F Probe: 175 °F

Cajun Double-smoked Ham

Servings: 12-15
Cooking Time: 300 Minutes

Ingredients:

- 1 (5- or 6-pound) bone-in smoked ham
- 1 batch Cajun Rub
- 3 tablespoons honey

Directions:

1. Supply your smoker with wood pellets and follow the start-up procedure. Preheat the grill, with the lid closed, to 225°F.

2. Generously season the ham with the rub and place it either in a pan or directly on the grill grate. Smoke it for 1 hour.

3. Drizzle the honey over the ham and continue to smoke it until the ham's internal temperature reaches 145°F.

4. Remove the ham from the grill and let it rest for 5 to 10 minutes, before thinly slicing and serving.

Savory Pork Belly Banh Mi

Servings: 4
Cooking Time: 420 Minutes

Ingredients:

- 2 Carrots, Sliced
- 1 Tbsp Cilantro, Minced
- 1 Tbsp Honey
- 2 Kirby Cucumbers, Sliced Thin
- 1 Lime, Zest & Juice
- 2 Tbsp Pickling Spice
- 1 Tbsp Ponzu
- 2 Lbs Pork Belly
- 1 Cup Rice Wine Vinegar
- 2 Tbsp Salt
- 4 Sandwich Buns
- 1 Small Daikon Radish, Sliced Thin
- To Taste, Smoky Salt & Cracked Pepper Rub
- 2 Tbsp Soy Sauce
- 1/2 Cup Sriracha Hot Sauce
- 4 Cloves Star Anise
- 1/2 Cup Sugar
- 1 Cup Water

Directions:

1. 30 minutes before you plan to put the belly on the smoker season liberally with the Smoky Salt and Cracked Pepper rub.

2. Supply your smoker with wood pellets and follow the start-up procedure. Preheat the grill, with the lid open, to 240° F. If using a gas or charcoal grill, set it up for low, indirect heat.

3. Place the belly on the smoker with a tin pan underneath the meat to catch the drippings. Smoke for 7 hours or until you reach an internal temp of 195 degrees. Remove the pork and let rest for 30 minutes.

4. Make the homemade pickles: Place pickling spice and star anise in a small sauce pan and toast. Once fragrant add vinegar and bring to a boil, cook for 3 minutes. Add the water, sugar, and salt and return to a boil, cook for 5 minutes. Strain the liquid and immediately pour over the vegetables, making sure the vegetables are submerged. Set in the fridge once cool.

5. Make the Sriracha Lime Sauce: Combine the sriracha, lime, soy sauce, honey, cilantro and ponzu in a mixing bowl and whisk until combined.

6. Assemble the sandwiches, placing sliced pork belly and homemade pickles on a roll before topping it with the sriracha lime sauce.

Smoked Blt Sandwich

Servings: 4
Cooking Time: 20 Minutes

Ingredients:

- 2 Pound thick-cut bacon
- 1/2 Cup mayonnaise
- 8 Slices Texas toast
- 2 Head butter lettuce
- 3 heirloom tomato, sliced

Directions:

1. Supply your smoker with wood pellets and follow the start-up procedure. Preheat the grill, with the lid closed, to 350° F.

2. When the grill is hot, place the bacon slices directly on the grill grate and cook for 15-20 minutes or until crispy. Grill: 350 °F

3. To build the sandwich, smear mayo on two pieces of toast. Layer lettuce leaves, tomatoes, bacon and top with the other piece of toast. Enjoy!

Sweet And Spicy Pork Roast

Servings: 2
Cooking Time: 60 Minutes

Ingredients:

- 2 Pound Pork, Loins
- 2/3 habanero peppers, seeded
- 2/3 Can coconut milk
- 1/3 Teaspoon Chinese five-spice powder
- 2/3 Tablespoon paprika
- 2/3 Teaspoon curry powder
- 2/3 Tablespoon lime juice
- 2/3 Tablespoon garlic, minced
- 2/3 Teaspoon freshly grated ginger

Directions:

1. Mix all ingredients, except pork, in a bowl. Rub the mixture onto your pork and let it sit overnight.
2. Supply your smoker with wood pellets and follow the start-up procedure. Preheat the grill, with the lid closed, to 300° F.
3. Place pork on hot grill. Cook for 1 to 1-1/2 hours, or until it reaches an internal temperature of 145-150°F for medium-rare to medium. Enjoy! Grill: 300 °F Probe: 150 °F

Pork & Pepperoni Burgers

Servings: 4
Cooking Time: 60 Minutes

Ingredients:

- 1lb (450g) bulk pork sausage, preferably Italian
- 1lb (450g) ground pork, well chilled
- 8 slices of bacon, preferably thick-cut
- 8oz (225g) grated mozzarella cheese, plus more
- 1 tsp Italian seasoning
- ½ cup pizza sauce
- 1½oz (40g) pepperoni, roughly chopped

Directions:

1. Wet your hands with cold water. In a large bowl, combine the sausage and ground pork until well mixed. Line a rimmed sheet pan with aluminum foil. Divide the meat into 4 equal-sized balls and place on the sheet pan. Spray the lower third of a soda can (including the bottom) with cooking spray. Firmly press the can into one of the meatballs to create a meat bowl with uniform sides. Gently twist or rock the can to remove. Use your hands to repair any cracks in the bowl.
2. Wrap 2 slices of bacon around the circumference of the bowl and secure with toothpicks. Repeat with the remaining meatballs, respraying the can with cooking spray as necessary. Chill for 1 hour.
3. Supply your smoker with wood pellets and follow the start-up procedure. Preheat the grill, with the lid closed, to 300° F.

4. Place the patties cup side up on the grate and grill for 30 minutes. Use paper towels to blot any grease that pools at the bottom of the cups.
5. Sprinkle 2 tablespoons of cheese into each cup. Top each patty with equal amounts of Italian seasoning, pizza sauce, and pepperoni. Generously sprinkle more cheese over the top. Continue to grill until the bacon crisps, the cheese melts, and the internal temperature reaches 160°F (71°C), about 20 to 30 minutes more.
6. Remove the burgers from the grill and rest for 3 minutes. Remove the toothpicks and serve immediately.

Amazing Bacon Cheese Fries

Servings: 2
Cooking Time: 25 Minutes

Ingredients:

- 2 Bacon, Strip
- 1/2 Cup Colby Jack Cheese, Shredded
- 1/2 Package Fries, Frozen
- 1/2 Cup Monterey Jack Cheese, Shredded

Directions:

1. Supply your smoker with wood pellets and follow the start-up procedure. Preheat the grill, with the lid open, to 350° F.
2. Place the bacon on the bacon rack and place on the grill. Cook until crispy, about 15 minutes.
3. Once slightly cooled, crumble the strips into small pieces and set it aside.
4. Grill the frozen French fries based on the package instructions, cooking on a pan in the instead of the oven.
5. Once fries are golden brown, sprinkle cheese and bacon on top of the fries, and return the pan to the grill and barbecue at 450°F for 1 minute. Remove from grill and enjoy!

Orange & Maple Baked Ham

Servings: 2
Cooking Time: 120 Minutes

Ingredients:

- 2/3 Cup orange juice
- 1/3 Cup maple syrup
- 1/3 Cup Marmalade, Orange
- 1/8 Cup Dijon mustard
- 1 1/3 Tablespoon apple cider vinegar
- 1/2 Teaspoon ground cinnamon
- 1/8 Teaspoon ground cloves
- 2/3 ham

Directions:

1. Supply your smoker with wood pellets and follow the start-up procedure. Preheat the grill, with the lid closed, to 325° F.

2.   Meanwhile, make the glaze: In a small saucepan, combine the orange juice, the maple syrup, marmalade, mustard, vinegar, cinnamon, and cloves.

3.   Warm over low heat, whisking to combine the ingredients. Remove from the heat and reserve.

4.   Place ham in large roasting pan lined with aluminum foil. Place pan on grill and cook for 1.5 hours. Grill: 325 ˚F

5.   Open grill and glaze ham with reserved mixture. Continue cooking for another 30 minutes or until a thermometer is inserted into the thickest part of the meat and reaches an internal temperatures of 135 degrees F. Grill: 325 ˚F Probe: 135 ˚F

6.   Remove ham from grill and allow to rest for 20 minutes before serving.

7.   Warm remaining sauce and serve with ham if desired. Enjoy!

SEAFOOD RECIPES

Grilled Garlic Shrimp With Cajun Dip

Servings: 4
Cooking Time: 15 Minutes

Ingredients:

- 1 Grated Garlic Cloves, Peeled
- 1 Tsp Lemon Juice
- ½ Cup Mayonnaise
- 2 Tbsp Olive Oil
- 1 ½ Tbsp Hickory Bacon Rub
- Scallions
- ½ Lb Shelled And Deveined Shrimp
- 1 Cup Sour Cream

Directions:

1. Supply your smoker with wood pellets and follow the start-up procedure. Preheat the grill, with the lid closed, to 350° F. If you're using a gas or charcoal grill, set it to medium heat.
2. In a glass mixing bowl, add mayonnaise, sour cream, Cajun seasoning, garlic, lemon juice, hot sauce, and Hickory Bacon. Whisk together until well combined.
3. Cajun shrimp: In a small bowl, add shrimp, olive oil, Cajun-style seasoning and Hickory Bacon seasoning and toss to combine. Set aside.
4. Transfer dip mixture into cast iron ramekin or small Dutch oven and cover with foil. Place on preheated grill and cook for 10-15 minutes, or until dip begins to bubble along the edges. At the same time, place cast iron pan on grill and add shrimp. Cook for about 3-5 minutes on each side or until shrimp are opaque.
5. Remove dip from grill and top with Cajun shrimp and scallions. Serve warm alongside garlic toast squares and enjoy!

Grilled Albacore Tuna With Potato-tomato Casserole

Servings: 8
Cooking Time: 20 Minutes

Ingredients:

- 6 Tuna Steaks, 6oz
- 1 Whole lemon zest
- 1 chile de árbol, thinly sliced
- 1 Tablespoon thyme
- 1 Tablespoon fresh parsley

Directions:

1. To make the fish: Season the fish with the lemon zest, chile, thyme, and parsley. Cover and refrigerate at least 4 hours.
2. Remove fish from the refrigerator 30 minutes before cooking to come to room temperature.

3. Season the fish with salt and pepper on both sides. Grill 2-3 minutes per side (next to the cast iron with the casserole) rotating it once or twice. The tuna should be well seared but still rare.

Simple Glazed Salmon Fillets

Servings: 2
Cooking Time: 25 Minutes

Ingredients:

- 4 (6-8 oz) center-cut salmon fillets, skin on
- Fin & Feather Rub
- 1/2 Cup mayonnaise
- 2 Tablespoon Dijon mustard
- 1 Tablespoon fresh lemon juice
- 1 Tablespoon fresh chopped tarragon or dill
- lemon wedges

Directions:

1. Season the fillets with the Traeger Fin & Feather Rub.
2. Make the Glaze: Combine the mayonnaise and mustard in a small bowl. Stir in the lemon juice and dill or tarragon.
3. Spread the flesh-side of the fillets with the glaze.
4. Supply your smoker with wood pellets and follow the start-up procedure. Preheat the grill, with the lid closed, to 350° F.
5. Arrange the salmon fillets on the grill grate, skin-side down. Grill for 25 to 30 minutes, or until the salmon is opaque and flakes easily with a fork. Grill: 350 ˚F
6. Transfer to a platter or plates, garnish with sliced lemons and chopped dill and serve immediately. Enjoy!

Honey-soy Garlic Salmon

Servings: 4
Cooking Time: 6 Minutes

Ingredients:

- 1 Tsp Chili Paste
- Chives, Chopped
- 2 Grate Garlic, Cloves
- 2 Tbsp Minced Ginger, Fresh
- 1 Tsp Honey
- 2 Tbsp Lemon, Juice
- 4 Salmon, Fillets (Skin Removed)
- 1 Tsp Sesame Oil
- 2 Tbsp Soy Sauce, Low Sodium

Directions:

1. Supply your smoker with wood pellets and follow the start-up procedure. Preheat the grill, with the lid closed, to 400° F.
2. Take the salmon and place it in a large resealable plastic bag, and then top with all remaining ingredients, except the chives.

Seal the plastic bag and toss evenly to coat the salmon. Marinade in the refrigerator for 20 minutes.

3. After the salmon has been marinading for 20 minutes, place salmon on a flat pan or right on the grates and grill for about 3 minutes, and then flip and grill on the second side for about 3 minutes. Turn off the Grill, remove the pan from grill, plate, garnish with chives, and enjoy!

Garlic Blackened Catfish

Servings: 4
Cooking Time: 10 Minutes

Ingredients:
- ½ Cup Cajun Seasoning
- ¼ Tsp Cayenne Pepper
- 1 Tsp Granulated Garlic
- 1 Tsp Ground Thyme
- 1 Tsp Onion Powder
- 1 Tsp Ground Oregano
- 1 Tsp Pepper
- 4 (5-Oz.) Skinless Catfish Fillets
- 1 Tbsp Smoked Paprika
- 1 Stick Unsalted Butter

Directions:
1. In a small bowl, combine the Cajun seasoning, smoked paprika, onion powder, granulated garlic, ground oregano, ground thyme, pepper and cayenne pepper.
2. Sprinkle fish with salt and let rest for 20 minutes.
3. Supply your smoker with wood pellets and follow the start-up procedure. Preheat the grill, with the lid closed, to 450° F. If you're using a gas or charcoal grill, set it up for medium-high heat. Place cast iron skillet on the grill and let it preheat.
4. While grill is preheating, sprinkle catfish fillets with seasoning mixture, pressing gently to adhere. Add half the butter to preheated cast iron skillet and swirl to coat, add more butter if needed. Place fillets in hot skillet and cook 3-5 minutes or until a dark crust has been formed. Flip and cook an additional 3-5 minutes or until the fish flakes apart when pressed gently with your finger.
5. Remove fish from grill and sprinkle evenly with fresh parsley. Serve with lemon wedges and enjoy!

Pacific Northwest Salmon

Servings: 4
Cooking Time: 75 Minutes

Ingredients:
- 1 (2-pound) half salmon fillet
- 1 batch Dill Seafood Rub
- 2 tablespoons butter, cut into 3 or 4 slices

Directions:
1. Supply your smoker with wood pellets and follow the start-up procedure. Preheat the grill, with the lid closed, to 180°F.
2. Season the salmon all over with the rub. Using your hands, work the rub into the flesh.
3. Place the salmon directly on the grill grate, skin-side down, and smoke for 1 hour.
4. Place the butter slices on the salmon, equally spaced. Increase the grill's temperature to 300°F and continue to cook until the salmon's internal temperature reaches 145°F. Remove the salmon from the grill and serve immediately.

Grilled Salmon

Servings: 4
Cooking Time: 25 Minutes

Ingredients:
- 1 (2-pound) half salmon fillet
- 3 tablespoons mayonnaise
- 1 batch Dill Seafood Rub

Directions:
1. Supply your smoker with wood pellets and follow the start-up procedure. Preheat the grill, with the lid closed, to 325°F.
2. Using your hands, rub the salmon fillet all over with the mayonnaise and sprinkle it with the rub.
3. Place the salmon directly on the grill grate, skin-side down, and grill until its internal temperature reaches 145°F. Remove the salmon from the grill and serve immediately.

Alder Smoked Scallops With Citrus & Garlic Butter Sauce

Servings: 4
Cooking Time: 35 Minutes

Ingredients:
- 2 Pound large dry sea scallops
- kosher salt
- freshly ground black pepper
- 8 Tablespoon salted butter, melted
- 1 Clove garlic, minced
- 1 Small orange
- 1/4 Teaspoon Worcestershire sauce
- 1 1/2 Teaspoon fresh chopped parsley or tarragon
- flat-leaf parsley, for serving

Directions:
1. Wash the scallops under cold running water and thoroughly pat dry on paper towels. Remove any tags of abductor muscle tissue you find on the sides of the scallops.

2.   Arrange the scallops on a baking sheet fitted with a cooling rack, and season with salt and pepper.

3.   Supply your smoker with wood pellets and follow the start-up procedure. Preheat the grill, with the lid closed, to 165° F.

4.   Place the baking sheet with the scallops on the grill grate and smoke for 20 minutes.

5.   While your scallops are smoking, make your sauce. Melt the butter in a small saucepan over medium-low heat. Add a pinch of salt, garlic, Worcestershire sauce, zest and juice from half of the orange, and parsley. Simmer for 5 minutes. Keep warm.

6.   Remove the baking sheet with the scallops from the grill and set aside. Increase the temperature to 400°F and preheat, lid closed. Optional: Place an oyster bed or oyster pan in the grill to preheat. These heavy iron pans are a great way to sear the scallops. Grill: 400 °F

7.   Return the baking sheet with the scallops to the grill, brush with the butter sauce, reserving some for serving. Roast until just opaque and tender, 10 to 15 minutes. The time will depend on how thick the scallops are. Do not overcook. If you are using an oyster pan, brush each compartment lightly with olive oil to prevent sticking. Spoon butter sauce on each of the scallops, reserving some for serving.

8.   Serve the scallops hot with a little more orange zest, fresh parsley and the the warm citrus and garlic butter sauce. Enjoy!

Oysters Margarita

Servings: 4
Cooking Time: 10minutes

Ingredients:

* 24 fresh oysters in the shell
* 4oz (120ml) freshly squeezed lime juice
* 2oz (60ml) tequila
* 2oz (60ml) orange liqueur, such as triple sec
* 6 tbsp cold butter, cut into 24 cubes
* crunchy salt, such as margarita rimming salt
* lime wedges
* hot sauce (optional)

Directions:

1.   Supply your smoker with wood pellets and follow the start-up procedure. Preheat the grill, with the lid closed, to 450° F.

2.   Carefully shuck each oyster to remove the top shell. Run your shucking knife under the oyster to release it from the bottom shell, but don't spill the juices. Discard the top shells, but keep the oysters in the bottom shells. Balance each oyster on a wire rack placed on a rimmed sheet pan.

3.   Place 1 teaspoon of lime juice, ½ teaspoon of tequila, ½ teaspoon of orange liqueur, and 1 cube of butter on each oyster.

4.   Place the pan on the grate and smoke until the butter has melted and the juices are bubbling, about 8 to 10 minutes. (The oysters should be just barely cooked.)

5.   Remove the pan from the grill. Sprinkle a pinch of salt on each oyster. Serve immediately with lime wedges and hot sauce (if using).

Barbecued Scallops

Servings: 4
Cooking Time: 10 Minutes

Ingredients:

* 1 pound large scallops
* 2 tablespoons olive oil
* 1 batch Dill Seafood Rub

Directions:

1.   Supply your smoker with wood pellets and follow the start-up procedure. Preheat the grill, with the lid closed, to 375°F.

2.   Coat the scallops all over with olive oil and season all sides with the rub.

3.   Place the scallops directly on the grill grate and grill for 5 minutes per side. Remove the scallops from the grill and serve immediately.

Baked Whole Fish In Sea Salt

Servings: 4
Cooking Time: 30 Minutes

Ingredients:

* 3 Pound Whole Branzino, (1.5 each)
* 10 Sprig thyme sprigs
* 1 Medium lemon, thinly sliced
* 5 Cup sea salt
* 10 Whole egg white
* olive oil
* 1 Whole lemon juice

Directions:

1.   Supply your smoker with wood pellets and follow the start-up procedure. Preheat the grill, with the lid closed, to High heat.

2.   Clip the fins and remove the gills from the fish. Stuff cavity with thyme and lemon slices. Whip the egg whites to soft peaks and fold in the sea salt.

3.   Place directly on the grill grate and bake for 30 minutes or until a thermometer poked through the salt crust and into the flesh of the fish registers an internal temperature of 135-140 degrees F. Remove fish from the grill and let stand 10 minutes.

4.   Using a wooden spoon, strike the crust to crack it open and brush remaining salt from the surface of the fish.

5.   Remove the skin and drizzle fish with good olive oil and a squeeze of lemon. Enjoy!

Grilled Mussels With Lemon Butter

Servings: 4
Cooking Time: 15 Minutes

Ingredients:

* 2 Pound Mussels, debearded, washed
* 5 Quart water
* 1/3 Cup salt
* 2 Clove garlic, minced
* 1/3 Cup white wine
* 1 Whole lemon juice
* 3 Tablespoon parsley, chopped
* 1 loaf French country bread

Directions:

1. Supply your smoker with wood pellets and follow the start-up procedure. Preheat the grill, with the lid closed, to 375° F.
2. Scrub mussels well in running water making sure to remove all dirt and barnacles.
3. Place clean mussels in a large bowl with 5 quarts (5 L) water and 1/3 cup (91 g) of salt for about 15 minutes.
4. Drain, rinse and repeat soaking method two more times to purge and remove all sand.
5. Melt butter in a saute pan over medium high heat. Add garlic and cook for 1 minute until fragrant. Add wine and bring to a simmer. Add mussels and lemon juice to the pan and toss to coat.
6. Cover with a tight fitting lid and transfer to the grill. Let the mussels steam 8-10 minutes. Remove from the grill and discard any unopened mussels.
7. Sprinkle with chopped parsley and transfer to a serving dish. Serve with sliced bread. Enjoy!

Smoked Honey Salmon

Servings: 2
Cooking Time: 25 Minutes

Ingredients:

* 1 lb. salmon fillets
* 1/2 tsp. pepper
* 1/4 tsp. salt
* 2 tbsp. sriracha
* 2 tsp. honey
* 2 tsp. chili sauce
* 1 tsp. lime juice
* 1/2 tsp. fish sauce

Directions:

1. Supply your smoker with wood pellets and follow the start-up procedure. Preheat the grill, with the lid closed, to 350° F.
2. Sprinkle the salmon with salt and pepper.
3. In a bowl, whisk together the sriracha, honey, chili sauce, lime juice, and fish sauce.
4. Once the grill is hot, place the salmon on the grill and leave for 15 minutes.
5. After 15 minutes, brush the salmon with the sriracha chili sauce and keep cooking for 5-10minutes. The salmon should be firm to the touch and crispy on the edges.
6. Serve hot!

Moules Marinières With Garlic Butter Sauce

Servings: 4
Cooking Time: 12 Minutes

Ingredients:

* 3lb (1.4kg) fresh mussels, scrubbed under cold running water and debearded
* lemon wedges
* crusty bread (optional)
* for the sauce
* 6 tbsp unsalted butter
* 3 garlic cloves, peeled and minced
* 1 cup dry white wine or hard cider
* 1 tbsp freshly squeezed lemon juice
* 2 tsp hot sauce, plus more
* coarse salt
* freshly ground black pepper
* 2 tbsp chopped fresh curly parsley or tarragon

Directions:

1. Supply your smoker with wood pellets and follow the start-up procedure. Preheat the grill, with the lid closed, to 450° F.
2. In a small saucepan on the stovetop over medium-low heat, make the sauce by melting the butter. Add the garlic and sauté for 1 to 2 minutes. Add the wine, lemon juice, and hot sauce. Season with salt and pepper to taste. Simmer for 5 minutes. Remove the saucepan from the heat and stir in the parsley. Keep warm.
3. Discard any mussels that are cracked or don't snap shut when tapped. Place the mussels in a large aluminum foil roasting pan and cover tightly with heavy-duty aluminum foil.
4. Place the pan on the grate and steam the mussels until the shells open, about 10 to 12 minutes. Remove the pan from the grill and use long-handled tongs to remove the foil from the pan. (Be careful of escaping steam.) Use the tongs to discard any mussels that don't open.
5. Pour the reserved garlic butter sauce over the mussels. Serve from the pan or transfer the mussels to a shallow serving bowl. Serve immediately with lemon wedges, additional hot sauce, and crusty bread (if using) to sop up the juices.

Traeger Crab Legs

Servings: 4

Cooking Time: 30 Minutes

Ingredients:

- 3 Pound crab legs, thawed and halved
- 1 Cup butter, melted
- 2 Tablespoon fresh lemon juice
- 2 Clove garlic, minced
- 1 Tablespoon Fin & Feather Rub or Old Bay Seasoning, plus more to taste
- lemon wedges
- Italian Parsley, chopped

Directions:

1. If the crab legs are too long to fit in the roasting pan, break them down at the joints by twisting, or use a heavy knife or cleaver. Split the shells open lengthwise. Transfer to the roasting pan.

2. Combine the butter, lemon juice and garlic; whisk to mix. Pour mixture over the crab legs, turning the legs to coat. Sprinkle the Traeger Fin & Feather Rub or Old Bay Seasoning over the legs.

3. Supply your smoker with wood pellets and follow the start-up procedure. Preheat the grill, with the lid closed, to 350° F.

4. Cook the crab legs, basting once or twice with the butter sauce from the bottom of the pan, for 20 to 30 minutes (depending on the size of the crab legs) or until warmed through. Grill: 350 ˚F

5. Transfer the crab legs to a large platter and divide the sauce and accumulated juices between 4 dipping bowls. Enjoy!

Mezcal Shrimp With Salsa De Molcajete

Servings: 4

Cooking Time: 14 Minutes

Ingredients:

- 18 to 24 jumbo shrimp, about 1½lb (680g) total, peeled and deveined
- ⅓ cup mezcal
- juice of ½ lime
- 2 tbsp extra virgin olive oil
- 2 tsp coarse salt
- 1 tsp ground cumin
- lime wedges
- for the salsa
- 2 Roma tomatoes
- 2 tomatillos, husked and washed
- 2 garlic cloves, peeled and impaled on a toothpick
- 1 jalapeño or serrano pepper
- 1 small white onion, halved
- ½ tsp coarse salt, plus more
- juice of ½ lime
- ¼ cup loosely packed fresh cilantro leaves

Directions:

1. Supply your smoker with wood pellets and follow the start-up procedure. Preheat the grill, with the lid closed, to 450° F.

2. In a large bowl, combine the shrimp, mezcal, lime juice, olive oil, salt, and ground cumin. Toss with your hands to mix thoroughly. Set aside for 15 minutes and then toss once more.

3. Begin to make the salsa by placing the tomatoes, tomatillos, garlic, jalapeño, and onion on the grate. Grill until they begin to char, about 3 minutes for the garlic and about 6 to 8 minutes for the other vegetables, turning as needed. Transfer the vegetables to a rimmed sheet pan. Remove the skewers from the garlic. Let everything cool. Coarsely chop the vegetables and leave them in separate piles.

4. Place the garlic in the molcajete and add the salt. Mash the garlic to a purée using the temolote. Add the onion and grind it into the garlic paste. Stir in the jalapeño (deseeded for a milder salsa), tomatoes, and tomatillos. Stir in the lime juice and cilantro leaves. Taste, adding salt. (If you don't own a molcajete or temolote, prepare the salsa using a small food processor.)

5. Drain the shrimp and discard the marinade. Thread the shrimp on wood or bamboo skewers. Place the shrimp on the grate and grill until they're white and opaque, about 4 to 6 minutes, tossing with tongs.

6. Transfer the shrimp to a platter. Serve with the salsa and lime wedges.

Baked Steelhead

Servings: 4

Cooking Time: 20 Minutes

Ingredients:

- 1 steelhead fillet
- 16-oz bottle Italian dressing
- 3 Tablespoon unsalted butter
- Blackened Saskatchewan Rub
- 1/2 shallot, minced
- 2 Clove garlic, minced
- 1 lemon

Directions:

1. Supply your smoker with wood pellets and follow the start-up procedure. Preheat the grill, with the lid closed, to 350° F.

2. Put butter in a small cast iron pan and place inside Traeger while preheating to soften. Pour Italian dressing over fillet to evenly coat.

3. Shake Traeger Blackened Saskatchewan rub evenly in a thin layer to cover dressing. Mince shallot and garlic.

Tequila & Lime Shrimp With Smoked Tomato Sauce

4. Remove butter from pre-heated grill, careful as the cast iron will be hot. Stir in shallots and garlic.

5. Spread a nice thick layer of mixture on the top-middle of the fillet. Cut lemon into thin slices and place on top of butter mix.

6. Place steelhead on the grill and cook for 20 to 30 minutes, until fish is flaky, being careful not to over cook.

7. Remove fillet from the grill. Enjoy!

Tequila & Lime Shrimp With Smoked Tomato Sauce

Servings: 4
Cooking Time: 6 Minutes

Ingredients:
- 24 to 28 jumbo shrimp, about 2lb (1kg) total, peeled and deveined
- 1 lime, quartered
- Smoked Tomato Sauce
- for the marinade
- ½ cup tequila or mezcal
- juice and zest of 1 lime
- 2 garlic cloves, peeled and roughly chopped
- ½ cup freshly squeezed orange juice
- ¼ cup extra virgin olive oil
- 2 tsp agave, light brown sugar, or low-carb substitute
- 2 tsp Mexican hot sauce, plus more
- 1½ tsp coarse salt
- 1 tsp baking soda
- 1 tsp chili powder
- ½ tsp ground cumin

Directions:
1. In a medium bowl, make the marinade by whisking together the ingredients. Whisk until the salt dissolves. Taste for seasoning, adding more hot sauce if desired.

2. Place the shrimp in a resealable plastic bag and pour the marinade over them, turning the bag several times to coat thoroughly. Refrigerate for 30 minutes.

3. Supply your smoker with wood pellets and follow the start-up procedure. Preheat the grill, with the lid closed, to 450° F.

4. Drain the shrimp and discard the marinade. Pat the shrimp dry with paper towels. Thread the shrimp on 4 bamboo skewers (preferably flat ones). Make sure all the shrimp face the same direction. Finish each skewer with a lime wedge.

5. Place the skewers on the grate and grill until the shrimp are white and opaque, about 2 to 3 minutes per side, turning once. (Don't overcook.)

6. Remove the shrimp from the grill. Serve immediately with the warm tomato sauce.

Lemon Shrimp Scampi

Servings: 3
Cooking Time: 10 Minutes

Ingredients:
- 2 Tsp Blackened Sriracha Rub Seasoning
- 1/2 Cup Butter, Cubed, Divided
- 1/2 Tsp Chili Pepper Flakes
- 3 Garlic Cloves, Minced
- To Taste, Lemon Wedges, For Serving
- 1 Lemon, Juice & Zest
- Linguine, Cooked
- 3 Tbsp Parsley, Chopped
- 1 1/2 Lbs Shrimp, Peeled & Deveined
- Toasted Baguette, For Serving

Directions:
1. Supply your smoker with wood pellets and follow the start-up procedure. Preheat the grill, with the lid closed, to medium-high heat. If using a gas or charcoal grill, set it up for medium-high heat.

2. Add half of the butter to the griddle, then sauté the garlic, Blackened Sriracha, and chili flakes for 1 minute, until fragrant.

3. Add the shrimp, turning occasionally for 2 minutes, until opaque.

4. Add the remaining butter, parsley, lemon zest and juice. Toss the shrimp to coat in lemon butter, then remove from the griddle, and transfer to a serving bowl.

5. Serve immediately, with fresh lemon wedges, and toasted baguette. Serve over linguine, spaghetti or zucchini noodles, if desired.

Sweet Smoked Salmon Jerky

Servings: 6
Cooking Time: 300 Minutes

Ingredients:
- 2 Quart water
- 3/4 Cup kosher salt
- 1 Cup Morton Tender Quick Home Meat Cure, optional
- 4 Cup dark brown sugar
- 2 Cup maple syrup, divided
- 1 (2-3 lb) wild caught salmon fillet, skinned and pin bones removed

Directions:
1. In a large nonreactive bowl, combine 2 quarts water, salt, curing salt (if using), brown sugar and 1 cup of the maple syrup. Stir with a long-handled spoon to dissolve the salts and sugar.

2. With a sharp, serrated knife, slice the salmon into 1/2 inch thick slices with the short side parallel to you on the cutting board. In other words, make your cuts from the head end to the tail end.

(This is considerably easier if the fish is frozen.) Cut each strip crosswise into 4 or 5 inch lengths.

3.   Immerse the strips in the brine, weighing down with a plate or a bag of ice. Cover with plastic wrap and refrigerate for 12 hours.

4.   Supply your smoker with wood pellets and follow the start-up procedure. Preheat the grill, with the lid closed, to 180° F.

5.   Drain the salmon strips and discard the brine. Arrange the salmon strips in a single layer directly on the grill grate. Smoke for several hours (5 to 6), or until the jerky is dry but not rock-hard. You want it to yield when you bite into it. Halfway through the smoking time, mix the remaining cup of maple syrup with 1/4 cup of warm water and brush the salmon strips on all sides with the mixture. Grill: 180 °F

6.   Transfer to a resealable bag while the jerky is still warm. Let the jerky rest for an hour at room temperature. Squeeze any air from the bag, and refrigerate the jerky. Enjoy!

Grilled Whole Steelhead Fillet

Servings: 6
Cooking Time: 30 Minutes

Ingredients:

- (2-1/2 to 3 lb) steelhead or salmon fillet, skin-on
- 2 Tablespoon Montana Mex Sweet Seasoning
- 1 Teaspoon Montana Mex Jalapeño Seasoning Blend
- 1 Teaspoon Montana Mex Mild Chile Seasoning Blend
- 2 Tablespoon Montana Mex Avocado Oil
- 2 Tablespoon freshly grated ginger
- 1 lemon, thinly sliced

Directions:

1.   Coat fillet evenly with all three dry seasonings, avocado oil, grated ginger and thinly sliced lemon.

2.   Supply your smoker with wood pellets and follow the start-up procedure. Preheat the grill, with the lid closed, to 380° F.

3.   Place the fish skin-side down on the grill grate and cook for 20 minutes. Grill: 380 °F

4.   Remove fillet from grill and let rest for 5 minutes. Enjoy!

Whole Vermillion Red Snapper

Servings: 6
Cooking Time: 20 Minutes

Ingredients:

- 1 Whole Vermillion Red Snapper, scaled & gutted
- 4 Clove garlic, chopped
- 1 Whole lemon, thinly sliced
- 2 Sprig rosemary sprigs
- sea salt and freshly ground black pepper

Directions:

1.   Supply your smoker with wood pellets and follow the start-up procedure. Preheat the grill, with the lid closed, to High heat.

2.   Stuff the cavity of the fish with chopped garlic. Sprinkle the fish with sea salt, pepper, rosemary, and lemon.

3.   Grill fish directly on the grill grate. Cook for 20-25 minutes. Serve. Enjoy!

Salmon Cakes With Homemade Tartar Sauce

Servings: 4
Cooking Time: 15 Minutes

Ingredients:

- 1 1/2 Cups Breadcrumb, Dry
- 1/2 Tablespoon Capers, Diced
- 1/4 Cup Dill Pickle Relish
- 2 Eggs
- 1 1/4 Cup Mayonnaise, Divided
- 1 Tablespoon Mustard, Grainy
- 1/2 Tablespoon Olive Oil
- 1/2 Red Pepper, Diced Finely
- 1/2 Tablespoon Sweet Rib Rub
- 1 Cup Cooked Salmon, Flaked

Directions:

1.   In a large bowl, mix together the salmon, eggs, ¼ cup mayonnaise, breadcrumbs, red bell pepper, Sweet Rib Rub, and mustard. Allow the mixture to sit for 15 minutes to hydrate the breadcrumbs.

2.   Supply your smoker with wood pellets and follow the start-up procedure. Preheat the grill, with the lid closed, to 350° F.

3.   In a small bowl, mix together the remaining mayonnaise, dill pickle relish, and diced capers. Set aside.

4.   Place the baking sheet on the grill to preheat. Once the baking sheet is hot, drizzle the olive oil over the pan and drop rounded tablespoons of the salmon mixture onto the sheet pan. Press the mixture down into a flat patty with a spatula. Allow to grill for 3 to 5 minutes, then flip and grill for 1 to 2 more minutes. Remove from the grill and serve with the reserved tartar sauce.

Garlic Grilled Shrimp Skewers

Servings: 3
Cooking Time: 6 Minutes

Ingredients:

- 1 pound large shrimp
- 1/4 cup olive oil
- 1/4 cup fresh cilantro, finely chopped
- 1/4 cup fresh parsley, finely chopped
- 4 cloves garlic, minced
- 1 tablespoon lemon juice

- 1/2 teaspoon salt
- 1/4 teaspoon black pepper
- Pinch cayenne pepper, adjust to spice preference

Directions:

1. Add the olive oil, herbs, and spices to a small mixing bowl and whisk together.
2. Place the shrimp in a bowl and pour 3/4 of the marinade on top of the shrimp. Mix together gently to coat the shrimp evenly.
3. Cover the bowl and marinate the shrimp for 30 minutes to an hour.
4. Thread the shrimp on the skewers and make sure to get all the good garlic and herbs from the bowl and spread on to the shrimp.
5. Supply your smoker with wood pellets and follow the start-up procedure. Preheat the grill, with the lid closed, to medium high heat.
6. Once the grill is hot, arrange the shrimp skewers on the grill and cook for 2-3 minutes per side, or until they turn pink and opaque.
7. Remove the shrimp skewers to a plate and spoon the remaining marinade on top before serving.

Smoked Mango Shrimp

Servings: 4
Cooking Time: 5 Minutes

Ingredients:

- 2 Tablespoon Olive Oil
- 1 Pound Raw Tail-On, Thawed And Deveined Shrimp, Uncooked

Directions:

1. Supply your smoker with wood pellets and follow the start-up procedure. Preheat the grill, with the lid closed, to 425° F. Rinse shrimp off in sink with cold water. Place in bowl and season generously with Mango Magic seasoning and olive oil. Toss well in bowl.
2. Thread several shrimp onto a skewer, so that they are all just touching each other. Repeat with other skewers and remaining shrimp.
3. Grill shrimp for 2 - 3 minutes on each side, or until pink and opaque all the way through. Remove from grill and serve immediately.

Grilled Crab Legs With Herb Butter

Servings: 2
Cooking Time: 15 Minutes

Ingredients:

- 12 Tablespoon butter
- 3 Tablespoon Fresh Herbs (Parsley, Chives, Tarragon), finely chopped
- 4 Pound King Crab Legs or Dungeness Crab Leg Clusters
- 3 Whole Lemons, cut into wedges

Directions:

1. Supply your smoker with wood pellets and follow the start-up procedure. Preheat the grill, with the lid closed, to 375° F.
2. Place the butter, garlic, herbs, and a pinch of salt into a small cast iron sauce pan. Place on grill for 5 minutes to melt. Remove from grill and stir. Grill: 375 °F
3. If using king crab legs, split down the center and pour herb butter over meat reserving a quarter for serving. If using crab clusters, toss clusters with herb butter in a large mixing bowl reserving a quarter for serving.
4. Place crab legs directly on the grill grate, meat side up. Grill for 5 to 10 minutes or until hot and beginning to develop a little char on the shell. Grill: 375 °F
5. Serve crab legs with lemon wedges and reserved herb butter. Enjoy!

Teriyaki Smoked Honey Tilapia

Servings: 4
Cooking Time: 120 Minutes

Ingredients:

- 4 tilapia fillets
- 1 cup teriyaki sauce
- 2/3 cup honey
- 1 tbsp sriracha sauce
- Green onions (optional)

Directions:

1. In a large bowl, make the marinade by mixing together the teriyaki sauce, honey,and sriracha. Make sure honey is dissolved and well blended.
2. Place the tilapia fillets in the marinade. Turn the fillets so they are completely coated. Cover with a plastic wrap and marinate in the fridge for about 2 hours.
3. Supply your smoker with wood pellets and follow the start-up procedure. Preheat the grill, with the lid closed, to 275° F.
4. Remove the tilapia fillets from the marinade and transfer them to the grill. Smoke the fillets until they reach an internal temperature of 145°F, about 2 hours.
5. Sprinkle with green onions if desired.

Cider Hot-smoked Salmon

Servings: 4

Cooking Time: 60 Minutes

Ingredients:

- 1 1/2 Pound Wild Caught Salmon Fillet, skinned, pin bones removed
- 12 Ounce apple juice or cider
- 4 Pieces juniper berries
- 1 Pieces Star Anise, Broken
- 1 Pieces bay leaf, coarsely crumbled
- 1/2 Cup kosher salt
- 1/4 Cup brown sugar
- 2 Teaspoon Blackened Saskatchewan Rub
- 1 Teaspoon coarse ground black pepper, divided

Directions:

1. Rinse the salmon fillet under cold running water and check for pin bones by running a finger over the fleshy part of the fillet. If you feel a bone, remove it with kitchen tweezers or a needle-nose pliers.

2. In a sturdy resealable plastic bag, combine the cider, crushed juniper berries, star anise, and bay leaf. Add the salmon fillet and put the bag in a bowl or pan in the refrigerator. Let sit for at least 8 hours, or overnight.

3. Remove the salmon from the bag and discard the cider mixture. Dry the salmon well on paper towels. Make the cure: In a small mixing bowl, combine the kosher salt, brown sugar, and Traeger rub.

4. Pour half into a shallow plate, or baking dish. Put the salmon fillet, skin-side down, on top of the cure. Generously sprinkle the top with the remaining cure, cover with plastic wrap, and refrigerate for 1 to 1-1/2 hours. Any longer, and the fish will get too salty.

5. Remove the salmon from the cure and pat dry with paper towels. Sprinkle the black pepper on top of the fillet.

6. Supply your smoker with wood pellets and follow the start-up procedure. Preheat the grill, with the lid closed, to 200° F.

7. Lay the salmon skin-side down on the grill grate. Cook for 1 hour, or until the internal temperature in the thickest part of the fish reaches 150 or the fish flakes easily when pressed with a finger or fork. Grill: 200 ˚F Probe: 150 ˚F

8. Let cool slightly. Turn the fillet over and remove the skin; it should come off in one piece.

9. If not serving immediately, let the salmon cool completely, then wrap in plastic wrap and refrigerate for up to 2 days. Transfer to a platter and serve with some or all of the suggested accompaniments. Enjoy!

Shrimp Cabbage Tacos With Lime Cream

Servings: 4

Cooking Time: 10 Minutes

Ingredients:

- 1/4 Cabbage, Shredded
- 2 Tsp Cilantro, Chopped
- Corn Tortillas
- 1/2 Lime, Wedges
- 1/4 Cup Mayonnaise
- Blackened Sriracha Rub
- 1/4 Red Bell Pepper, Chopped
- 1 Lb Shrimp, Peeled & Deveined
- 1/4 Cup Sour Cream
- 2 Tsp Vegetable Oil
- 1/2 White Onion, Chopped

Directions:

1. Place shrimp In a medium bowl. Season with Blackened Sriracha Rub, then drizzle with vegetable oil. Toss by hand to coat well then set aside.

2. In a small mixing bowl, stir together mayonnaise, sour cream, and fresh lime juice. Season to taste with Blackened Sriracha. Set aside.

3. In a small mixing bowl, combine jalapeño, onion, red bell pepper, and cilantro. Set aside.

4. Supply your smoker with wood pellets and follow the start-up procedure. Preheat the grill, with the lid closed, till over medium heat. If using a grill, preheat a cast iron skillet over medium-heat.

5. Place tortillas on the griddle to warm each side, then turn off the burner below.

6. Transfer shrimp to the hot griddle, and cook for 4 to 6 minutes, tossing occasionally, until opaque. For spicier shrimp, season with additional Blackened Sriracha.

7. Assemble tacos: shredded cabbage, shrimp, pepper mixture, then drizzle with sauce. Serve warm with fresh lime wedges.

Delicious Smoked Trout

Servings: 8

Cooking Time: 120 Minutes

Ingredients:

- 6 rainbow trout fillets
- Brine:
- 2 Tablespoons kosher salt
- 2 Tablespoons brown sugar
- 4 cups cool water

Directions:

1. For the brine, dissolve the kosher salt and brown sugar in water.

2. Place the trout fillets in the brine, skin side up, and brine the fillets for 15 minutes.

3. Supply your smoker with wood pellets and follow the start-up procedure. Preheat the grill, with the lid closed, to 180° F.

4. Remove the trout from the brine and transfer it to the grill grates.

5. Smoke the trout for 1.5 to 2 hours with the lid closed, depending on the thickness of your fillets.

6. Smoke until the trout reaches an internal temperature of 145 °F, or until the trout flakes easily.

7. Remove the trout from the smoker and serve warm, or let it cool completely and serve chilled with your favorite accouterments.

Flavour Fire Spiced Shrimp

Servings: 2
Cooking Time: 8 Minutes

Ingredients:
- 1 pound of extra large raw whole wild shrimp
- 1 tablespoon vegetable oil
- 1 tablespoon chili powder
- 1 teaspoon garlic powder
- 1/2 teaspoon onion powder
- 1/2 teaspoon cayenne pepper
- 1/4 teaspoon paprika
- 1/4 teaspoon dried oregano
- Pinch of Kosher salt

Directions:
1. Supply your smoker with wood pellets and follow the start-up procedure. Preheat the grill, with the lid closed, to High heat.

2. While grill is preheating, remove the shrimp shells, leaving the heads.

3. Butterfly shrimp by using a knife to cut each shrimp down the middle, from the head down to the tail.

4. Remove the vein, rinse off the shrimp and lightly dry off with paper towels.

5. Place the shrimp in a large bowl, sprinkle with all the seasonings and the oil.

6. Mix together, ensuring the mixture evenly covers each shrimp.

7. Using a skewer, impale the whole body of a shrimp, from head to tail. (Wrap them in aluminum foil if using wooden skewers).

8. Place the whole shrimp on the grill and cook for 3-4 minutes on each side (Or until shells turns pink and the shrimp is opaque).

9. Serve with your favorite sauce or condiment.

Spicy Crab Poppers

Servings: 8
Cooking Time: 30 Minutes

Ingredients:
- 18 Whole jalapeño
- 8 Ounce cream cheese, softened
- 1 Cup Canned Corn, drained
- 1/2 Cup Crab meat, lump
- 1 1/4 Teaspoon Old Bay Seasoning
- 2 Scallions, minced

Directions:
1. Cut each jalapeño in half lengthwise through the stem and remove the ribs and seeds.

2. Filling: In a mixing bowl, combine the cream cheese, corn, crab meat, scallions, and Old Bay Seasoning and stir until blended. Stir in the scallions. Spoon the filling into the jalapeño halves, mounding it slightly.

3. Arrange the poppers on a baking sheet covered with foil or parchment paper.

4. Supply your smoker with wood pellets and follow the start-up procedure. Preheat the grill, with the lid closed, to 350° F.

5. Roast the jalapeños for 25 to 30 minutes, or until the peppers have softened and the filling is hot and bubbling.

6. Let cool slightly before serving. Enjoy!

Seared Bluefin Tuna Steaks

Servings: 2
Cooking Time: 5 Minutes

Ingredients:
- 3 Whole Tuna, steak
- olive oil
- salt and pepper
- soy sauce
- Sriracha

Directions:
1. Lightly baste both sides of tuna steaks in olive oil; sprinkle sea salt and ground pepper on each side.

2. Supply your smoker with wood pellets and follow the start-up procedure. Preheat the grill, with the lid closed, to High heat.

3. Grill tuna steaks on each side for 2 to 2-1/2 minutes.

4. Remove tuna from grill and allow to cool slightly.

5. Cut into 1/2 - 3/4" pieces. Serve with a mixture of Soy Sauce and Sriracha. Enjoy!"

Bacon Wrapped Shrimp

Servings: 6
Cooking Time: 20 Minutes

Ingredients:

- 1 1/2 Pound Jumbo Shrimp, Peeled And Deveined
- 10 Strips Bacon
- Cheesy Grits, For Serving
- 1/4 Cup extra-virgin olive oil
- 2 Tablespoon lemon juice
- 1 Teaspoon Fresh Chopped Parsley
- 1 Tablespoon lemon zest
- 1 Teaspoon garlic, minced
- 1 Teaspoon salt
- 1/2 Teaspoon black pepper

Directions:

1. Rinse the shrimp under cold running water and dry thoroughly on paper towels.
2. Transfer to a re-sealable plastic bag or a bowl.
3. For the marinade: Combine the olive oil, lemon juice, lemon zest, garlic, salt, pepper, and parsley in a small jar with a tight-fitting lid and shake vigorously until combined.
4. Pour over the shrimp and refrigerate for 30 minutes to 1 hour.
5. Supply your smoker with wood pellets and follow the start-up procedure. Preheat the grill, with the lid closed, to 400° F.
6. Lay the bacon strips diagonally on the grill grate and grill for 10 to 12 minutes, or until the bacon is partially cooked but still very pliable.
7. Cut each strip in half width-wise. Leave the grill on.
8. Drain the shrimp, discarding the marinade. Wrap a strip of bacon around the body of each shrimp, securing with a toothpick. Grill for 4 minutes per side, turning once. Enjoy! Grill: 400 °F
9. Wrap a strip of bacon around the body of each shrimp, securing with a toothpick.
10. Grill for 4 minutes per side, turning once. Serve over cheesy grits, if desired. Enjoy!

Cajun Catfish

Servings: 6
Cooking Time: 15 Minutes

Ingredients:

- 2½ pounds catfish fillets
- 2 tablespoons olive oil
- 1 batch Cajun Rub

Directions:

1. Supply your smoker with wood pellets and follow the start-up procedure. Preheat the grill, with the lid closed, to 300°F.
2. Coat the catfish fillets all over with olive oil and season with the rub. Using your hands, work the rub into the flesh.
3. Place the fillets directly on the grill grate and smoke until their internal temperature reaches 145°F. Remove the catfish from the grill and serve immediately

Kimi's Simple Grilled Fresh Fish

Servings: 2
Cooking Time: 45 Minutes

Ingredients:

- 1 Cup soy sauce
- 1/3 Cup extra-virgin olive oil
- 1 Tablespoon garlic, minced
- 2 lemons, juiced
- fresh basil
- 4 Pound Fresh Fish, cut into portion-sized pieces

Directions:

1. Mix all ingredients to create sauce and cover fish in marinade for 45 minutes.
2. Supply your smoker with wood pellets and follow the start-up procedure. Preheat the grill, with the lid closed, to 140° F. Grill the marinated fish on the grill until it reaches an internal temperature of 140-145°F. Serve immediately, enjoy! Grill: 350 °F Probe: 145 °F

Bacon Wrapped Scallops

Servings: 8
Cooking Time: 20 Minutes

Ingredients:

- 24 jumbo deep sea diver scallops, dry-packed
- 1/2 Cup butter
- salt
- freshly ground black pepper
- 1 Clove garlic, minced
- 12 Slices thin-cut bacon, cut in half crosswise
- lemon wedges, for serving

Directions:

1. Remove the small, crescent-shaped muscle from the side of each scallop, if still attached. Dry the scallops thoroughly on paper towels, then transfer to a medium bowl.
2. Melt butter in a small saucepan, add garlic and cook for 1 minute. Let cool slightly then pour over the scallops. Season with salt and pepper and gently toss to coat.
3. Wrap a piece of bacon around each scallop and secure with a toothpick.
4. Supply your smoker with wood pellets and follow the start-up procedure. Preheat the grill, with the lid closed, to 400° F.
5. Arrange the scallops directly on the grill grate. Grill for 15 to 20 minutes, or until the scallop is opaque and the bacon has begun to crisp. If desired, you can turn the scallops on their side, bacon-

side down, turning occasionally to crisp the bacon. Do not overcook. Grill: 400 °F

6.   Transfer the scallops to a platter and serve with lemon wedges.

Grilled Lobster Tails With Smoked Paprika Butter

Servings: 4
Cooking Time: 10-12 Minutes

Ingredients:

- 4 lobster tails, each about 8 to 10oz (225 to 285g), thawed if frozen
- 3 lemons, 1 quartered lengthwise, 2 halved through their equators
- for the butter
- 1¼ cup unsalted butter, at room temperature
- 2 garlic cloves, peeled and finely minced
- 3 tbsp chopped fresh parsley
- 2 tbsp chopped fresh chives
- 1 tbsp freshly squeezed lemon juice
- 2 tsp finely chopped lemon zest
- 2 tsp smoked paprika
- 1 tsp coarse salt

Directions:

1.   Supply your smoker with wood pellets and follow the start-up procedure. Preheat the grill, with the lid closed, to 450° F.

2.   In a medium bowl, make the paprika butter by combining the ingredients. Beat with a wooden spoon until well blended.

3.   Use a sharp, heavy knife or sturdy kitchen shears to cut lengthwise through the top shell of each lobster tail in a straight line toward the tail fin. Gently loosen the meat from the bottom shell and sides. Lift the meat through the slit you just made so the meat sits on top of the shell. Slip a lemon quarter underneath the meat (between the meat and the bottom shell) to keep it elevated. Spread 1 tablespoon of paprika butter on top of each lobster. Melt the remaining butter and keep it warm.

4.   Place the lobster tails flesh side up and lemon halves cut sides down on the grate. Grill the lobsters until the flesh is white and opaque and the internal temperature of the lobster meat reaches 135 to 140°F (57 to 60°C), about 10 to 12 minutes, basting at least once with some of the melted butter. (Don't overcook or the lobster will become unpleasantly rubbery.)

5.   Transfer the lobsters and the lemon halves to a platter. Divide the remaining melted butter between 4 ramekins before serving.

Lemon Herb Grilled Salmon

Servings: 4

Cooking Time: 25 Minutes

Ingredients:

- 1 1/2 pounds salmon with skin
- 1/2 tablespoon lemon zest
- 1 tablespoon lemon juice
- 1 tablespoon unsalted butter
- 1/2 teaspoon sea salt
- 1/2 teaspoon ground black pepper
- 2 teaspoons freshly chopped dill
- 1 teaspoon freshly chopped parsley
- lemon slices for the garnish

Directions:

1.   Supply your smoker with wood pellets and follow the start-up procedure. Preheat the grill, with the lid closed, to 325° F.

2.   In a small bowl, combine the lemon zest, lemon juice, softened unsalted butter, dill, parsley, sea salt, and ground black pepper.

3.   Generously slather the top of the salmon fillet with the mixture and top with a slice of lemon. You may allow marinating for about 10 minutes or so to absorb the mixture.

4.   Place the salmon fillets on the hot grill grate, skin-side facing down.

5.   Cook the salmon for 20 to 25 minutes, until it reaches an internal temperature of 145 °F and flakes easily, or until the salmon is cooked to your preferred taste.

6.   Serve with lemon slices. Enjoy!

Grilled Shrimp Brochette

Servings: 6
Cooking Time: 20 Minutes

Ingredients:

- 1 Pound extra-large shrimp, peeled and deveined
- 6 Whole fresh jalapeños
- 8 Ounce block Monterey Jack cheese
- 1 Pound bacon
- 2 Tablespoon Meat Church The Gospel All-Purpose Rub
- oil

Directions:

1.   Fillet shrimp open slightly and set aside. Core the jalapeños and cut them into small slivers. Slice the cheese into similar-sized slivers as the peppers. Cut the bacon slices in half.

2.   Place one slice of jalapeño and one slice of cheese inside each shrimp. Wrap stuffed shrimp in a half piece of bacon and secure with a toothpick.

3.   After you have constructed all of the shrimp, season lightly with Meat Church The Gospel All-Purpose Rub.

4.   Supply your smoker with wood pellets and follow the start-up procedure. Preheat the grill, with the lid closed, to 425° F.

Florentine Shrimp Al Cartoccio

Servings: 4

Cooking Time: 13 Minutes

Ingredients:

- 6 tbsp unsalted butter, melted
- ½ cup heavy whipping cream
- ½ cup grated Parmesan cheese
- 2 garlic cloves, peeled and minced
- 1 cup thinly sliced button mushrooms, cleaned and destemmed
- 1 cup baby spinach leaves
- 2 tbsp chopped sun-dried, oil-packed tomatoes
- ½ tsp dried oregano
- ½ tsp dried basil
- ½ tsp crushed red pepper flakes, plus more
- ½ tsp coarse salt
- ½ tsp freshly ground black pepper
- 20 to 24 jumbo shrimp, about 1lb (450g) total, peeled and deveined
- sprigs of fresh rosemary, basil, thyme, or oregano

Directions:

1. Supply your smoker with wood pellets and follow the start-up procedure. Preheat the grill, with the lid closed, to 400° F.

2. In a large bowl, combine the butter and whipping cream. Stir in the Parmesan, garlic, mushrooms, spinach, tomatoes, oregano, basil, red pepper flakes, and salt and pepper. Add the shrimp and stir gently to coat.

3. Place four 12-inch (30.5cm) sheets of wide heavy-duty aluminum foil on a workspace and pull up the sides. Divide the shrimp mixture evenly between the sheets of foil. Roll and crimp the top and sides of the foil to create sealed packages.

4. Place the packets seam side up on the grate and grill until the shrimp are cooked through, about 10 to 13 minutes. (You can carefully open one package to check on the shrimp.)

5. Transfer the packets to plates. Carefully open the packets to avoid any steam. Scatter fresh herbs over the shrimp before serving.

Prosciutto-wrapped Scallops

Servings: 4

Cooking Time: 10 Minutes

Ingredients:

- 1½lb (680g) jumbo sea or diver scallops (size U-10)
- 8 to 10 thin slices of prosciutto, each halved lengthwise
- coarse salt
- freshly ground black pepper
- for the butter
- 8oz (225g) unsalted butter
- 2 tsp minced fresh curly or flat-leaf parsley
- 1½ tsp finely grated orange zest
- 1 tbsp freshly squeezed orange juice
- 1 tsp finely grated lemon zest
- 1 tsp finely grated lime zest
- ½ tsp coarse salt

Directions:

1. Supply your smoker with wood pellets and follow the start-up procedure. Preheat the grill, with the lid closed, to 450° F.

2. In a small saucepan on the stovetop over medium-low heat, make the citrus butter by melting the butter. Add the remaining ingredients and simmer for 3 to 5 minutes to blend the flavors. Keep warm.

3. Rinse the scallops under cold running water and dry with paper towels. Place each scallop on its side at the end of a piece of prosciutto and wrap the prosciutto around the scallop. Secure with a toothpick. Season the exposed sides of the scallop with salt and pepper.

4. Place the scallops exposed sides down on the grate and grill until the edges of the prosciutto begin to frizzle and the scallop is warm inside, about 3 to 5 minutes per side.

5. Transfer the scallops to a platter. Brush with some of the warm citrus butter before serving. Serve the remaining butter on the side.

Traeger Smoked Salmon

Servings: 6

Cooking Time: 240 Minutes

Ingredients:

- 1 (2-1/2 to 3 lb) salmon fillet
- 1/2 Cup kosher salt
- 1 Cup brown sugar, firmly packed
- 1 Tablespoon ground black pepper

Directions:

1. Remove all pin bones from salmon.

2. In a small bowl, combine salt, sugar and black pepper. Lay a large piece of plastic wrap on a flat surface that is at least 6 inches longer than the fillet. Spread 1/2 of the mixture on top of the plastic and lay the fillet skin side down on top of the cure. Top with the other 1/2 of the cure spreading it evenly over the top of the fillet. Fold up the edges of the plastic and wrap tightly.

3. Place the wrapped salmon fillet in the bottom of a flat, rectangle baking dish or hotel pan. Place another identical pan on

top of the fillet. Place a couple of cans or something heavy inside the top pan to weigh it down making sure the weight is distributed evenly.

4.   Transfer the weighted salmon to the refrigerator and cure for 4 to 6 hours.

5.   Remove the salmon from the plastic wrap and rinse the cure thoroughly (not rinsing thoroughly will result in a salty finished product). Place skin side down on a wire rack atop a sheet tray and pat dry. Place the sheet tray in the refrigerator and allow the salmon to dry overnight. This allows a tacky film called a pellicle to form on the surface of the salmon. The pellicle helps smoke adhere to the fish.

6.   Supply your smoker with wood pellets and follow the start-up procedure. Preheat the grill, with the lid closed, to 180° F.

7.   Place the salmon skin side down directly on the grill grate and smoke for 3 to 4 hours or until the internal temperature of the fish registers 140°F. Enjoy warm or chilled. Grill: 180 °F Probe: 140 °F

Traeger Baked Rainbow Trout

Servings: 2
Cooking Time: 20 Minutes

Ingredients:
- 2 Tablespoon olive oil, divided
- 2 Whole rainbow trout, gutted and cleaned, heads and tails still on
- 1/2 Teaspoon fresh dill
- 1/2 Teaspoon fresh thyme
- 1 Teaspoon Jacobsen Salt Co. Pure Kosher Sea Salt
- 1/2 Large onion, sliced
- 1 Large lemon, thinly sliced
- 1 Teaspoon freshly ground black pepper

Directions:
1.   Supply your smoker with wood pellets and follow the start-up procedure. Preheat the grill, with the lid closed, to 400° F.

2.   Grease a 9x13 inch baking dish with 1 tablespoon olive oil.

3.   Place trout in the prepared baking dish and coat fish with remaining olive oil. Season the inside and outside of fish with dill, thyme and salt. Stuff each fish with onion and lemon slices then grind pepper over the top. Place 1 lemon slice on each fish.

4.   Bake in the Traeger for 10 minutes. Add 2 tablespoons hot water to the baking dish. Continue baking until fish flakes easily with a fork, about 10 more minutes. Enjoy! Grill: 400 °F

Swordfish With Sicilian Olive Oil Sauce

Servings: 4
Cooking Time: 10 Minutes

Ingredients:

- 1/2 Cup extra-virgin olive oil, plus 2 tablespoons for oiling the fish
- 1 Whole lemon, juiced
- 2 Clove garlic, minced
- 3 Tablespoon finely chopped fresh parsley
- 1 Tablespoon finely chopped fresh oregano or 1 teaspoon dried oregano
- 1 Tablespoon brined capers, drained (optional)
- 4 (6 to 8 oz) swordfish, halibut, tuna or salmon steaks, 1 inch thick
- salt and pepper

Directions:
1.   Put 1/2 cup of olive oil in a small saucepan and warm over low heat.

2.   Whisk in lemon juice and 2 tablespoons hot water. Stir in garlic, parsley, oregano, capers (if using), and salt and pepper to taste (go easy on the salt if you're using capers). Keep warm.

3.   Supply your smoker with wood pellets and follow the start-up procedure. Preheat the grill, with the lid closed, to 400° F.

4.   Brush the fish steaks with 2 tablespoons of olive oil and season with salt and pepper. Grill: 400 °F

5.   Arrange on the grill grate and grill until the fish is opaque and flakes easily when pressed with a fork, about 18 minutes. (If you prefer your tuna or salmon on the rare side, cook them for less time.) Grill: 400 °F

6.   Transfer the fish steaks to a platter or plates and drizzle with the warm olive oil sauce.

7.   Serve the remaining sauce on the side. Enjoy!

Lemon Lobster Rolls

Servings: 4
Cooking Time: 35 Minutes

Ingredients:
- 1/2 Cup Butter
- 4 Hot Dog Bun(S)
- 1 Lemon, Whole
- 4 Lobster, Tail
- 1/4 Cup Mayo
- Pepper

Directions:
1.   Supply your smoker with wood pellets and follow the start-up procedure. Preheat the grill, with the lid closed, to 300° F.

2.   Using kitchen shears, cut the shell of the tail and crack in half so that the meat is exposed. Pour in butter and season with pepper. Place the tails meat side up on the grill and cook until the shell has turned red and the meat is white, about 35 minutes.

3.   Remove from the grill and separate the shell from the meat. Place the meat in a bowl with mayo, lemon juice and rind and season with pepper. Stir to combine and evenly distribute into the hot dog buns.

Smoked Crab Legs

Servings: 4
Cooking Time: 30 Minutes

Ingredients:

- 4 Whole crab legs
- 4 Tablespoon butter, melted
- 1/2 Cup Texas Spicy BBQ Sauce
- salt and pepper
- 1 Tablespoon Fin & Feather Rub

Directions:

1. Supply your smoker with wood pellets and follow the start-up procedure. Preheat the grill, with the lid closed, to 250° F.
2. Place the crab legs directly on the grill grate and smoke for 20 minutes. Grill: 250 °F
3. While the crab is smoking, make the sauce. In a medium bowl, combine melted butter, Traeger Texas Spicy BBQ sauce, salt, pepper and Traeger Fin & Feather Rub.
4. After 20 minutes of cooking, brush the crab legs with the BBQ sauce mixture. Continue to cook for another 10 minutes reserving the remaining sauce to serve. Remove crab legs from the grill, and serve with melted butter and BBQ sauce mixture. Enjoy!

Grilled Pepper Lobster Tails

Servings: 3
Cooking Time: 10 Minutes

Ingredients:

- Tt Black Pepper
- 3/4 Stick Butter, Room Temp
- 2 Tablespoons Chives, Chopped
- 1 Clove Garlic, Minced
- Lemon, Sliced
- 3 (7-Ounce) Lobster, Tail
- Tt Salt, Kosher

Directions:

1. Start your Grill on "SMOKE" with the lid open until a fire is established in the burn pot (3-7 minutes).
2. Supply your smoker with wood pellets and follow the start-up procedure. Preheat the grill, with the lid closed, to 350° F.
3. Blend butter, chives, minced garlic, and black pepper in a small bowl. Cover with plastic wrap and set aside.
4. Butterfly the tails down the middle of the softer underside of the shell. Don't cut entirely through the center of the meat. Brush the tails with olive oil and season with salt, to your liking.
5. Grill lobsters cut side down about 5 minutes until the shells are bright red in color. Flip the tails over and top with a generous tablespoon of herb butter. Grill for another 4 minutes, or until the lobster meat is an opaque white color.

6. Remove from the grill and serve with more herb butter and lemon wedges.

Barbecued Shrimp

Servings: 4
Cooking Time: 10 Minutes

Ingredients:

- 1 pound peeled and deveined shrimp, with tails on
- 2 tablespoons olive oil
- 1 batch Dill Seafood Rub

Directions:

1. Soak wooden skewers in water for 30 minutes.
2. Supply your smoker with wood pellets and follow the start-up procedure. Preheat the grill, with the lid closed, to 375°F.
3. Thread 4 or 5 shrimp per skewer.
4. Coat the shrimp all over with olive oil and season each side of the skewers with the rub.
5. Place the skewers directly on the grill grate and grill the shrimp for 5 minutes per side. Remove the skewers from the grill and serve immediately.

Lobster Tail

Servings: 2
Cooking Time: 25 Minutes

Ingredients:

- 2 lobster tails
- Salt
- Freshly ground black pepper
- 1 batch Lemon Butter Mop for Seafood

Directions:

1. Supply your smoker with wood pellets and follow the start-up procedure. Preheat the grill, with the lid closed, to 375°F.
2. Using kitchen shears, slit the top of the lobster shells, through the center, nearly to the tail. Once cut, expose as much meat as you can through the cut shell.
3. Season the lobster tails all over with salt and pepper.
4. Place the tails directly on the grill grate and grill until their internal temperature reaches 145°F. Remove the lobster from the grill and serve with the mop on the side for dipping.

Vodka Brined Smoked Wild Salmon

Servings: 4
Cooking Time: 60 Minutes

Ingredients:

- 1 Cup brown sugar
- 1 Tablespoon black pepper
- 1/2 Cup coarse salt
- 1 Cup vodka

- 1 (1-1/2 to 2 lb) wild caught salmon
- 1 lemon wedges
- capers

Directions:

1. In a small bowl, whisk together brown sugar, pepper, salt and vodka.
2. Place the salmon in a large resealable bag. Pour in marinade and massage into the salmon. Refrigerate for 2 to 4 hours.
3. Remove from bag, rinse and dry with paper towels.
4. Supply your smoker with wood pellets and follow the start-up procedure. Preheat the grill, with the lid closed, to 180° F.
5. Smoke the salmon, skin-side down for 30 minutes.
6. Increase grill temperature to 225°F and continue to cook salmon for an additional 45 to 60 minutes or until the internal temperature in the thickest part of the fish reaches 140°F or the fish flakes easily when pressed with a finger or fork. Grill: 225 °F Probe: 140 °F
7. Serve with lemons and capers. Enjoy!

Mexican Mahi Mahi With Baja Cabbage Slaw

Servings: 4
Cooking Time: 10 Minutes

Ingredients:

- 1½lb (680g) skinless mahi mahi, cod, or other firm white fish fillets
- coarse salt
- freshly ground black pepper
- chili powder
- lime wedges
- for the slaw
- 2 cups finely shredded green cabbage
- 2 cups finely shredded purple cabbage
- 4 tbsp reduced-fat mayo
- 2 tsp hot sauce, plus more
- 2 tsp freshly squeezed lime juice
- ½ tsp coarse salt
- for the marinade
- ¼ cup freshly squeezed orange juice
- ¼ cup freshly squeezed lime juice
- 2 tbsp extra virgin olive oil

Directions:

1. In a medium bowl, make the slaw by combining the ingredients. Stir well. Transfer to a serving bowl. Cover and refrigerate until ready to serve.
2. Place the fish fillets in a baking dish and pour the orange and lime juices and olive oil over them. Turn the fillets to coat thoroughly. Cover and refrigerate for 15 to 20 minutes.

3. Supply your smoker with wood pellets and follow the start-up procedure. Preheat the grill, with the lid closed, to 450° F.
4. Drain the fish and pat dry with paper towels. (Discard the marinade.) Season the fillets on both sides with salt and pepper and chili powder. Place the fillets on the grate and grill until golden brown, about 4 to 5 minutes per side, turning with a thin-bladed spatula.
5. Transfer the fish to a platter. Serve with the slaw and lime wedges.

Cedar Smoked Garlic Salmon

Servings: 6
Cooking Time: 60 Minutes

Ingredients:

- 1 Tsp Black Pepper
- 3 Cedar Plank, Untreated
- 1 Tsp Garlic, Minced
- 1/3 Cup Olive Oil
- 1 Tsp Onion, Salt
- 1 Tsp Parsley, Minced Fresh
- 1 1/2 Tbsp Rice Vinegar
- 2 Salmon, Fillets (Skin Removed)
- 1 Tsp Sesame Oil
- 1/3 Cup Soy Sauce

Directions:

1. Soak the cedar planks in warm water for an hour or more.
2. In a bowl, mix together the olive oil, rice vinegar, sesame oil, soy sauce, and minced garlic.
3. Add in the salmon and let it marinate for about 30 minutes.
4. Start your grill on smoke with the lid open until a fire is established in the burn pot (3-7 minutes).
5. Supply your smoker with wood pellets and follow the start-up procedure. Preheat the grill, with the lid closed, to 225° F.
6. Place the planks on the grate. Once the boards start to smoke and crackle a little, it's ready for the fish.
7. Remove the fish from the marinade, season it with the onion powder, parsley and black pepper, then discard the marinade.
8. Place the salmon on the planks and grill until it reaches 140°F internal temperature (start checking temp after the salmon has been on the grill for 30 minutes).
9. Remove from the grill, let it rest for 10 minutes, then serve.

Spicy Shrimp Skewers

Servings: 4
Cooking Time: 6 Minutes

Ingredients:

- 2 Pound shrimp, peeled and deveined
- 6 Thai chiles
- 6 Clove garlic
- 2 Tablespoon Winemaker's Napa Valley Rub
- 1 1/2 Teaspoon sugar
- 1 1/2 Tablespoon white vinegar
- 3 Tablespoon olive oil

Directions:

1.   If using bamboo skewers, place them in cold water to soak for 1 hour before grilling.
2.   Place shrimp in a bowl and set aside. Combine all remaining ingredients in a blender and blend until a coarse-textured paste is reached. Note: if a milder flavor is preferred, feel free to adjust amount of chiles to taste.
3.   Add chile-garlic mixture to the shrimp and place in fridge to marinate for at least 30 minutes.
4.   Remove from fridge and thread shrimp onto bamboo or metal skewers.
5.   Supply your smoker with wood pellets and follow the start-up procedure. Preheat the grill, with the lid closed, to 450° F.
6.   Place shrimp on grill and cook for 2 to 3 minutes per side or until shrimp are pink and firm to touch. Enjoy! Grill: 450 ˚F

Bbq Oysters

Servings: 4
Cooking Time: 6 Minutes

Ingredients:

- 1 Pound unsalted butter, softened
- 1 Tablespoon Meat Church Holy Gospel BBQ Rub
- 1 Bunch green onions, chopped
- 2 Clove garlic, minced
- 12 oysters
- 1/4 Cup seasoned breadcrumbs
- 8 Ounce shredded pepper jack cheese
- Sweet & Heat BBQ Sauce
- 1/2 Bunch green onions, minced

Directions:

1.   Supply your smoker with wood pellets and follow the start-up procedure. Preheat the grill, with the lid closed, to 375° F.
2.   For the compound butter: Combine butter, garlic, onion and Meat Church Rub thoroughly.
3.   Lay the butter on parchment paper or plastic wrap. Roll it up to form a log and tie each end with butcher's twine. Place in the freezer for an hour to solidify. You can use this butter on any grilled meat to enhance the flavor. You can also use a high-quality butter to replace the compound butter.
4.   Shuck the oysters, keeping all of the juice in the shell. Sprinkle the oysters with breadcrumbs and place directly on the Traeger. Cook them for 5 minutes. You will be looking for the edge of the oyster to start to curl slightly.
5.   After 5 minutes, place a spoonful of compound butter in the oysters. After the butter melts, add a pinch of pepper jack cheese.
6.   Remove the oysters after 6 minutes on the grill total. Top oysters with a squirt of Traeger Sweet & Heat BBQ Sauce and a few chopped onions. Allow to cool for 5 minutes, then enjoy!

Smoked Lobster Scampi

Servings: 2
Cooking Time: 30 Minutes

Ingredients:

- 1 Lobster Tail
- 1 Handful Pasta, Angel Hair
- 2 Tablespoon butter
- 1 Teaspoon garlic, minced
- 1/2 Teaspoon lemon juice
- 2 Teaspoon Parmesan cheese, grated
- 2 Tablespoon Sun Dried Tomato Pesto
- fresh parsley

Directions:

1.   Supply your smoker with wood pellets and follow the start-up procedure. Preheat the grill, with the lid closed, to 180° F.
2.   Use kitchen shears to cut along the top of the lobster on both sides to expose the meat. Place the lobster directly on the grill for 20-25 minutes, depending on the size of the lobster. Grill: 180 ˚F
3.   While lobster smokes, cook pasta according to packaged directions.
4.   After 20-25 minutes, take lobster off the grill and remove the meat from the tail. Cut meat into chunks.
5.   While the pasta is boiling, melt butter over medium high heat. Once butter starts to brown, add the garlic and lobster chunks. Toss in pan a few times then add lemon and parmesan. Set aside.
6.   When pasta has finished, place 1 tbsp of the sun dried tomato pesto on the bottom of a bowl or plate. Top with pasta, then finish with the lobster scampi. Garnish with parsley. Enjoy!

Smoky Crab Dip

Servings: 6
Cooking Time: 20 Minutes

Ingredients:

- 1/3 Cup mayonnaise
- 3 Ounce sour cream

- 1 Teaspoon smoked paprika
- 1/4 Teaspoon cayenne pepper
- 1 1/2 Pound Crab meat, lump
- salt and pepper
- scallions, chopped
- butter crackers

Directions:

1. Supply your smoker with wood pellets and follow the start-up procedure. Preheat the grill, with the lid closed, to 350° F.

2. Meanwhile, in a large bowl gently stir together all of the ingredients except the crackers, garnish scallions and the crab meat until thoroughly combined. Gently fold in the crab meat, being careful not to break it up too much.

3. Season to taste and transfer to an oven-safe serving dish.

4. Bake for 20 to 25 minutes, until bubbly and golden on top. Grill: 350 °F

5. Garnish with the additional chopped scallions and serve warm with butter crackers. Enjoy!

Planked Trout With Fennel, Bacon & Orange

Servings: 4
Cooking Time: 40minutes

Ingredients:

- 4 whole trout, each about 14 to 16oz (400 to 450g), cleaned and gutted, fins removed
- coarse salt
- freshly ground black pepper
- for the filling
- 1 large navel orange
- 4 slices of thick-cut bacon, diced
- 1 large fennel bulb, trimmed, halved, decored, and diced, green fronds reserved
- 4oz (110g) baby spinach, about 6 cups
- coarse salt
- freshly ground black pepper

Directions:

1. Supply your smoker with wood pellets and follow the start-up procedure. Preheat the grill, with the lid closed, to 450° F. Place 4 cedar planks on the grate and allow them to singe slightly on both sides. Remove them from the grill and place them on a heatproof surface to cool.

2. Lower the temperature to 300°F (149°C).

3. Slice 4 thin rounds from the center of the orange and then slice each in half for 8 pieces total. Zest the remainder of the orange and set aside.

4. In a cold skillet on the stovetop over medium heat, sauté the bacon, until the fat has rendered and the bacon is golden brown,

about 6 to 8 minutes, stirring frequently. Use a slotted spoon to transfer the bacon to paper towels to drain. Add the fennel to the fat in the skillet and cook until tender crisp, about 5 minutes. Add the spinach and stir until it wilts, about 1 to 2 minutes. Squeeze the juice of one of the reserved orange ends over the mixture. Add the drained bacon. Season with salt and pepper and then stir. Remove the skillet from the stovetop and set aside.

5. Rinse each trout inside and out under cold running water and pat dry with paper towels. Place three 12-inch (30.5cm) pieces of butcher's twine on each plank and place a trout on top. Season the inside of each fish with salt and pepper. Place two half-rounds of orange in each belly, rind side facing out. Top with some of the filling. Tie the trout with the butcher's twine and trim any ends. Repeat with the remaining trout.

6. Place the planks on the grate and cook the trout until they're cooked through, about 30 to 40 minutes.

7. Remove the planks from the grill and remove the twine. Top each trout with a few curls of orange zest and some reserved fennel fronds. Serve the trout on the planks.

Smoked Salt Cured Lox

Servings: 8
Cooking Time: 30 Minutes

Ingredients:

- 1 Cup kosher salt
- 1 Cup sugar
- 1 Tablespoon cracked black pepper
- 1 Whole lemon zest
- 1 Whole orange zest
- 1 Whole Packaged Dill, roughly chopped including stems
- 2 Pound salmon fillet, skin on

Directions:

1. Mix together salt, sugar, black pepper, lemon zest, orange zest, and dill.

2. Slice salmon in half. Coat all flesh of salmon completely with salt sugar mixture. Sandwich the 2 pieces together, flesh to flesh and completely cover with salt sugar mixture.

3. Wrap tightly with plastic wrap and place into a gallon zip top bag. Squeeze out as much air as possible. Place wrapped salmon into a baking dish and place something heavy on top like a pot filled with water or a brick wrapped in foil. Place into the refrigerator for 10 hours. After 10 hours, flip over and put the weight back on top. Refrigerate for another 10 hours.

4. Remove from refrigerator, unwrap and rinse of remaining salt with cold water. Pat dry and leave on counter for 1 hour.

5. Supply your smoker with wood pellets and follow the start-up procedure. Preheat the grill, with the lid closed, to 180° F.

6. Place salmon onto a baking pan. Fill another baking pan with ice and place baking pan with salmon over ice.

7. Place onto grill and smoke for 30 minutes. Remove from grill and slice thin. Grill: 180 ˚F

8. Serve with bagels, cream cheese, capers, dill, lemon wedges, sliced tomatoes, and red onion. Enjoy!

Garlic Bacon Wrapped Shrimp

Servings: 4

Cooking Time: 11 Minutes

Ingredients:
- 8 Bacon, Strip
- 1/4 Cup Butter Style Shortening (Melted)
- 1 Clove Garlic, Minced
- 1 Tsp Lemon, Juice
- Pepper
- Salt
- 16 (Peeled And Veined) Shrimp, Jumbo

Directions:
1. Supply your smoker with wood pellets and follow the start-up procedure. Preheat the grill, with the lid closed, to 450° F.
2. Take one slice of bacon, and wrap it around each piece of shrimp, and lock it in place with a wooden toothpick.
3. Place the shortening into a mixing bowl and whisk in the garlic and lemon juice. Brush each shrimp with the sauce on both sides.
4. Place on the grill, and barbecue for 11 minutes.
5. Turn the grill off, remove the shrimp, serve and enjoy!

Roasted Halibut With Spring Vegetables

Servings: 4

Cooking Time: 20 Minutes

Ingredients:
- 4 thick-cut halibut fillets
- 2 Tablespoon Fin & Feather Rub
- Butcher Paper
- 1 Pound Carrots, Peeled and Cut into 3/4" Inch Slices
- 1 Pound asparagus, ends trimmed
- 1/2 Pound Oyster Mushrooms
- 2 Tablespoon butter
- salt and pepper
- 1/2 Cup white wine

Directions:
1. Season the halibut fillets with Traeger Fin and Feather Rub.
2. To build the packets: Start with four sheets of parchment paper about twenty inches long. Fold in half, then open it back up.
3. Divide the carrots, asparagus, and mushrooms between the four pieces of parchment and top each with a little bit of butter.

Season with salt and pepper. Place a halibut fillet on top of the vegetables in each packet.

4. Next, fold the paper over so the two ends meet, enclosing the food. Beginning at either end of the center crease, make small, overlapping diagonal folds around the filling, sealing the packet tight. Before finishing the final fold, pour a little bit of wine in each packet then seal completely.
5. Supply your smoker with wood pellets and follow the start-up procedure. Preheat the grill, with the lid closed, to 500° F.
6. Place all four packets on a sheet tray and place in the grill. Cook for 7-10 minutes or until the internal temperature of the fish reaches 145˚F. Remove from the grill and place packet on a serving dish. Grill: 500 ˚F Probe: 145 ˚F
7. Using a knife or scissors, cut open each packet and fold the edges back. Finish with a little bit of lemon juice if desired. Enjoy!

Oysters In The Shell

Servings: 4

Cooking Time: 20 Minutes

Ingredients:
- 8 medium oysters, unopened, in the shell, rinsed and scrubbed
- 1 batch Lemon Butter Mop for Seafood

Directions:
1. Supply your smoker with wood pellets and follow the start-up procedure. Preheat the grill, with the lid closed, to 375˚F.
2. Place the unopened oysters directly on the grill grate and grill for about 20 minutes, or until the oysters are done and their shells open.
3. Discard any oysters that do not open. Shuck the remaining oysters, transfer them to a bowl, and add the mop. Serve immediately.

Charleston Crab Cakes With Remoulade

Servings: 4

Cooking Time: 45 Minutes

Ingredients:
- 1¼ cups mayonnaise
- ¼ cup yellow mustard
- 2 tablespoons sweet pickle relish, with its juices
- 1 tablespoon smoked paprika
- 2 teaspoons Cajun seasoning
- 2 teaspoons prepared horseradish
- 1 teaspoon hot sauce
- 1 garlic clove, finely minced
- 2 pounds fresh lump crabmeat, picked clean
- 20 butter crackers (such as Ritz brand), crushed

- 2 tablespoons Dijon mustard
- 1 cup mayonnaise
- 2 tablespoons freshly squeezed lemon juice
- 1 tablespoon salted butter, melted
- 1 tablespoon Worcestershire sauce
- 1 tablespoon Old Bay seasoning
- 2 teaspoons chopped fresh parsley
- 1 teaspoon ground mustard
- 2 eggs, beaten
- ¼ cup extra-virgin olive oil, divided

Directions:

1. For the remoulade:
2. In a small bowl, combine the mayonnaise, mustard, pickle relish, paprika, Cajun seasoning, horseradish, hot sauce, and garlic.
3. Refrigerate until ready to serve.
4. For the crab cakes:
5. Supply your smoker with wood pellets and follow the start-up procedure. Preheat, with the lid closed, to 375°F.
6. Spread the crabmeat on a foil-lined baking sheet and place over indirect heat on the grill, with the lid closed, for 30 minutes.
7. Remove from the heat and let cool for 15 minutes.
8. While the crab cools, combine the crushed crackers, Dijon mustard, mayonnaise, lemon juice, melted butter, Worcestershire sauce, Old Bay, parsley, ground mustard, and eggs until well incorporated.
9. Fold in the smoked crabmeat, then shape the mixture into 8 (1-inch-thick) crab cakes.
10. In a large skillet or cast-iron pan on the grill, heat 2 tablespoons of olive oil. Add half of the crab cakes, close the lid, and smoke for 4 to 5 minutes on each side, or until crispy and golden brown.
11. Remove the crab cakes from the pan and transfer to a wire rack to drain. Pat them to remove any excess oil.
12. Repeat steps 6 and 7 with the remaining oil and crab cakes.
13. Serve the crab cakes with the remoulade.

Wood-fired Halibut

Servings: 4
Cooking Time: 20 Minutes

Ingredients:
- 1 pound halibut fillet
- 1 batch Dill Seafood Rub

Directions:

1. Supply your smoker with wood pellets and follow the start-up procedure. Preheat the grill, with the lid closed, to 325°F.
2. Sprinkle the halibut fillet on all sides with the rub. Using your hands, work the rub into the meat.

3. Place the halibut directly on the grill grate and grill until its internal temperature reaches 145°F. Remove the halibut from the grill and serve immediately.

Smoked Sugar Halibut

Servings: 8
Cooking Time: 120 Minutes

Ingredients:
- 1/4 cup granulated sugar
- 1/4 cup brown sugar
- 1/2 cup kosher salt
- 1 tsp ground coriander
- 2 lbs fresh halibut

Directions:

1. In a small bowl, mix the sugars, salt,and coriander together. Season the halibut on all sides.
2. Wrap the halibut in plastic wrap, place on a rimmed sheet pan,and brine in the fridge for 3 hours.
3. Remove the plastic wrap and rinse the fish. Pat it dry. Set it on a drying rack over a sheet pan for 1-2 hours in the fridge.
4. Supply your smoker with wood pellets and follow the start-up procedure. Preheat the grill, with the lid closed, to 200° F. Smoke the fish for 2 hours or until its internal temperature reaches 140 °F.
5. Serve your preferred sauce with the fish.

Grilled Maple Syrup Salmon

Servings: 6
Cooking Time: 30 Minutes

Ingredients:
- 1 large salmon fillet (around 3 pounds)
- 1/2 cup salted butter (melted)
- 2 tablespoons soy sauce
- Salt and pepper
- 1/4 cup maple syrup

Directions:

1. Supply your smoker with wood pellets and follow the start-up procedure. Preheat the grill, with the lid closed, to 400° F.
2. Place the salmon fillet in a baking pan lined with parchment paper.
3. Sprinkle the fish with salt and pepper.
4. Add half of the melted butter to the salmon and place the baking pan on the grill.
5. Grill for 15-20 minutes or until fish is roughly 70% cooked. It will feel still gelatinous in the thickest parts of the salmon.
6. Combine the remaining melted butter, soy sauce, and maple syrup and pour over the salmon.It will run off the sides so use a spoon to pour it back over the fish. It's also perfectly fine that some will be left on the sides of the pan.

7. Cook for 5 to 10 additional minutes or until the fish is cooked through. The fish should be firm to the touch but still moist and soft when pressed on,and the ridges will flake or pull apart if pressed on.

Coconut Shrimp Jalapeño Poppers

Servings: 6
Cooking Time: 55 Minutes

Ingredients:

- 8 Whole shrimp, peeled and deveined
- 1/2 Teaspoon Chicken Rub, plus more as needed
- olive oil
- 6 Whole jalapeños
- 8 Ounce cream cheese, softened
- 2 Tablespoon fresh chopped cilantro
- 1/2 Cup unsweetened coconut flakes
- 12 Slices bacon

Directions:

1. Supply your smoker with wood pellets and follow the start-up procedure. Preheat the grill, with the lid closed, to 425° F.
2. Rinse and season the shrimp with the Traeger Chicken Rub.
3. Drizzle the shrimp with olive oil and cook on the Traeger for about 5 minutes per side, or until the shrimp is opaque. Grill: 425 °F
4. Remove the shrimp and let cool.
5. Reduce Traeger temperature to 350°F. Grill: 350 °F
6. Meanwhile, get those poppers going. Cut the jalapeños in half then remove the stems and seeds.
7. Chop the shrimp. Mix together the softened cream cheese, chopped shrimp, 1/2 teaspoon Traeger Chicken Rub and 2 tablespoons chopped cilantro.
8. Load a generous amount of the filling in each pepper half. Top with a sprinkle of coconut.
9. Wrap each stuffed pepper with a slice of bacon and place on a foil-lined baking sheet.
10. Cook the peppers on the Traeger for about 45 minutes, or until the bacon fat has rendered and the cream cheese is golden. Enjoy! Grill: 350 °F

Honey Balsamic Salmon

Servings: 2
Cooking Time: 25 Minutes

Ingredients:

- 1 Medium salmon fillet
- Fin & Feather Rub
- 1/2 Cup balsamic vinegar
- 1 Tablespoon minced garlic
- 2 Tablespoon honey

Directions:

1. Season the fillet with the Traeger Fin & Feather Rub.
2. Make the glaze: Combine the vinegar, garlic and honey in a small saucepan. Simmer over medium heat until reduced by half. Usually 10 to 15 minutes. The glaze will be properly reduced when it coats the back of a spoon. Using a basting brush, coat the fillet with the glaze.
3. Supply your smoker with wood pellets and follow the start-up procedure. Preheat the grill, with the lid closed, to 350° F.
4. Arrange the salmon fillet on the grill grate. Grill for 25 to 30 minutes, or until the salmon is opaque and flakes easily with a fork. Grill: 350 °F
5. Transfer to a platter or plates and serve immediately. If desired, heat any remaining glaze to a boil and drizzle over top of the salmon. Enjoy!

Grilled Fresh Fish

Servings: 2
Cooking Time: 15 Minutes

Ingredients:

- 1 Whole fillet of firm white fish: sea bass, halibut or cod
- Fin & Feather Rub
- 2 Whole lemons

Directions:

1. Supply your smoker with wood pellets and follow the start-up procedure. Preheat the grill, with the lid closed, to 325° F.
2. Season fish with Traeger Fin & Feather Rub and let sit for 30 minutes. Slice lemons in half.
3. Place the fish and the lemons (cut side down) directly on the grill grates. Cook for 10 to 15 minutes until the fish is flaky and is at least 145°F in the thickest part of fish. Be careful not to over cook.
4. Serve with the grilled lemons. Enjoy!

Citrus-smoked Trout

Servings: 6
Cooking Time: 120 Minutes

Ingredients:

- 6 to 8 skin-on rainbow trout, cleaned and scaled
- 1 gallon orange juice
- ½ cup packed light brown sugar
- ¼ cup salt
- 1 tablespoon freshly ground black pepper
- Nonstick spray, oil, or butter, for greasing
- 1 tablespoon chopped fresh parsley
- 1 lemon, sliced

Directions:

1. Fillet the fish and pat dry with paper towels.

2. Pour the orange juice into a large container with a lid and stir in the brown sugar, salt, and pepper.

3. Place the trout in the brine, cover, and refrigerate for 1 hour.

4. Cover the grill grate with heavy-duty aluminum foil. Poke holes in the foil and spray with cooking spray (see Tip).

5. Supply your smoker with wood pellets and follow the start-up procedure. Preheat, with the lid closed, to 225°F.

6. Remove the trout from the brine and pat dry. Arrange the fish on the foil-covered grill grate, close the lid, and smoke for 1 hour 30 minutes to 2 hours, or until flaky.

7. Remove the fish from the heat. Serve garnished with the fresh parsley and lemon slices.

Lemon Scallops Wrapped In Bacon

Servings: 4
Cooking Time: 20 Minutes

Ingredients:

- 3 Tbsp Lemon, Juice
- Pepper
- 12 Scallop

Directions:

1. Start your grill on smoke with the lid open until a fire is established in the burn pot (3-7 minutes).

2. Supply your smoker with wood pellets and follow the start-up procedure. Preheat the grill, with the lid closed, to 400° F. Cut the bacon rashers in half, wrap each half around a scallop and use a toothpick to keep it in place.

3. Next drizzle the lemon juice over the scallops, and then place them on a baking tray.

4. Place in the grill, and grill for about 15-20 minutes, or until the bacon is crisp, remove from the grill, then serve.

Grilled Lemon Lobster Tails

Servings: 3
Cooking Time: 7 Minutes

Ingredients:

- 6 lobster tails
- 1/4 cup melted butter
- 1/4 cup fresh lemon juice
- 1 tablespoon fresh dill
- 1 teaspoon salt
- 6 lime wedges

Directions:

1. Supply your smoker with wood pellets and follow the start-up procedure. Preheat the grill, with the lid closed, to 375° F.

2. Split the lobster tails in half place then back side down.

3. Cut down through the center to the shell the whole length of each tail.

4. Pull the shell back, exposing the meat.

5. Pat the lobster tails with paper towel to dry.

6. Combine in a small mixing bowl the butter, lemon juice, dill, and salt until the salt has dissolved.

7. Brush the mixture onto the flesh side of each lobster tail.

8. Place the lobster tails onto the grill and cook for 5 to 7 minutes, turning them once during the cooking process. (The shells should turn a bright pink).

9. Remove the heat.

10. Serve with lime wedges!

Thai-style Swordfish Steaks With Peanut Sauce

Servings: 4
Cooking Time: 8 Minutes

Ingredients:

- 4 center-cut swordfish steaks, each about 6oz (170g) and 1 inch (2.5cm) thick
- Peanut Sauce
- lime wedges
- for the marinade
- 1/2 cup light Thai-style unsweetened coconut milk
- 2 garlic cloves, peeled and smashed with a chef's knife
- juice and zest of 1 lime
- 1-inch (2.5cm) piece of fresh ginger, peeled and roughly chopped
- ½ Thai bird's eye chili pepper or serrano pepper, deseeded and thinly sliced, plus more
- 2 tbsp fresh cilantro leaves, coarsely chopped
- 1 tbsp Asian fish sauce
- 1 tbsp light soy sauce or liquid aminos
- 1 tbsp light brown sugar or low-carb substitute
- 1 tsp ground coriander
- ½ tsp ground turmeric

Directions:

1. In a medium bowl, make the marinade by whisking together the ingredients. Whisk until the brown sugar dissolves.

2. Place the swordfish steaks in a single layer in a nonreactive baking dish and pour the marinade over them, turning the steaks to coat thoroughly. Refrigerate for 1 hour.

3. Supply your smoker with wood pellets and follow the start-up procedure. Preheat the grill, with the lid closed, to 450° F.

4. Remove the swordfish from the marinade and scrape off any solids. (Discard the marinade.) Place the steaks on the grate and grill until the fish easily flakes when pressed with a fork, about 3 to 4 minutes per side, turning with a thin-bladed spatula.

5. Transfer the swordfish steaks to a platter. Serve with the peanut sauce and lime wedges.

Smoke-roasted Halibut With Mixed Herb Vinaigrette

Servings: 4
Cooking Time: 12 Minutes

Ingredients:
- 4 halibut fillets, each about 6 to 8oz (170 to 225g)
- for the vinaigrette
- 2 tbsp white wine vinegar or sherry vinegar, plus more
- ¼ tsp coarse salt, plus more
- ¼ tsp freshly ground black pepper, plus more
- ½ cup extra virgin olive oil
- 2 tbsp minced fresh herbs, such as dill, flat-leaf parsley, or oregano
- for serving
- 4 cups loosely packed baby arugula, spinach, or other mixed greens
- 1 lemon, cut lengthwise into 4 wedges

Directions:
1. Supply your smoker with wood pellets and follow the start-up procedure. Preheat the grill, with the lid closed, to 400° F.
2. In a small bowl, make the vinaigrette by whisking together the vinegar, and salt and pepper. Whisk until the salt dissolves. Continue to whisk while slowly adding the olive oil. Whisk until the vinaigrette is emulsified. Stir in the herbs. Taste, adding vinegar or salt and pepper to taste. Pour 1⁄3 of the vinaigrette into a separate container. Reserve the remainder.
3. Place the fillets on a rimmed sheet pan. Lightly brush both sides with the smaller portion of vinaigrette. (Dividing the vinaigrette into two containers prevents cross-contamination.) Lightly season with salt and pepper.
4. Place the fillets on the grate at an angle to the bars. Grill until the edges begin to look opaque, about 4 to 6 minutes. Gently turn and grill until the fish is cooked through, about 4 to 6 minutes more. (A fillet will break into clean flakes when pressed with a fork when it's done.)
5. Remove the fish from the grill. Place the greens in a large bowl and toss them with 2 to 3 tablespoons of the reserved vinaigrette (you want the greens lightly coated) and divide between 4 plates. Place a fillet on the greens on each plate. Drizzle a bit more of the vinaigrette over the top. Serve with lemon wedges.

Grilled Lemon Salmon

Servings: 4
Cooking Time: 60 Minutes

Ingredients:
- Dill, Fresh
- 1 Lemon, Sliced
- 1 1/2 - 2 Lbs Salmon, Fresh

Directions:
1. Supply your smoker with wood pellets and follow the start-up procedure. Preheat the grill, with the lid closed, to 225° F.
2. Place the salmon on a cedar plank. Lay the lemon slices along the top of the salmon. Smoke in your Grill for about 60 minutes.
3. Top with fresh dill and serve.

Garlic Blackened Salmon

Servings: 4
Cooking Time: 10 Minutes

Ingredients:
- 1 Tablespoon, Optional Cayenne Pepper
- 2 Cloves Garlic, Minced
- 2 Tablespoons Olive Oil
- 4 Tablespoons Sweet Rib Rub
- 2 Pound Salmon, Fillet, Scaled And Deboned

Directions:
1. Supply your smoker with wood pellets and follow the start-up procedure. Preheat the grill, with the lid closed, to 350° F.
2. Remove the skin from the salmon and discard. Brush the salmon on both sides with olive oil, then rub the salmon fillet with the minced garlic, cayenne pepper and Sweet Rib Rub.
3. Grill the salmon for 5 minutes on one side. Flip the salmon and then grill for another 5 minutes, or until the salmon reaches an internal temperature of 145°F. Remove from the grill and serve.

Grilled Artichoke Cheese Salmon

Servings: 12
Cooking Time: 270 Minutes

Ingredients:
- 28 Oz Artichoke Hearts, Whole, Canned
- 1/2 Cup Breadcrumbs
- 1/2 Cup Brown Sugar
- 8 Oz Cream Cheese
- 1 Tbsp Garlic Powder
- 1 Cup Italian Cheese Blend, Shredded
- 1/4 Cup Kosher Salt
- 1 Cup Mayonnaise
- 2 Tsp Olive Oil
- 1 Tbsp Onion Powder
- 1/2 Cup Parmesan Cheese
- 2 Tbsp Parsley, Chopped
- Blackened Sriracha Rub
- 1 1/4 Lbs Salmon, Fillet, Scaled And Deboned
- Sour Cream
- 1/2 Tsp White Pepper, Ground

Directions:

1.   In a small mixing bowl, whisk together the brown sugar, salt, garlic powder, onion powder, and white pepper. This will make twice the cure needed, so be sure and place the remaining half in a resealable plastic bag and save for smoking fish at a later date.

2.   Lay a sheet of plastic wrap on a sheet tray and sprinkle a thin layer of the cure on it. Place the salmon skin-side down on top of the cure, then sprinkle a couple tablespoons of cure on top. Gently press the cure on top of the salmon flesh, then wrap in plastic wrap.

3.   Refrigerate for 8 hours, or overnight.

4.   Remove salmon from the refrigerator and wash off the cure in the sink, under cold water.

5.   Blot salmon with a paper towel, then set salmon skin side on a wire rack. Dry at room temperature for two hours, or until a yellowish shimmer appears on the salmon.

6.   Supply your smoker with wood pellets and follow the start-up procedure. Preheat the grill, with the lid closed, to 250° F. If using a gas, charcoal or other grill, set it to low, indirect heat.

7.   Place the salmon in the upper cabinet. Smoke for 2 hours, then increase the grill temperature to 350° F to maintain a cabinet temperature of 225°F and smoke another 1 to 2 hours, until salmon reaches an internal temperature of 145° F.

8.   Remove salmon from the cabinet and set aside to rest for 15 minutes, then flake apart. Reserve ½ cup to top dip after grilling.

9.   While the salmon is resting, drain the artichokes, then skewer onto metal skewers (if using wooden skewers, make sure to soak in water for 1 hour prior to grilling, or you can use a grill basket as well).

10.   Season with Blackened Sriracha, then set on the grill. Grill for 2 to 3 minutes, until lightly browned.

11.   Remove from the grill, cool slightly, then roughly chop. Set aside.

12.   In a mixing bowl, combine shredded Italian cheese, grated parmesan, breadcrumbs and parsley. Set aside.

13.   Place cream cheese, mayonnaise, and sour cream in a cast iron skillet. Stir frequently, with a wooden spoon, for about 5 minutes, until the mixture is smooth.

14.   Carefully fold in flaked salmon and grilled artichoke hearts, then spread breadcrumb mixture over dip.

15.   Drizzle with olive oil, then close the grill lid and bake for 25 to 30 minutes, until dip begins to bubble around the edges, and cheese begins to caramelize on top.

16.   Remove dip from the grill, top with reserved salmon and a pinch of parsley. Serve warm with bagel chips, crackers, or crusty bread.

Grilled Oysters With Mignonette

Servings: 2
Cooking Time: 15 Minutes

Ingredients:
- 4 Cup rock salt
- 18 Large oysters
- 4 Tablespoon unsalted butter
- 2 Clove garlic, minced
- kosher salt
- 12 Medium lemon wedges, for serving
- 2 Tablespoon minced shallot
- 1/4 Cup red wine vinegar
- 1/2 Teaspoon freshly ground black pepper

Directions:
1.   Choose a shallow serving platter that will hold all of the oysters. Pour the rock salt onto the platter to create a 1/2 inch base. This will steady the oysters for serving.

2.   To prepare the oysters, check to ensure they are completely closed. Discard oysters that are not. Wash and lightly scrub the oysters to ensure there is no grit on the surface. This will prevent the grit from entering the oyster once shucked.

3.   Using a thick glove or kitchen towel, sturdy the oyster in the hand opposite of the one holding the knife. Using an oyster knife or very sturdy paring knife, locate the "hinge" on each oyster. Place the point of the knife in the hinge, and wiggle the tip of the knife into the oyster until it feels sturdy. Firmly turn the knife to apply a torquing pressure to gently open the oyster.

4.   Remove the top shell of the oyster. Using the tip of the knife, loosen the oyster from its shell, leaving the juices intact. Place each loosened oyster on its half shell on a baking sheet.

5.   Supply your smoker with wood pellets and follow the start-up procedure. Preheat the grill, with the lid closed, to 450° F.

6.   In a small saucepan, melt the butter over medium-low heat. Add the garlic and a generous pinch of salt, and cook until fragrant but not burned, about 1 minute. Remove from the heat. Grill: 450 °F

7.   For the Mignonette: Combine the minced shallot, red wine vinegar and 1/2 teaspoon freshly ground black pepper. Set aside.

8.   Spoon 1 teaspoon of the garlic butter sauce onto each oyster in its half shell. Carefully place each oyster directly on the grill grates, ensuring they don't slip. Close the lid and allow them to cook for 3 to 4 minutes, until the edges of the oysters have pulled away from the shell. Remove carefully with tongs to keep the juices and butter in the shells. Place directly on the rock salt to balance them. Serve immediately with the mignonette and lemon wedges to squeeze onto the oysters. Enjoy!

Grilled Lemon Shrimp Scampi

Servings: 4
Cooking Time: 6 Minutes

Ingredients:

- 1 ½ pounds medium shrimp, peeled and deveined
- ¼ cup olive oil
- ¼ cup lemon juice
- 3 tablespoons chopped fresh parsley
- 1 tablespoon minced garlic
- ground black pepper to taste
- ¼ teaspoon crushed red pepper flakes to taste

Directions:

1. In a large, non-reactive bowl, stir together the olive oil, lemon juice, parsley, garlic, and black pepper. Season with crushed red pepper, if desired. Add shrimp, and toss to coat. Marinate in the refrigerator for 30 minutes.
2. Supply your smoker with wood pellets and follow the start-up procedure. Preheat the grill, with the lid closed, to high heat.
3. Thread shrimp onto skewers, piercing once near the tail and once near the head. Discard any remaining marinade.
4. Lightly oil grill grate. Place the shrimp skewers on the grill grates.
5. Grill for 2 to 3 minutes per side, or until opaque.

Peper Fish Tacos

Servings: 12
Cooking Time: 10 Minutes

Ingredients:

- 1 Tsp Black Pepper
- 1/4 Tsp Cayenne Pepper
- 1 1/2 Lbs Cod Fish
- 1/2 Tsp Cumin
- 1 Tsp Garlic Powder
- 1 Tsp Oregano
- 1 1/2 Tsp Paprika, Smoked
- 1/2 Tsp Salt

Directions:

1. Supply your smoker with wood pellets and follow the start-up procedure. Preheat the grill, with the lid closed, to 350° F.
2. Mix together paprika, garlic powder, oregano, cumin, cayenne, salt and pepper. Sprinkle over cod.
3. Place the cod on your preheated for about 5 minutes per side. Toast tortillas over heat, if desired.
4. Break the cod into pieces, smash the avocado, slice the tomatoes in half and place evenly among the tortillas. Top with red onion, lettuce, jalapenos, sour cream, and cilantro. Spritz with lime juice and enjoy!

Summer Paella

Servings: 6
Cooking Time: 45 Minutes

Ingredients:

- 6 tablespoons extra-virgin olive oil, divided, plus more for drizzling
- 2 green or red bell peppers, cored, seeded, and diced
- 2 medium onions, diced
- 2 garlic cloves, slivered
- 1 (29-ounce) can tomato purée
- 1½ pounds chicken thighs
- Kosher salt
- 1½ pounds tail-on shrimp, peeled and deveined
- 1 cup dried thinly sliced chorizo sausage
- 1 tablespoon smoked paprika
- 1½ teaspoons saffron threads
- 2 quarts chicken broth
- 3½ cups white rice
- 2 (7½-ounce) cans chipotle chiles in adobo sauce
- 1½ pounds fresh clams, soaked in cold water for 15 to 20 minutes2 tablespoons chopped fresh parsley
- 2 lemons, cut into wedges, for serving

Directions:

1. Make the sofrito: On the stove top, in a saucepan over medium-low heat, combine ¼ cup of olive oil, the bell peppers, onions, and garlic, and cook for 5 minutes, or until the onions are translucent.
2. Stir in the tomato purée, reduce the heat to low, and simmer, stirring frequently, until most of the liquid has evaporated, about 30 minutes. Set aside. (Note: The sofrito can be made in advance and refrigerated.)
3. Supply your smoker with wood pellets and follow the start-up procedure. Preheat, with the lid closed, to 450°F.
4. Heat a large paella pan on the smoker and add the remaining 2 tablespoons of olive oil.
5. Add the chicken thighs, season lightly with salt, and brown for 6 to 10 minutes, then push to the outer edge of the pan.
6. Add the shrimp, season with salt, close the lid, and smoke for 3 minutes.
7. Add the sofrito, chorizo, paprika, and saffron, and stir together.
8. In a separate bowl, combine the chicken broth, uncooked rice, and 1 tablespoon of salt, stirring until well combined.
9. Add the broth-rice mixture to the paella pan, spreading it evenly over the other ingredients.
10. Close the lid and smoke for 5 minutes, then add the chipotle chiles and clams on top of the rice.
11. Close the lid and continue to smoke the paella for about 30 minutes, or until all of the liquid is absorbed.

12. Remove the pan from the grill, cover tightly with aluminum foil, and let rest off the heat for 5 minutes.

13. Drizzle with olive oil, sprinkle with the fresh parsley, and serve with the lemon wedges.

Seared Ahi Tuna Steak With Soy Sauce

Servings: 2
Cooking Time: 60 Minutes

Ingredients:
- 1/2 Cup Gluten Free Soy Sauce
- 1 Large Sushi Grade Ahi Tuna Steak, Patted Dry
- 1/4 Cup Lime Juice
- 2 Tablespoons Rice Wine Vinegar
- 2 Tablespoons Sesame Oil, Divided
- 2 Tablespoons Sriracha Sauce
- 4 Tablespoons Sweet Heat Rub
- 2 Cups Water

Directions:
1. Supply your smoker with wood pellets and follow the start-up procedure. Preheat the grill, with the lid closed, to 400° F. If using gas or charcoal, set it up for high heat over direct heat.

2. In the glass baking dish, pour in the water, soy sauce, lime juice, rice wine vinegar, 1 tablespoon sesame oil, sriracha sauce, and mirin. Whisk the marinade together with the whisk until everything is well combine. Place the ahi steak into the marinade and place the glass baking dish with the ahi steak in the refrigerator for 30 minutes. After 30 minutes, flip the ahi steak over so that the ahi has the chance to fully marinate on all sides, and allow to marinate for 30 more minutes.

3. After the tuna steak has finished marinating, drain off the marinade and pat the steak dry with paper towels on all sides. Pour the Sweet Heat Rub onto the plate and rub the remaining tablespoon of sesame oil generously on all sides of the tuna steak, and then gently place the tuna steak into the seasoning on the plate, turning on all sides to coat evenly.

4. Insert a temperature probe into the thickest part of the ahi steak and place the steak on the hottest part of the grill. Grill the ahi tuna steak for 45 seconds on each side, or just until the outside is opaque and has grill marks. Flip the steak and allow it to grill for another 45 seconds until the outside is just cooked through. The ahi tuna steak's internal temperature should be just at 115°F.

5. Remove the steak from the grill once it reaches 115°F, and immediately slice and serve. The inside of the steak should still be cool and ruby pink.

Spicy Lime Shrimp

Servings: 4
Cooking Time: 10 Minutes

Ingredients:
- 2 Tsp Chili Paste
- 1/2 Tsp Cumin
- 2 Cloves Garlic, Minced
- 1 Large Lime, Juiced
- 1/4 Tsp Paprika, Powder
- 1/4 Tsp Red Flakes Pepper
- 1/2 Tsp Salt

Directions:
1. In a bowl, whisk together the lime juice, olive oil, garlic, chili powder, cumin, paprika, salt, pepper, and red pepper flakes.

2. Then pour it into a resealable bag, add the shrimp, toss the coat, let it marinate for 30 minutes.

3. Supply your smoker with wood pellets and follow the start-up procedure. Preheat the grill, with the lid closed, to 400° F.

4. Next place the shrimp on skewers, place on the grill, and grill each side for about two minutes until it's done. One finished, remove the shrimp from the grill and enjoy!

Grilled Salmon Steaks With Dill Sauce

Servings: 4
Cooking Time: 8 Minutes

Ingredients:
- 4 salmon steaks, each about 6 to 8oz (170 to 225g) and 1 inch (2.5cm) thick
- extra virgin olive oil
- coarse salt
- freshly ground rainbow peppercorns or freshly ground black pepper
- lemon wedges
- for the sauce
- 1 cup reduced-fat mayo
- ⅓ cup light sour cream
- ¼ cup chopped fresh dill
- 2 tbsp freshly squeezed lemon juice
- coarse salt
- freshly ground black pepper
- sprigs of fresh dill

Directions:
1. Supply your smoker with wood pellets and follow the start-up procedure. Preheat the grill, with the lid closed, to 450° F.

2. In a small bowl, make the dill sauce by combining the mayo, sour cream, dill, and lemon juice. Mix until smooth. Season with salt and pepper to taste. Transfer to a serving bowl. Scatter the dill sprigs over the top. Cover and refrigerate until ready to serve.

3. Brush the salmon with olive oil and season with salt and pepper. Place the salmon on the grate at an angle to the bars. Grill until grill marks begin to appear, about 4 minutes. Use a thin-

bladed spatula to turn the salmon. Grill until the internal temperature reaches 140°F (60°C), about 4 minutes more.

4.   Transfer the salmon to a platter. Serve immediately with the lemon wedges and dill sauce.

Cajun-blackened Shrimp

Servings: 4
Cooking Time: 20 Minutes

Ingredients:
- 1 pound peeled and deveined shrimp, with tails on
- 1 batch Cajun Rub
- 8 tablespoons (1 stick) butter
- ¼ cup Worcestershire sauce

Directions:
1.   Supply your smoker with wood pellets and follow the start-up procedure. Preheat the grill, with the lid closed, to 450°F and place a cast-iron skillet on the grill grate. Wait about 10 minutes after your grill has reached temperature, allowing the skillet to get hot.
2.   Meanwhile, season the shrimp all over with the rub.
3.   When the skillet is hot, place the butter in it to melt. Once the butter melts, stir in the Worcestershire sauce.
4.   Add the shrimp and gently stir to coat. Smoke-braise the shrimp for about 10 minutes per side, until opaque and cooked through. Remove the shrimp from the grill and serve immediately.

Spiced Smoked Swordfish

Servings: 4
Cooking Time: 60 Minutes

Ingredients:
- 4 swordfish fillets (about 4 ounces each)
- For the brine:
- 1 gallon water
- ½ cup kosher salt
- ½ cup brown sugar
- For the rub:
- 1 tablespoon olive oil
- 1 tablespoon kosher salt
- 1 tablespoon coarse ground black pepper
- 1 tablespoon garlic powder
- 1 tablespoon onion powder

Directions:
1.   Make the brine by mixing the water, salt, and sugar in a large pot and stir. Add swordfish fillets to the bowl and refrigerate overnight in the mixture.
2.   Supply your smoker with wood pellets and follow the start-up procedure. Preheat the grill, with the lid closed, to 225° F.
3.   Remove the fillets from the brine, rinse, and blot dry.

4.   Brush a coat of olive oil on each fillet and mix salt, pepper, garlic powder, and onion powder in a small bowl for the rub. Apply the rub liberally to each fillet.
5.   Put the fillets skin-side down on the smoker and cook for about 1 hour or until the internal temperature in the thickest part of the fillets reaches 145 °F.
6.   Enjoy.

Grilled Salmon Gravlax

Servings: 4
Cooking Time: 10 Minutes

Ingredients:
- 1 center-cut salmon fillet, about 2lb (1kg), preferably wild caught, skin on
- ½ cup aquavit or vodka
- 4 whole juniper berries
- ¼ cup finely chopped fresh dill, plus more
- lemon wedges
- for the rub
- 3 tbsp granulated light brown sugar or low-carb substitute
- 2 tbsp coarse salt
- 2 tsp freshly ground black pepper
- 1 tsp freshly ground white pepper
- 1 tsp ground coriander

Directions:
1.   Run your fingers over the fillet, feeling for bones. Remove them with kitchen tweezers or needle-nosed pliers. Rinse the salmon under cold running water and pat dry with paper towels.
2.   Place the salmon skin side down in a nonreactive baking dish and pour the aquavit over it. Crush the berries with the flat of a chef's knife and add them to the dish. Cover and refrigerate for 1 hour.
3.   In a small bowl, make the rub by combining the ingredients.
4.   Remove the salmon from the aquavit and pat dry with paper towels. Discard the soaking liquid and juniper berries. Rinse out the baking dish and place the salmon in the dish. Lightly but evenly sprinkle the rub on the flesh side of the fillet and gently distribute it with your fingertips. Scatter the dill over the top. Cover the dish and refrigerate for 4 hours.
5.   Supply your smoker with wood pellets and follow the start-up procedure. Preheat the grill, with the lid closed, to 400° F.
6.   With a sharp knife, slice the fillet into 4 equal portions. Place the fillets on the grate and grill until the fish is somewhat opaque but still translucent in the center and the internal temperature reaches 125°F (52°C), about 3 to 5 minutes per side.
7.   Transfer the fillets to a platter. Scatter more dill over the top. Serve with lemon wedges.

Mango Rice Wine Thai Shrimp

Servings: 4
Cooking Time: 15 Minutes

Ingredients:
- 2 Tablespoons Brown Sugar
- 2 Tablespoons Mango Magic Seasoning
- 1 Pinch (Optional) Red Pepper Flakes
- 1/2 Tablespoons Rice Wine Vinegar
- 1 Pound Raw Tail-On, Thaw And Deveined Shrimp, Uncooked
- 2 Tablespoons Soy Sauce
- 1 Teaspoon Sriracha Hot Sauce
- 1/2 Cup Sweet Chili Sauce

Directions:
1. Supply your smoker with wood pellets and follow the start-up procedure. Preheat the grill, with the lid closed, to 425° F. Rinse shrimp off in sink with cold water. Place in bowl and put in all of the ingredients listed above. Let marinade for 2 - 4 hours.
2. Thread several shrimp onto a skewer, so that they are all just touching each other. Repeat with other skewers and remaining shrimp.
3. Grill shrimp for 2 - 3 minutes on each side, or until pink and opaque all the way through. Remove from grill and serve immediately.

Grilled Blackened Saskatchewan Salmon

Servings: 4
Cooking Time: 30 Minutes

Ingredients:
- 1 salmon fillets
- zesty Italian dressing
- Blackened Saskatchewan Rub
- lemon wedges

Directions:
1. Brush salmon with Italian dressing and season with Traeger Blackened Saskatchewan Rub.
2. Supply your smoker with wood pellets and follow the start-up procedure. Preheat the grill, with the lid closed, to 325° F.
3. Place salmon on the grill and cook for 20 to 30 minutes, until it reaches an internal temperature of 145°F and flakes easily. Remove salmon from grill. Serve with lemon wedges. Enjoy! Grill: 325 °F Probe: 145 °F

Grilled Hand Pulled Chicken

Servings: 4
Cooking Time: 90 Minutes

Ingredients:

- 2 Tablespoons Apple Cider Vinegar
- 1 Clove Garlic, Minced
- Juice Of Half Of A Lemon
- 1 Cup Mayo
- 1 Tablespoon Olive Oil
- ½ Teaspoon Paprika, Powder
- 2 Tablespoons Sugar
- 1, 3-4 Pound Chicken, Giblets Removed And Patted Dry
- 4 Tablespoons Champion Chicken Seasoning

Directions:

1. Supply your smoker with wood pellets and follow the start-up procedure. Preheat the grill, with the lid open, to 350° F.
2. In a large bowl, mix all the ingredients for the sauce together. Divide the sauce between two bowls and set aside.
3. On a clean, flat surface, lay your chicken breast side down. Using the kitchen shears, remove the spine and discard. Open the chicken up and flip the chicken over so that it lays breast side up. Press the breastbone down with the heel of your hand to flatten the chicken.
4. Generously rub the chicken with the olive oil and Champion Chicken. Place on the grill, skin-side up, on the grates. Grill for 1 ½ hours, basting with half the reserved sauce every 20 minutes, until the internal temperature reaches 175°F. Remove the chicken from the grill and cover loosely for 10 minutes.
5. Shred the chicken with forks and discard the skin and bones. Serve the chicken with the remaining white BBQ sauce.

Spiced Smoked Chicken Quarters

Servings: 4
Cooking Time: 120 Minutes

Ingredients:

- 4 chicken leg quarters
- For the rub:
- 2 tbsp paprika
- 1 tbsp thyme
- 2 tbsp chili powder
- 2 tbsp cayenne pepper
- 1 tbsp garlic powder
- 1 tbsp onion powder
- 1 tbsp kosher/table salt
- 2 tbsp black pepper
- 1 tbsp olive oil

Directions:

1. Supply your smoker with wood pellets and follow the start-up procedure. Preheat the grill, with the lid closed, to 220° F.
2. Pat down chicken pieces with a paper towel to make them dry. Cut off any excess fat that's visible on the outside of the meat.
3. Apply a thin layer of oil to the chicken skin. In a small bowl, combine all the BBQ rub ingredients thoroughly. Apply BBQ rub generously to your chicken thighs, rubbing in firmly and thoroughly.
4. Transfer chicken quarters to your smoker rack.Close the lid.
5. Cook until the quarters reach an internal temperature of 165°F, about 2 hours.
6. Once cooked, increase the grill temperature to medium heat. Cook for just a few minutes, turning regularly, for a crispy skin.

Smoked Deviled Eggs

Servings: 4
Cooking Time: 30 Minutes

Ingredients:

- 7 hard boiled eggs, cooked and peeled
- 3 Tablespoon mayonnaise
- 3 Teaspoon diced chives
- 1 Teaspoon brown mustard
- 1 Teaspoon apple cider vinegar
- hot sauce
- salt and pepper
- 2 Tablespoon cooked bacon, crumbled
- paprika

Directions:

1. Supply your smoker with wood pellets and follow the start-up procedure. Preheat the grill, with the lid closed, to 180° F.
2. Place cooked and peeled eggs directly on the grill grate and smoke eggs for 30 minutes. Grill: 180 °F
3. Remove from grill and allow eggs to cool. Slice the eggs lengthwise and scoop the egg yolks into a gallon zip top bag.
4. Add mayonnaise, chives, mustard, vinegar, hot sauce, salt, and pepper to the bag. Zip the bag closed and, using your hands, knead all of the ingredients together until completely smooth.
5. Squeeze the yolk mixture into one corner of the bag and cut a small part of the corner off. Pipe the yolk mixture into the hard boiled egg whites. Top the deviled eggs with crumbled bacon and paprika. Chill until ready to serve. Enjoy!

Crispy Spiced Chicken Wings

Servings: 10
Cooking Time: 75 Minutes

Ingredients:

- 5 pounds of chicken wings (flats and drumettes)
- 2 1/2 Tablespoons baking powder
- 1 teaspoon salt

Directions:

1. Dry your chicken wings thoroughly on all sides with a paper towel. Place them in a zip-top bag.
2. Add the baking powder and salt to the wings, close the bag, and toss to coat evenly.
3. Supply your smoker with wood pellets and follow the start-up procedure. Preheat the grill, with the lid closed, to 250° F, using your favorite wood. Place the wings directly on the grill grates, close the lid, and smoke for 30 minutes.
4. Increase the heat in your smoker to 425 degrees F and continue cooking for 45 more minutes, or until the internal temperature of the wing reads 175 degrees F. You can rotate or flip the wings as needed to maintain even cooking and avoid any hot spots on the grill.
5. Remove the wing from the grill and serve. You can serve plain, toss in your favorite BBQ seasoning, or hot sauce.

Smoked Boneless Chicken Thighs

Servings: 8 - 10
Cooking Time: 55 Minutes

Ingredients:

- 2 Tbsp Ginger Root, Grated
- 5 Lbs. Boneless Skinless Chicken Thighs
- ⅔ Cup Brown Sugar
- 2 Cups Chicken Broth
- 1 Tsp Chinese Five-Spice Powder
- 5 Garlic Cloves, Minced
- ¼ Cup Honey
- 1 Tbsp Sweet Heat Rub
- ½ Cup Soy Sauce
- 1 Yellow Onion, Minced

Directions:

1. Supply your smoker with wood pellets and follow the start-up procedure. Preheat the grill, with the lid closed, to 225° F. If using a gas or charcoal grill, set it up for low heat.
2. Remove chicken from marinade and place on a metal sheet tray. Using a mesh strainer, strain the marinade directly into a cast iron skillet.
3. Place skillet with marinade and chicken on the grill. Allow chicken to smoke for 10 minutes, then increase grill temperature to 400°F.

4. Grill an additional 15 minutes. Make sure to stir marinade periodically. The sauce will begin to reduce and thicken as it cooks.
5. After 15 minutes, baste chicken thighs with marinade, then flip and baste the other sides. Grill an additional 15 minutes, then baste again.
6. Cook until glaze has caramelized and thickened, then remove from grill and serve hot.

Glazed Bbq Half Chicken

Servings: 6
Cooking Time: 120 Minutes

Ingredients:

- Meat Church Bird Bath Poultry Brine
- 1/2 Gallon water or chicken stock
- 1 Whole chicken
- 1 Whole whole chicken
- Meat Church Holy Gospel BBQ Rub
- 1 Stick butter
- Cup favorite BBQ sauce
- 2 Teaspoon blackberry jelly, pepper jelly or your favorite jelly

Directions:

1. Mix the Meat Church Bird Bath Poultry Brine thoroughly in a 1/2 gallon of water or chicken stock. Feel free to be creative and add ingredients to enhance the flavor profile to your liking. Completely submerge the chicken in the brine mixture and place in the refrigerator overnight. We recommend 12 to 24 hours for this brine.
2. Remove the bird from the brine. Rinse off and pat dry with a paper towel.
3. Supply your smoker with wood pellets and follow the start-up procedure. Preheat the grill, with the lid closed, to 275° F.
4. Using a pair of chicken shears or a very sharp knife, remove the backbone. Do this by trimming along one side of the backbone from one end of the chicken to the other. Then repeat the process on the other side of the backbone and remove it completely. Open the chicken once the backbone is removed. At this point you can remove the breastbone if you like. Slice the bird in half using a sharp knife. Now you have 2 half chickens.
5. Apply Meat Church Holy Gospel BBQ Rub to all sides of the chicken; underneath and on top of the skin. We also recommend working your hands underneath the chicken skin and applying rub directly on the meat. This will ensure a really flavorful bite even if they don't get any skin.
6. Place the chicken halves and butter in a half steam pan and put the pan on the Traeger. Baste the chicken with the butter periodically throughout the cook.
7. Using an instant-read thermometer, remove the chicken from the grill when they reach an internal temperature of at least 165°F

in the deepest part of the breast, about 1-1/2 to 2 hours. Grill: 275 °F Probe: 165 °F

8.   For the glaze, mix the BBQ sauce, honey and jelly and heat in a small sauce pan.

Smoked Airline Chicken

Servings: 4
Cooking Time: 120 Minutes

Ingredients:

- 2 boneless chicken breasts with drumettes attached
- ½ cup soy sauce
- ½ cup teriyaki sauce
- ¼ cup canola oil
- ¼ cup white vinegar
- 1 tablespoon minced garlic
- ¼ cup chopped scallions
- 2 teaspoons freshly ground black pepper
- 1 teaspoon ground mustard

Directions:

1.   Place the chicken in a baking dish.

2.   In a bowl, whisk together the soy sauce, teriyaki sauce, canola oil, vinegar, garlic, scallions, pepper and ground mustard, then pour this marinade over the chicken, coating both sides.

3.   Refrigerate the chicken in marinade for 4 hours, turning over every hour.

4.   When ready to smoke the chicken, supply your smoker with wood pellets and follow the start-up procedure. Preheat, with the lid closed, to 250°F.

5.   Remove the chicken from the marinade but do not rinse. Discard the marinade.

6.   Arrange the chicken directly on the grill, close the lid, and smoke for 1 hour 30 minutes to 2 hours, or until a meat thermometer inserted in the thickest part of the meat reads 165°F.

7.   Let the meat rest for 3 minutes before serving.

Easy Rapid-fire Roast Chicken

Servings: 4
Cooking Time: 120 Minutes

Ingredients:

- 1 (4-pound) whole chicken, giblets removed
- Extra-virgin olive oil, for rubbing
- 3 tablespoons Greek seasoning
- Juice of 1 lemon
- Butcher's string

Directions:

1.   Supply your smoker with wood pellets and follow the start-up procedure. Preheat, with the lid closed, to 450°F.

2.   Rub the bird generously all over with oil, including inside the cavity.

3.   Sprinkle the Greek seasoning all over and under the skin of the bird, and squeeze the lemon juice over the breast.

4.   Tuck the chicken wings behind the back and tie the legs together with butcher's string or cooking twine.

5.   Put the chicken directly on the grill, breast-side up, close the lid, and roast for 1 hour to 1 hour 30 minutes, or until a meat thermometer inserted in the thigh reads 165°F.

6.   Let the meat rest for 10 minutes before carving.

Smoked Drumsticks

Servings: 2-4
Cooking Time: 25 Minutes

Ingredients:

- 1 pound chicken drumsticks
- 2 tablespoons olive oil
- 1 batch Sweet and Spicy Cinnamon Rub

Directions:

1.   Supply your smoker with wood pellets and follow the start-up procedure. Preheat the grill, with the lid closed, to 350°F.

2.   Coat the drumsticks all over with olive oil and season with the rub. Using your hands, work the rub into the meat.

3.   Place the drumsticks directly on the grill grate and smoke until their internal temperature reaches 170°F. Remove the drumsticks from the grill and serve immediately.

Chicken Tenders

Servings: 2-4
Cooking Time: 80 Minutes

Ingredients:

- 1 pound boneless, skinless chicken breast tenders
- 1 batch Chicken Rub

Directions:

1.   Supply your smoker with wood pellets and follow the start-up procedure. Preheat the grill, with the lid closed, to 180°F.

2.   Season the chicken tenders with the rub. Using your hands, work the rub into the meat.

3.   Place the tenders directly on the grill grate and smoke for 1 hour.

4.   Increase the grill's temperature to 300°F and continue to cook until the tenders' internal temperature reaches 170°F. Remove the tenders from the grill and serve immediately.

Smoked Avocado Turkey Tamale Pie

Servings: 6
Cooking Time: 240 Minutes

Ingredients:

- 1 Avocado, Diced (For Topping)
- 15 Oz Black Beans, Drained (For Filling)
- To Taste, Blackened Sriracha Rub Seasoning
- 2 Tsp Blackened Sriracha Rub Seasoning (For Filling)
- To Taste, Blackened Sriracha Rub Seasoning (For Polenta)
- 2 Tbsp Butter (For Polenta)
- 2 Tbsp Cilantro, Chopped (For Topping)
- 1 Cup Corn Kernels (For Filling)
- 2 Cups Enchilada Sauce (For Filling)
- 1/2 Jalapeño, Minced (For Topping)
- 2 Cups Milk Or Water (For Polenta)
- 1 Cup Polenta, Or Fine Cornmeal (For Polenta)
- 2 Scallions, Sliced (For Topping)
- 2 Cups Smoked Turkey Breast, Shredded (For Filling)
- 2 1/2 Lbs Split Turkey Breast , Bone-In
- 2 Cups Turkey Stock (For Polenta)
- 4 Oz White Cheddar, Shredded (For Polenta)
- 4 Oz White Cheddar, Shredded (For Topping)

Directions:

1.   Supply your smoker with wood pellets and follow the start-up procedure. Preheat the grill, with the lid closed, to 225° F. If using a gas or charcoal grill, set it up for low, indirect heat.

2.   Season the turkey breast with Blackened Sriracha, then transfer to the grill, on a rack, over indirect heat.

3.   Smoke the turkey breast for 2 ½ to 3 hours, until an internal temperature of 160° F. Remove the turkey from the grill, allow to rest for 20 minutes, then shred with 2 forks.

4.   While the turkey is resting, prepare the polenta:

5.   Place a deep, cast iron skillet on the grill, then increase the temperature to 375° F. Add chicken broth and milk to a skillet and bring to a boil.

6.   Whisk in the polenta, then reduce the heat to a simmer, stirring often for 5 minutes. Season with Blackened Sriracha, then stir in cheese and butter. Remove the skillet from the grill and smooth out the polenta in an even layer.

7.   In a large glass measuring cup or mixing bowl, combine the turkey, enchilada sauce, black beans, corn and Blackened Sriracha.

8.   Spoon the turkey mixture over the polenta, then top with 4 ounces of shredded cheese. Place on the grill, over indirect heat and bake for 20 to 25 minutes, until the filling is bubbling along the edge and the cheese is melted.

9.   Remove the skillet from the grill and allow it to rest for 10 minutes. Serve warm, garnished with avocado, scallions, jalapeño, and fresh cilantro.

Smo-fried Chicken

Servings: 4-6
Cooking Time: 55 Minutes

Ingredients:

- 1 egg, beaten
- ½ cup milk
- 1 cup all-purpose flour
- 2 tablespoons salt
- 1 tablespoon freshly ground black pepper
- 2 teaspoons freshly ground white pepper
- 2 teaspoons cayenne pepper
- 2 teaspoons garlic powder
- 2 teaspoons onion powder
- 1 teaspoon smoked paprika
- 8 tablespoons (1 stick) unsalted butter, melted
- 1 whole chicken, cut up into pieces

Directions:

1.   Supply your smoker with wood pellets and follow the start-up procedure. Preheat, with the lid closed, to 375°F.

2.   In a medium bowl, combine the beaten egg with the milk and set aside.

3.   In a separate medium bowl, stir together the flour, salt, black pepper, white pepper, cayenne, garlic powder, onion powder, and smoked paprika.

4.   Line the bottom and sides of a high-sided metal baking pan with aluminum foil to ease cleanup.

5.   Pour the melted butter into the prepared pan.

6.   Dip the chicken pieces one at a time in the egg mixture, and then coat well with the seasoned flour. Transfer to the baking pan.

7.   Smoke the chicken in the pan of butter ("smo-fry") on the grill, with the lid closed, for 25 minutes, then reduce the heat to 325°F and turn the chicken pieces over.

8.   Continue smoking with the lid closed for about 30 minutes, or until a meat thermometer inserted in the thickest part of each chicken piece reads 165°F.

9.   Serve immediately.

The Grilled Chicken Challenge

Servings: 4
Cooking Time: 60 Minutes

Ingredients:

- 1 (4 lb) whole chicken
- Chicken Rub

Directions:

1.   Supply your smoker with wood pellets and follow the start-up procedure. Preheat the grill, with the lid closed, to 375° F.

2. Rinse and pat dry the whole chicken (remove and discard giblets, if any). Lightly season the entire chicken, including the cavity with Traeger Chicken Rub (or similar rub of choice).

3. Place the chicken on the grill grate and cook for about 1 hour and 10 minutes. Remove chicken from grill when internal temperature of breast reaches 160℉. The temperature will continue to rise to 165℉ as the chicken rests. Check temperature periodically throughout as cook times will vary based on the weight of the chicken. Grill: 375 ℉ Probe: 160 ℉

4. Allow bird to rest until internal temperature of breast reaches 165℉, 15 to 20 minutes. Enjoy!

Jalapeno Chicken Sliders

Servings: 8-10
Cooking Time: 180 Minutes

Ingredients:

- 3 Pounds Boneless Skinless Chicken Breasts
- 8-10 Slices Cheese Of Choice
- 1/2 Cup Chicken Broth
- Pickled Jalapeños
- 1 Tsp Smoked Infused Sweet Mesquite Jalapeno Sea Salt
- 1/2 Cup Salsa Verde
- 1 Package Slider Buns
- 3 Tablespoons Sweet Heat Rub

Directions:

1. Add the chicken breasts, chicken broth, and salsa verde to a disposable aluminum foil pan. Season everything generously with Sweet Heat and 1 tsp of   Smoked Infused Sweet Mesquite Jalapeno Sea Salt. Cover tightly with aluminum foil.

2. Supply your smoker with wood pellets and follow the start-up procedure. Preheat the grill, with the lid open, to 275° F. Place the aluminum foil pan on the grill and cook for 3-4 hours, or until the chicken is completely cooked (165°F internal temperature), tender, and falling apart. Remove from the grill and let cool slightly.

3. Shred the chicken with the meat claws and toss with the Sweet Heat rub. Then, build the sliders: top the slider buns with a scoop of the pulled chicken, a slice cheese, and a few slices of pickled jalapeños. Serve immediately.

Smoked Chicken Leg & Thigh Quarters

Servings: 6
Cooking Time: 120 Minutes

Ingredients:

- 8 chicken legs (thigh and drumstick)
- 3 Tablespoon olive oil
- Pork & Poultry Rub

Directions:

1. Place the chicken pieces in a large mixing bowl. Pour oil over the chicken to coat each piece, then season to taste with the Traeger Pork & Poultry Rub. Massage the chicken pieces to encourage the oil and seasonings get under the skin. Cover and refrigerate for at least 1 to 2 hours.

2. Supply your smoker with wood pellets and follow the start-up procedure. Preheat the grill, with the lid closed, to 180° F.

3. Remove the chicken from the refrigerator, letting any excess oil drip back into the bowl. Grill: 180 ℉

4. Arrange the chicken on the grill grate and smoke for 1 hour. Increase Traeger temperature to 350℉ and continue to roast the chicken until the internal temperature in the thickest part of a thigh is 165℉ or the chicken is golden brown and the juices run clear, about 50 to 60 minutes. Grill: 350 ℉ Probe: 165 ℉

5. Remove from the grill and allow the chicken to rest for 8 to 10 minutes and serve. Enjoy!

Peanut Butter Chicken Wings

Servings: 4
Cooking Time: 35 Minutes

Ingredients:

- 1 Tsp Black Peppercorns, Ground
- 2 Tbsp Brown Sugar
- 4 Lbs Chicken Wings, Trimmed And Patted Dry
- 2 Tbsp Honey
- 1/4 Cup Peanut Butter
- 10 Oz Peanuts, Whole
- 2 Tsp Sweet Rib Rub
- 1/2 Red Onion, Minced
- 1/2 Cup Strawberry Preserves
- 1 Tbsp Thai Chili Sauce
- 1/4 Cup Worcestershire Sauce

Directions:

1. Place chicken wings in a 9 x13 glass baking dish. Pour mixture over chicken, cover with plastic wrap, and refrigerate for 2 hours.

2. Supply your smoker with wood pellets and follow the start-up procedure. Preheat the grill, with the lid open, to 400° F. Preheat griddle to medium-low flame. If using a gas or charcoal grill, set it to medium-high heat.

3. Place wings directly on grill grate, over indirect heat, and cook for 20 to 25 minutes, rotating wings every 5 minutes.

4. Meanwhile, place shelled peanuts on the griddle, turning occasionally with a metal spatula for 5 to 7 minutes, to lightly roast. Remove from the griddle and set aside to cool.

5. Remove wings from grill and allow to rest for 5 minutes. While wings are resting, shell the peanuts, and transfer to a resealable plastic bag. Use a rolling pin to crush the peanuts, then scatter peanuts on top of the chicken wings. Serve warm.

Smoked Spatchcocked Cornish Game Hens

Servings: 2
Cooking Time: 45 Minutes

Ingredients:
- 4 Cornish game hens
- 2 Ounce Big Game Rub

Directions:
1.   Place the game hen breast side down on a cutting board. Using poultry shears, cut from the neck to the tailbone to remove the backbone.
2.   Once backbone is removed, you will be able to see the inside of the bird. Make a small slit in the cartilage at the base of the breastbone to reveal the keel bone. Grab the bird with both hands on the ribs and open like a book, facing down towards the cutting board. Remove the keel bone. Cut small slits in the skin of the bird behind the legs and tuck the drumsticks into them to hold them in place.
3.   Season on both sides with Traeger Big Game Rub.
4.   Supply your smoker with wood pellets and follow the start-up procedure. Preheat the grill, with the lid closed, to 275° F.
5.   Place the game hens on the Traeger skin side up and cook until internal temperature reaches 160°F (about 45 minutes). Grill: 275 °F Probe: 160 °F
6.   Remove from Traeger and place on a cutting board; tent with foil. Let stand 10 minutes, then serve. Enjoy!

Spatchcocked Chicken With White Barbecue Sauce

Servings: 4
Cooking Time: 60 Minutes

Ingredients:
- 1 whole chicken, about 4 to 4½lb (1.8 to 2kg), preferably organic or farm raised
- extra virgin olive oil
- White Barbecue Sauce
- chopped fresh chives (optional)
- for the brine
- ½ gallon (1.9 liters) distilled water
- ½ cup kosher salt
- 2 tbsp light brown sugar or low-carb substitute
- for the rub
- ¼ cup coarse salt
- ¼ cup granulated light brown sugar or low-carb substitute
- ¼ cup sweet or smoked paprika
- 2 tbsp freshly ground black pepper
- 1 tbsp granulated garlic
- 2 tsp dried thyme
- ½ tsp ground cayenne

Directions:
1.   In a large stockpot on the stovetop over medium-high heat, make the brine by combining the ingredients. Bring the mixture to a boil. Stir until the salt and sugar dissolve. Remove the pot from the stovetop and let the brine cool to room temperature. Cover and refrigerate until cool.
2.   Remove the backbone of the chicken by using a sharp knife, starting at the tail and cutting through the rib bones. Repeat on the other side of the backbone. Fold the two halves backward to release the cartilaginous breastbone. (You might have to use a knife to slice through the thin skin on either side.) Remove the breastbone. Turn the chicken over and gently flatten it with the palm of your hand. Submerge the chicken in the brine. If it floats, place a resealable bag of ice on top. Refrigerate for 4 to 6 hours.
3.   Supply your smoker with wood pellets and follow the start-up procedure. Preheat the grill, with the lid closed, to 325° F.
4.   In a small bowl, make the rub by combining the ingredients.
5.   Rinse the chicken with cold running water and dry with paper towels. (Discard the brine.) Coat the skin with olive oil. Lightly dust the chicken on both sides with the rub. (Save the remainder for another grill session.) Tuck the wingtips behind the chicken's back.
6.   Place the chicken ribs side down on the grate and grill until the skin is nicely browned and the internal temperature in a thigh reaches 170°F (77°C), about 1 hour.
7.   Transfer the chicken to a platter. Spoon the white barbecue sauce over the chicken. Spread the sauce with a basting brush, letting it pool in places. Lightly scatter the chives over the top. Carve the chicken and serve with extra sauce on the side.

Wild West Wings

Servings: 4
Cooking Time: 60 Minutes

Ingredients:
- 2 pounds chicken wings
- 2 tablespoons extra-virgin olive oil
- 2 packages ranch dressing mix (such as Hidden Valley brand)
- ¼ cup prepared ranch dressing (optional)

Directions:
1.   Supply your smoker with wood pellets and follow the start-up procedure. Preheat, with the lid closed, to 350°F.
2.   Place the chicken wings in a large bowl and toss with the olive oil and ranch dressing mix.
3.   Arrange the wings directly on the grill, or line the grill with aluminum foil for easy cleanup, close the lid, and smoke for 25 minutes.

4. Flip and smoke for 20 to 35 minutes more, or until a meat thermometer inserted in the thickest part of the wings reads 165°F and the wings are crispy. (Note: The wings will likely be done after 45 minutes, but an extra 10 to 15 minutes makes them crispy without drying the meat.)

5. Serve warm with ranch dressing (if using).

Jamaican Jerk Chicken Quarters

Servings: 4
Cooking Time: 120 Minutes

Ingredients:
- 4 chicken leg quarters, scored
- ¼ cup canola oil
- ½ cup Jamaican Jerk Paste
- 1 tablespoon whole allspice (pimento) berries

Directions:
1. Supply your smoker with wood pellets and follow the start-up procedure. Preheat, with the lid closed, to 275°F.
2. Brush the chicken with canola oil, then brush 6 tablespoons of the Jerk paste on and under the skin. Reserve the remaining 2 tablespoons of paste for basting.
3. Throw the whole allspice berries in with the wood pellets for added smoke flavor.
4. Arrange the chicken on the grill, close the lid, and smoke for 1 hour to 1 hour 30 minutes, or until a meat thermometer inserted in the thickest part of the thigh reads 165°F.
5. Let the meat rest for 5 minutes and baste with the reserved jerk paste prior to serving.

Roasted Honey Bourbon Glazed Turkey

Servings: 8
Cooking Time: 240 Minutes

Ingredients:
- 1 Whole (18-20 lb) turkey
- 1/4 Cup Fin & Feather Rub
- 1/2 Cup bourbon
- 1/2 Cup honey
- 1/4 Cup brown sugar
- 3 Tablespoon apple cider vinegar
- 1 Tablespoon Dijon mustard
- salt and pepper

Directions:
1. Supply your smoker with wood pellets and follow the start-up procedure. Preheat the grill, with the lid closed, to 375° F. Truss the turkey legs together. Season the exterior of the bird and the cavity with Traeger Fin and Feather Rub.

2. Place the turkey directly on the grill grate and cook for 20-30 minutes at 375°F or until the skin begins to brown. Grill: 375 °F
3. After 30 minutes, reduce the temperature to 325°F and continue to cook until internal temperature registers 165°F when an instant read thermometer is inserted into the thickest part of the breast, about 3-4 hours. Grill: 325 °F Probe: 165 °F
4. For the Whiskey Glaze: Combine all ingredients in a small saucepan and bring to a boil. Reduce the temperature and let simmer 15-20 minutes or until thick enough to coat the back of a spoon. Remove from heat and set aside.
5. During the last ten minutes of cooking, brush the glaze on the turkey while on the grill and cook until the glaze is set, about 10 minutes. Remove from grill and let rest 10-15 minutes before carving. Enjoy! *Cook times will vary depending on set and ambient temperatures.

Smoked Turkey Breast

Servings: 2-4
Cooking Time: 120 Minutes

Ingredients:
- 1 (3-pound) turkey breast
- Salt
- Freshly ground black pepper
- 1 teaspoon garlic powder

Directions:
1. Supply your smoker with wood pellets and follow the start-up procedure. Preheat the grill, with the lid closed, to 180°F.
2. Season the turkey breast all over with salt, pepper, and garlic powder.
3. Place the breast directly on the grill grate and smoke for 1 hour.
4. Increase the grill's temperature to 350°F and continue to cook until the turkey's internal temperature reaches 170°F. Remove the breast from the grill and serve immediately.

Lemon Cajun Chicken Carbonara

Servings: 2
Cooking Time: 20 Minutes

Ingredients:
- 2 Slices Thick-Cut Bacon
- 1 Tbsp Cajun Seasoning
- 8 Oz. Chicken Breast
- 4 Egg, Yolk
- 1 Tbsp Garlic Clove, Minced
- 1 ¼ Cup Heavy Cream
- 2 Tbsp + 1 Tbsp Divided Italian Parsley
- 1 ½ Tbsp Divided Olive Oil
- ½ Cup Grated Parmesan Cheese

- ½ Tbsp Hickory Bacon Seasoning
- ¼ Tbsp Red Chili Flakes
- 1 Tbsp Scallions
- ½ Lb. Spaghetti

Directions:

1. Supply your smoker with wood pellets and follow the start-up procedure. Preheat the grill, with the lid open, to 400° F. If using a gas or charcoal grill, set the temp to medium-high heat. In a medium bowl, combine chicken, Hickory Bacon Seasoning, Cajun seasoning, and ½ tablespoon of olive oil. Toss to combine. Set aside or place in a bag and marinate in the refrigerator for 30 minutes to 1 hour.

2. Place tenders on preheated grill and cook for 3 minutes per side. Remove from grill and place on a cutting board to rest for 5 minutes. Slice thinly on the diagonal and set aside.

3. In a large stock pot, boil pasta per package instructions. Drain and set aside.

4. In a large skillet heat 1 tablespoon of oil over medium heat. Sauté bacon, stirring frequently, for 3 minutes or until crisp. Add garlic and cook for one minute. Lower heat to low and add in drained pasta. Using tongs, gently toss pasta to coat in oil and bacon.

5. In a mixing bowl, whisk together heavy cream, parmesan, egg yolks, and 2 tablespoons of parsley. Slowly pour over pasta, continuously stirring, as to not scramble eggs. After 2 minutes, the sauce will thicken. Add in chicken and lemon zest, and gently stir another minute. Transfer to serving dishes and garnish with additional parsley and red chili flakes.

Jalapeño- & Cheese-stuffed Chicken

Servings: 4
Cooking Time: 30 Minutes

Ingredients:

- 4 boneless, skinless chicken breasts, each about 6 to 8oz (170 to 225g)
- 8 strips of thin-sliced bacon
- for the filling
- 4oz (110g) light cream cheese, at room temperature
- ⅓ cup shredded pepper Jack or Cheddar cheese
- 2 jalapeños, destemmed, deseeded, and minced
- 2 tbsp reduced-fat mayo
- 1 tsp chili powder
- ½ tsp coarse salt

Directions:

1. Supply your smoker with wood pellets and follow the start-up procedure. Preheat the grill, with the lid closed, to 375° F.

2. In a large bowl, make the filling by combining the ingredients. Mix well.

3. Use a sharp, thin-bladed knife to cut a deep pocket in the side of each chicken breast, angling the knife toward the opposite side. (Don't cut all the way through.) Spoon ¼ of the cheese filling into the pocket of each breast and gently press the edges of the pocket together to enclose. Wrap 2 slices of bacon in a spiral pattern around each breast.

4. Place the chicken on the grate at an angle to the bars. Grill until the chicken is cooked through, the filling melts, and the bacon is golden brown, about 25 to 30 minutes.

5. Transfer the pockets to a platter. Let rest for 2 minutes before serving.

Loaded Chicken Fries

Servings: 4
Cooking Time: 20 Minutes

Ingredients:

- 8 Slices Bacon, Cooked And Diced
- 1 12 Oz Bag Cheese, Shredded
- 1 Bag Fries, Frozen
- 2 Tablespoons Green Onions, Diced
- ¼ Cup White Barbecue Sauce

Directions:

1. Supply your smoker with wood pellets and follow the start-up procedure. Preheat the grill, with the lid open, to 400° F.

2. Bake the fries on the baking sheet in your according to the manufacturer's instructions. Once the fries are done, remove them from the grill and reduce the temperature to 350°F.

3. Top the fries with the cheese, chicken and bacon. Place the fries back on the grill and cook for another 5-7 minutes, or until the chicken is warmed through and the cheese is melted. Remove the fries from the grill.

4. Top the fries with the white barbecue sauce and green onions and serve immediately.

Savory-sweet Turkey Legs

Servings: 4
Cooking Time: 300 Minutes

Ingredients:

- 1 gallon hot water
- 1 cup curing salt (such as Morton Tender Quick)
- ¼ cup packed light brown sugar
- 1 teaspoon freshly ground black pepper
- 1 teaspoon ground cloves
- 1 bay leaf
- 2 teaspoons liquid smoke
- 4 turkey legs
- Mandarin Glaze, for serving

Directions:

1. In a large container with a lid, stir together the water, curing salt, brown sugar, pepper, cloves, bay leaf, and liquid smoke until the salt and sugar are dissolved; let come to room temperature.
2. Submerge the turkey legs in the seasoned brine, cover, and refrigerate overnight.
3. When ready to smoke, remove the turkey legs from the brine and rinse them; discard the brine.
4. Supply your smoker with wood pellets and follow the start-up procedure. Preheat, with the lid closed, to 225°F.
5. Arrange the turkey legs on the grill, close the lid, and smoke for 4 to 5 hours, or until dark brown and a meat thermometer inserted in the thickest part of the meat reads 165°F.
6. Serve with Mandarin Glaze on the side or drizzled over the turkey legs.

Bacon Wrapped Turkey Legs

Servings: 8
Cooking Time: 180 Minutes

Ingredients:
- 1 Gallon water
- 1/4 Cup Rub
- 3 Cup Morton Tender Quick Home Meat Cure
- 1/2 Cup brown sugar
- 6 Whole black peppercorns
- 2 Whole bay leaves
- 8 (1-1/2 lb each) turkey legs
- 8 Slices bacon

Directions:
1. Plan ahead, these turkey legs brine overnight. In a large stockpot, combine one gallon of water, Traeger Rub, curing salt, brown sugar, peppercorns and bay leaves.
2. Bring to a boil over high heat to dissolve the salt and sugar granules. Take off of the heat and add in 1/2 gallon of water and ice. Make sure the brine is at least to room temperature, if not colder. (You may need to refrigerate the brine for an hour or so.)
3. Add the turkey legs making sure they are completely submerged in the brine.
4. After 24 hours, drain the turkey legs and discard the brine. Rinse the brine off the legs with cold water, then dry thoroughly with paper towels.
5. Supply your smoker with wood pellets and follow the start-up procedure. Preheat the grill, with the lid closed, to 250° F.
6. Lay the turkey legs directly on the grill grate.
7. After 2-1/2 hours, wrap a piece of bacon around each leg and finish cooking them for the last 30 to 40 minutes. Grill: 250 °F
8. The total cooking time for the legs will be 3 hours, or until the internal temperature reaches 165°F on an instant-read meat thermometer. Serve and enjoy! Grill: 250 °F Probe: 165 °F

Green Chile Chicken Enchiladas

Servings: 6
Cooking Time: 45 Minutes

Ingredients:
- 2 Cups Chicken, Shredded
- 1 (12 Oz) Package Colby Jack Cheese, Shredded
- 1 Enchilada Sauce, Can
- 1 Can Green Chile, Drained
- 1 Onion, Diced
- 1 Tablespoon Sweet Rib Rub
- 1 Cup Sour Cream
- 1 Package Flour Tortilla

Directions:
1. Supply your smoker with wood pellets and follow the start-up procedure. Preheat the grill, with the lid open, to 300° F.
2. In a bowl, mix - the chicken, green chiles, Sweet Heat seasoning, sour cream, diced onion, and half the bag of shredded cheese.
3. Place a large spoonful of the chicken mixture in the center of a tortilla and roll it up. Repeat with the remaining tortillas, then place in the baking pan, and pour the enchilada sauce over the tortilla pans. Top with the remainder of the shredded cheese.
4. Wrap the top of the pan tightly in aluminum foil and grill for 45 minutes or until the enchilada sauce is bubbly. Remove from the grill and serve.

Sweet And Spicy Smoked Wings

Servings: 2-4
Cooking Time: 85 Minutes

Ingredients:
- 1 pound chicken wings
- 1 batch Sweet and Spicy Cinnamon Rub
- 1 cup barbecue sauce

Directions:
1. Supply your smoker with wood pellets and follow the start-up procedure. Preheat the grill, with the lid closed, to 325°F.
2. Season the chicken wings with the rub. Using your hands, work the rub into the meat.
3. Place the wings directly on the grill grate and cook until they reach an internal temperature of 165°F.
4. Transfer the wings into an aluminum pan. Add the barbecue sauce and stir to coat the wings.
5. Reduce the grill's temperature to 250°F and put the pan on the grill. Smoke the wings for 1 hour more, uncovered. Remove the wings from the grill and serve immediately.

Smoked Turkey Legs

Servings: 4
Cooking Time: 300 Minutes

Ingredients:

- 1 Cup Rub
- 1/2 Cup Morton Tender Quick Home Meat Cure
- 1/2 Cup brown sugar
- 1 Tablespoon crushed allspice berries, optional
- 1 Tablespoon grains de poivre noir entiers
- 2 bay leaves
- 2 Teaspoon liquid smoke
- 4 turkey legs

Directions:

1. In a large stockpot, combine one gallon of warm water, the rub, curing salt, brown sugar, allspice (if using), peppercorns, bay leaves and liquid smoke.
2. Bring to a boil over high heat to dissolve the salt granules. Cool to room temperature. Add 1/2 gallon cold water and 4 cups ice; chill in the refrigerator.
3. Add the turkey legs, making sure they're completely submerged in the brine. After 24 hours, drain the turkey legs and discard the brine.
4. Rinse the brine off the legs with cold water, then dry thoroughly with paper towels. Brush off any clinging solid spices.
5. Supply your smoker with wood pellets and follow the start-up procedure. Preheat the grill, with the lid closed, to 250° F.
6. Lay the turkey legs directly on the grill grate.
7. Smoke for 4-5 hours, or until the internal temperature reaches 165°F on an instant-read meat thermometer. Make sure the probe doesn't touch bone or you'll get a false reading. Grill: 250 °F Probe: 165 °F
8. The turkey legs should be deeply browned. Don't be alarmed if the meat under the skin is pinkish: that's a chemical reaction to the cure and the smoke.
9. Serve immediately. Enjoy!

Bell Pepper Chicken Sliders

Servings: 5
Cooking Time: 20 Minutes

Ingredients:

- 16 Oz Chicken, Ground
- 1 Pepper, Anaheim
- Jalapeno Brat Burger Seasoning
- 1 Red Bell Peppers
- Spinach

Directions:

1. Supply your smoker with wood pellets and follow the start-up procedure. Preheat the grill, with the lid closed, to 400° F.
2. Put the ground chicken into a bowl and generously add the Jalapeno Brat Burger seasoning to the mixture.
3. Dice the Anaheim pepper and add it to the bowl as well.
4. Mix with your hands until the meat looks evenly coated.
5. Separate the meat out into 3oz balls, disperse or toss the remnants.
6. Use the 3-in-1 Burger press to create the perfect patty! If your chicken is too sticky to use the burger press, we put the 3oz balls into a tinfoil covered pan and placed that on the grill. Allow to cook 20-25 minutes, do not flip.
7. Add the buns to the grill if you'd like them toasted!
8. Remove the chicken sliders (and the buns) from the grill, add spinach, red peppers and whatever else you enjoy!

Kansas City Hot Fried Chicken

Servings: 4
Cooking Time: 25 Minutes

Ingredients:

- 1 Whole Chicken, cut into pieces
- 1 1/2 Cup buttermilk
- 2 Tablespoon hot sauce
- 4 Cup all-purpose flour
- 1 Teaspoon salt
- 1/2 Teaspoon black pepper
- 1/2 Tablespoon red pepper flakes
- 12 Ounce Bacon, Uncooked, Chopped
- vegetable oil

Directions:

1. Supply your smoker with wood pellets and follow the start-up procedure. Preheat the grill, with the lid closed, to 180° F.
2. Smoke the 4 pieces of chicken for about 10 min. Grill: 180 °F
3. Mix buttermilk and hot sauce together in a large bowl, keep mixture ultra chilled.
4. In a separate bowl, mix the dry ingredients and bacon together, set aside.
5. Remove chicken and place in ice-cold buttermilk mixture for about an hour in the refrigerator.
6. Heat Vegetable Oil in a frying pan to 370°F (195 C).
7. Remove chicken from the liquid and batter it in dry ingredient mixture, drop into frying oil for about 10-15 minutes.
8. Serve with pickled hot peppers. Enjoy!

Chicken Egg Rolls With Buffalo Sauce

Servings: 4
Cooking Time: 75 Minutes

Ingredients:

- 1/4 Cup Bleu Cheese, Crumbled
- 1/4 Cup Buffalo Sauce

- 1 Lb Chicken Breasts - Boneless, Skinless
- 4 Oz Cream Cheese, Softened
- 8 Egg Roll Wrappers
- 1/2 Jalapeno Pepper, Minced
- Pinch   Sweet Heat Rub
- 1/4 Red Bell Pepper, Chopped
- 4 Scallion, Sliced Thin
- 1/4 Cup Sour Cream
- 2 Cups Vegetable Oil

Directions:

1.   Supply your smoker with wood pellets and follow the start-up procedure. Preheat the grill, with the lid open, to 200° F. If using a gas or charcoal grill, set it up for low, indirect heat.

2.   Season chicken breasts with   Sweet Heat Rub, then place on the grill. Smoke for 1 hour, then remove from the grill, cool, shred, and set aside.

3.   Prepare the filling: In a mixing bowl, use a hand mixer to blend cream cheese, bleu cheese, Buffalo sauce and sour cream.

4.   Fold in scallions, jalapeño, red bell pepper, and shredded chicken.

5.   Prepare egg rolls: Lay an egg roll wrapper on a flat surface and add 3 tablespoons of filling to the middle.

6.   Fold the bottom of the wrapper over the top of the filling, then fold over each side. Brush the top point of the wrapper with warm water, then roll the wrapper tight. Transfer to a tray while filling the remaining wrappers.

7.   Increase the temperature of the grill to 425°F, then set a cast iron Dutch oven on the grill. Add vegetable oil and heat for 5 minutes.

8.   Place 3 egg rolls in heated oil and fry until golden, 1 to 2 minutes per side.

9.   Transfer to a wire rack to cool, then fry the remaining egg rolls, in batches.

10.   Cool egg rolls for 2 minutes, then slice in half and serve warm with celery sticks and extra Buffalo sauce for dipping.

Bbq Cheese Chicken Stuffed Bell Peppers

Servings: 4

Cooking Time: 15 Minutes

Ingredients:

- ½ Cup Barbecue Sauce
- 4 Bell Pepper
- ½ Cup Cheddar Cheese, Shredded
- 2 Cups Leftover Chicken, Chopped
- 2 Tablespoons Champion Chicken Seasoning

Directions:

1.   Wash and slice the bell peppers in half, long ways. Deseed them and set aside.

2.   Supply your smoker with wood pellets and follow the start-up procedure. Preheat the grill, with the lid open, to 350° F.

3.   In a large bowl, mix together the cheese, chicken, Champion Chicken Seasoning, and barbecue sauce, then stuff inside the pepper halves.

4.   Grill the peppers for 7-10 minutes or until the peppers are softened and the filling is heated through and melted. Remove from the grill and serve.

Savory Smoked Turkey Legs

Servings: 4

Cooking Time: 150 Minutes

Ingredients:

- 1 Cup Chicken Stock
- 2 Tbsp Blackened Sriracha Rub
- 4 Turkey Legs (Drumsticks)

Directions:

1.   Fire up your   pellet grill on SMOKE mode. With the lid open, let it run for 10 minutes.

2.   Supply your smoker with wood pellets and follow the start-up procedure. Preheat the grill, with the lid closed, to 225° F. If using a gas or charcoal grill, set it up for low, indirect heat.

3.   Combine turkey stock with 2 teaspoons of   Blackened Sriracha Rub.

4.   Place turkey legs on a sheet tray, then inject each with seasoned stock. Season the outside of the legs with remaining Blackened Sriracha.

5.   Place turkey legs directly on the grate of the smoking cabinet, and cook for 1 ½ hours.

6.   Increase temperature to 325°F, then transfer turkey legs to the bottom grill and cook for another 45 to 60 minutes, until the internal temperature reaches 170°F.

7.   Remove turkey from the grill, allow to rest for 10 minutes, then serve warm.

Roasted Christmas Goose

Servings: 8

Cooking Time: 120 Minutes

Ingredients:

- 5 1/2 Pound Goose
- 2 lemons
- 2 limes
- 2 Teaspoon salt
- 2 thyme sprigs
- 2 sage sprigs
- 1 Medium Apple, green

- 3 Tablespoon honey

Directions:

1. Supply your smoker with wood pellets and follow the start-up procedure. Preheat the grill, with the lid closed, to High heat.

2. Lightly score the breast and leg skin in a criss-cross pattern. This will help the fat to render down more quickly during cooking.

3. Grate the lemon and limes. Mix citrus zest with 2 teaspoons fine sea salt. Cut the lemons and lime into wedges.

4. Season cavity of the goose generously with salt, then rub the citrus mix well into the skin and sprinkle some inside the cavity.

5. Stuff goose with sage, thyme, lemons, limes and apples wedges. Place goose directly on the grill grate and cook for 40 minutes. Brush goose with honey and reduce temperature to 325°F.

6. Cook for 1-1/2 to 2 hours or until an instant read thermometer inserted in the thickest part of the breast reads 160°F. Grill: 325 °F Probe: 160 °F

7. Remove from grill, tent with foil and allow to rest for 30 minutes. Final internal temperature should be 165°F in the thickest part of the breast. Enjoy!

Easy Bbq Chicken Wings

Servings: 4
Cooking Time: 40 Minutes

Ingredients:
- 1 Pack Chicken Wings
- Extra Virgin Olive Oil
- Champion Chicken Seasoning

Directions:

1. Supply your smoker with wood pellets and follow the start-up procedure. Preheat the grill, with the lid closed, to 350° F.

2. Blot the defrosted chicken wings dry with paper towels.

3. Brush oil onto each side of the wings and sprinkle with seasoning.

4. Grill at 350° for 40 minutes or until wings are crispy. Flip halfway through. Serve hot.

Cheese Buffalo Chicken Wings

Servings: 4-6
Cooking Time: 25 Minutes

Ingredients:
- Bleu Cheese Dip
- ⅔ Cup Buffalo Sauce
- Celery
- 2 Lbs. Chicken Wings
- ½ Cup Sweet Heat Rub

Directions:

1. Supply your smoker with wood pellets and follow the start-up procedure. Preheat the grill, with the lid open, to 450° F. If using a gas or charcoal grill, set heat to high heat.

2. Rub wings generously with Sweet Heat Rub and transfer to wing rack.

3. Place rack on grill and cook for 20 minutes, rotating after 10 minutes.

4. Baste with sauce, then cover and grill an additional 5 to 7 minutes. Note: your cooking time will vary depending on the size of the wings. When done, wings should have an internal temperature of 165°F.

5. Remove wings from grill and transfer to a baking sheet and let rest for about 5 minutes.

6. Transfer wings to a large bowl and coat with the Buffalo Sauce. Shake the bowl around gently to combine or use a spatula to ensure every wing is coated.

7. Serve hot with extra sauce, celery, and bleu cheese dip.

Smoked Turkey Wings

Servings: 2
Cooking Time: 60 Minutes

Ingredients:
- 4 turkey wings
- 1 batch Sweet and Spicy Cinnamon Rub

Directions:

1. Supply your smoker with wood pellets and follow the start-up procedure. Preheat the grill, with the lid closed, to 180°F.

2. Using your hands, work the rub into the turkey wings, coating them completely.

3. Place the wings directly on the grill grate and cook for 30 minutes.

4. Increase the grill's temperature to 325°F and continue to cook until the turkey's internal temperature reaches 170°F. Remove the wings from the grill and serve immediately.

Big Game Roast Chicken

Servings: 4
Cooking Time: 60 Minutes

Ingredients:
- 1 whole chicken
- Big Game Rub

Directions:

1. Supply your smoker with wood pellets and follow the start-up procedure. Preheat the grill, with the lid closed, to 375° F.

2. Remove the neck and gizzards from the cavity of the bird. Rinse and wipe the outside and inside of the chicken with a paper towel. Tie chicken legs together with butcher twine and tuck wings.

3. Apply an even coat of the Traeger Big Game Rub to the inside and outside of the chicken.

4. Place chicken on the grill grate and cook for 60 minutes. After an hour, check the temperature of the bird in the thickest part of the leg. The temperature needs to be between 165 and 180°F. Check every 15 minutes if not up to temperature. When the leg reaches desired internal temperature, check the temperature of the breast. The breast needs to reach an internal temperature of 165°F before it is done. Grill: 375 °F Probe: 165 °F

5. Let bird rest for 15 to 20 minutes for slicing. Enjoy!

Juicy Jerk Chicken Kebabs

Servings: 4
Cooking Time: 12 Minutes

Ingredients:
- 1 Tablespoon All Spice, Ground
- 2 Lbs Chicken, Boneless/Skinless
- 1 Tablespoon Cinnamon, Ground
- 1/4 Cup Extra-Virgin Olive Oil
- 3 Garlic, Cloves
- 2 Inch Piece Ginger, Fresh
- 3 Green Onion
- 1 Lime, Juiced
- 1 Tablespoon Nutmeg, Ground
- 1 Cup Orange Juice, Fresh
- Pepper
- 1 Red Onion, Chopped
- Salt
- Skewers
- 1/4 Cup Soy Sauce
- 1/4 Cup Thyme, Fresh Sprigs

Directions:
1. Soak the bamboo skewers in water for about 30 minutes (the longer the better).
2. In a food processor, combine orange juice, oil, soy sauce, thyme, allspice, nutmeg, cinnamon, garlic, onions, ginger, lime juice, salt and pepper. Puree until smooth.
3. In a large resealable bag, pour all but 1/4 cup of the mixture in along with the sliced up chicken breasts. Seal the bag and marinate in the fridge for 2 - 3 hours.
4. Supply your smoker with wood pellets and follow the start-up procedure. Preheat the grill, with the lid open, to 450° F. Skewer the chicken and grill for about 7 minutes. Flip and continue grilling for about 5 minutes, or until the chicken is cooked through and grill marks appear. Serve with the remaining 1/4 cup of marinade.

Onion Turkey Burger Sliders

Servings: 5
Cooking Time: 30 Minutes

Ingredients:
- 1 Sweet Onion, Chopped
- 1 Pepper, Anaheim
- Bacon Cheddar Burger Seasoning
- Spinach
- 16 Oz Turkey, Ground

Directions:
1. Supply your smoker with wood pellets and follow the start-up procedure. Preheat the grill, with the lid closed, to 400° F.
2. Put the ground turkey into a bowl and generously add the Bacon Cheddar Burger seasoning to the mixture.
3. Dice the Anaheim pepper and add it to the bowl as well.
4. Dice about 1/3 of the sweet onion and add it to the bowl.
5. Mix with your hands until the meat looks evenly coated in seasoning and the veggies are evenly mixed.
6. Separate the meat out into 3oz balls, disperse or toss the remnants.
7. Use the 3-in-1 Burger press to create the perfect patty! Place the patties on the grill and cook for 15-20 minutes depending on their thickness. Flip every 5ish minutes.
8. Add the buns to the grill if you'd like them toasted!
9. Remove the turkey sliders (and the buns) from the grill, add spinach, and whatever you think will taste good!

Applewood-smoked Whole Turkey

Servings: 6-8
Cooking Time: 300 Minutes

Ingredients:
- 1 (10- to 12-pound) turkey, giblets removed
- Extra-virgin olive oil, for rubbing
- ¼ cup poultry seasoning
- 8 tablespoons (1 stick) unsalted butter, melted
- ½ cup apple juice
- 2 teaspoons dried sage
- 2 teaspoons dried thyme

Directions:
1. Supply your smoker with wood pellets and follow the start-up procedure. Preheat, with the lid closed, to 250°F.
2. Rub the turkey with oil and season with the poultry seasoning inside and out, getting under the skin.
3. In a bowl, combine the melted butter, apple juice, sage, and thyme to use for basting.
4. Put the turkey in a roasting pan, place on the grill, close the lid, and grill for 5 to 6 hours, basting every hour, until the skin is brown and crispy, or until a meat thermometer inserted in the thickest part of the thigh reads 165°F.
5. Let the bird rest for 15 to 20 minutes before carving.

Smoked Cheesy Chicken Quesadilla

Servings: 4-8

Cooking Time: 180 Minutes

Ingredients:

- 2-3 Boneless, Skinless Chicken Breasts
- 1 Jalapeno, Chopped
- 1 Onion, Chopped
- Sweet Heat Rub
- 1, Chopped Red Bell Pepper
- 1-2 Cups Salsa
- 3 Cups Shredded Cheddar Cheese
- 3 Cups Shredded Monterey Or Pepper Jack Cheese
- Taco Sauce
- 20 Taco-Size Tortilla

Directions:

1. Supply your smoker with wood pellets and follow the start-up procedure. Preheat the grill, with the lid closed, to 350° F. If you're using a gas or charcoal grill, set it up for medium heat. Preheat with lid closed for 10-15 minutes.

2. Sprinkle chicken breasts generously in Sweet Heat Rub and rub to coat evenly. Place chicken breasts directly on preheated grill grates and cook for 45 minutes, or until the chicken is completely cooked (165°F internal temperature), tender, and falling apart. Remove from the grill and let cool slightly. Shred with meat claws and set aside. Turn grill up to 375°F.

3. In a large bowl, add the shredded chicken, onion, red bell pepper, jalapeno, and taco sauce. Mix to combine then set aside.

4. Cut each tortilla in half. Add about 2 tablespoons each of the cheddar cheese, Monterey Jack cheese, and chicken mixture to each tortilla half. Roll the tortillas into cones, starting from the cut edge, making sure not to push the ingredients out of the tortilla.

5. Place the small bowl in the center of the pizza plan and begin to stack quesadilla cones in a ring around the bowl. The points of each cone should be in the center just touching the bowl. Sprinkle cheese over the layer and repeat another layer with the remaining cones, finishing with a final sprinkle of cheese.

6. Remove bowl from the center of the ring and place the pizza pan directly on the grill grates. Cook with the lid closed for 15-20 minutes, or until the cheese is melted and the edges are browned and crispy.

7. Fill small bowl with salsa and return to the center of the ring. Serve immediately and enjoy!

Roasted Beer Can Chicken

Servings: 4

Cooking Time: 60 Minutes

Ingredients:

- 1 Whole (3-5 lb) chicken
- Chicken Rub
- 1 Can beer

Directions:

1. Season chicken generously with Traeger Chicken Rub, including inside the cavity.

2. Tuck the wing tips back.

3. Supply your smoker with wood pellets and follow the start-up procedure. Preheat the grill, with the lid closed, to 350° F.

4. Open the can of beer and set the chicken on top of the beer. Make sure all but the bottom 1-1/2 inch of the beer can is in the cavity of the chicken. Tip: you can also place the beer can directly on the grill grates, then place the chicken on top.

5. Place the entire chicken and beer can directly on the grill grate. Cook for 60 to 75 minutes, or until the internal temperature registers 165°F in the thickest part of the breast. Grill: 350 °F Probe: 165 °F

6. Remove from the grill and onto a sheet tray and let rest 5 to 10 minutes. Before carving, lay the bird on its back and remove the beer can. Carve and enjoy!

Chicken Cordon Bleu Rollups

Servings: 8

Cooking Time: 30 Minutes

Ingredients:

- 4 boneless, skinless chicken breasts, each about 6 to 8oz (170 to 225g)
- garlic salt
- freshly ground black pepper
- 8 thin slices of Swiss cheese
- 8 thin slices of deli ham or prosciutto
- 4 tbsp unsalted butter, melted
- minced fresh parsley or chives

Directions:

1. Supply your smoker with wood pellets and follow the start-up procedure. Preheat the grill, with the lid closed, to 400° F.

2. Place each chicken breast between two sheets of plastic wrap and pound with a meat mallet or a rolling pin until each breast is ¼ inch (.5cm) thick. Place the breasts smooth side down on a workspace and lightly season with garlic salt and pepper. Top each breast with 2 slices of cheese and 2 slices of ham. Roll up the breasts and secure them with toothpicks that have been coated with vegetable oil. Brush the outside of the breasts with butter and lightly season with garlic salt and pepper.

3. Place the chicken rollups on the grate at an angle to the bars. Smoke for 25 to 30 minutes.

4. Transfer the rollups to a platter and let rest for 3 minutes. Remove the toothpicks. Scatter parsley over the top before serving.

Bbq Game Day Chicken Wings And Thighs

Servings: 6
Cooking Time: 50 Minutes

Ingredients:
- 10 chicken thighs
- 30 chicken wings
- 1/2 Cup olive oil
- 1/2 Cup Chicken Rub

Directions:
1. Place thighs and wings in a large bowl. Add the olive oil and Traeger Chicken Rub and mix well. Cover bowl and refrigerate for 3 to 8 hours.
2. Supply your smoker with wood pellets and follow the start-up procedure. Preheat the grill, with the lid closed, to 375° F.
3. Place chicken directly on the grill grate and cook for 45 minutes. Check the internal temperature of the chicken, it is considered done at 165°F, however, a finished temperature of 175 to 180°F results in a better texture in dark meat. Grill: 375 °F Probe: 165 °F
4. Once the finished temperature is reached, remove chicken from the grill and let rest for 5 to 10 minutes before serving. Enjoy!

Grilled Beantown Chicken Wings

Servings: 8
Cooking Time: 50 Minutes

Ingredients:
- 3 Pound chicken wings
- 1/4 Cup vegetable oil
- 1 1/2 Tablespoon Pork & Poultry Rub
- 1 Cup Irish Stout
- 1/2 Cup butter
- 2 Tablespoon apple jelly
- 1 Cup Frank's RedHot Sauce

Directions:
1. Rinse the chicken wings under cold running water and pat dry. With a sharp knife, cut the wings into three pieces through the joints. Discard the wing tips, or save for chicken stock.
2. Transfer the remaining "drumettes" and "flats" to a large a bowl. Add the oil and the Traeger Pork and Poultry shake, and toss with your hands to coat the wings evenly.
3. Make the beer sauce: In a small saucepan, bring the beer to a boil over high heat and reduce by half. Reduce the heat to medium-low and add the butter, stirring until melted. Stir in the apple jelly and the hot sauce. Keep warm.
4. Supply your smoker with wood pellets and follow the start-up procedure. Preheat the grill, with the lid closed, to 350° F.
5. Arrange the wings on the grill grate. Cook for 45 to 50 minutes, or until the chicken is no longer pink at the bone, turning once halfway through. Transfer the wings to a large clean bowl and pour the beer sauce over the wings, tossing to coat. Serve immediately. Grill: 350 °F

Gen's Old-fashioned Barbecued Chicken

Servings: 6
Cooking Time: 90 Minutes

Ingredients:
- 2 whole chickens, each about 4 to 4½lb (1.8 to 2kg)
- 6 tbsp unsalted butter, melted
- seasoned salt
- low-carb barbecue sauce

Directions:
1. Supply your smoker with wood pellets and follow the start-up procedure. Preheat the grill, with the lid closed, to 350° F.
2. Cut each chicken into 8 pieces: 2 wings, 2 breasts, 2 legs, 2 thighs. Rinse under cold running water and pat dry with paper towels. Place on a rimmed sheet pan. Brush with butter and season with seasoned salt.
3. Place the chicken skin side down on the grate and grill for 30 minutes. Turn and continue to grill until the internal temperature in the thickest part of a breast or a thigh reaches 165°F (74°C), about 45 minutes to 1 hour. During the last 10 minutes, brush the chicken with barbecue sauce.
4. Transfer the chicken to a platter. Serve with additional barbecue sauce.

Bbq Chicken Breasts

Servings: 6
Cooking Time: 25 Minutes

Ingredients:
- 6 boneless, skinless chicken breast
- 1 1/2 Cup Sweet & Heat BBQ Sauce
- salt and pepper
- 1 Tablespoon chopped parsley, for garnish

Directions:
1. Place chicken breasts and 1 cup of Traeger Sweet & Heat BBQ Sauce in a resealable bag or large bowl, and gently turn to cover chicken evenly in the sauce. Marinate in the refrigerator overnight.
2. Supply your smoker with wood pellets and follow the start-up procedure. Preheat the grill, with the lid closed, to 450° F.
3. Remove chicken from marinade and season with salt and pepper.

4.   Place chicken directly on the grill grate and cook for 10 minutes on each side flipping once or until internal temperature reaches 150°F.

5.   Brush on remaining 1/2 cup of Traeger Sweet & Heat BBQ Sauce while chicken is still on the grill, and continue to cook 5 to 10 minutes longer or until a finished internal temperature of 165°F.

6.   Remove chicken from grill and let rest 5 minutes before serving. Sprinkle with chopped parsley. Enjoy!

Lemon Chicken Breast

Servings: 6
Cooking Time: 15 Minutes

Ingredients:

- 1 Clove garlic, coarsely chopped
- 2 Teaspoon honey
- 2 Teaspoon kosher salt
- 1 Teaspoon freshly ground black pepper
- 2 Sprig fresh thyme leaves
- 1 lemon, zest and juice
- 1/2 Cup high-quality olive oil or vegetable oil
- 6 (6 oz) boneless, skinless chicken breasts
- 1 lemon, cut into wedges, for serving

Directions:

1.   To make the marinade, add the garlic, honey, salt, pepper, thyme, lemon juice and zest to a small mixing bowl. Whisk until the salt crystals and honey dissolve. Slowly whisk in the olive oil.

2.   Place the chicken breast in a large resealable plastic bag and pour the marinade over them, massaging the bag to distribute the marinade evenly.

3.   Refrigerate for 4 hours.

4.   Supply your smoker with wood pellets and follow the start-up procedure. Preheat the grill, with the lid closed, to 400° F.

5.   Drain the chicken breasts and discard the marinade.

6.   Arrange the chicken breasts directly on the grill grate and cook until the internal temperature reaches 165°F. Grill: 400 °F Probe: 165 °F

7.   If desired, grill the reserved lemon wedges alongside the chicken, cut sides down, for 15 minutes.

8.   Serve the chicken on a platter or plates with the lemon wedges.

Smoked Quarters

Servings: 2-4
Cooking Time: 120 Minutes

Ingredients:

- 4 chicken quarters
- 2 tablespoons olive oil
- 1 batch Chicken Rub
- 2 tablespoons butter

Directions:

1.   Supply your smoker with wood pellets and follow the start-up procedure. Preheat the grill, with the lid closed, to 180°F.

2.   Coat the chicken quarters all over with olive oil and season them with the rub. Using your hands, work the rub into the meat.

3.   Place the quarters directly on the grill grate and smoke for 1½ hours.

4.   Baste the quarters with the butter and increase the grill's temperature to 375°F. Continue to cook until the chicken's internal temperature reaches 170°F.

5.   Remove the quarters from the grill and let them rest for 10 minutes before serving.

Yucatán-spiced Chicken Thighs

Servings: 4
Cooking Time: 40 Minutes

Ingredients:

- 8 skin-on, bone-in chicken thighs, about 2½lb (1.2kg) total
- for the marinade
- 2oz (55g) achiote paste
- ¼ cup hot distilled water
- ¼ cup freshly squeezed orange juice
- 2 tbsp freshly squeezed lime juice
- 2 tbsp apple cider vinegar or distilled white vinegar
- 2 tbsp vegetable oil or extra virgin olive oil
- 2 garlic cloves, peeled and minced
- 1 tsp kosher salt, plus more
- 1 tsp dried Mexican oregano
- ½ tsp ground cumin
- ¼ tsp ground cinnamon

Directions:

1.   In a small bowl, make the marinade by using a fork to crumble the achiote paste. Add the hot water and mash the paste with the fork until blended. Whisk in the orange juice, lime juice, vinegar, oil, garlic, salt, oregano, cumin, and cinnamon.

2.   Place the chicken thighs in a resealable plastic bag. Pour the marinade over the chicken, turning and massaging the bag to thoroughly coat the chicken. Refrigerate for 2 hours.

3.   Supply your smoker with wood pellets and follow the start-up procedure. Preheat the grill, with the lid closed, to 400° F.

4.   Remove the chicken thighs from the marinade and let any excess drip off. (Discard the marinade.) Place the chicken thighs skin side down on the grate at an angle to the bars. Grill for 20 minutes and then turn. Continue to grill until the internal temperature in the thighs reaches 165°F (74°C), about 20 minutes more.

5.   Transfer the thighs to a platter and serve immediately.

Grilled Parmesan Chicken Wings

Servings: 4
Cooking Time: 25 Minutes

Ingredients:

- 4 Tbsp Butter
- 4 Lbs Chicken Wings, Trimmed And Patted Dry
- 4 Garlic Cloves, Chopped
- 2 Tbsp Olive Oil
- 1/2 Cup Parmesan Cheese, Grated
- 2 Tbsp Parsley, Chopped
- Champion Chicken Seasoning

Directions:

1. Lay chicken wings out on a sheet tray, blot with paper towel, then season with Champion Chicken.

2. Supply your smoker with wood pellets and follow the start-up procedure. Preheat the grill, with the lid open, to 400° F. If using a gas or charcoal grill, set it up for medium-high heat.

3. Transfer wings to grill and cook for 20 to 25 minutes, turning every 5 minutes, until lightly browned. Remove wings from the grill and set on a sheet tray. Place in the smoking cabinet to keep warm while preparing the garlic butter.

4. Melt butter and olive oil in a cast iron skillet, then add garlic and simmer until fragrant. Remove from the grill.

5. Transfer chicken wings to a large bowl and pour garlic butter over the wings. Add cheese and parsley, then toss well to coat. Serve warm with additional sprinkling of parmesan cheese.

Buffalo Wings

Servings: 2-3
Cooking Time: 35 Minutes

Ingredients:

- 1 pound chicken wings
- 1 batch Chicken Rub
- 1 cup Frank's Red-Hot Sauce, Buffalo wing sauce, or similar

Directions:

1. Supply your smoker with wood pellets and follow the start-up procedure. Preheat the grill, with the lid closed, to 300°F.

2. Season the chicken wings with the rub. Using your hands, work the rub into the meat.

3. Place the wings directly on the grill grate and smoke until their internal temperature reaches 160°F.

4. Baste the wings with the sauce and continue to smoke until the wings' internal temperature reaches 170°F.

Marinated Grilled Honey Chicken Wings

Servings: 4-6

Cooking Time: 30 Minutes

Ingredients:

- 1/2 Bottle Beer, Any Brand
- 2 Lbs Chicken Wings, Whole
- 2 Tablespoon Honey
- 1 Tablespoon   Sweet Heat Rub
- 2 Tablespoon Rice Wine Vinegar
- 1/2 Tablesoon Sesame Oil
- 1/4 Cup Soy Sauce
- 1 Tablespoon Sriracha Hot Sauce

Directions:

1. In a large glass or plastic bowl, combine the beer, soy sauce, honey, rice wine vinegar, sriracha, sesame oil and   Sweet Heat Seasoning. Whisk well to combine.

2. Add the chicken wings to the marinade and toss well to combine. Cover with plastic wrap and refrigerate for 2 hours and up to 24 hours.

3. Remove chicken wings from refrigerator, drain marinade and pat dry. Supply your smoker with wood pellets and follow the start-up procedure. Supply your smoker with wood pellets and follow the start-up procedure. Preheat the grill, with the lid open, to 350° F. Place the wings on a grill pan and grill for 20-25 minutes, or until the wings' internal temperature is 165F. Remove from the grill, serve and enjoy!

Smoked Turkey

Servings: 6
Cooking Time: 420 Minutes

Ingredients:

- 1 (12-16 lb) fresh or frozen turkey, thawed, giblets removed
- 1 Cup Rub
- 1 1/2 Tablespoon minced garlic
- 1 Cup sugar
- 1/2 Cup Worcestershire sauce
- 2 Tablespoon canola oil

Directions:

1. Ensure the turkey is fully thawed and remove any giblets. Pour 3 gallons of water in a 5 gallon non-metal bucket.

2. Add Traeger rub, garlic, sugar, and Worcestershire sauce and mix until sugars are completely dissolved.

3. Place the turkey, breast side down, into the bucket with the brine. Make sure the turkey is completely submerged.

4. Cover bucket and place in refrigerator overnight.

5. Remove turkey from brine and pat dry. Rub canola oil over entire outside of turkey and place breast side up into disposable aluminum roasting pan.

6. Supply your smoker with wood pellets and follow the start-up procedure. Preheat the grill, with the lid closed, to 225° F.

7. Place the turkey on the grill and smoke for 2 1/2 to 3 hours Grill: 180 ˚F

8. Increase grill temperature to 350˚F and cook for 3-1/2 to 4 hours, or until the internal temperature reaches 165˚F in the thickest part of the breast. Grill: 350 ˚F Probe: 165 ˚F

9. Remove from grill and allow to rest for 30 minutes before carving. Enjoy!

Cheesy Buffalo Chicken Pinwheels

Servings: 8
Cooking Time: 10 Minutes

Ingredients:
- 2 T Bleu Cheese, Crumbled
- ½ Cup Buffalo Wing Sauce, Divided
- 1-2, Boneless And Skinless Chicken Breast
- ½ Cup Colby Cheese, Shredded
- 4 Oz. Cream Cheese
- 4, 10” Diameter Flour Tortillas
- 2 Scallions, Thinly Sliced [Reserve 1 Tsp Of Green For Garnish]

Directions:
1. Supply your smoker with wood pellets and follow the start-up procedure. Preheat the grill, with the lid closed, to 375° F. If you're using a gas or charcoal grill, set it up for medium heat. Remove chicken from refrigerator place on grill. Grill chicken for 10 min, turning once. Allow to rest 10 minutes, then shred.

2. In a food processor, add remaining buffalo wing sauce, cream cheese, Colby cheese, bleu cheese, and scallions. Process on low for 20 seconds. Add shredded chicken breast to mixture and pulse about 8 times, or until mixture is fully combined.

3. Place tortillas on a flat work surface and divide filling into quarters. Spread mixture evenly over each tortilla with a rubber spatula.

4. Roll up tortillas and place seam side down on cutting board. Refrigerate for 10 minutes, then slice into ½ inch pieces. Transfer to serving platter and garnish with remaining scallions. Serve with extra buffalo sauce or ranch dressing.

Apricot Glazed Ham

Servings: 8
Cooking Time: 60 Minutes

Ingredients:
- 1 Cup Apricot Preserves
- 1/2 Cup apricot brandy
- 1/4 Cup honey
- 1/4 Cup brown sugar, firmly packed
- 1/4 Teaspoon ground cloves
- 6 Ounce Apricot Nectar, bottled or ginger ale
- 1 Large ham
- fresh parsley
- apricot, halved

Directions:
1. Supply your smoker with wood pellets and follow the start-up procedure. Preheat the grill, with the lid closed, to 325° F.

2. In a saucepan, stir together the apricot preserves, apricot brandy, honey, brown sugar, cloves, and apricot nectar and simmer over medium heat until the preserves, honey, and brown sugar have melted. Set aside and keep warm.

3. Place ham in large roasting pan lined with aluminum foil. Place pan on grill and cook for 1.5 hours.

4. Open Grill and glaze ham with reserved mixture. Continue cooking for another 30 minutes or until a thermometer is inserted into the thickest part of the meat and reaches an internal temperatures of 135 degrees F. Probe: 135 ˚F

5. Garnish the platter with the parsley and apricots, if desired. Enjoy!

Whole Smoked Honey Chicken

Servings: 4
Cooking Time: 40 Minutes

Ingredients:
- 1 Tablespoon Honey
- 1 ½ Lemon
- 4 Tablespoons Champion Chicken Seasoning
- 4 Tablespoons Unsalted Butter
- 1, 4 Pound Chicken, Giblets Removed And Patted Dry

Directions:
1. Supply your smoker with wood pellets and follow the start-up procedure. Preheat the grill, with the lid open, to 225° F.

2. In a small saucepan, melt together the butter and honey over low heat. Squeeze ½ lemon into the honey mixture and remove from the heat.

3. Smoke the chicken, skin side down until the chicken is lightly browned and the skin releases from the grate without ripping, about 6-8 minutes.

4. Turn the chicken over and baste with the honey butter mixture.

5. Continue to smoke the chicken, basting every 45 minutes, until the thickest part of the chicken reaches 160°F.

Smoked Thanksgiving Turkey

Servings: 6 - 8
Cooking Time: 300 Minutes

Ingredients:
- 1 Turkey Brining Kits
- 12 – 14 Lbs Turkey
- 1 Gallon Water, Cold
- 4 Cups + 1 Gallon Water, Warm

Directions:
1. Start by defrosting the turkey overnight in the refrigerator.
2. Once turkey has been defrosted begin to make the brine by adding 4 cups of water and the brine mixture to a large stockpot.
3. Bring the mixture to a boil and add 1 gallon of cold water.
4. Place the turkey in the brine bag and pour the brine mixture over the turkey and refrigerate 1 hour per pound.
5. Once turkey has been brined rinse the turkey with cold water and set on a pan.
6. Using the seasoning in the brine box, season the turkey. Once turkey has been seasoned, supply your smoker with wood pellets and follow the start-up procedure. Preheat the grill, with the lid closed, to 275° F.
7. Place your turkey in the smoker and place the temperature probe in the deepest part of the breast. Cook at 275 until the breast and thigh meat internal temperature has reached 165°F to 170°F.
8. Remove the turkey from the smoker, let cool, and cut the turkey into your desired pieces. Enjoy!

Cider-brined Turkey

Servings: 8
Cooking Time: 180 Minutes

Ingredients:
- 1 whole turkey, about 12 to 14lb (4.5 to 5.4kg), thawed if frozen
- 1 white onion, peeled and sliced into quarters
- 1 apple, cut into wedges
- 2 celery stalks, sliced into 2-inch (5cm) pieces
- sprigs of fresh sage, rosemary, parsley, or thyme
- 8 tbsp unsalted butter, at room temperature
- coarse salt
- freshly ground black pepper
- for the brine
- 1 quart (1 liter) apple cider or apple juice
- 3 quarts (3 liters) cold distilled water
- ¾ cup coarse salt
- ½ cup light brown sugar or low-carb substitute
- 3 garlic cloves, peeled and smashed with a chef's knife
- 3 bay leaves

Directions:
1. In a large food-safe bucket, make the brine by combining the apple cider, water, salt, and brown sugar. Stir until the salt and sugar dissolve. Add the garlic and bay leaves. Submerge the turkey in the brine. If it floats, place a resealable bag of ice on top. Refrigerate for at least 8 hours and up to 16 hours.
2. Supply your smoker with wood pellets and follow the start-up procedure. Preheat the grill, with the lid closed, to 350° F.
3. Remove the turkey from the brine and pat dry with paper towels. Discard the brine. Place the onion, apple, celery, and herbs in the main cavity. Tie the legs together with butcher's twine. Fold the wings behind the back. Rub the outside with butter. Lightly season with salt and pepper.
4. Place the turkey breast side up on a wire rack in a shallow roasting pan. Place the pan on the grate and roast the turkey until the internal temperature in the thickest part of a thigh reaches 165°F (74°C), about 2½ to 3 hours.
5. Transfer the turkey to a cutting board and let rest for 20 minutes. (Save the drippings to make from-scratch turkey gravy.) Carve the turkey and arrange the meat on a large platter before serving.

Spiced Bbq Turkey

Servings: 8
Cooking Time: 120 Minutes

Ingredients:
- 1 Bay Leaf
- 1/2 Tsp Black Peppercorns, Ground
- Pinch Chili Flakes
- 4 Garlic Cloves, Peeled And Smashed
- 1/4 Cup Honey
- 3/4 Cup Honey Chipotle Bbq Sauce
- 1 Honeysuckle White® Turkey, Thawed
- 1 Tsp Kosher Salt
- 1/4 Cup Olive Oil
- 3 Thyme Sprigs
- 1 Cup Turkey Stock
- 3 Cups Water
- 2 Tbsp Worcestershire Sauce

Directions:
1. Rinse Honeysuckle White® turkey thoroughly under cold water, then blot dry with paper towels. Place on a greased rack of a roasting pan. Set aside.
2. Prepare the injection solution: in a saucepot, whisk together the turkey stock, honey, olive oil, smashed garlic, Worcestershire sauce, salt, pepper, and chili flakes. Add in the thyme sprigs and bay leaf. Bring mixture to a boil, then simmer for 5 minutes. Remove from heat, cool for 30 minutes, then strain.

3. Using an injection needle, inject the solution throughout the turkey. Rub 1 tablespoon of solution over the top of the turkey. Add water to the bottom of the roasting pan. Set aside.

4. Supply your smoker with wood pellets and follow the start-up procedure. Preheat the grill, with the lid closed, to 450° F. If using a gas or charcoal grill, set it up for high heat.

5. Transfer the turkey to the grill and roast for 100 to 120 minutes, until an internal temperature of 165° F is reached, rotating every 30 minutes. Tent with foil after 30 minutes, then brush all over with BBQ sauce during the final 10 minutes of roasting time.

6. Remove from the grill, and allow the turkey to rest for 30 minutes, then carve and serve warm.

Green Goddess Chicken Legs

Servings: 4
Cooking Time: 40 Minutes

Ingredients:
- 2 Pound chicken legs
- 2 Cup Prepared "Green Goddess" Dressing
- 1/4 Cup parsley, chopped
- 1 Tablespoon paprika

Directions:
1. Place the chicken legs in a large resealable plastic bag. Combine the Green Goddess dressing as well as the parsley and paprika. Pour over the chicken legs. Refrigerate for 2 to 8 hours.

2. Supply your smoker with wood pellets and follow the start-up procedure. Preheat the grill, with the lid closed, to 350° F. Drain the chicken legs. Arrange the legs directly on the grill grate and grill, turning once, for 40 to 50 minutes, or until the legs are golden brown and cooked through. Serve at once. Grill: 350 °F

Roasted Prosciutto Stuffed Chicken

Servings: 2
Cooking Time: 35 Minutes

Ingredients:
- 2 Whole boneless, skinless chicken breast
- salt and pepper
- 2 Tablespoon Dijon mustard
- 2 Slices Prosciutto Ham
- 4 Pieces mozzarella cheese
- 1 Large Tomatoes, sliced
- 4 Large basil leaves
- 2 Tablespoon olive oil
- Toothpicks

Directions:
1. Supply your smoker with wood pellets and follow the start-up procedure. Preheat the grill, with the lid closed, to 225° F.

2. While grill heats up, use a sharp knife to fillet each chicken breast in two. Open up each half, by pounding with a meat tenderizer.

3. Season each breast half with salt and pepper to taste. Rub mustard on both sides. Place a slice of proscuitto on the inside of the breast followed by a slice of mozzarella, a slice of tomato and a basil leaf. Drizzle olive oil on top.

4. Fold chicken breast back in half and secure with toothpicks. Brush outside of stuffed breast with olive oil.

5. Place directly on the grill grate. Cook for 6 to 7 minutes per side, or until chicken reaches an internal temperature of 160 degrees F.

Bbq Pulled Turkey Sandwiches

Servings: 6
Cooking Time: 120 Minutes

Ingredients:
- 6 Whole Turkey Thighs
- Pork & Poultry Rub
- 1 1/2 Cup chicken broth
- 1 Cup 'Que BBQ Sauce
- 6 Whole Kaiser Buns, Split

Directions:
1. Season turkey thighs on both sides with the Traeger Pork & Poultry rub.

2. Supply your smoker with wood pellets and follow the start-up procedure. Preheat the grill, with the lid closed, to 180° F.

3. Arrange the turkey thighs directly on the grill grate and smoke for 30 minutes.

4. Transfer the thighs to a sturdy disposable aluminum foil or roasting pan. Pour the broth around the thighs. Cover the pan with foil or a lid.

5. Increase temperature to 325°F and preheat, lid closed. Roast the thighs until they reach an internal temperature of 180°F. Grill: 325 °F Probe: 180 °F

6. Remove pan from the grill, but leave grill on. Let the turkey thighs cool slightly until they can be comfortably handled.

7. Pour off the drippings and reserve. Remove the skin and discard.

8. Pull the turkey meat into shreds with your fingers and return the meat to the roasting pan.

9. Add 1 cup or more of your favorite Traeger BBQ Sauce along with some of the drippings.

10. Recover the pan with foil and reheat the BBQ turkey on the Traeger for 20 to 30 minutes.

11. Serve with toasted buns if desired. Enjoy!

Easy Grilled Chicken Shawarma

Servings:

Cooking Time: 16 Minutes

Ingredients:

- 2 lbs to 2 ¼ lb chicken thighs
- Shawarma Marinade
- 2 tablespoons ground cumin
- 2 tablespoons ground coriander
- 8 garlic cloves, minced
- 2 teaspoons kosher salt
- 6 tablespoons olive oil
- 1/4 teaspoon cayenne pepper
- 2 teaspoon turmeric
- 1 teaspoon ground ginger
- 1 teaspoon ground black pepper
- 2 teaspoon allspice

Directions:

1. Supply your smoker with wood pellets and follow the start-up procedure. Preheat the grill, with the lid closed, to medium-high heat. Place all marinade ingredients in a bowl and mix, or pulse in a food processor to make a paste.

2. Rub chicken on all sides with the marinade and let sit 20 minutes.

3. Place the chicken on the grill racks, closing the lid to the BBQ, until all sides have nice grill marks, about 8 minutes each side. Move to the warming rack until cooked all the way through, about 10 minutes.

4. Enjoy the chicken shawarma over Israeli salad, or with rice and veggies, or with pita bread and tzatziki.

Fried Chicken Sliders

Servings: 8

Cooking Time: 30 Minutes

Ingredients:

- 8 Slider Buns
- ½ Cup Buttermilk
- 4 Horizontally Cut Chicken Breasts
- 2 Cups Flour, All-Purpose
- 1 Tablespoon Hot Sauce
- ¼ Cup Mayonnaise
- 2 Quarts Cooking Canola Or Soybean Oil
- ½ Cup Spicy Bread And Butter Pickle Slices
- ½ Tablespoon Champion Chicken Seasoning

Directions:

1. Supply your smoker with wood pellets and follow the start-up procedure. Preheat the grill, with the lid open, to 350° F. If you're using a gas or charcoal grill, set it up for medium heat.

2. Place a deep cast iron pan on the grill and fill it with about 3 inches of cooking oil. Place a temperature probe into the oil.

3. While the oil heats, combine the buttermilk, hot sauce and Champion Chicken seasoning in a resealable plastic bag. Seal and shake to mix, then place the chicken in the bag and turn to coat.

4. Place the flour on a plate and dip the chicken in the flour to coat. Place the chicken on a wire rack set on a baking sheet and allow the coated chicken to set for 10 minutes, then dip again in the flour.

5. Once the oil in the cast iron pan reaches 350°F, place a temperature probe in a piece of chicken and fry the chicken, 2-3 pieces at a time. The oil temperature in the pan will drop by 25-30 degrees, so make sure not to put more than 3 pieces of chicken in the pan or your chicken will be greasy.

6. Fry the chicken until golden brown, crispy, and the internal temperature of the chicken is 170°F. Remove the chicken and place on a plate lined with paper towels. Allow the chicken to drain and rest for 5 minutes. Fry the remaining chicken pieces, reinserting the temperature probe.

7. Once the chicken is all fried, place the chicken on the slider buns, top with spicy bread and butter pickles, and a swoop of mayo, serve immediately.

Smoked Chicken Fajita Quesadillas

Servings: 4

Cooking Time: 45 Minutes

Ingredients:

- 2 Chicken, Boneless/Skinless
- 1 Tsp Chilli, Powder
- 1 Tsp Garlic Powder
- 1/2 Green Bell Pepper, Sliced
- 1 Cup Mexican Cheese, Shredded
- 1/2 Onion, Sliced
- 1/2 Tsp Oregano
- 1 Tsp Paprika, Powder
- 1/4 Tsp Pepper
- 1/2 Red Bell Peppers
- Salsa
- Sour Cream
- 4 Tortilla
- 1/2 Yellow Bell Pepper, Sliced

Directions:

1. Supply your smoker with wood pellets and follow the start-up procedure. Preheat the grill, with the lid open, to 350° F.

2. Combine spices in a bowl and season chicken breasts. Leave a little bit of seasoning for the vegetables.

3. Place chicken on the grates and cook for 30 minutes, flipped halfway through.

4.   In a Vegetable Basket, combine all vegetables and season with the remaining spice mixture.

5.   Open up the flame broiler and saute over the open flame for about 15 minutes, or until the vegetables are cooked to your liking.

6.   On a tortilla, layer cheese, vegetables, sliced chicken and more cheese. Fold the tortilla and place over the open flame on your Grill. Sear until the tortilla is nicely toasted and the cheese is melted. Cut and serve with salsa and sour cream.

Smoked Bourbon & Orange Brined Turkey

Servings: 8
Cooking Time: 180 Minutes

Ingredients:
- 1 Orange Brine and Turkey Rub Kit
- 4 Quart water
- 1 Cup bourbon
- 1 (12-14 lb) turkey, fresh or thawed
- 1 Tablespoon butter, melted
- 1 Tablespoon Grand Mariner or other orange-flavored liquor

Directions:
1.   Mix Orange Brine seasoning (from Traeger Orange Brine & Turkey Rub Kit) with one quart of water. Boil for 5 minutes. Remove from heat, add 3 quarts of cold water and bourbon. Refrigerate until completely cooled.

2.   Place turkey breast side down in a large container. Pour cooled brine mix over bird. Add cold water until bird is submerged. Refrigerate for 24 hours.

3.   Remove turkey and discard brine. Blot turkey dry with paper towels.

4.   Combine butter and Grand Marnier and coat outside of turkey. Season outside of turkey with Traeger Turkey Rub (from Orange Brine & Turkey Rub Kit).

5.   Supply your smoker with wood pellets and follow the start-up procedure. Preheat the grill, with the lid closed, to 225° F.

6.   Smoke turkey, breast up, for 2 hours. Grill: 225 °F

7.   Increase grill temperature to 350°F and roast turkey until the internal temperature of the thickest part of the thigh reaches 165F, 2 to 3 hours, depending on size of turkey. Grill: 350 °F Probe: 165 °F

8.   Let rest 20 to 30 minutes before serving. Enjoy!

Lemon Parmesan Chicken Wings

Servings: 4 -8
Cooking Time: 30 Minutes

Ingredients:
- 2 Tablespoons Unsalted Butter, Melted
- 2 Lbs Chicken Wings, Trimmed And Patted Dry
- 3 Cloves Garlic, Minced
- Juice Of 1 Lemon
- 2 Tablespoons Mustard, Dijon
- ¼ Cup Olive Oil
- ¼ Cup Shredded Parmesan Cheese
- 2 Tablespoons Parsley, Chopped
- 2 Tablespoons Champion Chicken Seasoning

Directions:
1.   Supply your smoker with wood pellets and follow the start-up procedure. Preheat the grill, with the lid open, to 350° F. If you are using a charcoal or gas grill, set the temperature to medium high heat.

2.   In a large resealable bag, combine the olive oil, minced garlic, lemon zest, lemon juice, Dijon mustard, Champion Chicken Seasoning, and chopped parsley. Seal the resealable bag and give it a good shake to mix the ingredients.

3.   Once the chicken has finished marinating, remove the chicken from the marinade and drain. Place the chicken wings on the wing rack.

4.   Place the wing rack on the grill and insert a temperature probe into the thickest part of one of the wings. Grill the wings for 5 minutes, then rotate, and grill for another 5-10 minutes, or until the internal temperature of the wings reaches 165°F.

5.   Toss the wings in the large bowl with the melted butter and shredded Parmesan until well coated. Serve immediately.

Bbq Smoked Turkey Jerky

Servings: 4 - 6
Cooking Time: 120 Minutes

Ingredients:
- 2 Tablespoons Apple Cider Vinegar
- 2 Tablespoons (Any Kind) Barbecue Sauce
- 1 Tablespoon Quick Curing Salt
- ½ Cup Soy Sauce
- 4 Tablespoons Sweet Sweet Rib Rub
- 2 Pounds Boneless Skinless Turkey Breast
- ¼ Cup Water

Directions:
1.   In a large bowl, combine the soy sauce, water, barbecue sauce, apple cider vinegar, quick curing salt, and 2 tablespoons of the Sweet Rib Rub. Whisk together until well combined and pour into a large, resealable plastic bag.

2.   Using a sharp knife, slice the turkey into ¼ inch slices with the grain (this is easier if the meat is partially frozen). Trim off any fat, skin or connective tissue and discard.

3.   Place the turkey slices into the plastic bag, seal, and massage the marinade into the turkey. Refrigerate for 24 hours.

4.   Once the jerky is ready to go, remove the turkey from the refrigerator, drain the marinade and discard. Pat the turkey dry

with paper towels and sprinkle all sides generously with the remaining Sweet Rib Rub.

5. Supply your smoker with wood pellets and follow the start-up procedure. Preheat the grill, with the lid closed, to 180° F. If you're using a sawdust or charcoal smoker, set it up for medium low heat.

6. Place the turkey slices directly onto the smoker grates and smoke for 2-4 hours, or until the jerky is chewy but still bends slightly.

7. Transfer the jerky to a resealable plastic bag while the jerky is still warm and allow it to sit at room temperature for 1 hour. Squeeze any air from the bag and place in the refrigerator. It will keep for several weeks.

Garlic Sriracha Buffalo Chicken Wings

Servings: 6-8
Cooking Time: 160 Minutes

Ingredients:
- 1 Cup Buffalo Sauce
- 6 Lbs Chicken Wings
- 2 Tbsp Garlic Powder
- 1 Tsp Pepper
- Divided By 2 Tbsp And ½ Tbsp   Sweet Heat Rub
- 1 Tsp Salt
- ⅓ Cup, Divided Sriracha Sauce

Directions:
1. In a non-stick sauce pot, add the remaining Sriracha and buffalo sauce. Stir to combine and set aside.
2. Supply your smoker with wood pellets and follow the start-up procedure. Preheat the grill, with the lid open, to 250° F. If using a gas or charcoal grill, set it to low heat with indirect heat. Place marinated wings directly on grill grate and cook (covered) for 1 hour 15 minutes.
3. Flip wings and baste each piece with Sriracha sauce. Season with additional   Sweet Heat Rub, cover, and continue to grill for an additional 1 hour 15 minutes.
4. Remove wings from grill and place on sheet tray. Baste with additional sauce, then open Sear Slide and return wings to the grill. Grill for 3-5 minutes, rotating often, until wings begin to char lightly.
5. Transfer wings to a serving tray, baste with remaining sauce and serve!

Traeger Mandarin Wings

Servings: 2
Cooking Time: 30 Minutes

Ingredients:

- 1 Bottle (12 oz) mandarin orange sauce
- Beef Rub
- Chicken Rub
- 2 Pound chicken wings, flats and drumettes separated

Directions:
1. Coat chicken wings with mandarin sauce. Sprinkle Traeger Beef Rub and Traeger Chicken Rub onto wings. Marinate for at least 30 minutes.
2. Supply your smoker with wood pellets and follow the start-up procedure. Preheat the grill, with the lid closed, to 350° F.
3. Place wings directly on the grill grate and cook for 30 minutes. Enjoy! Grill: 350 °F Probe: 165 °F

Grilled Honey Chicken Kabobs

Servings: 4
Cooking Time: 14 Minutes

Ingredients:
- 1 pound boneless skinless chicken breasts (cut into 1 inch pieces)
- 1/4 cup olive oil
- 1/3 cup soy sauce
- 1/4 cup honey
- 1 teaspoon minced garlic
- salt and pepper to taste
- 1 red bell pepper (cut into 1 inch pieces)
- 1 yellow bell pepper (cut into 1 inch pieces)
- 2 small zucchini (cut into 1 inch slices)
- 1 red onion (cut into 1 inch pieces)
- 1 tablespoon chopped parsley

Directions:
1. In a large bowl combine the olive oil, soy sauce, honey, garlic and salt and pepper, and whisk.
2. Add the chicken, bell peppers, zucchini and red onion to the bowl,tossing to thoroughly coat.
3. Cover and refrigerate for 1 to 8 hours.
4. Soak wooden skewers in cold water for at least 30 minutes. Supply your smoker with wood pellets and follow the start-up procedure. Preheat the grill, with the lid closed, to high heat.
5. Thread the chicken and vegetables onto the skewers.
6. Cook for 5-7 minutes on each side or until chicken is cooked through.
7. To serve, sprinkle with parsley. Enjoy!

Asian Chicken Sliders

Servings: 4
Cooking Time: 10 Minutes

Ingredients:

- 1½lb (680g) ground chicken, preferably a mix of breast and thigh meat
- 1 large egg, beaten
- ½ cup panko breadcrumbs or crushed chicharróns
- 2 scallions, trimmed, white and green parts finely minced
- 2 garlic cloves, peeled and finely minced
- ¼ cup loosely packed minced cilantro leaves
- 2 tbsp sambal oelek
- 1 tbsp light soy sauce
- 2 tsp peeled and minced fresh ginger
- 1 tsp coarse salt
- 1 tsp freshly ground black pepper
- vegetable oil
- for serving
- 8 slider buns
- reduced-fat mayo
- fresh baby arugula or spinach leaves
- pickled onions (optional)

Directions:

1. Supply your smoker with wood pellets and follow the start-up procedure. Preheat the grill, with the lid closed, to 450° F.
2. In a large bowl, combine all the ingredients except the vegetable oil. Wet your hands with cold water. Knead the mixture until it's somewhat sticky and the ingredients are incorporated. Form the mixture into 8 equal-sized patties. Lightly oil the patties on both sides with the oil.
3. Place the patties on the grate and grill until the internal temperature reaches 165°F (74°C), about 4 to 5 minutes per side.
4. Transfer each patty to the bottom half of each bun. Top with a dollop of mayo, a few arugula or spinach leaves, and drained pickled onions (if using). Top each slider with the top half of the bun. Run a knotted bamboo skewer through the top of each slider before serving.

Spatchcocked Turkey

Servings: 10-14
Cooking Time: 120 Minutes

Ingredients:

- 1 whole turkey
- 2 tablespoons olive oil
- 1 batch Chicken Rub

Directions:

1. Supply your smoker with wood pellets and follow the start-up procedure. Preheat the grill, with the lid closed, to 350°F.
2. To remove the turkey's backbone, place the turkey on a work surface, on its breast. Using kitchen shears, cut along one side of the turkey's backbone and then the other. Pull out the bone.
3. Once the backbone is removed, turn the turkey breast-side up and flatten it.

4. Coat the turkey with olive oil and season it on both sides with the rub. Using your hands, work the rub into the meat and skin.
5. Place the turkey directly on the grill grate, breast-side up, and cook until its internal temperature reaches 170°F.
6. Remove the turkey from the grill and let it rest for 10 minutes, before carving and serving.

Bbq Chicken Tostada

Servings: 4
Cooking Time: 50 Minutes

Ingredients:

- 4 Whole boneless, skinless chicken thighs
- salt and pepper
- 8 Whole Corn Tostada
- Refried Beans
- lettuce
- green onion, coarsely chopped
- cilantro, chopped
- guacamole

Directions:

1. Supply your smoker with wood pellets and follow the start-up procedure. Preheat the grill, with the lid closed, to 350° F.
2. While grill heats, trim excess fat and skin from chicken thighs.
3. Season with a light layer of salt and pepper.
4. Place chicken thighs on the grill grate and cook for 35 minutes.
5. Check internal temperature; chicken is done when a thermometer inserted reads 175 degrees F. Remove from the grill and let rest for 10 minutes before shredding.
6. Place tostadas on grill while chicken is resting for 5 minutes.
7. Build tostadas starting with refried beans, sliced lettuce, shredded chicken, tomatoes, green onions, cilantro, guacamole. Enjoy!

Asian Bbq Chicken

Servings: 4
Cooking Time: 60 Minutes

Ingredients:

- 1 Whole whole chicken
- Asian BBQ Rub
- 1 Whole ginger ale

Directions:

1. Rinse chicken in cold water and pat dry with paper towels. Cover the chicken all over with Traeger Asian BBQ rub; make sure to drop some in the inside too. Place in large bag or bowl and cover and refrigerate for 12 to 24 hours.

2. Supply your smoker with wood pellets and follow the start-up procedure. Preheat the grill, with the lid closed, to 375° F.

3. Open your can of ginger ale and take a few big gulps. Set the can of soda on a stable surface. Take the chicken out of the fridge and place the bird over top of the soda can. The base of the can and the two legs of the chicken should form a sort of tripod to hold the chicken upright.

4. Stand the chicken in the center of your hot grate and cook the chicken till the skin is golden brown and the internal temperature is about 165°F on a instant-read thermometer, approximately 40 minutes to 1 hour.

5. De-throne chicken. Enjoy!

County Fair Turkey Legs

Servings: 4
Cooking Time: 90 Minutes

Ingredients:
- 4 turkey legs, each about 1lb (450g)
- for the brine
- ½ gallon (1.9 liters) distilled water
- ½ cup kosher salt
- ¼ cup light brown sugar or low-carb substitute
- 2½ tsp pink curing salt #1
- 1 tsp liquid smoke (optional)

Directions:
1. In a stockpot on the stovetop over medium-high heat, make the brine by combining the ingredients. Bring the mixture to a boil. Stir until the salts and sugar dissolve. Remove the pot from the stovetop and let the brine cool to room temperature. Cover and refrigerate until cool.

2. Submerge the turkey legs in the brine. If they float, place a resealable bag of ice on top. Refrigerate for 24 hours, turning from time to time so the legs cure evenly.

3. Supply your smoker with wood pellets and follow the start-up procedure. Preheat the grill, with the lid closed, to 325° F.

4. Remove the turkey legs from the brine and discard the liquid. Rinse the legs under cold running water and pat dry with paper towels.

5. Place the turkey legs on the grate and grill for 45 minutes. Turn and continue to cook until the turkey skin is nicely browned and the internal temperature in a leg reaches 170 to 175°F (77 to 79°C), about 45 minutes. (Turkey legs have a lot of connective tissue and they seem to turn out better when cooked to a slightly higher temperature.)

6. Remove the legs from the grill and serve warm or cold.

Injected Drunken Smoked Turkey Legs

Servings: 4
Cooking Time: 30 Minutes

Ingredients:
- 1 Bottle Frank's RedHot Sauce
- 1/2 Cup butter
- 1 Cup brown sugar
- 1/2 Cup whiskey or bourbon
- 3 Clove garlic, minced
- 1 Teaspoon Cajun seasoning
- 1/2 Cup chicken stock
- 6 Large turkey legs

Directions:
1. In a large pot, mix together all ingredients except the turkey legs. Bring to a boil. Let cool and pour the marinade into a resealable bag, then add in the turkey legs. Allow them to marinate for 24 hours in the fridge.

2. Remove the turkey legs from the bag, saving the marinade.

3. Bring half of marinade to a boil and reserve for basting.

4. Dilute the other half of marinade with chicken stock. Fill the meat injector with the marinade/chicken stock mixture and insert it into the meaty parts of the turkey leg in several places. Inject turkey legs with marinade until they plump up.

5. Supply your smoker with wood pellets and follow the start-up procedure. Preheat the grill, with the lid closed, to 250° F.

6. Place the turkey legs on the grill grate and cook for 1-1/2 to 3 hours, depending on the thickness of the legs, or until the internal temp registers 165°F on an instant-read thermometer. Baste the legs with the reserved, boiled marinade every 45 minutes. Enjoy! Grill: 250 ˚F Probe: 165 ˚F

Smoked Whole Chicken

Servings: 6-8
Cooking Time: 240 Minutes

Ingredients:
- 1 whole chicken
- 2 cups Tea Injectable (using Not-Just-for-Pork Rub)
- 2 tablespoons olive oil
- 1 batch Chicken Rub
- 2 tablespoons butter, melted

Directions:
1. Supply your smoker with wood pellets and follow the start-up procedure. Preheat the grill, with the lid closed, to 180°F.

2. Inject the chicken throughout with the tea injectable.

3. Coat the chicken all over with olive oil and season it with the rub. Using your hands, work the rub into the meat.

4. Place the chicken directly on the grill grate and smoke for 3 hours.

5. Baste the chicken with the butter and increase the grill's temperature to 375°F. Continue to cook the chicken until its internal temperature reaches 170°F.

6. Remove the chicken from the grill and let it rest for 10 minutes, before carving and serving.

Smoked Ditch Chicken

Servings: 2
Cooking Time: 60 Minutes

Ingredients:
- 3 pheasant breasts or quarters
- Blackened Saskatchewan Rub
- 3 Tablespoon Smoky Okie's Rooster Booster Poultry Seasoning
- 1 white onion
- 1 red bell pepper
- 4 Tablespoon olive oil
- salt and pepper
- 1 Box Uncle Ben's Ready Rice Pilaf

Directions:
1. Supply your smoker with wood pellets and follow the start-up procedure. Preheat the grill, with the lid closed, to 275° F.
2. Clean and rinse pheasant breasts and thighs; place in a large resealable bag.
3. Add a liberal amount of Traeger Blackened Saskatchewan Rub and Rooster Booster. Shake vigorously and set aside.
4. Slice the onions into thin sections. Quarter the peppers, removing the core.
5. Brush onions and peppers lightly with olive oil and lightly apply salt and pepper.
6. Place the vegetables on tin foil on one side of the grill. Give the vegetables an ample head start on the pheasant (at least an hour), as pheasant is lean and will cook quickly.
7. After allowing the vegetables to smoke for at least an hour, place the pheasant on the grill, keeping the grill at 275°F. Cook for 30 to 45 minutes. Remove the pheasant and vegetables from the grill and serve over a bed of rice pilaf. Enjoy! Grill: 275 °F

Cranberry Turkey Breast

Servings: 6
Cooking Time: 90 Minutes

Ingredients:
- 1 Bay Leaf
- 1/2 Tsp Black Pepper
- 3 Tbsp Butter, Divided
- 1 Celery Rib, Chopped
- To Taste, Cracked Black Pepper
- 4 Oz Cremini Mushrooms
- 1/2 Cup Dried Cranberries
- 2 Garlic Cloves, Minced
- 1 Package, Approx 2Lbs Honeysuckle White Turkey Breast, Boneless
- 1/2 Cup Marsala Wine
- 1 Tbsp Olive Oil
- 1 Rosemary Sprigs
- 1/2 Tsp Rubbed Sage
- 1/2 Tsp Salt
- To Taste, Sea Salt
- 6 Oz Stuffing Mix
- 1 1/4 Cup Turkey Stock, Divided
- 1 Yellow Onion, Chopped

Directions:
1. Supply your smoker with wood pellets and follow the start-up procedure. Preheat the grill, with the lid closed, to 325° F. If using a gas or charcoal grill, set it up for medium-low heat.
2. Melt the butter 1 tablespoon of butter and olive oil in a large skillet over medium heat. Add the onions and celery and cook, stirring frequently, until soft, 3 minutes.
3. Add the garlic and mushrooms and continue to cook for 5 minutes, until the mushrooms are slightly browned.
4. Deglaze with marsala wine, using a wooden spoon to scrape up any browned bits from the bottom of the pan.
5. Add the dried cranberries, black pepper, sage, and salt and simmer for 2 minutes, then remove from the heat.
6. Fold the stuffing into the vegetable mixture, then slowly pour over turkey stock, until stuffing is moistened.
7. Place the Honeysuckle White® Turkey Breast on a large cutting board, skin-side down, then butterfly it. Season with salt and pepper, then spoon over ⅓ of the stuffing, leaving an inch border.
8. Roll the turkey breast, starting at the side with less skin. Use butcher's twine to truss the turkey breast and secure the stuffing. Place in a cast iron skillet, top remaining butter, season with salt and pepper. Place a sprig of rosemary on top, add remaining ¼ cup of stock around the turkey, along with 1 bay leaf. Transfer to the grill.
9. Cook the turkey for 1 to 1 ½ hours, until an internal temperature of 165°F is reached.
10. Remove stuffed turkey breast from the grill, rest for 15 minutes, then slice and serve warm, with remaining stuffing.

Smoked Whiskey Peach Pulled Chicken

Servings: 6-8
Cooking Time: 45 Minutes

Ingredients:
- 3-4 pound whole chicken
- 1 cup peach juice
- 1/4 cup whiskey
- 1/4 cup melted butter
- 1/4 cup Hey Grill Hey's Sweet BBQ Rub
- 1/2 cup Whiskey Peach BBQ sauce

Directions:
1. Supply your smoker with wood pellets and follow the start-up procedure. Preheat the grill, with the lid closed, to 225°F, using a mild fruit wood like a peach.
2. Remove any giblets or neck from inside of the chicken and pat dry.
3. In a jar, combine the peach juice, whiskey, and melted butter. Inject this mixture into your chicken in several spots. Be sure to inject in at least 3 different places in each breast, 2 places in the thighs, and 1 time in each leg.
4. Season your chicken generously on all sides with the Sweet BBQ Rub. Place in the middle of your grill and close the lid. Smoke for 45 minutes per pound of chicken.
5. Brush liberally with the whiskey peach BBQ sauce once the internal temperature of your meat reaches 150 degrees.
6. Check the temperature in both the thighs and the breasts and when your internal temperature reads consistently 160 degrees F, remove the chicken to a rimmed serving platter or baking sheet and cover tightly with foil to allow the chicken to come up to 165 degrees F and rest for 20 minutes.
7. Shred the chicken and set it onto your serving platter. Discard the carcass or save for homemade stock. Drizzle your smoked pulled chicken with more of the Whiskey Peach Barbecue Sauce and serve on toasted buns.

Bbq Turkey Drumsticks

Servings: 6
Cooking Time: 120 Minutes

Ingredients:
- 1/2 Tbsp Black Pepper
- 1 Tbsp Brown Sugar
- 1/2 Tsp Cayenne Pepper
- 1/2 Tbsp Coriander, Ground
- 1/2 Tbsp Granulated Garlic
- 1 Package, Approx 4 Lbs Honeysuckle White® Turkey Drumsticks
- 1 Tbsp Kosher Salt

- 2 Tbsp Olive Oil

Directions:
1. Supply your smoker with wood pellets and follow the start-up procedure. Preheat the grill, with the lid open, to 225° F. If using a gas or charcoal grill, set it up for low, indirect heat.
2. Place Honeysuckle White® Turkey Legs on a sheet tray, coat with olive oil, then season with a blend of salt pepper, cayenne, brown sugar, granulated garlic, and ground coriander.
3. Place turkey legs in the smoking cabinet and smoke for 1 ½ hours, checking the internal temperature after 1 hour.
4. Increase the temperature to 325°F, transfer the turkey legs to the bottom grill grate and cook for another 25 to 30 minutes, until the internal temperature reaches 170°F.
5. Remove turkey drumsticks from the grill, allow to rest for 10 minutes, then serve warm.

Cornish Game Hens

Servings: 4
Cooking Time: 60 Minutes

Ingredients:
- 4 Cornish game hens
- 4 Tablespoon butter, melted
- Chicken Rub
- 4 Sprig rosemary or sage, plus more for garnish

Directions:
1. Rinse the Cornish game hens under cold running water, inside and out. (Game hens do not usually come with giblets, but check the cavity for them before rinsing. If you find giblets, freeze them for chicken stock, if desired.)
2. Dry thoroughly with paper towels. Tuck the wings behind the backs and tie the legs together with butcher's string.
3. Rub the outside of each hen with the melted butter. Season with Traeger Chicken Rub. Slip a sprig of rosemary into the main cavity of each hen.
4. Supply your smoker with wood pellets and follow the start-up procedure. Preheat the grill, with the lid closed, to 375° F.
5. Roast the hens for 50 to 60 minutes, or until the juices run clear and the internal temperature of the thigh, when read on an instant-read meat thermometer, is 165°F. Grill: 375 °F Probe: 165 °F
6. Transfer the hens to a platter or plates and let rest for 5 minutes.
7. Garnish with a sprig of rosemary before serving. Enjoy!

Bbq Chicken Drumsticks

Servings: 4
Cooking Time: 120 Minutes

Ingredients:

- 8 chicken drumsticks
- 2 Tablespoon Chicken Rub
- 1/2 Cup 'Que BBQ Sauce

Directions:

1. Season each drumstick and let rest for 20 minutes.

2. Supply your smoker with wood pellets and follow the start-up procedure. Preheat the grill, with the lid closed, to 275° F.

3. Hang the drumsticks on the leg hanger (alternatively, place directly on the grill grate flipping halfway through) and cook for 1 hour. Grill: 275 °F

4. Remove the drumsticks from the hanger (or grate) and place in a pan. Grill: 275 °F Probe: 190 °F

5. Cover with foil and cook for 45 more minutes or until meat reaches an internal temperature of 190 degrees F. Grill: 275 °F Probe: 190 °F

6. Remove the foil and sauce all drumsticks in the pan.

7. Cook for an additional 15 minutes so sauce can set. Grill: 275 °F

8. Remove from Traeger and let rest for 15 minutes before serving. Enjoy!

Smoked Chicken With Apricot Bbq Glaze

Servings: 4
Cooking Time: 60 Minutes

Ingredients:

- 2 Whole Chickens, halved
- 4 Tablespoon Chicken Rub
- 1 Cup Apricot BBQ Sauce

Directions:

1. Supply your smoker with wood pellets and follow the start-up procedure. Preheat the grill, with the lid closed, to 375° F.

2. Season chicken with Chicken Rub and place on grill meat side up. Cook 1 hour or until internal temperature has reached 160°F in the breast and 175°F in the leg. Grill: 375 °F Probe: 160 °F

3. Baste each chicken half with a bit of the Apricot BBQ glaze and return to grill for 10 minutes. Grill: 375 °F

4. Remove chicken from the grill and allow to rest 5-10 minutes. Portion each half by removing the leg and cutting each breast in half leaving you with four legs and 8 breast pieces. Serve with your favorite vegetables or sides. Enjoy!

Wood-fired Chicken Breasts

Servings: 2-4
Cooking Time: 45 Minutes

Ingredients:

- 2 (1-pound) bone-in, skin-on chicken breasts
- 1 batch Chicken Rub

Directions:

1. Supply your smoker with wood pellets and follow the start-up procedure. Preheat the grill, with the lid closed, to 350°F.

2. Season the chicken breasts all over with the rub. Using your hands, work the rub into the meat.

3. Place the breasts directly on the grill grate and smoke until their internal temperature reaches 170°F. Remove the breasts from the grill and serve immediately.

VEGETABLES RECIPES

Roasted Hasselback Potatoes By Doug Scheiding

Servings: 6
Cooking Time: 120 Minutes

Ingredients:

- 6 Large russet potatoes
- 1 Pound bacon
- 1/2 Cup butter
- salt
- black pepper
- 1 Cup cheddar cheese
- 3 Whole scallions

Directions:

1. To cut potatoes, place two wooden spoons on either side of the potato (this prevents your knife from going all the way through). Slice potato into thin chips leaving about 1/4" attached on the bottom.
2. Freeze bacon slices for about 30 minutes then cut into small pieces about the size of a stamp. Place these in the cracks between every other slice.
3. Place the potato in a large cast iron skillet. Top the potato with slices of hard butter (you can also place thin slivers of cold butter between the potato slices with the bacon if desired). Season with salt and pepper.
4. Supply your smoker with wood pellets and follow the start-up procedure. Preheat the grill, with the lid closed, to 350° F.
5. Place the cast iron directly on the grill grate and cook for two hours. Top potatoes with more butter and baste with melted butter every 30 minutes.
6. In the last 10 minutes of cooking, sprinkle with cheddar and return to grill to melt.
7. To finish, top with chives or scallions. Enjoy!

Roasted Mashed Potatoes

Servings: 8
Cooking Time: 40 Minutes

Ingredients:

- 5 Pound Yukon Gold potatoes
- 1 1/2 Stick butter, softened
- 1 1/2 Cup heavy whipping cream, room temperature
- kosher salt
- white pepper

Directions:

1. Supply your smoker with wood pellets and follow the start-up procedure. Preheat the grill, with the lid closed, to 300° F.

2. Peel and cut potatoes into 1/2 inch cubes. Place the potatoes in a shallow baking dish with 1/2 cup water and cover. Bake until tender, about 40 minutes. Grill: 300 ˚F
3. In a medium saucepan, combine cream and butter. Cook over medium heat until butter is melted.
4. Remove potatoes from the grill and drain water.
5. Transfer potatoes to a bowl and mash using a potato masher. Gradually add in cream and butter mixture and mix using the masher. Be careful not to overwork or the potatoes will becomes gluey. Season with salt and pepper to taste. Enjoy!

Broccoli-cauliflower Salad

Servings: 4
Cooking Time: 25 Minutes

Ingredients:

- 1½ cups mayonnaise
- ½ cup sour cream
- ¼ cup sugar
- 1 bunch broccoli, cut into small pieces
- 1 head cauliflower, cut into small pieces
- 1 small red onion, chopped
- 6 slices bacon, cooked and crumbled (precooked bacon works well)
- 1 cup shredded Cheddar cheese

Directions:

1. In a small bowl, whisk together the mayonnaise, sour cream, and sugar to make a dressing.
2. In a large bowl, combine the broccoli, cauliflower, onion, bacon, and Cheddar cheese.
3. Pour the dressing over the vegetable mixture and toss well to coat.
4. Serve the salad chilled.

Roasted Potato Poutine

Servings: 6
Cooking Time: 40 Minutes

Ingredients:

- 4 Large russet potatoes
- Tablespoon olive oil or vegetable oil
- Prime Rib Rub
- Cup chicken or beef gravy (homemade or jarred)
- 1 1/2 Cup white or yellow cheddar cheese curds
- freshly ground black pepper
- 2 Tablespoon scallions

Directions:

1. Supply your smoker with wood pellets and follow the start-up procedure. Preheat the grill, with the lid closed, to 500° F.

2.   Scrub the potatoes and slice into fries, wedges or preferred shape.

3.   Put potatoes into a large mixing bowl and coat with oil. Season generously with Traeger Prime Rib rub.

4.   Tip the potatoes onto a rimmed baking sheet and spread in a single layer, cut sides down.

5.   Roast for 20 minutes, then using a spatula, turn the potatoes to the other cut side. Continue to roast until the potatoes are tender and golden brown, about 15 to 20 minutes more.

6.   While potatoes cook, warm the gravy on the stovetop or in a heat-proof saucepan on your Traeger.

7.   To assemble the poutine, arrange the potatoes in a large shallow bowl or on a serving platter. Distribute the cheese curds on top. Pour the hot gravy evenly over the potatoes and cheese curds.

8.   Season with black pepper and garnish with thinly sliced scallions. Serve immediately. Enjoy!

Salt Crusted Baked Potatoes

Servings: 4
Cooking Time: 60 Minutes

Ingredients:

- 6 russet potatoes, scrubbed and dried
- 3 Tablespoon canola oil
- 1 Tablespoon kosher salt
- butter
- sour cream
- Chives, fresh
- Bacon Bits
- cheddar cheese

Directions:

1.   In a large bowl, coat the potatoes in canola oil and sprinkle heavily with salt.

2.   Supply your smoker with wood pellets and follow the start-up procedure. Preheat the grill, with the lid closed, to 450° F.

3.   Place the potatoes directly on the grill grate and bake for 30-40 minutes, or until soft in the middle when pricked with a fork. Serve loaded with your favorite toppings. Enjoy! Grill: 450 ˚F

Grilled Street Corn

Servings: 6
Cooking Time: 10 Minutes

Ingredients:

- 6 ears corn, husked
- 1 As Needed extra-virgin olive oil
- 1/4 Cup mayonnaise
- 1 Tablespoon ancho or guajillo chile powder
- 1/2 Cup chopped cilantro, plus more for serving
- 1 lime, zested and juiced
- salt
- 1/2 Cup Cotija cheese
- 1 As Needed cilantro, finely chopped

Directions:

1.   Supply your smoker with wood pellets and follow the start-up procedure. Preheat the grill, with the lid closed, to 450° F.

2.   Brush corn with oil and place on grill, turning occasionally.

3.   While corn is on the grill, mix mayonnaise with chile powder, cilantro, lime juice and zest in a bowl. Season with salt.

4.   After about 10 minutes corn should be cooked through and slightly charred on the outside. Remove from grill.

5.   Top corn with chile mayonnaise then sprinkle on the Cotija cheese and chopped cilantro. Enjoy!

Roasted Asparagus

Servings: 4
Cooking Time: 30 Minutes

Ingredients:

- 1 Bunch asparagus
- 2 Tablespoon olive oil, plus more as needed
- Veggie Rub

Directions:

1.   Coat asparagus with olive oil and Veggie Rub, stirring to coat all pieces.

2.   Supply your smoker with wood pellets and follow the start-up procedure. Preheat the grill, with the lid closed, to 350° F.

3.   Place asparagus directly on the grill grate for 15-20 minutes.

4.   Remove from grill and enjoy!

Twice-smoked Potatoes

Servings: 16
Cooking Time: 95 Minutes

Ingredients:

- 8 Idaho, Russet, or Yukon Gold potatoes
- 1 (12-ounce) can evaporated milk, heated
- 1 cup (2 sticks) butter, melted
- ½ cup sour cream, at room temperature
- 1 cup grated Parmesan cheese
- ½ pound bacon, cooked and crumbled
- ¼ cup chopped scallions
- Salt
- Freshly ground black pepper
- 1 cup shredded Cheddar cheese

Directions:

1.   Supply your smoker with wood pellets and follow the start-up procedure. Preheat, with the lid closed, to 400°F.

2. Poke the potatoes all over with a fork. Arrange them directly on the grill grate, close the lid, and smoke for 1 hour and 15 minutes, or until cooked through and they have some give when pinched.

3. Let the potatoes cool for 10 minutes, then cut in half lengthwise.

4. Into a medium bowl, scoop out the potato flesh, leaving ¼ inch in the shells; place the shells on a baking sheet.

5. Using an electric mixer on medium speed, beat the potatoes, milk, butter, and sour cream until smooth.

6. Stir in the Parmesan cheese, bacon, and scallions, and season with salt and pepper.

7. Generously stuff each shell with the potato mixture and top with Cheddar cheese.

8. Place the baking sheet on the grill grate, close the lid, and smoke for 20 minutes, or until the cheese is melted.

Bacon Wrapped Corn On The Cob

Servings: 4
Cooking Time: 21 Minutes

Ingredients:
- 4 Whole Corn, ears
- 8 Slices bacon
- 1 Teaspoon freshly ground black pepper
- 1 Teaspoon chili powder
- 1 To Taste Parmesan cheese, grated

Directions:
1. Peel back the corn husks, remove silk strings and rinse corn under cold water.

2. Wrap 2 pieces of bacon around each ear of corn, securing with toothpicks.

3. Dust each ear of corn with some chili powder and cracked black pepper.

4. Supply your smoker with wood pellets and follow the start-up procedure. Preheat the grill, with the lid closed, to 375° F.

5. Place the ears of corn directly on the Traeger and grill for approximately 20 minutes or until the bacon is cooked crisp. Grill: 375 °F

6. Take the corn off the Traeger. Carefully remove the toothpicks and season with a little more chili powder and a grating of parmesan cheese, if desired. Serve & enjoy!

Grilled Asparagus And Hollandaise Sauce

Servings: 4
Cooking Time: 10 Minutes

Ingredients:
- 1 Pound asparagus
- 2 Teaspoon red pepper flakes
- 2 Tablespoon olive oil
- salt and pepper
- 4 egg yolk
- 1 Tablespoon lemon juice
- 1/2 Cup butter, melted
- cayenne pepper
- salt

Directions:
1. Supply your smoker with wood pellets and follow the start-up procedure. Preheat the grill, with the lid closed, to 375° F.

2. In a large bowl, mix asparagus with olive oil, red pepper flakes and salt. Arrange asparagus on a cooking sheet and take to the grill. Cook for approximately 10 to 15 minutes. Grill: 375 °F

3. In an aluminum bowl, whisk the egg yolks well. Add the lemon juice and whisk until creamy.

4. Place bowl over a double boiler, over low heat, making sure that it does not touches the water.

5. While whisking, add the melted butter slowly. Whisk until it doubles the volume. Take off the heat, still whisking and add the cayenne pepper and salt.

6. Arrange asparagus over a serving plater. Pour hollandaise sauce over asparagus and serve. Enjoy!

Traeger Smoked Coleslaw

Servings: 8
Cooking Time: 20 Minutes

Ingredients:
- 1 Head purple cabbage, shredded
- 1 Head green cabbage, shredded
- 1 Cup shredded carrots
- 2 scallions, thinly sliced
- 1 1/2 Cup mayonnaise
- 1/8 Cup white wine vinegar
- 1 Teaspoon celery seed
- 1 Teaspoon sugar
- salt and pepper

Directions:
1. Supply your smoker with wood pellets and follow the start-up procedure. Preheat the grill, with the lid closed, to 180° F.

2. Spread cabbage and carrots out on a sheet tray and place directly on the grill grates. Smoke for 20 to 25 minutes or until cabbage picks up desired amount of smoke. Grill: 180 °F

3. Remove from grill and transfer to the refrigerator immediately to cool. While cabbage is cooling, make the dressing.

4. For the dressing, combine all ingredients in a small bowl and mix well.

5. Place smoked cabbage and carrots in a large bowl and pour dressing over them. Stir to coat well.

6. Transfer to a serving dish and sprinkle with scallions. Enjoy!

Grilled Corn On The Cob With Parmesan And Garlic

Servings: 6
Cooking Time: 30 Minutes

Ingredients:

- 4 Tablespoon butter, melted
- 2 Clove garlic, minced
- salt and pepper
- 8 ears fresh corn
- 1/2 Cup shaved Parmesan
- 1 Tablespoon chopped parsley

Directions:

1. Supply your smoker with wood pellets and follow the start-up procedure. Preheat the grill, with the lid closed, to 450° F.
2. Place butter, garlic, salt and pepper in a medium bowl and mix well.
3. Peel back corn husks and remove the silk. Rub corn with half of the garlic butter mixture.
4. Close husks and place directly on the grill grate. Cook for 25 to 30 minutes, turning occasionally until corn is tender. Grill: 450 °F
5. Remove from grill, peel and discard husks. Place corn on serving tray, drizzle with remaining butter and top with Parmesan and parsley.

Smoked Asparagus Soup

Servings: 4
Cooking Time: 40 Minutes

Ingredients:

- Pound Asparagus Spears
- 1 Tablespoon olive oil
- salt and pepper
- 1/2 yellow onion, diced
- 1 Tablespoon butter
- 2 Clove garlic, minced
- 1 1/2 Cup chicken stock
- 1 1/2 Cup cream
- 2 Stalk Raw Asparagus, Shaved

Directions:

1. Supply your smoker with wood pellets and follow the start-up procedure. Preheat the grill, with the lid closed, to 180° F.
2. Drizzle 1 pound of asparagus with olive oil and season with salt and pepper. Place directly on the grill grate and smoke for 20-30 minutes. Taste along the way to assess smoke level pulling earlier if needed. Grill: 180 °F
3. Place 1 Tbsp butter in a saucepan and melt over medium heat. Add onion and garlic and saute for 2-3 minutes or until onion is translucent.
4. Remove asparagus from the grill and cut into 1" pieces. Place asparagus in the pan with the onions and add stock and cream. Bring to a simmer.
5. Remove from heat and puree using a blender or immersion blender until smooth.
6. Season with salt and pepper and serve. Top with fresh shaved asparagus, sprinkle with salt, pepper, and smoked paprika if desired. Enjoy!

Smoked Pico De Gallo

Servings: 4
Cooking Time: 30 Minutes

Ingredients:

- 3 Cup diced Roma tomatoes
- 1 jalapeño, diced
- 1/2 red onion, diced
- 1/2 Bunch cilantro, finely chopped
- 2 lime, juiced
- salt
- olive oil

Directions:

1. Supply your smoker with wood pellets and follow the start-up procedure. Preheat the grill, with the lid closed, to 180° F.
2. Place the diced tomatoes on a small sheet pan spreading them into a thin layer. Place the sheet pan directly on the grill and smoke for 30 minutes. Grill: 180 °F
3. When the tomatoes are finished, toss all ingredients in a medium bowl and finish with lime juice, salt and olive oil to taste. Serve and enjoy!

Traeger Baked Potato Torte

Servings: 6
Cooking Time: 25 Minutes

Ingredients:

- 6 Yukon Gold potatoes, sliced 1/4 inch thick
- 2 Stick butter, melted
- 3 Clove garlic, crushed
- 2 Tablespoon rosemary, chopped
- 1 Cup Parmesan cheese, grated
- salt and pepper

Directions:

1. Supply your smoker with wood pellets and follow the start-up procedure. Preheat the grill, with the lid closed, to 375° F.

2.   While the Traeger is heating up, peel and slice the potatoes (make sure to put them in water so they will not oxidize). Melt the butter and combine it with the crushed garlic.

3.   Grease a 12" cast iron pan with butter and start to layer the torte. The layers should go as follows, potatoes, butter garlic mixture, rosemary, parmesan, continue layering to the top of the pan, about 4 to 5 layers.

4.   Place the pan in the Traeger and bake for 20 to 25 minutes, or until the potatoes are fully cooked. If the top of the torte starts to darken before it is finished cooking, reduce the heat to 325°F. Serve hot and enjoy! Grill: 375 °F

Smoked Macaroni Salad

Servings: 4
Cooking Time: 20 Minutes

Ingredients:

- 1 Pound macaroni, uncooked
- 1/2 Small red onion, diced
- 1 green bell pepper, diced
- 1/2 Cup shredded carrot
- 1 Cup mayonnaise
- 3 Tablespoon white wine vinegar
- 2 Tablespoon sugar
- salt
- black pepper

Directions:

1.   Bring a large stock pot of salted water to a boil over medium heat and cook pasta according to package directions. Make sure to cook to al dente, strain, and rinse under cold water.

2.   Supply your smoker with wood pellets and follow the start-up procedure. Preheat the grill, with the lid closed, to 225° F.

3.   Spread cooked pasta out on a sheet tray and place sheet tray directly on the grill grate. Smoke for 20 minutes, remove from heat, and transfer directly to the refrigerator to cool. Grill: 225 °F

4.   While the pasta is cooling mix the dressing. Place all ingredients in a medium bowl and whisk to combine.

5.   When pasta is cool combine chopped veggies, smoked pasta and dressing in a large bowl.

6.   Cover with plastic wrap and place in the fridge for 20 minutes before serving. Enjoy!

Roasted Pumpkin Seeds

Servings: 8
Cooking Time: 40 Minutes

Ingredients:

- 1 Whole Pumpkin, seeds
- olive oil or vegetable oil
- Jacobsen Salt Co. Pure Kosher Sea Salt

Directions:

1.   As soon as possible after removing the seeds from the pumpkin, rinse pumpkin seeds under cold water in a colander and pick out the pulp and strings.

2.   Place the pumpkin seeds in a single layer on an oiled baking sheet, stirring to coat. Supply your smoker with wood pellets and follow the start-up procedure. Preheat the grill, with the lid closed, to 180° F.

3.   Place the baking sheet with the seeds on the grill grate, close the lid, and smoke for 20 minutes. Grill: 180 °F

4.   Sprinkle your seeds with salt and turn the temperature on your grill up to 325°F. Roast the seeds until toasted, about 20 minutes. Check and stir seeds after the first 10 minutes. Grill: 325 °F

5.   Seeds will be brown because they were smoked before being roasted. Enjoy!

Stuffed Jalapenos

Servings: 8
Cooking Time: 60 Minutes

Ingredients:

- 40 Whole jalapeño
- 8 Ounce cream cheese, room temperature
- 1 Cup Sharp Cheddar Grated
- 1 1/2 Teaspoon Pork & Poultry Rub
- 2 Tablespoon sour cream
- 1 Whole (14 oz) cocktail sausages
- 20 Whole Slices of Smoked Bacon, Cut in Half

Directions:

1.   Wash and dry the peppers. Cut the stem ends off with a paring knife, and using the same knife or a small metal spoon, carefully scrape the seeds and ribs out of each pepper. Set aside.

2.   In a small bowl, combine the cream cheese, grated cheese, Traeger Pork and Poultry Rub, and the sour cream.

3.   Transfer the mixture to a sturdy resealable plastic bag and trim 1/2-inch off one of the lower corners with a scissors. Squeeze the cream cheese mixture into each pepper, filling each a little over the halfway point.

4.   Stuff one sausage into each pepper. Wrap the outside of each with a piece of bacon, securing with 1 or 2 toothpicks.

5.   Arrange the peppers on a foil-lined baking sheet. Supply your smoker with wood pellets and follow the start-up procedure. Preheat the grill, with the lid closed, to 180° F, and smoke the peppers for 1 to 1-1/2 hours.

6.   Increase the heat to 350 degrees F and continue to cook for 20 to 30 minutes, or until the bacon begins to render its fat and crisp. Enjoy! Grill: 350 °F

Roasted Olives

Servings: 4
Cooking Time: 45 Minutes

Ingredients:

- 2 Cup mixed olives
- 3 Sprig fresh rosemary
- 2 Clove garlic, minced
- 2 Tablespoon orange zest
- 1/3 Cup extra-virgin olive oil
- 2 Tablespoon orange juice
- 1/2 Teaspoon red pepper flakes

Directions:

1. Combine the olives, rosemary, garlic, orange zest, red pepper flakes, olive oil, and orange juice in a glass oven-safe pie plate or baking dish. Cover with foil.
2. Supply your smoker with wood pellets and follow the start-up procedure. Preheat the grill, with the lid closed, to 300° F.
3. Roast the olives for 45 minutes, stirring once or twice. Serve warm in an attractive bowl. Enjoy! Grill: 300 ˚F

Grilled Asparagus And Spinach Salad

Servings: 8
Cooking Time: 10 Minutes

Ingredients:

- 4 Fluid Ounce apple cider vinegar
- 8 Fluid Ounce Honey Bourbon BBQ Sauce
- 2 Bunch asparagus, ends trimmed
- 3 Fluid Ounce extra-virgin olive oil
- 2 Ounce Beef Rub
- 24 Ounce Spinach, fresh
- 4 Ounce candied pecans
- 4 Ounce feta cheese

Directions:

1. Combine apple cider vinegar and Traeger Apricot BBQ Sauce to create salad dressing.
2. Supply your smoker with wood pellets and follow the start-up procedure. Preheat the grill, with the lid closed, to High heat.
3. Toss the asparagus with Olive Oil and the Beef Shake. Put asparagus in the Traeger Grilling Basket and move the basket to the grill grate.
4. Grill for about 10 minutes. Remove the asparagus once it is cooked. Grill: 350 ˚F
5. Place the hot asparagus right on top of the bowl of spinach.
6. Add candied pecans, feta cheese & salad dressing then toss and serve. Enjoy!

Red Potato Grilled Lollipops

Servings: 4
Cooking Time: 25 Minutes

Ingredients:

- 8 Large red bliss potatoes, halved
- 2 Clove garlic, minced
- 2 Sprig rosemary, minced
- 2 Tablespoon olive oil
- 1 Teaspoon salt
- 1/2 Teaspoon black pepper
- 5 Wooden Skewers, soaked in water
- 1/4 Cup Parmesan cheese, grated

Directions:

1. Supply your smoker with wood pellets and follow the start-up procedure. Preheat the grill, with the lid closed, to 450° F.
2. Halve potatoes and poke each several times with a fork.
3. Put the potatoes in a large bowl and toss with the minced garlic, rosemary leaves, a few tablespoons of olive oil, kosher salt, and pepper. Microwave the potatoes for 4 minutes. Gently toss potatoes and microwave for another 3 minutes.
4. Skewer potato halves threading about 4 or 5 potato halves on each skewer. Brush potatoes with olive oil.
5. Place the potato skewers on the Traeger, cut side down, and grill until the sides begin to brown (4-7 minutes).
6. Flip and grill skin side down for another 7-10 minutes.
7. They are done when a sharp knife tip easily penetrates the sides. Remove potatoes from grill and top with grated parmesan cheese. Enjoy!

Baked Breakfast Mini Quiches

Servings: 8
Cooking Time: 15 Minutes

Ingredients:

- cooking spray
- 1 Tablespoon extra-virgin olive oil
- 1/2 yellow onion, diced
- 3 Cup Spinach, fresh
- 10 eggs
- 4 Ounce shredded cheddar, mozzarella or Swiss cheese
- 1/4 Cup fresh basil
- 1 Teaspoon kosher salt
- 1/2 Teaspoon black pepper

Directions:

1. Spray a 12-cup muffin tin generously with cooking spray.
2. In a small skillet over medium heat, warm the oil. Add the onion and cook, stirring frequently, until softened, about 7 minutes. Add the spinach and cook until wilted, about 1 minute longer.

3.   Transfer to a cutting board to cool, then chop the mixture so the spinach if broken up a little.

4.   Supply your smoker with wood pellets and follow the start-up procedure. Preheat the grill, with the lid closed, to 350° F.

5.   In a large bowl, whisk the eggs until frothy. Add the cooled onions and spinach, cheese, basil, 1 tsp salt and 1/2 tsp pepper. Stir to combine. Divide egg mixture evenly among the muffin cups.

6.   Place tray on the grill and bake until the eggs have puffed up, are set, and are beginning to brown, about 18 to 20 minutes. Grill: 350 °F

7.   Serve immediately, or allow to cool on a wire rack, then refrigerate in an air tight container for up to 4 days. Enjoy!

Butternut Squash

Servings: 4
Cooking Time: 45 Minutes

Ingredients:
- 1 Whole butternut squash
- Veggie Rub
- Blackened Saskatchewan Rub
- olive oil

Directions:
1.   Cut squash in half and lightly coat with mixture of olive oil, Traeger Veggie Shake, and Traeger Blackened Saskatchewan.

2.   Wrap in foil with 1/2 cup (120mL) of water.

3.   Supply your smoker with wood pellets and follow the start-up procedure. Preheat the grill, with the lid closed, to 450° F.

4.   Place squash on grill for 45 minutes. Remove from grill and unwrap. Enjoy!

Steak Fries With Horseradish Creme

Servings: 6
Cooking Time: 25 Minutes

Ingredients:
- 5 Potatoes, Baking
- 2 Tablespoon extra-virgin olive oil
- 1 Teaspoon butter
- 3 Clove garlic, crushed
- 1 Teaspoon onion powder
- 2 Teaspoon Jacobsen Salt Co. Pure Kosher Sea Salt
- 1 Teaspoon black pepper

Directions:
1.   Wash the potatoes thoroughly, and cut them in eighths, then toss them in the olive oil, butter, crushed garlic, onion powder, salt, and pepper.

2.   Supply your smoker with wood pellets and follow the start-up procedure. Preheat the grill, with the lid closed, to 450° F.

3.   In order to get great grill marks, line up the wedges on the front of the grill and the back of the grill, turning to get grill marks on all sides.

4.   Once they have been seared, move them to the center of the grill and finish cooking about ten more minutes, serve hot with the horseradish mayo. Enjoy!

Baked Winter Squash Au Gratin

Servings: 8
Cooking Time: 45 Minutes

Ingredients:
- 2 Cup heavy cream
- salt and pepper
- 3 Cup shredded Gruyere cheese
- 4 Clove garlic, diced
- 2 Tablespoon butter
- 3 yellow potatoes, peeled and cubed
- 1 butternut squash seeded, peeled and cubed
- 1 acorn squash seeded, peeled and cubed

Directions:
1.   Supply your smoker with wood pellets and follow the start-up procedure. Preheat the grill, with the lid closed, to 375° F.

2.   In a medium saucepan, cook the cream, stirring constantly, until it comes to a low boil. Add salt, pepper, garlic and shredded Gruyere cheese. Stir until cheese is melted.

3.   Grease a 9x13 inch baking dish with 2 tablespoons of butter. In a large mixing bowl, combine potatoes, butternut and acorn squash. Stir in the cheese sauce. Place mixture in the prepared baking dish and place in grill.

4.   Cook for 45 minutes or until potatoes and squash are fork tender. Remove from grill and let cool for 10 minutes before serving. Enjoy! Grill: 375 °F

Parmesan Roasted Cauliflower

Servings: 4
Cooking Time: 40 Minutes

Ingredients:
- 1 Head cauliflower, cut into florets
- 1 Medium onion, sliced
- 4 Clove garlic, unpeeled
- 4 Tablespoon olive oil
- salt
- black pepper
- 1 Teaspoon fresh thyme
- 1/2 Cup Parmesan cheese, grated

Directions:
1.   Supply your smoker with wood pellets and follow the start-up procedure. Preheat the grill, with the lid closed, to 400° F.

2. On a baking tray, mix together cauliflower, onion, thyme, garlic, olive oil, salt and pepper.

3. Place tray on preheated grill and cook until cauliflower is firm and almost tender (about 25 minutes). Grill: 400 °F

4. Sprinkle cauliflower with Parmesan cheese and continue to cook on the Traeger for another 10 to 15 minutes. Cauliflower should be tender and the Parmesan crisp. Serve immediately, enjoy!

Smoked Parmesan Herb Popcorn

Servings: 2
Cooking Time: 15 Minutes

Ingredients:
- 4 Tablespoon butter
- 2 Teaspoon Italian Seasoning
- 1 Teaspoon garlic powder
- 1 Teaspoon salt
- 1/4 Cup popcorn kernels
- 1/2 Cup Parmesan cheese, grated

Directions:
1. Supply your smoker with wood pellets and follow the start-up procedure. Preheat the grill, with the lid closed, to 250° F.

2. In a small saucepan, melt the butter over medium heat. Add Italian seasoning, garlic powder, and salt and stir to combine. Remove from heat and set aside.

3. Add 1/4 cup of popcorn to a brown paper lunch bag. Fold the top of the bag over twice to close. Place the bag in the microwave and microwave on high for 1 to 2 minutes, or until there are about 5 seconds between pops. Open the bag with care and dump into a large mixing bowl.

4. Pour butter mixture of popcorn in a bowl and toss to combine. Dump popcorn onto a baking sheet and place in grill.

5. Smoke for 10 minutes; remove from grill. Toss with parmesan cheese to serve. Enjoy! Grill: 250 °F

Baked Heirloom Tomato Tart

Servings: 4
Cooking Time: 45 Minutes

Ingredients:
- 1 Whole Puff Pastry Sheet
- 2 Pound heirloom tomatoes, various shapes and sizes
- 1/2 Tablespoon kosher salt
- 1/2 Cup Ricotta Cheese
- 5 Whole eggs
- 1 To Taste salt and pepper
- 1/2 Teaspoon thyme leaves
- 1/2 Teaspoon red pepper flakes
- 4 Sprig thyme

Directions:

1. Supply your smoker with wood pellets and follow the start-up procedure. Preheat the grill, with the lid closed, to 350° F.

2. Place the puff pastry on a parchment lined sheet tray, and make a cut ¾ of the way through the pastry, ½" from the edge.

3. Slice the tomatoes and season with salt. Place on a sheet tray lined with paper towels.

4. In a small bowl combine the ricotta, 4 of the eggs, salt, thyme leaves, red pepper flakes and black pepper. Whisk together until combined. Spread the ricotta mixture over the puff pastry, staying within ½" from the edge.

5. In a small bowl whisk the last egg. Brush the egg wash onto the exposed edges of the pastry.

6. Place the sheet tray directly on the grill grate and bake for 45 minutes, rotating half-way through. Grill: 350 °F

7. When the edges are browned and the moisture from the tomatoes has evaporated, remove from the grill and let cool 5-7 minutes before serving. Enjoy!

Grilled Ratatouille Salad

Servings: 4
Cooking Time: 25 Minutes

Ingredients:
- 1 Whole sweet potatoes
- 1 Whole red onion, diced
- 1 Whole zucchini
- 1 Whole Squash
- 1 Large Tomato, diced
- vegetable oil
- salt and pepper

Directions:
1. Supply your smoker with wood pellets and follow the start-up procedure. Preheat the grill, with the lid closed, to High heat.

2. Slice all vegetables to a ¼ inch thickness.

3. Lightly brush each vegetable with oil and season with Traeger's Veggie Shake or salt and pepper.

4. Place sweet potato, onion, zucchini, and squash on grill grate and grill for 20 minutes or until tender, turn halfway through.

5. Add tomato slices to the grill during the last 5 minutes of cooking time.

6. For presentation, alternate vegetables while layering them vertically. Enjoy!

Roasted Artichokes With Garlic Butter

Servings: 2
Cooking Time: 60 Minutes

Ingredients:

- 2 Large artichokes
- 3 Tablespoon olive oil
- sea salt
- 1 Stick unsalted butter
- 2 Clove garlic, chopped
- 2 Tablespoon chives, parsley, tarragon or cilantro
- 1 lemon

Directions:

1. Supply your smoker with wood pellets and follow the start-up procedure. Preheat the grill, with the lid closed, to 375° F.
2. Meanwhile, break off and discard any small outer leaves on the artichokes. Use a knife to slice off the tops of the artichokes, then using scissors, cut off any thorns on the remaining artichoke leaves. Trim the very bottom of the stem, then peel the tough and fibrous outer layer of the stem. Finally, cut artichokes in half and rinse off.
3. Transfer artichokes to a large mixing bowl, drizzle with olive oil and generously sprinkle with sea salt. Toss to coat the artichokes thoroughly. Grill: 375 °F
4. Add the artichokes to the grill, cut side down, and roast at 375°F until the artichoke bottoms are tender when poked with a fork or knife, about 50 to 60 minutes. Grill: 375 °F
5. When artichokes are almost done, add butter, chopped garlic and a pinch of sea salt to a small sauce pan and melt slowly over medium-low heat. Once the butter melts all the way and starts to bubble slightly, add the herbs.
6. When the artichokes are done, transfer to a butcher paper lined tray with the cut sides up. Drizzle half the garlic butter and squeeze half of the lemon over the artichokes. Add a small sprinkle of sea salt over the artichokes.
7. Serve with a ramekin of the remaining butter for dipping and extra wedges of lemon. Enjoy! Chef Tip: You can also serve with a ramekin of good mayonnaise mixed with a bit of hot sauce.

Chef Curtis' Famous Chimichurri Sauce

Servings: 4
Cooking Time: 5 Minutes

Ingredients:

- 2 Whole lemon, halved
- 2 Medium flat-leaf Italian parsley, washed and chopped with the majority of stems cut off
- 4 Clove garlic, diced
- 1/4 Cup red wine vinegar
- 1/2 Teaspoon black pepper
- 1/4 Cup extra-virgin olive oil
- 1 Teaspoon salt

Directions:

1. Supply your smoker with wood pellets and follow the start-up procedure. Preheat the grill, with the lid closed, to 450° F.
2. Place lemon halves directly on the grill grate and cook for 5 minutes or until grill marks appear. Grill: 450 °F
3. Take lemons off grill and juice. Combine all of the ingredients in a food processor or blender and purée until smooth, or leave slightly chunky for some texture.
4. Add additional olive oil to taste for a milder flavor if preferred. Serve on protein or as a dip. Enjoy!

Roasted Garlic Herb Fries

Servings: 4
Cooking Time: 45 Minutes

Ingredients:

- 4 Whole russet potatoes
- 1 Teaspoon salt
- 2 Tablespoon avocado oil
- 1 Teaspoon fresh chopped rosemary
- 1 Teaspoon fresh chopped thyme
- 2 Clove garlic, minced
- 2 Teaspoon flake salt
- 1 Teaspoon chopped parsley, for garnish

Directions:

1. Supply your smoker with wood pellets and follow the start-up procedure. Preheat the grill, with the lid closed, to 425° F.
2. Chop potatoes into fries, (a mandolin works great for this) and place directly into an ice water bath with 1 teaspoon salt for 15 to 30 minutes.
3. Combine oil, rosemary, thyme and garlic in a big bowl. Remove potatoes from ice water and dry thoroughly with paper towels.
4. Toss potatoes in the oil mixture and place them on 2 to 3 parchment-lined baking sheets in a single layer. Sprinkle the flake salt over the fries.
5. Place baking sheets on the grill and roast for 30 minutes, flip the fries, then cook for an additional 15 minutes until golden and crispy. Dust with parsley. Grill: 425 °F
6. Serve with your favorite dipping sauce, side dish or as a nacho base.

Grilled Zucchini Squash Spears

Servings: 4
Cooking Time: 10 Minutes

Ingredients:

- 4 Medium zucchini
- 2 Tablespoon olive oil
- 1 Tablespoon sherry vinegar
- 2 thyme, leaves pulled
- salt and pepper

Directions:

1. Clean the zucchini and cut the ends off. Cut each in half lengthwise, then each half into thirds.

2. Combine remaining ingredients in a medium Ziplock bag and add the spears. Toss and mix well to coat the zucchini.

3. Supply your smoker with wood pellets and follow the start-up procedure. Preheat the grill, with the lid closed, to 350° F.

4. Remove the spears from the bag and place directly on the grill grate cut side down.

5. Cook for 3-4 minutes per side, until grill marks appear and zucchini is tender. Grill: 350 °F

6. Remove from grill and finish with more thyme leaves if desired. Enjoy!

Potluck Salad With Smoked Cornbread

Servings: 6
Cooking Time: 45 Minutes

Ingredients:

- 1 cup all-purpose flour
- 1 cup yellow cornmeal
- 1 tablespoon sugar
- 2 teaspoons baking powder
- 1 teaspoon salt
- 1 cup milk
- 1 egg, beaten, at room temperature
- 4 tablespoons (½ stick) unsalted butter, melted and cooled
- Nonstick cooking spray or butter, for greasing
- ½ cup milk
- ½ cup sour cream
- 2 tablespoons dry ranch dressing mix
- 1 pound bacon, cooked and crumbled
- 3 tomatoes, chopped
- 1 bell pepper, chopped
- 1 cucumber, seeded and chopped
- 2 stalks celery, chopped (about 1 cup)
- ½ cup chopped scallions

Directions:

1. For the cornbread:

2. In a medium bowl, combine the flour, cornmeal, sugar, baking powder, and salt.

3. In a small bowl, whisk together the milk and egg. Pour in the butter, then slowly fold this mixture into the dry ingredients.

4. Supply your smoker with wood pellets and follow the start-up procedure. Preheat, with the lid closed, to 375°F.

5. Coat a cast iron skillet with cooking spray or butter.

6. Pour the batter into the skillet, place on the grill grate, close the lid, and smoke for 35 to 45 minutes, or until the cornbread is browned and pulls away from the side of the skillet.

7. Remove the cornbread from the grill and let cool, then coarsely crumble.

8. For the salad:

9. In a small bowl, whisk together the milk, sour cream, and ranch dressing mix.

10. In a medium bowl, combine the crumbled bacon, tomatoes, bell pepper, cucumber, celery, and scallions.

11. In a large serving bowl, layer half of the crumbled cornbread, half of the bacon-veggie mixture, and half of the dressing. Toss lightly.

12. Repeat the layering with the remaining cornbread, bacon-veggie mixture, and dressing. Toss again.

13. Refrigerate the salad for at least 1 hour. Serve cold.

Smoked Pickled Green Beans

Servings: 4
Cooking Time: 45 Minutes

Ingredients:

- 1 Pound Green Beans, blanched
- 1/2 Cup salt
- 1/2 Cup sugar
- 1 Tablespoon red pepper flakes
- 2 Cup white wine vinegar
- 2 Cup ice water

Directions:

1. Supply your smoker with wood pellets and follow the start-up procedure. Preheat the grill, with the lid closed, to 180° F.

2. Place the blanched green beans on a mesh grill mat and place mat directly on the grill grate. Smoke the green beans for 30-45 minutes until they've picked up the desired amount of smoke. Remove from grill and set aside until the brine is ready. Grill: 180 °F

3. In a medium sized saucepan, bring all remaining ingredients, except ice water, to a boil over medium high heat on the stove. Simmer for 5-10 minutes then remove from heat and steep 20 minutes more. Pour brine over ice water to cool.

4. Once brine has cooled, pour over the green beans and weigh them down with a few plates to ensure they are completely submerged. Let sit 24 hours before use. Enjoy!

Sweet Potato Marshmallow Casserole

Servings: 6

Cooking Time: 60 Minutes

Ingredients:

- 5 Yams
- 1 1/2 Stick butter
- 1/2 Cup brown sugar
- 1 Teaspoon vanilla
- 1 Teaspoon kosher salt
- 1 Teaspoon cracked black pepper
- 1 Marshmallows, miniature
- 1/4 Unsalted Butter, Softened

Directions:

1. Supply your smoker with wood pellets and follow the start-up procedure. Preheat the grill, with the lid closed, to 375° F.

2. Pierce the skin of the yams with a fork a few times. Place on a baking sheet or foil tin inside the grill and let roast for 50 minutes or until extremely softened. Grill: 375 °F

3. Remove yams from the grill and set aside until cool enough to handle. While the potatoes cool, with a stiff whisk, whip together 1/2 cup softened butter, the brown sugar, vanilla, salt and pepper.

4. Remove and discard skins from sweet potatoes and mash until smooth. Fold in the butter mixture and transfer to a cast iron pan.

5. Place cast iron on the grill and bake for 15-20 minutes. Remove from the grill, top with marshmallows and dot with remaining 1/4 cup butter.

6. Place back in the grill for 15 minutes until warm and the marshmallows are golden. Enjoy! Grill: 375 °F

Roasted Sheet Pan Vegetables

Servings: 4
Cooking Time: 25 Minutes

Ingredients:

- 1 Small head purple cauliflower, stemmed and cut into 2 inch florets
- 1 Small head yellow cauliflower, stemmed and cut into 2 inch florets
- 4 Cup butternut squash
- 2 Cup oyster or shiitake mushrooms, rinsed and sliced
- 3 Tablespoon olive oil
- 2 Teaspoon kosher salt
- freshly ground black pepper
- 1/4 Cup chopped flat-leaf parsley

Directions:

1. Supply your smoker with wood pellets and follow the start-up procedure. Preheat the grill, with the lid closed, to 450° F.

2. In a large mixing bowl, combine all of the vegetables. Drizzle olive oil over the top, along with kosher salt and a generous grinding of black pepper.

3. Using your hands, toss the vegetables until they are evenly coated.

4. Spread out onto 1 or 2 half sheet pans or baking sheets, ensuring there is a little space between the veggies. (If they are too crowded, the vegetables will steam instead of roast and you won't get that crispy texture.)

5. Place the sheet pans on the grill and cook for 15 minutes. Open and stir, then close the lid and continue to cook until the vegetables are brown around the edges, about 5 to 15 minutes longer. Grill: 450 °F

6. Toss with parsley and serve immediately. The vegetables are also delicious at room temperature. Enjoy!

Roasted Sweet Potato Steak Fries

Servings: 4
Cooking Time: 40 Minutes

Ingredients:

- 3 Whole sweet potatoes
- 4 Tablespoon extra-virgin olive oil
- salt and pepper
- 2 Tablespoon fresh chopped rosemary

Directions:

1. Supply your smoker with wood pellets and follow the start-up procedure. Preheat the grill, with the lid closed, to 450° F.

2. Cut sweet potatoes into wedges and toss with olive oil, salt, pepper and rosemary. Spread on a parchment lined baking sheet and put in the grill. Cook for 15 minutes then flip and continue to cook until lightly browned and cooked through, about 40 to 45 minutes total. Grill: 450 °F

3. Serve with your favorite dipping sauce. Enjoy! Grill: 450 °F

Baked Loaded Tater Tots

Servings: 6
Cooking Time: 35 Minutes

Ingredients:

- 2 Pound frozen tater tots
- 1 Can Black Beans
- 1 1/2 Cup leftover chili
- 1 Cup leftover queso
- 1 red onion, finely diced
- 1/2 Cup chopped cilantro
- 1/2 Cup sour cream
- 1 jalapeños, sliced

Directions:

1. Supply your smoker with wood pellets and follow the start-up procedure. Preheat the grill, with the lid closed, to 375° F.

2. Spread frozen tots out on a sheet tray and place directly on the grill grate.

3. Cook for 20 to 25 minutes or until tots are crispy. Grill: 375 °F

4. Top with warmed chili, queso and beans. Place back on the grill for 15 minutes. Grill: 375 °F

5. Remove from grill and top with red onion, cilantro, sour cream and jalapeño. Enjoy!

Smoked Mushrooms

Servings: 4
Cooking Time: 45 Minutes

Ingredients:
- Pound Mushrooms, fresh
- 1/2 Cup apple cider vinegar
- 1/2 Cup soy sauce
- 1 Teaspoon Blackened Saskatchewan Rub

Directions:
1. Clean mushrooms and place in a large Ziploc bag. Add apple cider vinegar, soy sauce and rub.

2. Mix well and allow to marinate in the refrigerator for at least 2 hours.

3. Supply your smoker with wood pellets and follow the start-up procedure. Preheat the grill, with the lid closed, to 350° F.

4. Place cast iron skillet inside grill for 20 minutes to warm up.

5. Add the mushrooms and marinade slowly into the cast iron skillet.

6. Cook uncovered for 15 minutes, then cover the skillet and cook another 30 minutes until mushrooms are tender. Grill: 350 °F

7. Remove skillet from grill and let mushrooms cool down for 5 minutes before serving. Enjoy!

Roasted New Potatoes

Servings: 4
Cooking Time: 25 Minutes

Ingredients:
- 2 Pound small new potatoes
- 3 Tablespoon butter, melted
- 2 Tablespoon olive oil
- 2 Tablespoon whole mustard seeds
- salt and pepper
- 2 Tablespoon freshly minced chives
- 2 Tablespoon freshly minced parsley

Directions:

1. Place potatoes in a colander and rinse with cold water. Dry on paper towels and transfer to a rimmed baking sheet large enough to hold them in a single layer.

2. Drizzle the potatoes with butter and olive oil, then sprinkle them with the mustard seeds. Season with salt and pepper.

3. Supply your smoker with wood pellets and follow the start-up procedure. Preheat the grill, with the lid closed, to 400° F.

4. Place the baking sheet with the potatoes on the grill grate. Roast for about 25 minutes shaking the pan once or twice, until potatoes are tender and the skins are slightly wrinkled. Grill: 400 °F

5. Transfer potatoes to a bowl or platter. Top with fresh chives and parsley. Enjoy!

Grilled Asparagus & Honey-glazed Carrots

Servings: 4
Cooking Time: 35 Minutes

Ingredients:
- 1 Bunch asparagus, woody ends removed
- 1 Pound Carrots, peeled
- 2 Tablespoon olive oil
- sea salt
- 2 Tablespoon honey
- lemon zest

Directions:

1. Rinse all vegetables under cold water. Drizzle asparagus with olive oil and a generous sprinkling of sea salt. Generously drizzle carrots with honey and lightly sprinkle with sea salt.

2. Supply your smoker with wood pellets and follow the start-up procedure. Preheat the grill, with the lid closed, to 350° F.

3. Place carrots on the grill first and cook for 10-15 minutes, then add asparagus and cook both for another 15 to 20 minutes, or until they're done to your liking. Grill: 350 °F

4. Top the asparagus with some fresh lemon zest. Enjoy!

Baked Bacon Green Bean Casserole

Servings: 6
Cooking Time: 50 Minutes

Ingredients:
- 1 1/2 Pound Green Beans, fresh
- 1 Can cream of mushroom soup
- 1/2 Cup milk
- 1/2 Teaspoon Worcestershire sauce
- 1/2 Teaspoon black pepper
- 2/3 Cup French's Original Crispy Fried Onions
- 8 Slices bacon
- 1/4 Cup red bell pepper, diced

* 2/3 French's Original Crispy Fried Onions

Directions:

1.   In a mixing bowl, combine beans, soup, milk, Worcestershire sauce, black pepper, 2/3 cup of the onions, 6 of the slices of crumbled bacon, and red bell pepper. Transfer to a 1-1/2 quart casserole dish.

2.   Supply your smoker with wood pellets and follow the start-up procedure. Preheat the grill, with the lid closed, to 350° F.

3.   Cook casserole until the filling is hot and bubbling, 35 to 40 minutes. Grill: 350 ˚F

4.   Top with remaining onions and the last 2 slices of crumbled bacon and cook for 5 to 10 minutes more, or until the onions are crisp and beginning to brown. Serve, enjoy! Grill: 350 ˚F

Baked Sweet Potatoes

Servings: 8
Cooking Time: 60 Minutes

Ingredients:
* 1 Cup butter, softened
* 1/4 Cup pure maple syrup
* 1/2 Teaspoon ground cinnamon
* 8 Medium sweet potatoes

Directions:

1.   Make the Maple-Cinnamon Butter: In a mixing bowl, combine the butter, maple syrup, and cinnamon and whip with a wooden spoon. (Alternatively, blend the ingredients using a hand-held mixer or a stand mixer.) Transfer to a small bowl, cover, and chill until serving time.

2.   Supply your smoker with wood pellets and follow the start-up procedure. Preheat the grill, with the lid closed, to 375° F. Arrange the sweet potatoes on the grill grate and bake until soft, 1 to 1-1/2 hours, depending on the size of the potatoes. Make a slit in the side of each, and squeeze the ends gently to fluff.

3.   Serve hot with the Maple-Cinnamon Butter. Enjoy!

Mashed Red Potatoes

Servings: 4
Cooking Time: 40 Minutes

Ingredients:
* 8 Large red potatoes
* salt
* black pepper
* 1/2 Cup heavy cream
* 1/4 Cup butter

Directions:

1.   Supply your smoker with wood pellets and follow the start-up procedure. Preheat the grill, with the lid closed, to 180° F.

2.   Slice red potatoes in half, lengthwise then cut in half again to make quarters. Season potatoes with salt and pepper.

3.   Increase the heat to High and preheat. Once the grill is hot, set potatoes directly on the grill grate. Grill: 450 ˚F

4.   Every 15 minutes flip potatoes to ensure all sides get color. Continue to do this until potatoes are fork tender.

5.   When tender, mash potatoes with cream, butter, salt, and pepper to taste. Serve warm, enjoy!

Smoked Jalapeño Poppers

Servings: 4
Cooking Time: 60 Minutes

Ingredients:
* 12 Medium jalapeño
* 6 Slices bacon, cut in half
* 8 Ounce cream cheese
* 2 Tablespoon Pork & Poultry Rub
* 1 Cup grated cheese

Directions:

1.   Supply your smoker with wood pellets and follow the start-up procedure. Preheat the grill, with the lid closed, to 180° F. For optimal flavor, use Super Smoke if available.

2.   Slice the jalapeños in half lengthwise. Scrape out any seeds and ribs with a small spoon or paring knife. Mix softened cream cheese with Traeger Pork & Poultry rub and grated cheese. Spoon mixture onto each jalapeño half. Wrap with bacon and secure with a toothpick.

3.   Place the jalapeños on a rimmed baking sheet. Place on grill and smoke for 30 minutes. Grill: 180 ˚F

4.   Increase the grill temperature to 375˚F and cook an additional 30 minutes or until bacon is cooked to desired doneness. Serve warm, enjoy! Grill: 375 ˚F

Roasted Vegetable Napoleon

Servings: 4
Cooking Time: 30 Minutes

Ingredients:
* 2 Whole sweet potatoes
* 2 Whole zucchini
* 2 Whole Squash
* 1 Whole red onion
* 2 Whole Bell Pepper, Red
* salt and pepper

Directions:

1.   Supply your smoker with wood pellets and follow the start-up procedure. Preheat the grill, with the lid closed, to High heat.

2.   Salt and pepper all vegetables and grill them on both sides. Begin with the peppers and onions as they will take a little longer to cook. Grill: 450 ˚F

Portobello Marinated Mushroom

Servings: 2
Cooking Time: 15 Minutes

Ingredients:

- 1 Teaspoon chopped thyme
- 1 Teaspoon rosemary, chopped
- 1 Teaspoon Oregano, chopped
- 3 Tablespoon extra-virgin olive oil
- 1 To Taste Jacobsen Salt Co. Pure Kosher Sea Salt
- 1 To Taste pepper
- 6 Whole Portobello Mushroom
- 2 Whole russet potatoes

Directions:

1. Supply your smoker with wood pellets and follow the start-up procedure. Preheat the grill, with the lid closed, to 450° F.
2. Mix fresh herbs, olive oil, salt, and pepper together in a bowl. Rub over mushrooms. Grill both sides of mushrooms for approximately 2-3 minutes on each side. Grill: 450 ˚F
3. Clean the potatoes and slice into long strips.
4. Heat the oil on the Traeger in a sauce pan; drop the potatoes in the hot oil and fry for 7-8 minutes. Let the potatoes cool slightly on a sheet pan. Enjoy! Grill: 450 ˚F

Roasted Jalapeño Poppers

Servings: 2
Cooking Time: 30 Minutes

Ingredients:

- 8 Slices Bacon, Center Cut
- 2 Cup cream cheese
- 2 Ounce Cheese, sharp cheddar
- 1/2 Cup green onions, minced
- 2 Teaspoon fresh squeezed lime juice
- 4 Tablespoon Seeded Tomato, Chopped
- 4 Tablespoon cilantro, chopped
- 1/2 Teaspoon kosher salt
- 2 Small garlic clove, minced
- 12 Whole Jalapeños

Directions:

1. Supply your smoker with wood pellets and follow the start-up procedure. Preheat the grill, with the lid closed, to 350° F.
2. Place 2 bacon slices directly on the grill grate and cook 10-15 minutes until cooked through and crispy flipping halfway through. Remove from grill, but leave the grill on. When cool enough to handle, coarsely chop the bacon and reserve. Grill: 350 ˚F
3. In the bowl of a stand mixer, combine cream cheese, cheddar cheese, green onions, chopped bacon, lime juice, tomatoes, cilantro, salt and garlic. Mix on medium speed with a paddle until combined. Transfer mixture to a piping bag.
4. Cut the tops off the jalapeños and remove the seeds and ribs with a small paring knife.
5. Pipe the filling into each pepper so that the filling comes up a 1/4” over the top of the pepper. Place the tops back on each pepper.
6. With a rolling pin, flatten out the remaining six slices of bacon until they are 1/8” thick. Cut each slice in half. Wrap 1/2 a bacon slice around each pepper and secure with a toothpick.
7. Place the peppers in the Traeger Jalapeno Popper Tray. Place the tray directly on the grill grate and cook for 30-40 minutes until the peppers are tender, bacon is crispy, and cheese is melted. Enjoy! Grill: 350 ˚F

Roasted Green Beans With Bacon

Servings: 4
Cooking Time: 20 Minutes

Ingredients:

- 1 1/2 Pound green beans, ends trimmed
- 4 Strips bacon, cut into small pieces
- 4 Tablespoon extra-virgin olive oil
- 2 Clove garlic, minced
- 1 Teaspoon kosher salt

Directions:

1. Supply your smoker with wood pellets and follow the start-up procedure. Preheat the grill, with the lid closed, to 350° F.
2. Toss all ingredients together and spread out evenly on a sheet tray.
3. Place the tray directly on the grill grate and roast until the bacon is crispy and beans are lightly browned, about 20 minutes. Enjoy! Grill: 450 ˚F

Double-smoked Cheese Potatoes

Servings: 12
Cooking Time: 35 Minutes

Ingredients:

- 4 large baking potatoes (12 to 14 ounces each—preferably organic)
- 1 1/2 tablespoons bacon fat or butter, melted, or extra virgin olive oil
- Coarse salt (sea or kosher) and freshly ground black pepper
- 4 strips artisanal bacon (like Nueske’s), cut crosswise into 1/4-inch slivers
- 6 tablespoons (3/4 stick) cold unsalted butter, thinly sliced
- 2 scallions, trimmed, white and green parts finely chopped (about 4 tablespoons)
- 2 cups coarsely grated smoked or regular white cheddar cheese (about 8 ounces)
- 1/2 cup sour cream

- Spanish smoked paprika (pimentón) or sweet paprika, for sprinkling

Directions:

1. Supply your smoker with wood pellets and follow the start-up procedure. Preheat the grill, with the lid closed, to 400° F.Add enough wood for 1 hour of smoking as specified by the manufacturer.

2. Scrub the potatoes on all sides with a vegetable brush. Rinse well under cold running water and blot dry with paper towels. Prick each potato several times with a fork (this keeps the spud from exploding and facilitates the smoke absorption). Brush or rub the potato on all sides with the bacon fat and season generously with salt and pepper.

3. Place the potatoes on the smoker rack. Smoke until the skins are crisp and the potatoes are tender in the center (they'll be easy to pierce with a slender metal skewer), about 1 hour.

4. Meanwhile, place the bacon in a cold skillet and fry over medium heat until browned and crisp, 3 to 4 minutes. Drain off the bacon fat (save the fat for future potatoes).

5. Transfer the potatoes to a cutting board and let cool slightly. Cut each potato in half lengthwise. Using a spoon, scrape out most of the potato flesh, leaving a 1/4-inch-thick shell. (It's easier to scoop the potatoes when warm.) Cut the potato flesh into 1/2-inch dice and place in a bowl.

6. Add the bacon, 4 tablespoons of the butter, the scallions, and cheese to the potato flesh and gently stir to mix. Stir in the sour cream and salt and pepper to taste; the mixture should be highly seasoned. Stir as little and as gently as possible so as to leave some texture to the potatoes.

7. Spoon the potato mixture back into the potato shells, mounding it in the center. Top each potato half with a thin slice of the remaining butter and sprinkle with paprika. The potatoes can be prepared up to 24 hours ahead to this stage, covered, and refrigerated.

8. Just before serving, preheat your smoker to 400 °F. Add enough wood for 30 minutes of smoking. Place the potatoes in a shallow aluminum foil pan and re-smoke them until browned and bubbling, 15 to 20 minutes.

Whole Roasted Cauliflower With Garlic Parmesan Butter

Servings: 4
Cooking Time: 45 Minutes

Ingredients:

- 1 Whole head cauliflower
- 1/4 Cup olive oil
- salt and pepper
- 1/2 Cup butter, melted
- 1/4 Cup shredded Parmesan cheese
- 2 Clove garlic, minced

- 1/2 Tablespoon chopped parsley

Directions:

1. Supply your smoker with wood pellets and follow the start-up procedure. Preheat the grill, with the lid closed, to 450° F.

2. Brush the cauliflower with olive oil and season liberally with salt and pepper.

3. Put cauliflower in a cast iron skillet, place directly on the grill grate and cook for 45 minutes until golden brown and the center is tender.

4. While the cauliflower is cooking, combine the melted butter, parmesan, garlic and parsley in a small bowl.

5. During the last 20 minutes of cooking, baste the cauliflower with the melted butter mixture.

6. Remove the cauliflower from the grill and top with extra parmesan and parsley if desired. Enjoy!

Roasted Jalapeno Cheddar Deviled Eggs

Servings: 6
Cooking Time: 30 Minutes

Ingredients:

- 7 Eggs, hard boiled
- 3 Tablespoon mayonnaise
- 1 Teaspoon brown mustard
- 1 Teaspoon apple cider vinegar
- 1 Dash hot sauce
- 1 jalapeño pepper, seeded and minced
- salt and pepper
- 1/2 Cup shredded cheddar cheese
- paprika

Directions:

1. Supply your smoker with wood pellets and follow the start-up procedure. Preheat the grill, with the lid closed, to 180° F.

2. Place your eggs directly on the grill grate and smoke for 30 minutes.

3. Remove from the grill and allow the eggs to cool. Smoking the eggs will give them a slightly yellowed color, but an intense smoky flavor. If a classic white egg is your preference, then skip this step.

4. Slice the eggs lengthwise and scoop the egg yolks directly into a gallon zip top bag.

5. Add the mayo, mustard, vinegar, hot sauce, roasted jalapeños and salt and pepper to the bag.

6. Zip the bag closed and, using your hands, knead all of the ingredients together in the bag until completely smooth.

7. Squeeze the yolk mixture into one corner of the bag and then cut the corner off. Pipe the yolk mixture into the whites.

8. Sprinkle with the finely shredded cheddar or paprika and chill until you are ready to serve. Enjoy!

Roasted Beet & Bacon Salad

Servings: 4
Cooking Time: 45 Minutes

Ingredients:
- 2 Medium raw beets, peeled and thinly sliced
- 8 Slices bacon
- 1/4 Cup raw pecans or walnuts
- 2 Medium ripe pears, sliced
- 2 Large avocados, diced
- 1 Head red leaf lettuce or baby spinach, torn into bite-size pieces
- 1/4 Cup champagne vinaigrette

Directions:
1. Supply your smoker with wood pellets and follow the start-up procedure. Preheat the grill, with the lid closed, to 400° F.
2. Place beets on a foil-lined baking sheet and top with bacon. Place baking sheet directly on the grill grate (while preheating) and cook for 25 minutes. Grill: 400 °F
3. Toss to coat beets in rendered bacon fat.
4. Spread everything out in a single layer and continue to cook for another 15 minutes, or until beets are tender and bacon is crispy. Grill: 400 °F
5. Add pecans or walnuts and roast for 5 more minutes. Spoon out nuts and place on paper towels to drain and cool.
6. Once bacon is cool to the touch, roughly chop into medium pieces.
7. Place bacon, beets, nuts, pears, avocado and lettuce in a large salad bowl. Drizzle with champagne vinaigrette, toss to coat, and serve. Enjoy!

Grilled Fingerling Potato Salad

Servings: 6
Cooking Time: 15 Minutes

Ingredients:
- 10 Whole scallions
- 2/3 Cup extra-virgin olive oil, divided
- 1 1/2 Pound fingerling potatoes, cut in half lengthwise
- pepper
- 2 Teaspoon kosher salt, divided, plus more as needed
- 2 Tablespoon rice vinegar
- 2 Teaspoon lemon juice
- 1 Small jalapeño, sliced

Directions:
1. Supply your smoker with wood pellets and follow the start-up procedure. Preheat the grill, with the lid closed, to 450° F.

2. Brush the scallions with oil and place on the grill.
3. Cook until lightly charred, about 2 to 3 minutes. Remove and let cool. Grill: 450 °F
4. Once the scallions have cooled, slice and set aside.
5. Brush the fingerling potatoes with oil (reserving 1/3 cup for later use), then salt and pepper. Place cut-side down on the grill until cooked through, about 4 to 5 minutes. Grill: 450 °F
6. In a bowl, whisk the remaining 1/3 cup olive oil, 1 teaspoon salt, rice vinegar and lemon juice. Next mix in the scallions, potatoes and sliced jalapeño.
7. Season with salt and pepper, and serve. Enjoy!

Butter Braised Green Beans

Servings: 6
Cooking Time: 60 Minutes

Ingredients:
- 24 Ounce thin fresh green beans, trimmed or whole frozen green beans, thawed
- 8 Tablespoon butter, melted
- Veggie Rub or coarse salt
- freshly ground black pepper

Directions:
1. Supply your smoker with wood pellets and follow the start-up procedure. Preheat the grill, with the lid closed, to 325° F.
2. Put the green beans in a pile on a rimmed baking sheet and pour the melted butter over them. Using tongs, spread the beans out in the pan and season with Traeger Veggie Rub and black pepper.
3. Roast the beans for about 1 hour, stirring and lifting with tongs every 20 minutes or so. The beans should be very tender, shriveled, and lightly browned in places. Transfer to a serving bowl and serve while hot. Enjoy!

Roasted Pickled Beets

Servings: 8
Cooking Time: 60 Minutes

Ingredients:
- 6 Medium Red Beets, scrubbed and trimmed
- 1 Cup red wine vinegar
- 1/2 Cup sugar
- 10 Whole peppercorns
- 1 Cup water
- 1 1/2 Teaspoon coarse salt
- 8 whole cloves
- 2 Pieces Star Anise, Broken
- 1 cinnamon stick, broken in half

Directions:

1. Make a foil pouch large enough to enclose the beets. Poke a few holes in the top to allow steam to escape.

2. Supply your smoker with wood pellets and follow the start-up procedure. Preheat the grill, with the lid closed, to 350° F.

3. Roast the beets until they are tender, 50 to 60 minutes. Carefully remove the foil and allow the beets to cool until they can be comfortably handled. Grill: 350 ˚F

4. Slip the skins off with your fingers. (You may wish to wear latex gloves to avoid staining your hands.) Cut the beets into quarters or slices. (Candy cane beets are especially pretty when sliced.)

5. In the meantime, make the brine: Bring the vinegar, sugar, salt, and water to a boil in a small saucepan over high heat.

6. Put the cloves, peppercorns, star anise, and cinnamon in a clean lidded jar, such as a canning jar

7. Add the beets to the jar. Pour the hot brine over the beets. Put the lid on the jar. Cool the beets to room temperature, then refrigerate for 3 to 5 days before serving. Enjoy!

Traeger Grilled Whole Corn

Servings: 4
Cooking Time: 25 Minutes

Ingredients:

- 3 green onions
- 6 Tablespoon butter, softened
- 1 Teaspoon chile powder
- 1 Teaspoon toasted sesame seeds
- 4 ears corn, in husk

Directions:

1. Supply your smoker with wood pellets and follow the start-up procedure. Preheat the grill, with the lid closed, to 325° F.

2. Place green onions directly on the grill grate and cook 15 minutes until lightly charred. Remove from grill and set aside.

3. Sesame-Chile Butter: Take butter out of fridge and let soften. Chop up charred green onions and add to butter along with chile powder and sesame seeds. Mash all ingredients together.

4. Grill corn, rotating occasionally, until husks are blackened (some will flake and fall off) and kernels are tender with some browned and charred spots, about 25 to 35 minutes. Grill: 325 ˚F

5. Let corn cool slightly, then shuck. Serve with the Sesame-Chile Butter. Enjoy

Baked Sweet Potato Casserole With Marshmallow Fluff

Servings: 6
Cooking Time: 60 Minutes

Ingredients:

- 3 Pound sweet potatoes

- 1/2 Cup milk
- 1 Cup brown sugar
- 3 eggs
- 4 Tablespoon butter
- 1/2 Teaspoon salt
- 3 egg white
- 1 Pinch salt
- 1 Pinch ground cinnamon

Directions:

1. Supply your smoker with wood pellets and follow the start-up procedure. Preheat the grill, with the lid closed, to 375° F.

2. Rinse, dry and pierce the sweet potatoes and place in grill whole. Cook for 45 minutes or until fork tender. Remove from grill and peel. Grill: 375 ˚F

3. Once peeled, mash the sweet potatoes in a large bowl with the milk, brown sugar, eggs, butter and salt. Place mashed potatoes in a baking dish and cook for 35 minutes. Grill: 375 ˚F

4. While the potatoes bake, make the fluff. Make a double boiler by bringing a small pot of water to a simmer, then placing the bowl of your stand mixer or another large stainless steel bowl atop the water.

5. Add the 3 egg whites, 2/3 cup brown sugar, a pinch of salt and a pinch of cinnamon to the bowl and whisk continuously until the sugar dissolves and the liquid is warm to the touch.

6. Transfer the bowl from the stovetop to your stand mixer and use the whisk attachment to whip the whites on medium-high speed until it turns glossy with stiff peaks, about 5-8 minutes.

7. Once the casserole has finished baking, use a rubber spatula to cover the sweet potato mixture with the fluff. Use the back of the spatula to create dramatic peaks.

8. Return to the grill for 5-7 minutes, or until the fluff starts to turn golden and the peaks are just shy of burnt. Remove from grill and enjoy!

Tater Tot Bake

Servings: 4
Cooking Time: 15 Minutes

Ingredients:

- 1 Whole frozen tater tots
- salt and pepper
- 1 Cup sour cream
- 1 Cup shredded cheddar cheese, divided
- 1/2 Cup bacon, chopped
- 1/4 Cup green onion, diced

Directions:

1. Supply your smoker with wood pellets and follow the start-up procedure. Preheat the grill, with the lid closed, to 375° F.

2. Line a baking sheet with aluminum foil for easy clean up and spread frozen tater tots onto sheet.

3. Sprinkle with Veggie Shake or salt and pepper to taste.

4. Place the baking sheet on the preheated grill grate and cook the tater tots for 10 minutes.

5. Drizzle sour cream over cooked tater tots.

6. Sprinkle the cheese, bacon bits and green onions on top of the tater tots.

7. Turn heat up to High heat and cook for 5 more minutes until the cheese melts and serve immediately. Enjoy!

Smoked & Loaded Baked Potato

Servings: 4
Cooking Time: 60 Minutes

Ingredients:
- 6 Yukon Gold or russet potatoes
- 8 Slices bacon
- 1/2 Cup butter, melted
- 1 Cup sour cream
- 1 1/2 Cup shredded cheddar cheese, divided
- salt and pepper
- 1 Bunch green onions, thinly sliced

Directions:

1. Supply your smoker with wood pellets and follow the start-up procedure. Preheat the grill, with the lid closed, to 375° F.

2. Poke potatoes with a fork, then place straight onto the grill. Cook for 1 hour. Grill: 375 ˚F

3. At the same time, cook bacon on a baking sheet on the grill for about 20 minutes; remove, cool and crumble. Grill: 375 ˚F

4. Once potatoes are done, remove and allow to cool for 15 minutes.

5. Cut each potato lengthwise, creating long halves. Use a small spoon to scoop out about 70% of the potato to make a boat, keeping a thick layer of potato near skin.

6. Place excess potato in a bowl and reserve. Lightly mash extra potato with a fork; add butter, sour cream, 1/2 cup cheese and season with salt and pepper.

7. Take the potato skins and fill with potato mixture, then sprinkle with extra cheese and bacon.

8. Place back on grill for about 10 minutes or until warm and cheese has melted. Garnish with green onions and extra sour cream. Enjoy! Grill: 375 ˚F

Roasted Tomatoes

Servings: 2
Cooking Time: 180 Minutes

Ingredients:
- 3 Large ripe tomatoes
- 1/2 Tablespoon kosher salt
- 1 Teaspoon coarse ground black pepper
- 1/4 Teaspoon sugar
- 1/4 Teaspoon thyme or basil
- olive oil

Directions:

1. Line a rimmed baking sheet with parchment paper.

2. Supply your smoker with wood pellets and follow the start-up procedure. Preheat the grill, with the lid closed, to 225° F.

3. Remove the stem end from each tomato and cut the tomatoes into 1/2 inch thick slices.

4. Combine the salt, pepper, sugar and thyme or basil in a small bowl and mix.

5. Pour olive oil into the well of a dinner plate.

6. Dip one side of each tomato slice in the olive oil and arrange on the baking sheet. Dust the tomato slices with the seasoning mixture.

7. Arrange the pan directly on the grill grate and roast the tomatoes until the juices stop running and the edges have contracted, about 3 hours. Remove from grill and enjoy!

Braised Creamed Green Beans

Servings: 4
Cooking Time: 25 Minutes

Ingredients:
- 6 Tablespoon butter
- 2 Clove garlic, pressed or minced
- 1 shallot, thinly sliced
- 1 Cup heavy cream
- 1 Pinch ground nutmeg
- salt
- 3 Pound mixed greens such as kale, chard or collards; washed, stems removed and torn into bite sized pieces

Directions:

1. Supply your smoker with wood pellets and follow the start-up procedure. Preheat the grill, with the lid closed, to 325° F.

2. In a saucepan, heat 2 tablespoons of the butter over high heat until it foams. Add the garlic and shallot and cook over medium-low heat, stirring, until softened and golden, about 5 minutes.

3. Add the cream, bring to a simmer and cook until slightly thickened, about 10 minutes.

4. Add the nutmeg and salt to taste. Using a hand blender, purée until smooth.

5. In a cast iron pan, heat the remaining 4 tablespoons butter over high heat until it foams.

6. Add the greens and cook until tender but still bright green, about 5 minutes.

7. Sprinkle with salt and add the cream mixture. Cover and transfer to the grill.

8. Braise greens for 15-20 minutes until the cream is bubbling and greens are tender. Grill: 325 ˚F

9. Season to taste with nutmeg and salt. Serve hot. Enjoy!

Blt Pasta Salad

Servings: 6
Cooking Time: 45 Minutes

Ingredients:
- 1 pound thick-cut bacon
- 16 ounces bowtie pasta, cooked according to package directions and drained
- 2 tomatoes, chopped
- ½ cup chopped scallions
- ½ cup Italian dressing
- ½ cup ranch dressing
- 1 tablespoon chopped fresh basil
- 1 teaspoon salt
- 1 teaspoon freshly ground black pepper
- 1 teaspoon garlic powder
- 1 head lettuce, cored and torn

Directions:
1. Supply your smoker with wood pellets and follow the start-up procedure. Preheat, with the lid closed, to 225°F.
2. Arrange the bacon slices on the grill grate, close the lid, and cook for 30 to 45 minutes, flipping after 20 minutes, until crisp.
3. Remove the bacon from the grill and chop.
4. In a large bowl, combine the chopped bacon with the cooked pasta, tomatoes, scallions, Italian dressing, ranch dressing, basil, salt, pepper, and garlic powder. Refrigerate until ready to serve.
5. Toss in the lettuce just before serving to keep it from wilting.

Grilled Chili-lime Corn

Servings: 8
Cooking Time: 45 Minutes

Ingredients:
- 12 Corn, ears
- 1 Teaspoon chili powder
- 1/2 Teaspoon onion powder
- 1 Teaspoon Leinenkugel's Summer Shandy Rub
- 2 lime, juiced
- 1 Tablespoon lime zest

Directions:
1. Soak the ears of corn, still in their husk, in water for 4 to 8 hours.
2. Supply your smoker with wood pellets and follow the start-up procedure. Preheat the grill, with the lid closed, to 350° F.
3. Place corn directly on grill grates. Turn corn every 15 minutes for 45 minutes total cooking time. Grill: 350 °F
4. Combine chili powder, onion powder, Summer Shandy rub, lime juice, lime zest and butter in an oven safe dish and place in grill for 10 minutes. Remove corn and butter from the grill.
5. Pull corn husk back, but not off and remove corn silk. Using the corn husk as a handle, brush the corn with the melted chili-lime butter. Enjoy!

Smoked Beet-pickled Eggs

Servings: 4
Cooking Time: 30 Minutes

Ingredients:
- 6 Eggs, hard boiled
- 1 Red Beets, scrubbed and trimmed
- 1 Cup apple cider vinegar
- 1 Cup Beet, juice
- 1/4 Onion, Sliced
- 1/3 Cup granulated sugar
- 3 Cardamom
- 1 star anise

Directions:
1. Supply your smoker with wood pellets and follow the start-up procedure. Preheat the grill, with the lid closed, to 275° F.
2. Place the peeled hard boiled eggs directly on the grill and smoke for 30 minutes. Grill: 275 °F
3. Put the smoked eggs in a quart size glass jar with the cooked/chopped beets in the bottom.
4. In a medium sauce pan, add the vinegar, beet juice, onion, sugar, cardamom and anise.
5. Bring to a boil and cook, uncovered, until sugar has dissolved and the onions are translucent (about 5 minutes).
6. Remove from the heat and let cool for a few minutes.
7. Pour the vinegar and onions mixture over the eggs and beets in the jar, covering the eggs completely.
8. Securely close with the jar lid. Refrigerate up to a month. Enjoy!

Smoked Mashed Potatoes

Servings: 6
Cooking Time: 45 Minutes

Ingredients:
- 2 Pound red bliss potatoes, washed and diced medium
- chicken stock or water
- 1/2 Stick salted butter
- 1 Cup whole milk
- 1/2 Cup sour cream
- 1/2 Cup shredded or grated Parmesan cheese
- kosher salt
- freshly ground black pepper
- 1/2 Cup fresh sliced green onions

Directions:

1.   Place the diced red potatoes into a small saucepan or stockpot and cover with chicken stock or water.

2.   Bring to a boil and cook on a simmer until fork tender, then cook 4 to 5 minutes past that until soft.

3.   Supply your smoker with wood pellets and follow the start-up procedure. Preheat the grill, with the lid closed, to 400° F.

4.   In a separate ovenproof pan, such as a cast iron skillet, add butter and milk and place in the Traeger during start up, until melted (approximately 7 to 10 minutes). Grill: 400 °F

5.   Carefully remove the butter/milk mixture from the Traeger using heatproof gloves.

6.   Drain the potatoes and place into a large bowl. Add the melted butter/milk mixture and slowly mash.

7.   Add sour cream, cheese and green onions, then season to taste with salt and pepper.

8.   Place into the cast iron skillet, then place the skillet back into the Traeger and cook until the potatoes have a slight crust and are bubbling, about 15 minutes. Grill: 400 °F

9.   Carefully remove the mashed potatoes from the Traeger using heatproof gloves. Allow to cool for 5 minutes. Scoop and enjoy!

Carolina Baked Beans

Servings: 12-15
Cooking Time: 180 Minutes

Ingredients:
- 3 (28-ounce) cans baked beans (I like Bush's brand)
- 1 large onion, finely chopped
- 1 cup The Ultimate BBQ Sauce
- ½ cup light brown sugar
- ¼ cup Worcestershire sauce
- 3 tablespoons yellow mustard
- Nonstick cooking spray or butter, for greasing
- 1 large bell pepper, cut into thin rings
- ½ pound thick-cut bacon, partially cooked and cut into quarters

Directions:
1.   Supply your smoker with wood pellets and follow the start-up procedure. Preheat, with the lid closed, to 300°F.

2.   In a large mixing bowl, stir together the beans, onion, barbecue sauce, brown sugar, Worcestershire sauce, and mustard until well combined

3.   Coat a 9-by-13-inch aluminum pan with cooking spray or butter.

4.   Pour the beans into the pan and top with the bell pepper rings and bacon pieces, pressing them down slightly into the sauce.

5.   Place a layer of heavy-duty foil on the grill grate to catch drips, and place the pan on top of the foil. Close the lid and cook

for 2 hours 30 minutes to 3 hours, or until the beans are hot, thick, and bubbly.

6.   Let the beans rest for 5 minutes before serving.

Baked Garlic Duchess Potatoes

Servings: 8
Cooking Time: 60 Minutes

Ingredients:
- 12 Medium Potatoes, Yukon gold
- salt
- 5 Large Egg Yolk
- 2 Clove garlic, minced
- 1.24 Cup heavy cream
- 3/4 Cup sour cream
- 10 Tablespoon butter, melted
- black pepper

Directions:
1.   Place potatoes in a large pot and fill with water. Season with salt. Bring to a boil over medium-high heat.

2.   Reduce heat and simmer until a paring knife easily slides through potatoes, about 25 to 35 minutes. Drain and let cool slightly.

3.   Supply your smoker with wood pellets and follow the start-up procedure. Preheat the grill, with the lid closed, to 450° F.

4.   Whisk together egg yolks, garlic, cream, sour cream, butter, and pepper in a large bowl. Season with salt.

5.   Peel potatoes and push flesh through a ricer or a food mill directly into bowl with egg mixture. Fold in the egg mixture being careful not to overmix.

6.   Transfer to a 3-quart baking dish and bake until golden brown and slightly puffed, about 30–40 minutes. Enjoy! Grill: 450 °F

Roasted Fall Vegetables

Servings: 6
Cooking Time: 30 Minutes

Ingredients:
- 1/2 Pound Potatoes, new
- 2 Tablespoon olive oil
- salt and pepper
- 1/2 Pound Butternut Squash, diced
- 1/2 Pound fresh Brussels sprouts
- 1 Pint mushrooms, sliced

Directions:
1.   Supply your smoker with wood pellets and follow the start-up procedure. Preheat the grill, with the lid closed, to 200° F.

2.   Toss potatoes and squash with olive oil, salt and pepper and spread out on a sheet tray.

3.   Place directly on the grill grate and cook for 15 minutes. Add brussels sprouts and mushrooms and toss to coat.

4.   Cook another 15-20 minutes until veggies are lightly browned and cooked through.

5.   Adjust seasoning as needed. Enjoy!

Skillet Potato Cake

Servings: 4
Cooking Time: 40 Minutes

Ingredients:

- 8 Tablespoon butter, melted
- 2 Pound russet potatoes, peeled and thinly sliced
- 3 Tablespoon kosher salt
- 2 Tablespoon freshly ground black pepper
- thyme

Directions:

1.   Supply your smoker with wood pellets and follow the start-up procedure. Preheat the grill, with the lid closed, to 375° F.

2.   Brush the bottom of a cast iron skillet with part of the melted butter. Place potato slices vertically around the outer edges then fill in the middle in the same fashion.

3.   Pour additional melted butter over the top of the layers and sprinkle with salt and pepper.

4.   Place skillet in grill and cook for 35 to 40 minutes or until potatoes are fork tender and golden brown.

5.   Garnish with a sprinkle of fresh thyme over the top of the potatoes. Enjoy!

Baked Artichoke Parmesan Mushrooms

Servings: 8
Cooking Time: 30 Minutes

Ingredients:

- 8 Cremini Mushroom Caps
- 6 1/2 Ounce artichoke hearts
- 1/3 Cup Parmesan cheese, grated
- 1/4 Cup mayonnaise
- 1/2 Teaspoon garlic salt
- your favorite hot sauce
- paprika

Directions:

1.   Clean the mushrooms with a damp paper towel. Remove the stems and discard or save for another use.

2.   Using a small spoon, scoop out the inside (gills, etc.). Combine the artichoke hearts, parmesan, mayonnaise, garlic salt, and hot sauce and mix well.

3.   Mound the filling in the mushroom caps. Dust the tops with paprika.

4.   Arrange the mushrooms in an oven-safe baking dish.

5.   Supply your smoker with wood pellets and follow the start-up procedure. Preheat the grill, with the lid closed, to 350° F.

6.   Bake the mushrooms (uncovered) until the filling is bubbling and just beginning to brown, about 25 to 30 minutes. Serve immediately. Grill: 350 ˚F

7.   For a simple variation, stuff the mushrooms with your favorite bulk sausage and bake on your Traeger as directed above. Enjoy!

Grilled Broccoli Rabe

Servings: 4
Cooking Time: 10 Minutes

Ingredients:

- 4 Tablespoon extra-virgin olive oil
- 4 Bunch broccoli rabe or broccolini
- kosher salt
- 1 lemon, halved

Directions:

1.   Supply your smoker with wood pellets and follow the start-up procedure. Preheat the grill, with the lid closed, to 450° F.

2.   On a platter or in a mixing bowl, drizzle the olive oil over the broccoli rabe. Use your hands to mix thoroughly, coating the vegetables evenly with the oil. Season with sea salt.

3.   Place the broccoli rabe in one layer directly on the lowest grill grate. Close the lid and cook for 5 to 10 minutes. You want there to be some color and slight char on the first side. Flip and cook for a few more minutes. Grill: 450 ˚F

4.   Transfer the broccoli rabe to a serving platter and squeeze the juice of half a lemon evenly over the top.

5.   Serve with more lemon wedges on the side. Enjoy!

Baked Sweet And Savory Yams By Bennie Kendrick

Servings: 6
Cooking Time: 60 Minutes

Ingredients:

- 3 Medium Yams
- 3 Tablespoon extra-virgin olive oil
- honey
- Goat Cheese
- 1/2 Cup brown sugar
- 1/2 Cup Pecans, pieces

Directions:

1. Supply your smoker with wood pellets and follow the start-up procedure. Preheat the grill, with the lid closed, to 350° F.

2. While Traeger comes to temperature, wash yams and poke a few holes all over. Wrap yams in foil.

3. Bake for 45-60 minutes or until knife tender. You don't want to overcook and get the yams too soft because you want to be able to cut each yam into rounds.

4. Once yams have cooled to the touch, cut each into 1/4" rounds. Lightly coat each round with oil olive and place on sheet tray.

5. Sprinkle each top with brown sugar. Using a teaspoon, place desired amount of goat cheese on each round. Next top with chopped pecans. Finally, drizzle Bee Local honey over each round.

6. Based on how sweet you like your yams, you can add more brown sugar and honey.

7. After complete, place your sheet tray back in the grill and cook, lid closed, for another 20 minutes. Enjoy!

Spicy Asian Brussels Sprouts

Servings: 4
Cooking Time: 10 Minutes

Ingredients:
- 2 Cup fresh Brussels sprouts
- 2 Tablespoon vegetable oil
- 1 Tablespoon Asian BBQ Rub
- 1/4 Cup Thai sweet chile sauce

Directions:
1. Supply your smoker with wood pellets and follow the start-up procedure. Preheat the grill, with the lid closed, to 350° F.

2. Spread the halved brussel sprouts in a single layer on a lined cookie sheet. Drizzle with the oil and toss to coat.

3. Sprinkle the brussel sprouts evenly with an Asian BBQ rub and put the cookie sheet on the grill. Close the lid and cook for 7-8 minutes. Grill: 350 °F

4. Toss the brussels sprouts in the Thai Chili Sauce and return to the grill for an additional 3-4 minutes, or until the sprouts are crisp-tender. Grill: 350 °F

5. Serve immediately. Enjoy!

Grilled Beer Cabbage

Servings: 4
Cooking Time: 50 Minutes

Ingredients:
- 2 Cabbage, head
- 1 Tablespoon extra-virgin olive oil
- 1 Teaspoon salt
- 1 Teaspoon freshly ground black pepper
- 14 Fluid Ounce Guinness Extra Stout

Directions:
1. Clean and core cabbages. Drizzle with olive oil and salt and pepper. Rub into the cabbage.

2. Supply your smoker with wood pellets and follow the start-up procedure. Preheat the grill, with the lid closed, to 180° F.

3. Place cabbages directly on grill grate; smoke for 15 to 20 minutes. Remove from grill and thickly slice cabbage. Grill: 180 °F

4. Place sliced cabbage in cast-iron skillet. Pour beer over cabbage and return to grill.

5. Increase temperature to 375°F and cook for 30 minutes, or until cabbage has reached desired softness. Grill: 375 °F

6. Serve with corned beef. Enjoy!

Baked Stuffed Avocados

Servings: 6
Cooking Time: 15 Minutes

Ingredients:
- 4 avocados, halved and pit removed
- 8 eggs
- 2 Cup shredded cheddar cheese
- 1/4 Cup cherry tomatoes, halved
- 4 Slices Bacon, cooked & chopped
- salt and pepper
- 1 scallion, thinly sliced

Directions:
1. Supply your smoker with wood pellets and follow the start-up procedure. Preheat the grill, with the lid closed, to 450° F.

2. After removing the pit from the avocado, scoop out a little of the flesh to make enough room to fit 1 egg per half.

3. Fill the bottom of a cast iron pan with kosher salt and nestle the avocado halves into the salt, cut side up. The salt helps to keep them in place while cooking, like ice with oysters.

4. Crack one egg into each half, top with shredded cheddar cheese, cherry tomatoes and bacon. Season with salt and pepper to taste.

5. Place the cast iron pan directly on the grill grate and bake the avocados for 12 to 15 minutes until the cheese is melted and the egg is just set. Grill: 450 °F

6. Remove from the grill and let rest 5 to 10 minutes. Top with sliced scallions and enjoy!

Roasted New Potatoes With Compound Butter

Servings: 4
Cooking Time: 45 Minutes

Ingredients:
- 2 Pound Small Red, White or Purple Potatoes (or Combination of All Three)

- 3 Tablespoon olive oil
- salt and pepper
- 2 Stick Butter, unsalted
- 1 Tablespoon shallot, minced
- 3 Tablespoon Finely Chopped Herbs, Such As Tarragon, Parsley, Basil or Combination
- 2 Teaspoon kosher salt

Directions:

1. Supply your smoker with wood pellets and follow the start-up procedure. Preheat the grill, with the lid closed, to 400° F. Cut the potatoes in half and place in a large mixing bowl. Cover with the olive oil, a teaspoon of salt and generous grinding of pepper.

2. Place on a large baking sheet so there is space between the potatoes. Place on the grill and roast for 45 minutes to 1 hour, until crispy skinned. Toss once during cooking. Grill: 400 ℉

3. To make the butter: Place it in a medium sized shallow mixing bowl. Use a wooden spoon or strong spatula to break it up and soften it even more. Sprinkle the shallot, herbs, and salt over the butter, then use the spoon to combine the ingredients. Taste, adding more salt or herbs if necessary. Reserve a few tablespoons of the butter to serve on the potatoes.

4. To freeze the butter for future use, place a foot long piece of plastic wrap on the counter. Spread the butter out into a 6" log across the long direction of the plastic wrap towards the bottom. Begin to roll the plastic wrap away from you to roll it into a log, twisting the sides of the plastic wrap like a candy wrapper to secure.

5. Using your hands, shape the log into an even cylinder. Once it's wrapped tightly, place in the freezer. Then when more is needed, simply slice off coins of it to serve over grilled steak, chicken, veggies, or roasted potatoes. The butter holds well in the freezer for up to one month. Enjoy! *Cook times will vary depending on set and ambient temperatures.

Green Bean Casserole

Servings: 6
Cooking Time: 25 Minutes

Ingredients:

- 1/2 Stick butter
- 1 Small onion
- 1/2 Cup sliced button mushrooms
- 4 Can green beans, drained
- 2 Can cream of mushroom soup
- 1 Teaspoon Lawry's Seasoned Salt
- pepper
- 1 Can French's Original Crispy Fried Onions
- 1 Cup grated sharp cheddar cheese

Directions:

1. Supply your smoker with wood pellets and follow the start-up procedure. Preheat the grill, with the lid closed, to 375° F.

2. Melt butter in a cast iron skillet and add onions and mushrooms, stirring occasionally until softened.

3. Add drained green beans and cream of mushroom soup and stir gently to combine.

4. Season with seasoned salt and pepper and sprinkle the top with grated cheddar cheese and fried onions.

5. Bake for 25 minutes. Serve warm, enjoy! Grill: 375 ℉

Sicilian Stuffed Mushrooms

Servings: 6
Cooking Time: 25 Minutes

Ingredients:

- 12 Medium Fresh Mushrooms, about 1-1/2 inches in diameter
- 4 Ounce cream cheese, room temperature
- 1/4 Cup Parmesan cheese, grated
- 1/4 Cup shredded mozzarella cheese
- 8 Whole Pimento Stuffed Green Olives, chopped
- 3 Tablespoon Pepperoni, finely diced
- 1 1/2 Tablespoon Sun Dried Tomatoes, drained & minced
- 1/4 Teaspoon freshly ground black pepper

Directions:

1. Dampen a paper towel and wipe the outside of the mushrooms clean. Remove the stem. Using a small spoon, scoop out the inside of the mushroom leaving a shell.

2. Filling: In a small mixing bowl, beat together the cream cheese, Parmesan, and mozzarella. Stir in olives, pepperoni, tomatoes, basil, and pepper.

3. Mound the filling in the mushroom caps. Set each filled cap into the well of a muffin tin.

4. Supply your smoker with wood pellets and follow the start-up procedure. Preheat the grill, with the lid closed, to 350° F.

5. Arrange the muffin tin on the grill grate and bake the mushrooms for 25 to 30 minutes, or until the mushrooms are tender and the filling is beginning to brown.

6. Transfer to a serving plate or platter. Enjoy!

Roasted Tomatoes With Hot Pepper Sauce

Servings: 4
Cooking Time: 60 Minutes

Ingredients:

- 2 Pound fresh Roma tomatoes
- 3 Tablespoon parsley, chopped
- 2 Tablespoon garlic, chopped
- salt and pepper

- 1/2 Cup extra-virgin olive oil
- 1 Pound Spaghetti
- Hot peppers

Directions:

1. Supply your smoker with wood pellets and follow the start-up procedure. Preheat the grill, with the lid closed, to 400° F.

2. Wash tomatoes and cut them in half, lengthwise. Place them in a baking dish cut side up.

3. Sprinkle with chopped parsley, garlic, add salt and black pepper and pour 1/4 cup (100 mL)of olive oil over them.

4. Place on pre-heated grill and bake for 1 1/2 hours. Tomatoes will shrink and the skins will be partly blackened. Grill: 400 °F

5. Remove tomatoes from baking dish and place in a food processor leaving the cooked oil, and puree them.

6. Drop pasta into boiling salted water and cook until tender. Drain and toss immediately with the pureed tomatoes.

7. Add the remaining 1/4 cup (60mL) of raw olive oil and crumbled hot red pepper to taste. Toss and serve. Enjoy!

Christmas Brussel Sprouts

Servings: 6
Cooking Time: 50 Minutes

Ingredients:
- 1/2 Pound thick-cut bacon
- 1 Medium onion, diced
- 2 Pound fresh Brussels sprouts
- 2 Tablespoon olive oil
- salt and pepper

Directions:

1. Supply your smoker with wood pellets and follow the start-up procedure. Preheat the grill, with the lid closed, to 350° F.

2. Place bacon directly on grill grate and cook for 15-20 minutes, or until lightly browned. Remove from grill and set aside on paper towel lined plate.

3. Slice onion in half and then slice into 1⁄4 inch moons and add to large mixing bowl. Slice brussels sprouts in half lengthwise and add to bowl.

4. Cut reserved bacon into 1⁄2 inch pieces and add to bowl. Drizzle with olive oil and sprinkle with salt and pepper. Toss to coat and pour into baking pan.

5. Turn the temperature on grill to 375 and place baking pan on grill. Roast for 30 minutes mixing halfway through cooking. Grill: 375 °F

Smoked Bbq Onion Brussels Sprout

Servings: 4
Cooking Time: 110 Minutes

Ingredients:

- 4 strip bacon
- 1 onion minced
- 2 cloves garlic minced
- 1 lb brussels sprouts stems trimmed and cut in half
- 1 tbsp BBQ Spice Blend
- 1/2 cup Apple Habanero Bar-B-Que Sauce (or other BBQ sauce)

Directions:

1. Supply your smoker with wood pellets and follow the start-up procedure. Preheat the grill, with the lid closed, to High heat. Place a cast iron skillet over the highest heat spot and cook the bacon until crisp.

2. Remove the bacon from pan and drain, reserving the bacon fat in the pan.

3. Reduce the heat on your smoker to 250°F.

4. Add the onions, garlic, and brussels to the pan and toss to coat in the bacon drippings. Sprinkle the BBQ spice blend over top.

5. Cover the lid and allow to smoke for 1 to 1 1/2 hours, until the sprouts are fork tender.

6. For the last 20 minutes of smoking, toss the brussels sprouts in half of the barbecue sauce.

7. Remove the sprouts from the smoker.

8. Chop the bacon and add it and the remaining barbecue sauce to the pan of sprouts, tossing to coat.

9. Serve hot.

Grilled Cabbage Steaks With Warm Bacon Vinaigrette

Servings: 4
Cooking Time: 10 Minutes

Ingredients:

- 3 Strips thick-cut lean bacon, cut into 1/4 inch strips
- 1 Large shallot, minced
- 2 Tablespoon sherry vinegar
- 1 Tablespoon whole grain mustard
- 1 Teaspoon chopped thyme
- 2 Tablespoon olive oil, plus more as needed
- 1 Head green cabbage, cut into 3/4 inch thick slices (about 6 steaks)
- salt and pepper

Directions:

1. Supply your smoker with wood pellets and follow the start-up procedure. Preheat the grill, with the lid closed, to 450° F.

2. For the Vinaigrette: In a large skillet, cook the bacon in 2 tablespoons olive oil over medium-high heat until browned and crisp. Remove bacon from heat and stir in the shallot, vinegar, mustard and thyme then set aside.

3.   Brush cabbage steaks with olive oil and season with salt and pepper. Place cabbage steaks directly on grill grate and grill for 5 minutes per side. Grill: 450 ˚F

4.   Remove cabbage steaks from grill and drizzle with bacon vinaigrette. Enjoy!

Baked Kale Chips

Servings: 4
Cooking Time: 20 Minutes

Ingredients:
*   2 Bunch kale, leaves washed and stems removed
*   1 As Needed extra-virgin olive oil
*   1 To Taste sea salt

Directions:
1.   Dry the kale leaves well and lay them out on a sheet tray. Drizzle lightly with olive oil and sprinkle with sea salt.
2.   Supply your smoker with wood pellets and follow the start-up procedure. Preheat the grill, with the lid closed, to 250° F.
3.   Place the sheet tray directly on the grill grate and cook until kale is lightly browned and crispy, about 20 minutes. Enjoy! Grill: 250 ˚F

Cast Iron Potatoes

Servings: 4
Cooking Time: 60 Minutes

Ingredients:
*   4 Tablespoon butter, cut into cubes
*   2 1/2 Pound potatoes, peeled and cut into 1/8 inch slices
*   1/2 Large sweet onion, thinly sliced
*   salt
*   black pepper
*   1 1/2 Cup grated mild cheddar or jack cheese
*   2 Cup milk
*   paprika

Directions:
1.   Butter the inside of a cast iron skillet and layer half the potato slices on the bottom. Top with half the onions. Season with salt and pepper.
2.   Sprinkle 1 cup of the cheese over the potatoes and onions and dot with half the butter. Layer the remaining potatoes and onions on top. Dot with remaining butter.
3.   Pour the milk into the skillet. Cover the skillet tightly with aluminum foil.
4.   Supply your smoker with wood pellets and follow the start-up procedure. Preheat the grill, with the lid closed, to 350° F.
5.   Bake for 1 hour, or until the potatoes are very tender. Grill: 350 ˚F
6.   Remove the foil and top with the remaining 1/2 cup of cheese. Bake for 30 minutes more (uncovered) until the cheese is lightly browned. Dust the top with paprika and serve immediately.

Roasted Red Pepper White Bean Dip

Servings: 4
Cooking Time: 40 Minutes

Ingredients:
*   4 Whole garlic
*   4 Tablespoon extra-virgin olive oil
*   2 Bell Pepper, Red
*   3 Tablespoon Dill Weed, fresh
*   3 Tablespoon chopped flat-leaf parsley
*   2 Can cannellini beans, mashed
*   4 Teaspoon lemon juice
*   1 1/2 Teaspoon salt

Directions:
1.   Roasting the garlic and red peppers:
2.   Supply your smoker with wood pellets and follow the start-up procedure. Preheat the grill, with the lid closed, to 400° F.
3.   Peel away the outside layers of the garlic husk. Cut off the top of the garlic bulb, exposing each of the individual cloves. Drizzle olive oil over the top of the head of garlic and rub it in. Wrap the garlic in foil, completely covering it. Put the head of garlic and the two red peppers (washed and dried) on the Traeger.
4.   Roast the garlic for 25-30 minutes and the peppers for about 40 minutes. Rotate the peppers a quarter-turn every 10 minutes until the exterior is blistered and blackened. Grill: 400 ˚F
5.   Pull the peppers off the grill and put them in a bowl. Cover the bowl with plastic wrap and leave them for 15 minutes. The steam will loosen the skins so that they slip off like a drumstick covered in barbecue sauce.
6.   Peel off the pepper skin. Cut off the stems and scrape out the seeds and they're ready to use.
7.   As for the garlic, let it cool and then pull out the individual cloves as needed.
8.   The dip:
9.   In a blender put the roasted red peppers, 4 cloves of roasted garlic, dill, parsley, drained and rinsed beans, olive oil, lemon juice and salt.
10. Blend until the dip is smooth and creamy. You may need to scrape down the sides of the blender a couple of times. If it's having difficulty blending or looks too thick add more olive oil or lemon juice. (Add more lemon juice if it tastes like it needs more acid or brightness.) Enjoy!

Roasted Do-ahead Mashed Potatoes

Servings: 6
Cooking Time: 50 Minutes

Ingredients:
*   5 Pound Yukon Gold or russet potatoes
*   9 Tablespoon butter

- 8 Ounce cream cheese
- 1/2 Cup milk
- salt and pepper

Directions:

1. Peel the potatoes and cut into chunks that are roughly the same size. Cover with cold water and add a teaspoon of salt. Bring to a boil over high heat, then reduce the heat to medium and simmer the potatoes until they are tender.

2. Drain the potatoes and return them to the pot. Stir over low heat for 2 to 3 minutes to evaporate any excess moisture.

3. Mash the potatoes with a hand-held potato masher. (Alternative, rice the potatoes using a ricer.) Incorporate 8 tbsp butter and cream cheese. Add milk until the potatoes are of a good consistency. Stir in salt and pepper to taste.

4. Butter the inside of a casserole dish. Spread the potatoes out in an even layer in the casserole dish, smoothing the top with a spatula. Cool, cover, and refrigerate if not cooking right away. Before cooking, let the potatoes warm to room temperature (about an hour).

5. Supply your smoker with wood pellets and follow the start-up procedure. Preheat the grill, with the lid closed, to 350° F.

6. Bake the potatoes for 45 to 50 minutes, or until hot through. Grill: 350 ˚F

APPETIZERS AND SNACKS

Chicken Wings With Teriyaki Glaze

Servings: 4
Cooking Time: 50 Minutes

Ingredients:

- 16 large chicken wings, about 3lb (1.4kg) total
- 1 to 1½ tbsp toasted sesame oil
- for the glaze
- ½ cup light soy sauce or tamari
- ¼ cup sake or sugar-free dark-colored soda
- ¼ cup light brown sugar or low-carb substitute
- 2 tbsp mirin or 1 tbsp honey
- 1 garlic clove, peeled, minced or grated
- 2 tsp minced fresh ginger
- 1 tsp cornstarch mixed with 1 tbsp distilled water (optional)
- for serving
- 1 tbsp toasted sesame seeds
- 2 scallions, trimmed, white and green parts sliced sharply diagonally

Directions:

1. Supply your smoker with wood pellets and follow the start-up procedure. Preheat the grill, with the lid closed, to 350° F.
2. Place the chicken wings in a large bowl, add the sesame oil, and turn the wings to coat thoroughly.
3. Place the wings on the grate at an angle to the bars. Grill for 20 minutes and then turn. Continue to cook until the wings are nicely browned and the meat is no longer pink at the bone, about 20 minutes more.
4. To make the glaze, in a saucepan on the stovetop over medium-high heat, combine the ingredients and bring the mixture to a boil. Reduce the glaze by 1/3, about 6 to 8 minutes. If you prefer your glaze to be glossy and thick, add the cornstarch and water mixture to the glaze and cook until it coats the back of a spoon, about 1 to 2 minutes more.
5. Transfer the wings to an aluminum foil roasting pan. Pour the glaze over them, turning to coat thoroughly. Place the pan on the grate and cook the wings until the glaze sets, about 5 to 10 minutes.
6. Transfer the wings to a platter. Scatter the sesame seeds and scallions over the top. Serve with plenty of napkins.

Bacon-wrapped Jalapeño Poppers

Servings: 12
Cooking Time: 30 Minutes

Ingredients:

- 8 ounces cream cheese, softened
- ½ cup shredded Cheddar cheese
- ¼ cup chopped scallions
- 1 teaspoon chipotle chile powder or regular chili powder
- 1 teaspoon garlic powder
- 1 teaspoon salt
- 18 large jalapeño peppers, stemmed, seeded, and halved lengthwise
- 1 pound bacon (precooked works well)

Directions:

1. Supply your smoker with wood pellets and follow the start-up procedure. Preheat, with the lid closed, to 350°F. Line a baking sheet with aluminum foil.
2. In a small bowl, combine the cream cheese, Cheddar cheese, scallions, chipotle powder, garlic powder, and salt.
3. Stuff the jalapeño halves with the cheese mixture.
4. Cut the bacon into pieces big enough to wrap around the stuffed pepper halves.
5. Wrap the bacon around the peppers and place on the prepared baking sheet.
6. Put the baking sheet on the grill grate, close the lid, and smoke the peppers for 30 minutes, or until the cheese is melted and the bacon is cooked through and crisp.
7. Let the jalapeño poppers cool for 3 to 5 minutes. Serve warm.

Bacon Pork Pinwheels (kansas Lollipops)

Servings: 4-6
Cooking Time: 20 Minutes

Ingredients:

- 1 Whole Pork Loin, boneless
- To Taste salt and pepper
- To Taste Greek Seasoning
- 4 Slices bacon
- To Taste The Ultimate BBQ Sauce

Directions:

1. When ready to cook, start the smoker and set temperature to 500F. Preheat, lid closed, for 10 to 15 minutes.
2. Trim pork loin of any unwanted silver skin or fat. Using a sharp knife, cut pork loin length wise, into 4 long strips.
3. Lay pork flat, then season with salt, pepper and Cavender's Greek Seasoning.
4. Flip the pork strips over and layer bacon on unseasoned side. Begin tightly rolling the pork strips, with bacon being rolled up on the inside.
5. Secure a skewer all the way through each pork roll to secure it in place. Set the pork rolls down on grill and cook for 15 minutes.

6.   Brush BBQ Sauce over the pork. Turn each skewer over, then coat the other side. Let pork cook for another 5-10 minutes, depending on thickness of your pork. Enjoy!

Bayou Wings With Cajun Rémoulade

Servings: 8
Cooking Time: 40 Minutes

Ingredients:

*   16 large whole chicken wings or 32 drumettes and flats, about 3lb (1.4kg) total
*   for the rub
*   1 tbsp kosher salt
*   1 tsp freshly ground black pepper
*   1 tsp paprika
*   ½ tsp ground cayenne, plus more
*   ½ tsp garlic powder
*   ½ tsp celery salt
*   ½ tsp dried thyme
*   2 tbsp vegetable oil
*   for the rémoulade
*   1¼ cups reduced-fat mayo
*   ¼ cup Creole-style or whole grain mustard
*   2 tbsp horseradish
*   2 tbsp pickle relish
*   1 tbsp freshly squeezed lemon juice
*   1 tsp paprika, plus more
*   1 tsp hot sauce, plus more
*   1 tsp Worcestershire sauce
*   coarse salt
*   for serving
*   lemon wedges
*   pickled okra (optional)

Directions:

1.   Supply your smoker with wood pellets and follow the start-up procedure. Preheat the grill, with the lid closed, to 350° F.

2.   If using whole wings, cut through the two joints, separating them into drumettes, flats, and wing tips. (Discard the wing tips or save them for chicken stock.) Alternatively, leave the wings whole. Place the chicken in a resealable plastic bag.

3.   In a small bowl, make the rub by combining the ingredients. Mix well. Pour the rub over the wings and toss them to thoroughly coat. Refrigerate for 2 hours.

4.   In a small bowl, make the Cajun rémoulade by whisking together the mayo, mustard, horseradish, pickle relish, lemon juice, paprika, hot sauce, and Worcestershire. Season with salt to taste. The mixture should be highly seasoned. Transfer to a serving bowl and lightly dust with paprika. Cover and refrigerate until ready to serve.

5.   Remove the wings from the refrigerator and allow the excess marinade to drip off. Place the wings on the grate at an angle to the bars. Grill for 20 minutes and then turn. (They'll brown more

evenly but will also have less of a tendency to stick.) Continue to cook until the wings are nicely browned and the meat is no longer pink at the bone, about 20 minutes more.

6.   Remove the wings from the grill and pile them on a platter. Serve with the Cajun rémoulade, lemon wedges, and pickled okra (if using).

Pulled Pork Loaded Nachos

Servings: 4
Cooking Time: 10 Minutes

Ingredients:

*   2 cups leftover smoked pulled pork
*   1 small sweet onion, diced
*   1 medium tomato, diced
*   1 jalapeño pepper, seeded and diced
*   1 garlic clove, minced
*   1 teaspoon salt
*   1 teaspoon freshly ground black pepper
*   1 bag tortilla chips
*   1 cup shredded Cheddar cheese
*   ½ cup The Ultimate BBQ Sauce, divided
*   ½ cup shredded jalapeño Monterey Jack cheese
*   Juice of ½ lime
*   1 avocado, halved, pitted, and sliced
*   2 tablespoons sour cream
*   1 tablespoon chopped fresh cilantro

Directions:

1.   Supply your smoker with wood pellets and follow the start-up procedure. Preheat, with the lid closed, to 375°F.

2.   Heat the pulled pork in the microwave.

3.   In a medium bowl, combine the onion, tomato, jalapeño, garlic, salt, and pepper, and set aside.

4.   Arrange half of the tortilla chips in a large cast iron skillet. Spread half of the warmed pork on top and cover with the Cheddar cheese. Top with half of the onion-jalapeño mixture, then drizzle with ¼ cup of barbecue sauce.

5.   Layer on the remaining tortilla chips, then the remaining pork and the Monterey Jack cheese. Top with the remaining onion-jalapeño mixture and drizzle with the remaining ¼ cup of barbecue sauce.

6.   Place the skillet on the grill, close the lid, and smoke for about 10 minutes, or until the cheese is melted and bubbly. (Watch to make sure your chips don't burn!)

7.   Squeeze the lime juice over the nachos, top with the avocado slices and sour cream, and garnish with the cilantro before serving hot.

Citrus-infused Marinated Olives

Servings: 6
Cooking Time: 30 Minutes

Ingredients:

- 1½ cups mixed brined olives, with pits
- ½ cup extra virgin olive oil
- 1 tbsp freshly squeezed lemon juice
- 1 garlic clove, peeled and thinly sliced
- 1 tsp smoked Spanish paprika
- 2 sprigs of fresh rosemary
- 2 sprigs of fresh thyme
- 2 bay leaves, fresh or dried
- 1 small dried red chili pepper, deseeded and flesh crumbled, or ¼ tsp crushed red pepper flakes
- 3 strips of orange zest
- 3 strips of lemon zest

Directions:

1. Supply your smoker with wood pellets and follow the start-up procedure. Preheat the grill, with the lid closed, to 180° F.
2. Drain the olives, reserving 1 tablespoon of brine. Spread the olives in a single layer in an aluminum foil roasting pan. Place the pan on the grate and cook the olives for 30 minutes, stirring the olives or shaking the pan once or twice.
3. In a small saucepan on the stovetop over low heat, warm the olive oil. Whisk in the lemon juice and the reserved 1 tablespoon of brine. Stir in the garlic and paprika. Add the rosemary, thyme, bay leaves, chili pepper, and orange and lemon zests. Warm over low heat for 10 minutes. Remove the saucepan from the heat.
4. Transfer the olives and olive oil mixture to a pint jar. Tuck the aromatics around the sides of the jar. Let cool and then cover and refrigerate for up to 5 days. Let the olives come to room temperature before serving.

Chorizo Queso Fundido

Servings: 4-6
Cooking Time: 20 Minutes

Ingredients:

- 1 poblano chile
- 1 cup chopped queso quesadilla or queso Oaxaca
- 1 cup shredded Monterey Jack cheese
- ¼ cup milk
- 1 tablespoon all-purpose flour
- 2 (4-ounce) links Mexican chorizo sausage, casings removed
- ⅓ cup beer
- 1 tablespoon unsalted butter
- 1 small red onion, chopped
- ½ cup whole kernel corn
- 2 serrano chiles or jalapeño peppers, stemmed, seeded, and coarsely chopped
- 1 tablespoon minced garlic
- 1 tablespoon freshly squeezed lime juice
- 1 teaspoon ground cumin
- 1 teaspoon salt
- 1 teaspoon freshly ground black pepper
- 1 tablespoon chopped fresh cilantro
- 1 tablespoon chopped scallions
- Tortilla chips, for serving

Directions:

1. Supply your smoker with wood pellets and follow the start-up procedure. Preheat, with the lid closed, to 350°F.
2. On the smoker or over medium-high heat on the stove top, place the poblano directly on the grate (or burner) to char for 1 to 2 minutes, turning as needed. Remove from heat and place in a closed-up lunch-size paper bag for 2 minutes to sweat and further loosen the skin.
3. Remove the skin and coarsely chop the poblano, removing the seeds; set aside.
4. In a bowl, combine the queso quesadilla, Monterey Jack, milk, and flour; set aside.
5. On the stove top, in a cast iron skillet over medium heat, cook and crumble the chorizo for about 2 minutes.
6. Transfer the cooked chorizo to a small, grill-safe pan and place over indirect heat on the smoker.
7. Place the cast iron skillet on the preheated grill grate. Pour in the beer and simmer for a few minutes, loosening and stirring in any remaining sausage bits from the pan.
8. Add the butter to the pan, then add the cheese mixture a little at a time, stirring constantly.
9. When the cheese is smooth, stir in the onion, corn, serrano chiles, garlic, lime juice, cuvmin, salt, and pepper. Stir in the reserved chopped charred poblano.
10. Close the lid and smoke for 15 to 20 minutes to infuse the queso with smoke flavor and further cook the vegetables.
11. When the cheese is bubbly, top with the chorizo mixture and garnish with the cilantro and scallions.
12. Serve the chorizo queso fundido hot with tortilla chips.

Grilled Guacamole

Servings: 6
Cooking Time: 30 Minutes

Ingredients:

- 3 large avocados, halved and pitted
- 1 lime, halved
- ½ jalapeño, deseeded and deveined
- ½ small white or red onion, peeled
- 2 garlic cloves, peeled and skewered on a toothpick

- 1 tsp coarse salt, plus more
- 1½ tbsp reduced-fat mayo
- 2 tbsp chopped fresh cilantro
- 2 tbsp crumbled queso fresco (optional)
- tortilla chips

Directions:

1. Supply your smoker with wood pellets and follow the start-up procedure. Preheat the grill, with the lid closed, to 225° F.

2. Place the avocados, lime, jalapeño, and onion cut sides down on the grate. Use the toothpicks to balance the garlic cloves between the bars. Smoke for 30 minutes. (You want the vegetables to retain most of their rawness.)

3. Transfer everything to a cutting board. Remove the garlic cloves from the toothpick and roughly chop. Sprinkle with the salt and continue to mince the garlic until it begins to form a paste. Scrape the garlic and salt into a large bowl.

4. Scoop the avocado flesh from the peels into the bowl. Squeeze the juice of ½ lime over the avocado. Mash the avocados but leave them somewhat chunky. Finely dice the jalapeño. Dice 2 tablespoons of onion. (Reserve the remaining onion for another use.) Add the jalapeño, onion, mayo, and cilantro to the bowl. Stir gently to combine. Taste for seasoning, adding more salt, lime juice, and jalapeño as desired.

5. Transfer the guacamole to a serving bowl. Top with the queso fresco (if using). Serve with tortilla chips.

Pigs In A Blanket

Servings: 4-6
Cooking Time: 15 Minutes

Ingredients:

- 2 Tablespoon Poppy Seeds
- 1 Tablespoon Dried Minced Onion
- 2 Teaspoon garlic, minced
- 2 Tablespoon Sesame Seeds
- 1 Teaspoon salt
- 8 Ounce Original Crescent Dough
- 1/4 Cup Dijon mustard
- 1 Large egg, beaten

Directions:

1. When ready to cook, start your smoker at 350 degrees F, and preheat with lid closed, 10 to 15 minutes.

2. Mix together poppy seeds, dried minced onion, dried minced garlic, salt and sesame seeds. Set aside.

3. Cut each triangle of crescent roll dough into thirds lengthwise, making 3 small strips from each roll.

4. Brush the dough strips lightly with Dijon mustard. Put the mini hot dogs on 1 end of the dough and roll up.

5. Arrange them, seam side down, on a greased baking pan. Brush with egg wash and sprinkle with seasoning mixture.

6. Bake in smoker until golden brown, about 12 to 15 minutes.

7. Serve with mustard or dipping sauce of your choice. Enjoy!

Simple Cream Cheese Sausage Balls

Servings: 5
Cooking Time: 30 Minutes

Ingredients:

- 1 pound ground hot sausage, uncooked
- 8 ounces cream cheese, softened
- 1 package mini filo dough shells

Directions:

1. Supply your smoker with wood pellets and follow the start-up procedure. Preheat, with the lid closed, to 350°F.

2. In a large bowl, using your hands, thoroughly mix together the sausage and cream cheese until well blended.

3. Place the filo dough shells on a rimmed perforated pizza pan or into a mini muffin tin.

4. Roll the sausage and cheese mixture into 1-inch balls and place into the filo shells.

5. Place the pizza pan or mini muffin tin on the grill, close the lid, and smoke the sausage balls for 30 minutes, or until cooked through and the sausage is no longer pink.

6. Plate and serve warm.

Deviled Eggs With Smoked Paprika

Servings: 6
Cooking Time: 30 Minutes

Ingredients:

- 6 large eggs
- 3 tbsp reduced-fat mayo, plus more
- 1 tsp Dijon or yellow mustard
- ½ tsp Spanish smoked paprika or regular paprika, plus more
- dash of hot sauce
- coarse salt
- freshly ground black pepper
- for garnishing
- small sprigs of fresh parsley, dill, tarragon, or cilantro
- chopped chives
- minced scallions
- Mustard Caviar
- sliced green or black olives
- celery leaves
- sliced radishes
- diced bell peppers
- sliced cherry tomatoes
- fresh or pickled jalapeños
- sliced or diced pickles
- slivers of sun-dried tomatoes

- bacon crumbles
- smoked salmon
- Hawaiian black salt
- Caviar

Directions:

1. Supply your smoker with wood pellets and follow the start-up procedure. Preheat the grill, with the lid closed, to 180° F.

2. On the stovetop over medium-high heat, bring a saucepan of water to a boil. (Make sure there's enough water in the saucepan to cover the eggs by 1 inch [5cm].) Use a slotted spoon to gently lower the eggs into the water. Lower the heat to maintain a simmer. Set a timer for 13 minutes.

3. Prepare an ice bath by combining ice and cold water in a large bowl. Carefully transfer the eggs to the ice bath when the timer goes off.

4. When the eggs are cool enough to handle, gently tap them all over to crack the shell. Carefully peel the eggs. Rinse under cold running water to remove any clinging bits of shell, but don't dry the eggs. (A damp surface will help the smoke adhere to the egg whites.)

5. Place the eggs on the grate and smoke until the eggs take on a light brown patina from the smoke, about 25 minutes. Transfer the eggs to a cutting board, handling them as little as possible.

6. Slice each egg in half lengthwise with a sharp knife. Wipe any yolk off the blade before slicing the next egg. Gently remove the yolks and place them in a food processor. Pulse to break up the yolks. Add the mayo, mustard, paprika, and hot sauce. Season with salt and pepper to taste. Pulse until the filling is smooth. Add additional mayo 1 teaspoon at a time if the mixture is a little dry. (It shouldn't be too loose either.)

7. Spoon the filling into each egg half or pipe it in using a small resealable plastic bag. You can also use a pastry bag fitted with a fluted tip.

8. Place the eggs on a platter and lightly dust with paprika. Accompany with one or more of the suggested garnishes.

Smoked Cashews

Servings: 6
Cooking Time: 60 Minutes

Ingredients:

- 1 pound roasted, salted cashews

Directions:

1. Supply your smoker with wood pellets and follow the start-up procedure. Preheat the grill, with the lid closed, to 120°F.

2. Pour the cashews onto a rimmed baking sheet and smoke for 1 hour, stirring once about halfway through the smoking time.

3. Remove the cashews from the grill, let cool, and store in an airtight container for as long as you can resist.

Pig Pops (sweet-hot Bacon On A Stick)

Servings: 24
Cooking Time: 30 Minutes

Ingredients:

- Nonstick cooking spray, oil, or butter, for greasing
- 2 pounds thick-cut bacon (24 slices)
- 24 metal skewers
- 1 cup packed light brown sugar
- 2 to 3 teaspoons cayenne pepper
- ½ cup maple syrup, divided

Directions:

1. Supply your smoker with wood pellets and follow the start-up procedure. Preheat, with the lid closed, to 350°F.

2. Coat a disposable aluminum foil baking sheet with cooking spray, oil, or butter.

3. Thread each bacon slice onto a metal skewer and place on the prepared baking sheet.

4. In a medium bowl, stir together the brown sugar and cayenne.

5. Baste the top sides of the bacon with ¼ cup of maple syrup.

6. Sprinkle half of the brown sugar mixture over the bacon.

7. Place the baking sheet on the grill, close the lid, and smoke for 15 to 30 minutes.

8. Using tongs, flip the bacon skewers. Baste with the remaining ¼ cup of maple syrup and top with the remaining brown sugar mixture.

9. Continue smoking with the lid closed for 10 to 15 minutes, or until crispy. You can eyeball the bacon and smoke to your desired doneness, but the actual ideal internal temperature for bacon is 155°F

10. Using tongs, carefully remove the bacon skewers from the grill. Let cool completely before handling.

Chuckwagon Beef Jerky

Servings: 6
Cooking Time: 300 Minutes

Ingredients:

- 2½lb (1.2kg) boneless top or bottom round steak, sirloin tip, flank steak, or venison
- 1 cup sugar-free dark-colored soda
- 1 cup cold brewed coffee
- ½ cup light soy sauce
- ¼ cup Worcestershire sauce
- 2 tbsp whiskey (optional)
- 2 tsp chili powder
- 1½ tsp garlic salt
- 1 tsp onion powder
- 1 tsp pink curing salt

Directions:

1. Slice the meat into ¼-inch-thick (.5cm) strips, trimming off any visible fat or gristle. (Slice against the grain for more tender jerky and with the grain for chewier jerky.) Place the meat in a large resealable plastic bag.

2. In a small bowl, whisk together the soda, coffee, soy sauce, Worcestershire sauce, whiskey (if using), chili powder, garlic salt, onion powder, and curing salt (if using). Whisk until the salt dissolves. Pour the mixture over the meat and reseal the bag. Refrigerate for 24 to 48 hours, turning the bag several times to redistribute the brine.

3. Supply your smoker with wood pellets and follow the start-up procedure. Preheat the grill, with the lid closed, to 150° F.

4. Drain the meat and discard the brine. Place the strips of meat in a single layer on paper towels and blot any excess moisture.

5. Place the meat in a single layer on the grate and smoke for 4 to 5 hours, turning once or twice. (If you're aware of hot spots on your grate, rotate the strips so they smoke evenly.) To test for doneness, bend one or two pieces in the middle. They should be dry but still somewhat pliant. Or simply eat a piece to see if it's done to your liking.

6. For the best texture, when you remove the meat from the grill, place the still-warm jerky in a resealable plastic bag and let rest for 30 minutes. (You might see condensation form on the inside of the bag, but the moisture will be reabsorbed by the meat.) Or let the meat cool completely and then store in a resealable plastic bag or covered container. The jerky will last a few days at room temperature but will last longer (up to 2 weeks) if refrigerated.

Smoked Cheese

Servings: 4
Cooking Time: 150 Minutes

Ingredients:

- 1 (2-pound) block medium Cheddar cheese, or your favorite cheese, quartered lengthwise

Directions:

1. Supply your smoker with wood pellets and follow the start-up procedure. Preheat the grill, with the lid closed, to 90°F.

2. Place the cheese directly on the grill grate and smoke for 2 hours, 30 minutes, checking frequently to be sure it's not melting. If the cheese begins to melt, try flipping it. If that doesn't help, remove it from the grill and refrigerate for about 1 hour and then return it to the cold smoker.

3. Remove the cheese, place it in a zip-top bag, and refrigerate overnight.

4. Slice the cheese and serve with crackers, or grate it and use for making a smoked mac and cheese.

Roasted Red Pepper Dip

Servings: 8
Cooking Time: 45 Minutes

Ingredients:

- 4 red bell peppers, halved, destemmed, and deseeded
- 1 cup English walnuts, divided
- 1 small white onion, peeled and coarsely chopped
- 2 garlic cloves, peeled and smashed with a chef's knife
- ¼ cup extra virgin olive oil, plus more
- 1 tbsp balsamic vinegar or balsamic glaze
- 1 tsp honey (eliminate if using balsamic glaze)
- 1 tsp coarse salt, plus more
- 1 tsp ground cumin
- 1 tsp smoked paprika
- ½ to 1 tsp Aleppo red pepper flakes, plus more
- ¼ cup fresh white breadcrumbs (optional)
- distilled water (optional)
- assorted crudités or wedges of pita bread

Directions:

1. Supply your smoker with wood pellets and follow the start-up procedure. Preheat the grill, with the lid closed, to 400° F.

2. Place the peppers skin side down on the grate and grill until the skins blister and the flesh softens, about 30 minutes. Transfer the peppers to a bowl and cover with plastic wrap. Let cool to room temperature. Remove the skins with a paring knife or your fingers. Coarsely chop or tear the peppers.

3. Place ¾ cup of walnuts in an aluminum foil roasting pan. Place the pan on the grate and toast for 10 to 15 minutes, stirring twice. Remove the pan from the grill and let the walnuts cool.

4. Place the peppers, onion, garlic, and walnuts in a food processor fitted with the chopping blade. Pulse several times. Add the olive oil, balsamic vinegar, honey, salt, cumin, paprika, and red pepper flakes. Process until the mixture is fairly smooth. Taste for seasoning, adding more salt or red pepper flakes (if desired). (If the mixture is too loose, add breadcrumbs until the texture is to your liking. If it's too thick, add olive oil or water 1 tablespoon at a time.)

5. Transfer the dip to a serving bowl. Use the back of a spoon to make a shallow depression in the center. Top with the remaining ¼ cup of walnuts and drizzle olive oil in the depression. Serve with crudités or pita bread.

Delicious Deviled Crab Appetizer

Servings: 30
Cooking Time: 10 Minutes

Ingredients:

- Nonstick cooking spray, oil, or butter, for greasing
- 1 cup panko breadcrumbs, divided
- 1 cup canned corn, drained
- ½ cup chopped scallions, divided
- ½ red bell pepper, finely chopped
- 16 ounces jumbo lump crabmeat
- ¾ cup mayonnaise, divided
- 1 egg, beaten
- 1 teaspoon salt
- 1 teaspoon freshly ground black pepper
- 2 teaspoons cayenne pepper, divided
- Juice of 1 lemon

Directions:

1. Supply your smoker with wood pellets and follow the start-up procedure. Preheat, with the lid closed, to 425°F.
2. Spray three 12-cup mini muffin pans with cooking spray and divide ½ cup of the panko between 30 of the muffin cups, pressing into the bottoms and up the sides. (Work in batches, if necessary, depending on the number of pans you have.)
3. In a medium bowl, combine the corn, ¼ cup of scallions, the bell pepper, crabmeat, half of the mayonnaise, the egg, salt, pepper, and 1 teaspoon of cayenne pepper.
4. Gently fold in the remaining ½ cup of breadcrumbs and divide the mixture between the prepared mini muffin cups.
5. Place the pans on the grill grate, close the lid, and smoke for 10 minutes, or until golden brown.
6. In a small bowl, combine the lemon juice and the remaining mayonnaise, scallions, and cayenne pepper to make a sauce.
7. Brush the tops of the mini crab cakes with the sauce and serve hot.

Smoked Turkey Sandwich

Servings: 1
Cooking Time: 15 Minutes

Ingredients:

- 2 slices sourdough bread
- 2 tablespoons butter, at room temperature
- 2 (1-ounce) slices Swiss cheese
- 4 ounces leftover Smoked Turkey
- 1 teaspoon garlic salt

Directions:

1. Supply your smoker with wood pellets and follow the start-up procedure. Preheat the grill, with the lid closed, to 375°F.
2. Coat one side of each bread slice with 1 tablespoon of butter and sprinkle the buttered sides with garlic salt.
3. Place 1 slice of cheese on each unbuttered side of the bread, and then put the turkey on the cheese.
4. Close the sandwich, buttered sides out, and place it directly on the grill grate. Cook for 5 minutes. Flip the sandwich and cook for 5 minutes more. Remove the sandwich from the grill, cut it in half, and serve.

Sriracha & Maple Cashews

Servings: 10
Cooking Time: 60 Minutes

Ingredients:

- 2 tbsp unsalted butter
- 3 tbsp pure maple syrup
- 1 tbsp sriracha
- 1 tsp coarse salt (use only if nuts are unsalted)
- 2½ cups unsalted cashews

Directions:

1. Supply your smoker with wood pellets and follow the start-up procedure. Preheat the grill, with the lid closed, to 250° F.
2. In a small saucepan on the stovetop over low heat, melt the butter. Add the maple syrup, sriracha, and salt (if using). Stir until combined. Add the nuts and stir gently to coat thoroughly.
3. Spread the nuts in a single layer in an aluminum foil roasting pan coated with cooking spray. Place the pan on the grate and smoke the nuts until they're lightly toasted, about 1 hour, stirring once or twice.
4. Remove the pan from the grill and let the nuts cool for 15 minutes. They'll be sticky at first but will crisp up. Break them up with your fingers and store at room temperature in an airtight container, such as a lidded glass jar.

Jalapeño Poppers With Chipotle Sour Cream

Servings: 8
Cooking Time: 45 Minutes

Ingredients:

- 3 strips of thin-sliced bacon
- 12 large jalapeños, red, green, or a mix
- 8oz (225g) light cream cheese, at room temperature
- 1 cup shredded pepper Jack, Monterey Jack, or Cheddar cheese
- 1 tsp chili powder
- ½ tsp garlic salt
- smoked paprika
- for the sour cream
- 1¼ cups light sour cream

- juice of ½ lime
- ½ to 1 canned chipotle peppers in adobo sauce, finely minced, plus 1 tsp of sauce, plus more
- 1 tbsp minced fresh cilantro leaves
- ½ tsp coarse salt, plus more

Directions:

1. Supply your smoker with wood pellets and follow the start-up procedure. Preheat the grill, with the lid closed, to 375° F.

2. Line a rimmed sheet pan with aluminum foil and place a wire rack on top. Place the bacon in a single layer on the wire rack. Place the pan on the grate and grill until the bacon is crisp and golden brown, about 20 minutes. Transfer the bacon to paper towels to cool and then crumble. Set aside.

3. In a small bowl, make the chipotle sour cream by whisking together the ingredients. Add more salt, chipotle peppers, or adobe sauce to taste. Cover and refrigerate.

4. Slice the jalapeños lengthwise through their stems. Scrape out the veins and seeds with the edge of a small metal spoon.

5. In a small bowl, beat together the cream cheese, shredded cheese, chili powder, and garlic salt. Stir in the crumbled bacon. Mound the cream cheese mixture in the jalapeño halves. Line another rimmed sheet pan with aluminum foil and place a wire rack on top. Place the jalapeños filled side up in a single layer on the wire rack.

6. Place the sheet pan on the grate and roast the jalapeños until the filling has melted and the peppers have softened, about 20 to 25 minutes. (They should no longer look bright in color.) Remove the pan from the grill and let the peppers rest for 5 minutes.

7. Transfer the poppers to a platter and lightly dust with paprika. Serve with the chipotle sour cream.

Cold-smoked Cheese

Servings: 6
Cooking Time: 180 Minutes

Ingredients:

- 2lb (1kg) well-chilled hard or semi-hard cheese, such as:
- Edam
- Gouda
- Cheddar
- Monterey Jack
- pepper Jack
- goat cheese
- fresh mozzarella
- Muenster
- aged Parmigiano-Reggiano
- Gruyère
- blue cheese

Directions:

1. Unwrap the cheese and remove any protective wax or coating. Cut into 4-ounce (110g) portions to increase the surface area.

2. If possible, move your smoker to a shady area. Place 1 resealable plastic bag filled with ice on top of the drip pan. This is especially important on a warm day because you want to keep the interior temperature of the grill between 70 and 90°F (21 and 32°C) or below.

3. Place a grill mat on one side of the grate. Place the cheese on the mat and allow space between each piece.

4. Fill your smoking tube or pellet maze (see Cast Iron Skillets and Grill Pans) with pellets or sawdust and light according to the manufacturer's instructions. Place the smoking tube on the grate near—but not on—the grill mat. When the tube is smoking consistently, close the grill lid.

5. Smoke the cheese for 1 to 3 hours, replacing the pellets or sawdust and ice if necessary. Monitor the temperature and make sure the cheese isn't beginning to melt. Carefully lift the mat with the cheese to a rimmed baking sheet and let the cheese cool completely before handling.

6. Package the smoked cheese in cheese storage paper or bags or vacuum-seal the cheese, labeling each. (While you can wrap the cheese tightly in plastic wrap, the cheese will spoil faster.) Let the cheese rest for at least 2 to 3 days before eating. It will be even better after 2 weeks.

COCKTAILS RECIPES

Smoked Berry Cocktail

Servings: 2
Cooking Time: 15 Minutes

Ingredients:

- 1/2 Cup strawberries, stemmed
- 1/2 Cup blackberries
- 1/2 Cup blueberries
- 8 Ounce bourbon or iced tea
- 2 Ounce lime juice
- 3 Ounce simple syrup
- soda water
- fresh mint, for garnish

Directions:

1. Supply your smoker with wood pellets and follow the start-up procedure. Preheat the grill, with the lid closed, to 180° F.
2. Wash berries well, spread them on a clean cookie sheet and place on the grill. Smoke berries for 15 minutes. Grill: 180 ˚F
3. Remove berries from grill and transfer to a blender. Puree berries until smooth then pass through a fine mesh strainer to remove seeds.
4. To create a layered cocktail, pour 2 ounces of berry puree in the bottom of a glass. Next, pour 2 ounces of bourbon or iced tea over the back of a spoon into the glass, then 1/2 ounce lime juice and 1/2 ounce simple syrup, top with soda water and ice. Finish with mint or extra berries for garnish.
5. Repeat the same process for 3 more servings. Enjoy!

Smoking Gun Cocktail

Servings: 2
Cooking Time: 45 Minutes

Ingredients:

- 2 Jar vermouth soaked cocktail onions
- 3 Ounce vodka
- 1 Ounce dry vermouth

Directions:

1. Supply your smoker with wood pellets and follow the start-up procedure. Preheat the grill, with the lid closed, to 180° F.
2. To make the smoked onion vermouth: Pour jar of vermouth soaked cocktail onions onto a shallow sheet pan. Smoke for 45 minutes. Remove from grill and set aside to chill. Grill: 180 ˚F
3. To make the cocktail: Add vodka, 1 teaspoon liquid from the smoked onions and dry vermouth to a mixing glass. Shake and strain into a chilled martini glass.
4. Garnish with smoked cocktail onions on a skewer. Enjoy!

Traeger Smoked Daiquiri

Servings: 2
Cooking Time: 25 Minutes

Ingredients:

- 2 limes, sliced
- 2 Tablespoon granulated sugar
- 3 Ounce Rum
- 1 Ounce Smoked Simple Syrup
- 1 1/2 Ounce lime juice

Directions:

1. Supply your smoker with wood pellets and follow the start-up procedure. Preheat the grill, with the lid closed, to 350° F.
2. Toss the lime slices with granulated sugar and place directly on the grill grate. Cook 20-25 minutes or until grill marks form. Remove from grill and cool. Grill: 350 ˚F
3. In a mixing glass add rum, Traeger Simple Syrup, and fresh lime juice. Add ice to the mixing glass and shake. Strain contents into a chilled glass.
4. Garnish with a grilled lime wheel. Enjoy!

In Traeger Fashion Cocktail

Servings: 2
Cooking Time: 20 Minutes

Ingredients:

- 2 Whole orange peel
- 2 Whole lemon peel
- 3 Ounce bourbon
- 1 Ounce Smoked Simple Syrup
- 6 Dash Bitters Lab Charred Cedar & Currant Bitters

Directions:

1. Supply your smoker with wood pellets and follow the start-up procedure. Preheat the grill, with the lid closed, to 350° F.
2. Place the lemon and orange peel directly on the grill grate and cook 20 to 25 minutes or until lightly browned. Grill: 350 ˚F
3. Add bourbon, Traeger Smoked Simple Syrup and bitters to a mixing glass and stir over ice. Stir until glass is chilled and contents are well diluted.
4. Strain into a new glass over fresh ice and garnish with grilled lemon and orange peel. Enjoy!

Smoked Apple Cider

Servings: 2

Cooking Time: 30 Minutes

Ingredients:

- 32 Ounce apple cider
- 2 cinnamon sticks
- 4 whole cloves
- 3 star anise
- 2 Pieces orange peel
- 2 Pieces lemon peel

Directions:

1. Supply your smoker with wood pellets and follow the start-up procedure. Preheat the grill, with the lid closed, to 225° F.

2. Combine the cider, cinnamon stick, star anise, clove, lemon and orange peel in a shallow baking dish.

3. Place directly on the grill grate and smoke for 30 minutes. Remove from grill, strain and transfer to four mugs. Grill: 225 ˚F

4. Finish with a slice of apple and a cinnamon stick to serve. Enjoy!

Grilled Blood Orange Mimosa

Servings: 4

Cooking Time: 15 Minutes

Ingredients:

- 3 blood orange, halved
- 2 Tablespoon granulated sugar
- 1 Bottle sparkling wine
- thyme sprigs, for garnish

Directions:

1. Supply your smoker with wood pellets and follow the start-up procedure. Preheat the grill, with the lid closed, to 375° F.

2. When the grill is hot, dip the cut side of the orange halves in sugar and place cut side down directly on the grill grate. Grill: 375 ˚F

3. Grill the oranges for 10-15 minutes or until grill marks develop. Grill: 375 ˚F

4. Remove from the grill and let cool at room temperature.

5. When cool enough to handle, juice the oranges and strain through a fine strainer removing any pulp.

6. Pour 5 oz of sparkling wine into each glass and top with 1 oz blood orange juice.

7. Garnish with a sprig of thyme. Enjoy!

Sunset Margarita

Servings: 2

Cooking Time: 55 Minutes

Ingredients:

- 4 oranges
- 2 Cup plus 1 teaspoon agave
- 1/2 Cup water
- 1 Ounce burnt orange agave
- 3 Ounce reposado tequila
- 1 1/2 Ounce fresh squeezed lime juice
- Jacobsen Salt Co. Cherrywood Smoked Salt

Directions:

1. Supply your smoker with wood pellets and follow the start-up procedure. Preheat the grill, with the lid closed, to 350° F.

2. For the Burnt Orange Agave Syrup: Cut one orange in half and brush cut side with agave. Place cut side down directly on the grill grate and grill for 15 minutes or until grill marks develop. Grill: 350 ˚F

3. While the orange halves are grilling, slice the other orange and brush both sides of the slices with agave. Place slices directly on the grill grate next to the halves and cook for 15 minutes or until grill marks develop. Grill: 350 ˚F

4. Remove orange halves from grill grate and let cool. After they have cooled, juice halves and strain. Set aside.

5. Combine 1/4 cup water and agave in a shallow dish and mix well. Remove orange slices from the grill and place in the agave mixture, reserving a few for garnish.

6. Reduce the grill temperature to 180 degrees F and place the shallow dish with agave and oranges directly on the grill grate. Smoke for 40 minutes. Remove from heat and strain. Set aside. Grill: 180 ˚F

7. To Mix Drink: Rim glass with Jacobsen Smoked Salt. Combine tequila, fresh lime juice, grilled orange juice and burnt orange agave syrup in a glass. Add ice and shake well.

8. Strain into a rimmed glass over clean ice. Garnish with a grilled orange slice. Enjoy!

Ryes And Shine Cocktail

Servings: 2

Cooking Time: 30 Minutes

Ingredients:

- 2 lemon, cut into wheels for garnish
- 6 Tablespoon granulated sugar
- 2 Ounce rye
- 1 Ounce bourbon
- 3 Ounce lemon juice
- 1 Ounce Smoked Simple Syrup
- 6 Dash Fernet-Branca

Directions:

1. Supply your smoker with wood pellets and follow the start-up procedure. Preheat the grill, with the lid closed, to 325° F.

2. Toss lemon wheels with granulated sugar to coat on both sides. Place wheels directly on the grill grate and cook for 15 minutes on each side or until grill marks form. Grill: 325 °F

3. Add rye, bourbon, lemon juice, Traeger Smoked Simple Syrup and Fernet-Branca to a shaker and shake until slightly diluted (about 10 to 15 seconds).

4. Pour into a fresh glass, serve neat and garnish with a grilled lemon wheel. Enjoy!

Grilled Peach Sour Cocktail

Servings: 2
Cooking Time: 15 Minutes

Ingredients:

- 2 peach, sliced
- 2 Tablespoon sugar
- 1 1/2 Ounce Smoked Simple Syrup
- 4 Ounce bourbon
- 6 Dash Bitters Lab Apricot Vanilla Bitters
- 2 Sprig fresh thyme, for garnish

Directions:

1. Supply your smoker with wood pellets and follow the start-up procedure. Preheat the grill, with the lid closed, to 325° F.

2. Toss peach slices with granulated sugar and place directly on grill grate. Cook for 20 minutes or until grill marks form. Remove from grill and let cool. Grill: 325 °F

3. Place peaches and Traeger Smoked Simple Syrup into tin and muddle. Peaches should form about an ounce of juice during the muddling. Once completed, add remaining ingredients and shake.

4. Pour contents into glass over fresh ice and garnish with fresh thyme. Enjoy!

Zombie Cocktail Recipe

Servings: 2
Cooking Time: 45 Minutes

Ingredients:

- fresh squeezed orange juice
- pineapple juice
- 2 Ounce light rum
- 2 Ounce dark rum
- 2 Ounce lime juice
- 1 Ounce Smoked Simple Syrup
- 6 Ounce smoked orange and pineapple juice
- 2 grilled orange peel, for garnish
- 2 grilled pineapple chunks, for garnish

Directions:

1. Supply your smoker with wood pellets and follow the start-up procedure. Preheat the grill, with the lid closed, to 180° F.

2. Smoked Orange and Pineapple Juice: Pour equal parts fresh squeezed orange juice and pineapple juice into a shallow sheet pan and smoke for 45 minutes. Remove and let cool. Measure out 3 ounces of juice and reserve any remaining juice in the refrigerator for future use. Grill: 180 °F

3. Add dark and light rums, 3 ounces smoked orange and pineapple juice, lime juice and Traeger Smoked Simple Syrup to a mixing glass.

4. Add ice, shake and strain over clean ice into a Tiki glass.

5. Garnish with a grilled orange peel and grilled pineapple. Enjoy!

Smoked Hot Buttered Rum

Servings: 4
Cooking Time: 30 Minutes

Ingredients:

- 2 Cup water
- 1/4 Cup brown sugar
- 1/2 Stick butter, melted
- 1 Teaspoon ground cinnamon
- 1/4 Teaspoon ground nutmeg
- ground cloves
- salt
- 6 Ounce Rum

Directions:

1. Supply your smoker with wood pellets and follow the start-up procedure. Preheat the grill, with the lid closed, to 180° F.

2. In a shallow baking dish, combine 2 cups water with all ingredients except for the rum and place directly on the grill grate. Smoke for 30 minutes. Grill: 180 °F

3. Remove from the grill and pour into the pitcher of a blender. Process until somewhat frothy.

4. Pour 1.5 ounces of rum each into 4 glasses. Split hot butter mixture evenly between the four glasses.

5. Garnish with a cinnamon stick and freshly grated nutmeg. Enjoy!

Strawberry Mule Cocktail

Servings: 2
Cooking Time: 15 Minutes

Ingredients:

- 8 grilled strawberries, plus more for serving
- 3 Ounce vodka
- 1 Ounce Smoked Simple Syrup
- 1 Ounce lemon juice
- 6 Ounce ginger beer
- fresh mint leaves

Directions:

1. Supply your smoker with wood pellets and follow the start-up procedure. Preheat the grill, with the lid closed, to 400° F.

2. Place strawberries directly on the grill grate and cook 15 minutes or until grill marks appear. Grill: 400 °F

3. For the cocktail: Add vodka, grilled strawberries, Traeger Smoked Simple Syrup and lemon juice to a shaker. Shake vigorously.

4. Double strain into a fresh glass or copper mug with crushed ice.

5. Top with ginger beer and garnish with extra grilled strawberries and fresh mint. Enjoy!

Garden Gimlet Cocktail

Servings: 2
Cooking Time: 45 Minutes

Ingredients:

- 2 Cup honey
- 4 lemons, zested
- 4 Sprig rosemary, plus more for garnish
- 1/2 Cup water
- 4 Slices cucumber
- 1 1/2 Ounce lime juice
- 3 Ounce vodka

Directions:

1. Supply your smoker with wood pellets and follow the start-up procedure. Preheat the grill, with the lid closed, to 180° F.

2. To make smoked lemon and rosemary honey syrup, thin 1 cup honey by adding 1/4 cup water to a shallow pan. Add lemon zest and 2 sprigs rosemary.

3. Place the pan directly on the grill grate and smoke 45 minutes to an hour. Remove from heat, strain and cool. Grill: 180 °F

4. In a cocktail shaker, muddle the cucumbers and 1oz of the smoked lemon and rosemary honey syrup.

5. After muddling, add lime juice, vodka, and ice. Shake and double strain into a coup glass.

6. Garnish with a sprig of rosemary. Enjoy!

Grilled Hawaiian Sour

Servings: 2
Cooking Time: 15 Minutes

Ingredients:

- 2 Whole pineapple, trimmed and sliced
- 1/2 Cup palm sugar
- 3 Ounce bourbon
- 2 Ounce grilled pineapple juice
- 2 Ounce Smoked Simple Syrup
- 10 Ounce lemon juice
- 2 grilled pineapple chunk, for garnish
- 2 pineapple leaf, for garnish

Directions:

1. Supply your smoker with wood pellets and follow the start-up procedure. Preheat the grill, with the lid closed, to 350° F.

2. For the Grilled Pineapple Juice: Dust pineapple slices with palm sugar. Place directly on the grill grate and cook for 8 minutes per side. Grill: 350 °F

3. Remove from grill and let cool. Reserve a few pieces for garnish. Run remaining pineapple pieces through centrifugal juicer to extract juice.

4. To Make the Drink: Add bourbon, grilled pineapple juice, simple syrup and lemon juice to a cocktail strainer with ice. Shake vigorously. Double strain into a chilled coupe glass. Garnish with grilled pineapple chunk and pineapple leaf. Enjoy!

Smoked Pomegranate Lemonade Cocktail

Servings: 2
Cooking Time: 45 Minutes

Ingredients:

- 32 Ounce POM Juice
- 2 Cup pomegranate seeds
- 3 Ounce vodka
- 8 Ounce lemonade
- lemon wheel, for garnish
- fresh mint, for garnish

Directions:

1. Supply your smoker with wood pellets and follow the start-up procedure. Preheat the grill, with the lid closed, to 225° F.

2. For the Smoked Pomegranate Ice Cubes: Pour one small container of POM juice and 1 cup of pomegranate seeds into a shallow sheet pan. Smoke on the Traeger for 45 minutes. Pull off grill and let sit until cooled. Grill: 180 °F

3. Pour smoked POM juice into ice molds of your choice and put into freezer.

4. When ready to serve, place the frozen pomegranate cubes into a mason jar. Pour vodka and lemonade over the ice cubes.

5. Garnish with a lemon wheel and fresh mint. Enjoy!

Smoked Mulled Wine

Servings: 10
Cooking Time: 60 Minutes

Ingredients:
- 2 Bottle red wine
- 1/2 Cup whiskey
- 1/2 Cup white rum
- 1/2 Cup honey
- 1 cinnamon stick
- 2 pods star anise
- 4 whole cloves
- 1 (3 in) orange peel

Directions:
1. Supply your smoker with wood pellets and follow the start-up procedure. Preheat the grill, with the lid closed, to 180° F.
2. In a shallow baking dish, combine wine, whiskey, rum, honey, cinnamon stick, star anise, cloves and orange peel. Stir well until combined.
3. Place the dish directly on the grill grate and smoke for one hour until the mixture is warm. Grill: 180 ˚F
4. Remove from grill and ladle into mugs leaving the mulling spices behind. Garnish with fresh cinnamon sticks, anise, orange zest or a combination. Enjoy!

Batter Up Cocktail

Servings: 2
Cooking Time: 60 Minutes

Ingredients:
- 2 whole nutmeg
- 4 Ounce Michter's Bourbon
- 3 Teaspoon pumpkin puree
- 1 Ounce Smoked Simple Syrup
- 2 Large egg

Directions:
1. Supply your smoker with wood pellets and follow the start-up procedure. Preheat the grill, with the lid closed, to 180° F.
2. Place whole nutmeg on a sheet tray and place in the grill. Smoke 1 hour. Remove from grill and let cool. Grill: 180 ˚F
3. Add everything to a shaker and shake without ice. Add ice, then shake and strain into a chilled highball glass.
4. Garnish with grated, smoked nutmeg. Enjoy!

Smoked Ice Mojito Slurpee

Servings: 2
Cooking Time: 30 Minutes

Ingredients:
- water
- 1 Cup white rum
- 1/2 Cup lime juice
- 1/4 Cup Smoked Simple Syrup
- 12 Whole fresh mint leaves
- 4 Sprig mint
- 4 Whole lime wedge, for garnish

Directions:
1. Supply your smoker with wood pellets and follow the start-up procedure. Preheat the grill, with the lid closed, to 180° F.
2. For optimal flavor, use Super Smoke if available. Grill: 180 ˚F
3. Remove water from grill and pour smoked water into ice cube trays. Place in freezer until frozen.
4. Add rum, lime juice, Traeger Smoked Simple Syrup, mint and smoked ice to a blender.
5. Blend until a slushy consistency and pour into glasses.
6. Garnish with a mint sprig and lime wedge. Enjoy!

Grilled Frozen Strawberry Lemonade

Servings: 4
Cooking Time: 15 Minutes

Ingredients:
- 1 Pound fresh strawberries
- 1/2 Cup turbinado sugar
- 8 lemon, halved
- 1/4 Cup Cointreau
- 1/4 Cup simple syrup
- 2 Cup ice
- 1 Cup Titos Vodka

Directions:
1. Supply your smoker with wood pellets and follow the start-up procedure. Preheat the grill, with the lid closed, to High heat.
2. Dip the lemon halves in turbinado sugar and place directly on the grill grate. Toss the strawberries with remaining sugar and place next to the lemons.
3. Cook until grill marks develop on both, about 15 min for lemons and 10 min for strawberries.
4. Remove from heat and let cool.
5. Juice grilled lemons straining out any seeds or pulp. Pour into a blender pitcher.
6. Remove stems from grilled strawberries and place in blender pitcher with lemon juice. Add simple syrup, vodka, cointreau, and 2 cups of ice.
7. Puree until smooth and transfer to 4-6 glasses. Garnish with grilled strawberries and grilled lemon slices if desired. Enjoy!

Smoked Sangria

Servings: 6
Cooking Time: 45 Minutes

Ingredients:

- 1 (750 ml) medium-bodied red wine
- 1/4 Cup Grand Marnier
- 1/4 Cup Smoked Simple Syrup
- 1 Cup fresh cranberries
- 1 Whole apple, sliced
- 2 Whole limes, sliced
- 4 cinnamon stick
- soda water

Directions:

1. Supply your smoker with wood pellets and follow the start-up procedure. Preheat the grill, with the lid closed, to 180° F.
2. In a shallow dish, combine red wine, Grand Marnier, Traeger Smoked Simple Syrup and cranberries, and place directly on the grill grate.
3. Smoke for 30 to 45 minutes or until the liquid picks up desired amount of smoke. Remove from grill and place in the fridge to cool. Grill: 180 ˚F
4. When the mixture has cooled, place in a large pitcher. Add sliced apples, limes, cinnamon sticks and ice to pitcher.
5. Top with soda water, if desired. Enjoy!

Smoked Pumpkin Spice Latte

Servings: 4
Cooking Time: 45 Minutes

Ingredients:

- 1 Small sugar pumpkin
- olive oil
- 1 Can sweetened condensed milk
- 1 Cup whole milk
- 2 Tablespoon Smoked Simple Syrup
- 1 Teaspoon pumpkin pie spice
- pinch of salt
- cinnamon
- whipped cream
- shaved nutmeg
- 8 Ounce smoked cold brew coffee

Directions:

1. Supply your smoker with wood pellets and follow the start-up procedure. Preheat the grill, with the lid closed, to 325° F.
2. Cut the sugar pumpkin in half, scoop out the seeds and discard. Place the pumpkin halves cut side up on a baking sheet and brush lightly with olive oil.
3. Place the sheet tray directly on the grill grate and cook 45 minutes or until the flesh is tender. Remove from heat and place on the counter to cool. Grill: 325 ˚F
4. When the pumpkin is cool enough to handle, scoop out the flesh and mash until smooth.
5. Place 3 Tbsp of the pumpkin puree in a separate bowl and reserve the remaining for another use.
6. Add the sweetened condensed milk, whole milk, Traeger Smoked Simple Syrup, pumpkin pie seasoning and salt to the pumpkin puree. Whisk to combine.
7. Pour the cold brew over ice, add desired amount of pumpkin spice creamer and top with whipped cream, cinnamon, and shaved nutmeg if desired. Enjoy!

Fig Slider Cocktail

Servings: 2
Cooking Time: 15 Minutes

Ingredients:

- 2 peach, halved
- 4 oranges
- honey
- sugar
- 2 Teaspoon orange fig spread
- 1 Ounce fresh lemon juice
- 4 Ounce bourbon
- 3 Ounce honey glazed grilled orange juice

Directions:

1. Supply your smoker with wood pellets and follow the start-up procedure. Preheat the grill, with the lid closed, to 325° F.
2. Pit the peach and cut in half. Cut one of the oranges in half. Glaze the peach and orange cut sides with honey and set directly on the grill grate until the honey caramelizes and fruit has grill marks. Grill: 325 ˚F
3. Cut the second orange into wheels and coat with granulated sugar on both sides. Place directly on the grill grate and cook 15 minutes each side or until grill marks form. Grill: 325 ˚F
4. In a mixing tin, add grilled peaches, bourbon, orange fig spread, fresh lemon juice and honey glazed orange juice.
5. Shake vigorously to blend the juices and fig spread. Strain over clean ice. Garnish with grilled orange wheel. Enjoy!

Bacon Old-fashioned Cocktail

Servings: 2
Cooking Time: 20 Minutes

Ingredients:

- 16 Slices bacon
- 1/2 Cup warm water (110˚F to 115˚F)
- 1500 mL bourbon

* 1/2 Fluid Ounce maple syrup
* 4 Dash Angostura bitters
* 2 fresh orange peel

Directions:

1. Smoke bacon prior to making Old Fashioned using this recipe for Applewood Smoked Bacon.
2. To Make Bacon: Supply your smoker with wood pellets and follow the start-up procedure. Preheat the grill, with the lid closed, to 325° F.
3. Place bacon in a single layer on a cooling rack that fits inside a baking sheet pan. Cook in Traeger for 15-20 minutes or until bacon is browned and crispy. Reserve bacon for later. Let the fat cool slightly; you'll use the fat to infuse the bourbon. Grill: 325 °F
4. Combine 1/4 cup of warm (not hot) liquid bacon fat with the entire contents of a 750ml bottle of bourbon in a glass or heavy plastic container.
5. Use a fork to stir well. Let it sit on the counter for a few hours, stirring every so often.
6. After about four hours, put bourbon fat mixture into the freezer. After about an hour, the fat will congeal and you can simply scoop it out with a spoon. You can fine-strain the mixture through a sieve to remove all fat if desired.
7. Combine ingredients with ice and stir until cold. Strain over fresh ice in an Old Fashioned glass and garnish with reserved bacon and orange peel. Enjoy!

Smoked Salted Caramel White Russian

Servings: 4
Cooking Time: 20 Minutes

Ingredients:

* 16 Ounce half-and-half
* salted caramel sauce
* 6 Ounce vodka
* 6 Ounce Kahlúa

Directions:

1. Supply your smoker with wood pellets and follow the start-up procedure. Preheat the grill, with the lid closed, to 180° F.
2. Pour the half-and-half in a shallow baking dish and place directly on the grill grate. In another shallow baking dish, pour 2 to 3 cups of water and place on the grill next to the half-and-half.
3. Smoke both the half-and-half and water for 20 minutes. Remove from the grill and let cool. Grill: 180 °F
4. Place the half-and-half in the fridge until ready to use. Pour the smoked water into ice cube trays and transfer to the freezer until completely frozen.
5. Separate the smoked ice cubes into four glasses. Drizzle the salted caramel sauce around the inside of the glass.

6. Pour 1-1/2 ounce vodka and 1-1/2 ounce Kahlúa into each of the glasses and top with the smoked half-and-half. Enjoy!

Smoky Scotch & Ginger Cocktail

Servings: 2
Cooking Time: 60 Minutes

Ingredients:

* 1 Ounce ginger syrup
* 1/2 Ounce brandied cherry juice
* 1/2 Ounce agave nectar
* 4 Ounce scotch
* 1 1/2 Ounce lemon juice
* 2 Slices grilled lemon, for garnish
* 2 cherry, for garnish

Directions:

1. Supply your smoker with wood pellets and follow the start-up procedure. Preheat the grill, with the lid closed, to 180° F.
2. For the smoked ginger cherry syrup: Place ginger syrup, cherry juice and agave nectar in a shallow dish and place the dish directly on the grill grate.
3. Smoke for 60 minutes, or until the mixture has picked up the smoke flavor. Remove from grill and allow to cool for 30 minutes. Grill: 180 °F
4. Place smoked ginger cherry syrup, scotch and lemon juice into a shaker tin and shake with ice. Strain into a glass over fresh ice and garnish with a grilled lemon wheel and cherry. Enjoy!

A Smoking Classic Cocktail

Servings: 2
Cooking Time: 60 Minutes

Ingredients:

* 2 Bottle Angostura orange bitters
* 10 sugar cubes
* 8 Ounce Champagne
* lemon twist

Directions:

1. Supply your smoker with wood pellets and follow the start-up procedure. Preheat the grill, with the lid closed, to 180° F.
2. For the Smoked Orange Bitters: In a small skillet, combine 1 bottle of Angostura orange bitters with a splash of water and 4 sugar cubes.
3. Place skillet on the grill grate and smoke for 60 minutes. Cool the smoked bitters and put back into the bottle. Grill: 180 °F
4. Add a sugar cube to each Champagne flute and soak the sugar cubes with the smoked bitters.
5. Add champagne and a lemon twist in a flute glass. Enjoy!

Cran-apple Tequila Punch With Smoked Oranges

Servings: 2
Cooking Time: 15 Minutes

Ingredients:

- 6 Cup apple juice, chilled
- 6 Cup light cranberry cocktail
- 1 Cup cranberries, fresh or thawed
- 3 Large oranges, halved
- 1 Cup sugar, for rimming glasses
- 2 Tablespoon lemon juice
- 2 Cup reposado tequila
- 1 Cup orange-flavored liqueur, such as Grand Marnier or Cointreau
- 2 Bottle sparkling wine (such as prosecco) or sparkling water

Directions:

1. Combine 1 cup each of the apple and cranberry juices, then pour into ice cube trays. If the cube molds are big enough, place a few cranberries into each cube. Freeze for 6 hours to overnight.
2. Supply your smoker with wood pellets and follow the start-up procedure. Preheat the grill, with the lid closed, to 180° F.
3. Place the orange halves cut-side down on the grill and smoke for 15 minutes. Remove from the grill and juice oranges. Reserve smoked orange juice. Grill: 180 ˚F
4. When ready to serve, place the sugar on a flat plate. Pour the lemon juice into a bowl that will fit the rim of each glass.
5. Carefully dip the rim of each glass in the lemon juice, then dip in the sugar to create a 1/8" sugar rim. Turn the glass right-side up and allow to dry for a few minutes before using.
6. Just before serving, mix the remaining apple juice, cranberry cocktail and smoked orange juice with the tequila, orange liqueur, and sparkling wine in a large bowl or pitcher. Taste, adding more of any ingredient to meet your preference.
7. When ready to serve, place a few ice cubes in each glass, then pour a cup of the punch over the top. Alternatively, place all of the ice cubes in the punch bowl and allow guests to help themselves. Enjoy!

Smoked Cold Brew Coffee

Servings: 8
Cooking Time: 120 Minutes

Ingredients:

- 12 Ounce coarse ground coffee
- heavy cream or milk
- sugar

Directions:

1. Place half the coffee grounds in a plastic container and slowly pour 3-1/2 cups water over the top of the grounds. Add remaining grounds and pour another 3-1/2 cups water over the top in a circular motion.
2. Press the grounds down into the water using the back of a spoon. Cover and transfer to the refrigerator and let sit for 18 to 24 hours.
3. Remove from refrigerator and strain into a clean container through a fine mesh strainer or double layer of cheese cloth.
4. Supply your smoker with wood pellets and follow the start-up procedure. Preheat the grill, with the lid closed, to 180° F.
5. Pour cold brew into a shallow baking dish and place directly on the grill grate. Smoke for 1 to 2 hours depending on desired level of smoke. Grill: 180 ˚F
6. Remove from grill and place over an ice bath to cool. Drink as is over ice, with cream or sugar or use in your favorite coffee recipes. Enjoy!

Smoked Hibiscus Sparkler

Servings: 4
Cooking Time: 30 Minutes

Ingredients:

- 1/2 Cup sugar
- 2 Tablespoon dried hibiscus flowers
- 1 Bottle sparkling wine
- crystallized ginger, for garnish

Directions:

1. Supply your smoker with wood pellets and follow the start-up procedure. Preheat the grill, with the lid closed, to 180° F.
2. Place water in a shallow baking dish and place directly on the grill grate. Smoke the water for 30 minutes or until desired smoke flavor is achieved. Grill: 180 ˚F
3. Pour water into a small saucepan and add sugar and hibiscus flowers. Bring to a simmer over medium heat and cook until sugar is dissolved.
4. Strain out the hibiscus flowers and transfer your simple syrup to a small container and refrigerate until chilled.
5. Pour 1/2 ounce smoked hibiscus simple syrup in the bottom of a champagne glass and top with sparkling wine.
6. Drop in a few pieces of crystallized ginger to garnish. Enjoy!

Smoked Jacobsen Salt Margarita

Servings: 2

Cooking Time: 1 Day

Ingredients:

- kosher sea salt
- 3 Cup Jacobsen Co. Honey
- 6 Ounce tequila
- 4 Ounce fresh squeezed lime juice
- 1/2 Cup Jacobsen Salt Co. Cherrywood Smoked Salt or smoked kosher salt
- 2 Ounce simple syrup
- 2 Teaspoon orange liqueur

Directions:

1. If making your own smoked salt, take kosher sea salt (however much you want to smoke) and spread it out on a tray.

2. Supply your smoker with wood pellets and follow the start-up procedure. Preheat the grill, with the lid closed, to 165° F.

3. Place tray of salt directly on the grill grate and smoke for about 24 hours, stirring the salt every 8 hours. Once it has smoked for 24 hours, take off grill and use in all your favorite dishes. Note: If you want to skip the long smoke session, use Jacobsen Salt Co. Cherrywood Smoked Salt. Grill: 165 °F

4. Simple Syrup: Put the honey and 1 cup water in a small saucepan. Cook over low heat, stirring, for about 20 min.

5. Fill a cocktail shaker with ice. Add tequila, lime juice, simple syrup and orange liqueur. Cover and shake until mixed and chilled, about 30 seconds.

6. Place smoked salt on a plate. Press the rim of a chilled rocks glass into the salt to rim the edge. Strain margarita into the glass. Enjoy!

Smoked Barnburner Cocktail

Servings: 2

Cooking Time: 45 Minutes

Ingredients:

- 16 Ounce fresh raspberries
- 1/2 Cup Smoked Simple Syrup
- 1 1/2 Ounce smoked raspberry syrup
- 3 Ounce reposado tequila
- 1 Ounce lime juice
- 1 Ounce lemon juice
- 2 grilled lime wheel, for garnish

Directions:

1. Supply your smoker with wood pellets and follow the start-up procedure. Preheat the grill, with the lid closed, to 180° F.

2. For Smoked Raspberry Syrup: Place fresh raspberries on a grill mat and smoke for 30 minutes. After the raspberries have been smoked, reserve a few for garnish and place the remainder into a shallow sheet pan with Traeger Smoked Simple Syrup. Grill: 180 °F

3. Place sheet pan on the grill grate and smoke for 45 minutes. Remove from grill and let cool. Strain through a fine mesh sieve discarding solids. Transfer the syrup to the refrigerator until ready to use. Makes about 1/2 cup of smoked raspberry syrup. Grill: 180 °F

4. For cocktail: Add 3/4 ounce smoked raspberry syrup, tequila, lime juice and lemon juice with ice into a mixing glass. Shake and pour over clean ice. Garnish with smoked raspberries and a grilled lime wheel. Enjoy!

Smoked Pineapple Hotel Nacional Cocktail

Servings: 2

Cooking Time: 20 Minutes

Ingredients:

- 2 pineapple
- 1/2 Cup water
- 1/2 Cup sugar
- 3 Fluid Ounce white rum
- 1 1/2 Fluid Ounce lime juice
- 1 1/2 Fluid Ounce Pineapple Syrup
- 1 Fluid Ounce apricot brandy
- 2 Dash Angostura bitters

Directions:

1. For the Syrup: Supply your smoker with wood pellets and follow the start-up procedure. Preheat the grill, with the lid closed, to 180° F.

2. Trim both ends of the pineapple, discard the ends. Cut the pineapple into slices about 3/4" thick. Don't worry about the skin, it doesn't hurt to leave it on. Place the pineapple slices on the grill and smoke for about 15 minutes on each sideTrim both ends of the pineapple and discard the ends. Cut the pineapple into slices about 3/4 inch thick. Don't worry about the skin, it doesn't hurt to leave it on. Place the pineapple slices on the grill and smoke for about 15 minutes per side. Grill: 180 °F

3. While the pineapple is smoking, combine 1/4 cup water and sugar in a saucepan over low heat, stirring constantly, until sugar is dissolved. Pour syrup into a large bowl and set aside.

4. When the pineapple is done cooking, cut each slice into eight or so wedges and add the wedges to the bowl with the simple syrup, tossing to coat and cover.

5. Leave the mixture to macerate for at least 4 hours (or up to 24) in the refrigerator, stirring from time to time.

6. Strain the syrup into a clean bowl through a fine-mesh strainer and press on the pineapple with a ladle to extract as much

liquid as possible. You can bottle and refrigerate the syrup for up to 4 days.

7.   To make the cocktail: Combine the rum, lime juice, pineapple syrup, apricot brandy, and bitters in a cocktail shaker or mixing glass. Fill with ice cubes and shake until cold.

8.   Strain into a chilled cocktail glass. Garnish with a lime wheel and serve. Enjoy!

Dublin Delight Cocktail

Servings: 2
Cooking Time: 20 Minutes

Ingredients:
- 2 orange, sliced
- 3 Fluid Ounce Teeling Whiskey
- 1 1/2 Fluid Ounce Smoked Simple Syrup
- 6 Dash aromatic bitters
- 6 Fluid Ounce Guinness beer
- 2 Amarena cherry, for garnish

Directions:
1.   Supply your smoker with wood pellets and follow the start-up procedure. Preheat the grill, with the lid closed, to 450° F.

2.   Place orange slices directly on the grill grate and cook 20 to 25 minutes. Remove from grill and let cool. Grill: 450 °F

3.   In a mixing glass, add whiskey, Traeger Smoked Simple Syrup and bitters. Add ice and shake. Pour over a beer glass filled with ice and top off with cold Guinness.

4.   Garnish with a grilled orange slice and Amarena cherry. Enjoy!

Grilled Peach Mint Julep

Servings: 2
Cooking Time: 45 Minutes

Ingredients:
- 2 Whole peach
- 4 Ounce whiskey
- 2 Cup sugar
- 4 Tablespoon pink peppercorns
- 20 Whole fresh mint leaves, plus more for garnish
- 2 lime wedge, for garnish
- 4 Ounce bourbon

Directions:
1.   For the Grilled Whiskey Peaches: cut peach into slices, then soak peach slices in whiskey in the refrigerator for 4 to 6 hours.

2.   For the Pink Peppercorn Simple Syrup: In a shallow pan, combine sugar, 1 cup water and pink peppercorns.

3.   Supply your smoker with wood pellets and follow the start-up procedure. Preheat the grill, with the lid closed, to 180° F.

4.   Cook syrup down on the grill for 30 minutes, or until desired smoke flavor has been reached. Remove from the grill. Grill: 180 °F

5.   Increase Traeger temperature to 350°F and preheat. Place the whiskey peach slices directly on the grill grate and cook 10 to 12 minutes or until peaches soften and get grill marks. Grill: 350 °F

6.   To make the Julep: Muddle 1/2 ounce Pink Peppercorn Simple Syrup with 10 fresh mint leaves and 4 slices of grilled whiskey peaches.

7.   Add crushed ice over the rim of the glass. Pour bourbon over the crushed ice and stir. Garnish with 1 large sprig of mint and fresh lime. Enjoy!

Smoked Irish Coffee

Servings: 2
Cooking Time: 15 Minutes

Ingredients:
- 10 Ounce hot coffee
- 1/2 Cup heavy cream
- 1 Tablespoon sugar
- 2 Ounce Irish whiskey
- freshly grated nutmeg, for garnish (optional)

Directions:
1.   Supply your smoker with wood pellets and follow the start-up procedure. Preheat the grill, with the lid closed, to 180° F.

2.   Place the coffee and cream in separate shallow baking dishes and place both directly on the grill grate. Smoke for 10 to 15 minutes until the liquids pick up a slight smoke flavor. Grill: 180 °F

3.   Remove from the grill and cool the cream. When the cream is cool, add sugar and whip in a stand mixer or by hand to soft peaks.

4.   Pour the hot coffee into two mugs then add 2 ounces of whiskey to each.

5.   Top with smoked whipped cream and finish with freshly grated nutmeg, if desired. Enjoy!

Smoked Texas Ranch Water

Servings: 4
Cooking Time: 60 Minutes

Ingredients:
- 3 Whole limes
- 1 Tablespoon Blackened Saskatchewan Rub
- 12 Ounce blanco tequila
- 24 Ounce Topo Chico or other sparkling mineral water
- 8 Slices jalapeño, optional

Directions:

1. Supply your smoker with wood pellets and follow the start-up procedure. Preheat the grill, with the lid closed, to 225° F.
2. Cut two of the limes in half and sprinkle with Traeger Blackened Saskatchewan Rub. Place the four lime halves on the edge of the grill grate and smoke for 1 hour. Remove from grill and set aside to cool. Grill: 225 °F
3. Pour some of the rub onto a small plate. Cut the third lime into 1/4 wedges and use the lime to rub the rim of 4 cocktail glasses, turn the glasses upside down, and into the rub to salt the rim.
4. Place several ice cubes into your rimmed glasses and pour 3 ounces tequila, 6 ounces Topo Chico, squeeze the juice of one smoked lime (discard after squeezing), and add one fresh lime wedge to each. If using the jalapeño, add one or two slices to each glass (muddle if desired).
5. Stir to combine and enjoy!

Traeger Old Fashioned

Servings: 2
Cooking Time: 60 Minutes

Ingredients:
- 2 orange
- 2 Cup cherries
- 3 Ounce bourbon
- 1 Ounce Smoked Simple Syrup
- 8 Dash Bitters Lab Apricot Vanilla Bitters

Directions:
1. Supply your smoker with wood pellets and follow the start-up procedure. Preheat the grill, with the lid closed, to 180° F.
2. While Traeger preheats, slice whole orange into wheels.
3. Place cherries on a small sheet pan and place in the Traeger. Place orange slices directly on the grill grate.
4. Smoke cherries for 1 hour and oranges for 25 minutes, depending on taste, before removing from the grill. Let oranges and cherries cool. Grill: 180 °F
5. Pour bourbon into glass, followed by Traeger Smoked Simple Syrup and bitters. Add ice and stir for 45 seconds or until drink is well-diluted.
6. Strain contents into new glass over fresh ice. Skewer orange wheel and add cherry for garnish. Enjoy!

Traeger Boulevardier Cocktail

Servings: 2
Cooking Time: 60 Minutes

Ingredients:
- 4 oranges
- 1/2 Cup honey
- 1500 mL rye whiskey
- 1 1/2 Ounce Campari
- 1 1/2 Ounce sweet vermouth
- 2 Tablespoon granulated sugar
- 3 Ounce grilled orange infused rye

Directions:
1. Supply your smoker with wood pellets and follow the start-up procedure. Preheat the grill, with the lid closed, to 350° F.
2. Slice 2 oranges in half and coat cut side with honey. Peel remaining orange and place peels on the grill. Cook 20 to 25 minutes. Grill: 350 °F
3. Remove from grill and let cool. Place orange halves cut side down directly on the grill grate and cook 20 to 30 minutes or until dark grill marks appear. Remove orange halves and allow to cool. Grill: 350 °F
4. Place orange halves into a bottle of rye whiskey and let steep for 10 to 12 hours. The longer they steep, the sweeter and more pronounced the orange flavor will be.
5. Add all ingredients into a mixing glass and stir until diluted. Strain into a fresh coupe glass and serve neat.
6. Garnish with grilled orange peel. Enjoy!

Grilled Rabbit Tail Cocktail

Servings: 2
Cooking Time: 25 Minutes

Ingredients:
- 1 1/2 Ounce lemon juice
- 4 Ounce Apple Brandy
- 1 Ounce orange juice
- 1 Ounce Smoked Simple Syrup

Directions:
1. Supply your smoker with wood pellets and follow the start-up procedure. Preheat the grill, with the lid closed, to 350° F.
2. Place lemon halves directly on the grill grate and cook for 20-25 minutes or until grill marks appear. Remove from grill and let cool. Once cool enough to handle, juice the lemons then chill and reserve the juice. Grill: 350 °F
3. Using the proportions listed above and considering the size and consumption rate of your tailgate crew or party, mix all the above ingredients in a large thermos and top with a bit of ice.
4. Using 6-8 oz glasses or cups, guests can serve themselves from the thermos and garnish each drink with a grilled apple slice. Enjoy!

Traeger Paloma Cocktail

Servings: 2
Cooking Time: 25 Minutes

Ingredients:
- 4 grapefruit, halved
- Smoked Simple Syrup
- 10 Stick cinnamon
- 3 Ounce reposado tequila
- 1 Ounce lime juice
- 1 Ounce Smoked Simple Syrup
- grilled lime, for garnish
- cinnamon stick, for garnish

Directions:
1. Supply your smoker with wood pellets and follow the start-up procedure. Preheat the grill, with the lid closed, to 350° F.
2. Grilled Grapefruit Juice: Cut 2 grapefruits in half. Place a cinnamon stick in each grapefruit half and glaze with Traeger Smoked Simple Syrup. Place on grill grate and cook for 20 minutes or until edges start to burn and it acquires grill marks. Remove from heat and let cool. Grill: 350 °F
3. After grapefruits have cooled, squeeze and strain juice. It should yield 10 to 12 ounces of juice.
4. In a mixing glass, add tequila, lime juice, Traeger Smoked Simple Syrup and 2 ounces of the grilled grapefruit juice.
5. Add ice and shake. Strain over ice in an old fashioned glass.
6. Add a grilled lime slice and cinnamon stick to garnish. Enjoy!

Smoked Grape Lime Rickey

Servings: 4
Cooking Time: 45 Minutes

Ingredients:
- 1/2 Pound red grapes
- 1/2 Cup plus 1 tablespoon sugar
- 1/2 Cup water
- 1 limes, sliced
- 2 limes, halved
- 1 Tablespoon sugar
- 1 L lemon lime soda

Directions:
1. Supply your smoker with wood pellets and follow the start-up procedure. Preheat the grill, with the lid closed, to 180° F.
2. Rinse grapes well and place in a shallow baking dish. Combine 1/2 cup sugar and water and stir until sugar dissolves. Pour over grapes.
3. Place the baking dish directly on the grill grate and smoke for 30 to 40 minutes until grapes are tender. Grill: 180 °F
4. Remove from the grill and pour entire contents of the baking dish in a blender. Puree on high until smooth then pass the mixture through a fine mesh strainer.

5. Increase Traeger temperature to 350°F. Grill: 350 °F
6. Toss the lime slices and lime halves with 1 tablespoon sugar and place directly on the grill grate. Cook for 15 to 20 minutes or until grill marks develop. Remove from grill and set slices aside. When cool enough to handle, juice grilled lime halves. Grill: 350 °F
7. To build the drink, fill a pint glass with ice. Pour in 1-1/2 ounce grilled lime juice, 1-1/2 ounce smoked grape syrup and top off with soda. Garnish with grilled lime slice. Enjoy!

Honey Glazed Grapefruit Shandy Cocktail

Servings: 2
Cooking Time: 20 Minutes

Ingredients:
- 4 grapefruits
- 4 Tablespoon honey
- granulated sugar
- 2 Ounce bourbon
- 1 Ounce Smoked Simple Syrup
- 4 Ounce honey glazed grilled grapefruit, juiced
- 2 Bottle Ballast Point Grapefruit Sculpin

Directions:
1. Supply your smoker with wood pellets and follow the start-up procedure. Preheat the grill, with the lid closed, to 375° F.
2. For the honey glazed grapefruit: Slice one grapefruit in half and coat with 2 tablespoons honey.
3. Take the other grapefruit and slice into wheels. Toss the wheels in granulated sugar until well coated.
4. Place the grapefruit halves and wheels directly on the grill grate, cut side down, and cook for 20 to 30 minutes. Remove from grill and set the wheels aside. Grill: 375 °F
5. Squeeze the grapefruit halves into a measuring cup. It should yield about 2 oz juice.
6. Pour the grapefruit juice into a shaker and add bourbon and Traeger Smoked Simple Syrup then top with ice. Shake for 10-15 seconds.
7. Strain into glass, add ice and fill with beer. Garnish with the grilled grapefruit wheel. Enjoy!

Smoked Plum And Thyme Fizz Cocktail

Servings: 2
Cooking Time: 60 Minutes

Ingredients:
- 6 fresh plums
- 4 Fluid Ounce vodka

- 1 1/2 Fluid Ounce fresh lemon juice
- 2 Ounce smoked plum and thyme simple syrup
- 4 Fluid Ounce club soda
- 2 Slices smoked plum, for garnish
- 2 Sprig fresh thyme, for garnish
- 8 Sprig thyme
- 2 Cup Smoked Simple Syrup

Directions:

1.   Supply your smoker with wood pellets and follow the start-up procedure. Preheat the grill, with the lid closed, to 180° F.

2.   Cut plums in half and remove the pit. Place the plum halves directly on the grill grate and smoke for 25 minutes. Grill: 180 °F

3.   For the Plum and Thyme Simple Syrup: After 25 minutes, remove plums from the grill and cut into quarters. Add plums and thyme sprigs to 1 cup of Traeger Smoked Simple Syrup. Smoke the mixture for 45 minutes. Remove from grill, strain and let cool. Grill: 180 °F

4.   Add vodka, fresh lemon juice and smoked plum and thyme simple syrup to a mixing glass.

5.   Add ice and shake. Strain over clean ice, top off with club soda and garnish with a piece of thyme and slice of smoked plum. Enjoy!

Grilled Peach Smash Cocktail

Servings: 2
Cooking Time: 10 Minutes

Ingredients:

- 2 peach, sliced and grilled
- 10 fresh mint leaves
- 1 1/2 Ounce Smoked Simple Syrup
- 4 Ounce bourbon
- 2 mint sprig, for garnish

Directions:

1.   Supply your smoker with wood pellets and follow the start-up procedure. Preheat the grill, with the lid closed, to 375° F.

2.   Cut the peach into 6 slices and brush with Traeger Smoked Simple Syrup. Place directly on the grill grate and cook 10 to 12 minutes or until peaches soften and get grill marks. Grill: 375 °F

3.   In a mixing glass, add 3 slices of grilled peaches, 5 mint leaves and Traeger Smoked Simple Syrup.

4.   Muddle ingredients to release oils of the mint and juices from the grilled peaches. Add bourbon and crushed ice.

5.   Shake and pour into a stemless wine glass. Top off with more crushed ice. Garnish with a grilled peach and mint sprig. Enjoy!

Smoked Eggnog

Servings: 4
Cooking Time: 60 Minutes

Ingredients:

- 2 Cup whole milk
- 1 Cup heavy cream
- 4 egg yolk
- Cup sugar
- 3 Ounce bourbon
- 1 Teaspoon vanilla extract
- 1 Teaspoon nutmeg
- 4 egg white
- whipped cream

Directions:

1.   Plan ahead, this recipe requires chill time.

2.   Supply your smoker with wood pellets and follow the start-up procedure. Preheat the grill, with the lid closed, to 180° F.

3.   Pour the milk and the cream into a baking pan and smoke on the Traeger for 60 minutes. Grill: 180 °F

4.   Meanwhile, in the bowl of a stand mixer, beat the egg yolks until they lighten in color. Gradually add 1/3 cup sugar and continue to beat until sugar completely dissolves.

5.   After the milk and cream have smoked, add them along with the bourbon, vanilla and nutmeg into the egg mixture and stir to combine.

6.   Place the egg whites in the bowl of a stand mixer and beat to soft peaks. When you lift the beaters the whites will make a peak that slightly curls down.

7.   With the mixer still running, gradually add 1 tablespoon of sugar and beat until stiff peaks form.

8.   Gently fold the egg whites into the cream mixture and then whisk to thoroughly combine.

9.   Chill eggnog for a couple hours to let the flavors meld. Garnish with a dash of nutmeg and whipped cream on top. Enjoy!

Traeger Gin & Tonic

Servings: 2
Cooking Time: 45 Minutes

Ingredients:

- 1/2 Cup berries
- 2 orange, sliced
- 4 Tablespoon granulated sugar
- 3 Ounce gin
- 1 Cup tonic water
- 2 Sprig fresh mint, for garnish

Directions:

1.   Supply your smoker with wood pellets and follow the start-up procedure. Preheat the grill, with the lid closed, to 180° F.

2.   For the Smoked Berries: Spread mixed fresh berries on a sheet pan and place directly on the grill grate. Smoke for 30 minutes then remove from grill. Grill: 180 °F

3.   For the Orange Slices: Increase the grill temperature to 450°F and preheat, lid closed for 15 minutes. Grill: 450 °F

4.   Toss the orange slices with granulated sugar and place directly on grill grate. Cook for about 5 minutes, turning once or until the slices have developed grill marks. Grill: 450 °F

5.   Pour gin into a glass, add ice and berries, then top with tonic water. Garnish with a fresh mint sprig and grilled orange wheel. Enjoy!

Smoke And Bubz Cocktail

Servings: 2
Cooking Time: 45 Minutes

Ingredients:
- 16 Ounce POM Juice
- 2 Cup pomegranate seeds
- 6 Ounce sparkling white wine
- 2 lemon twist, for garnish
- 2 Teaspoon pomegranate seeds

Directions:
1.   Supply your smoker with wood pellets and follow the start-up procedure. Preheat the grill, with the lid closed, to 180° F.

2.   For the Smoked Pomegranate Juice: Pour POM juice and a cup of pomegranate seeds into a shallow sheet pan. Smoke on the Traeger for 45 minutes. Pull off grill, strain, discard seeds and let sit until chilled. Grill: 180 °F

3.   Add 1-1/2 ounces of the smoked pomegranate juice to the bottom of a champagne flute.

4.   Add sparkling white wine, a few fresh pomegranate seeds and a lemon twist to garnish. Enjoy!

Smoked Raspberry Bubbler Cocktail

Servings: 2
Cooking Time: 45 Minutes

Ingredients:
- 2 Cup fresh raspberries
- Smoked Simple Syrup
- 8 Ounce sparkling wine

Directions:
1.   Supply your smoker with wood pellets and follow the start-up procedure. Preheat the grill, with the lid closed, to 180° F.

2.   Smoked Raspberry Syrup: Place 1 cup fresh raspberries on a grill mat and smoke for 30 minutes. Grill: 180 °F

3.   After the raspberries have been smoked, set a few aside for garnish. Place the remainder into a shallow sheet pan with Traeger Smoked Simple Syrup. Place back on the grill grate and let smoke for 45 minutes. Remove from heat and allow to cool. Strain and refrigerate until ready to use. Grill: 180 °F

4.   Place 1 ounce of the smoked raspberry syrup in the bottom of a champagne flute and top off with sparkling white wine or champagne.

5.   Garnish with smoked raspberries. Enjoy!

Smoky Mountain Bramble Cocktail

Servings: 2
Cooking Time: 15 Minutes

Ingredients:
- 16 Ounce blackberries
- 2 Cup sugar
- 10 smoked blackberries
- 3 Ounce vodka
- 1 1/2 Ounce Alpine Distilling Preserve Liqueur
- 1 1/2 Ounce lemon juice
- 1 Ounce smoked blackberry syrup

Directions:
1.   Supply your smoker with wood pellets and follow the start-up procedure. Preheat the grill, with the lid closed, to 180° F.

2.   To make Smoked Blackberry Simple Syrup: Place blackberries on a grill mat and smoke for 15 to 20 minutes. Grill: 180 °F

3.   Combine 1 cup water and sugar in a small sauce pan and warm over medium heat until sugar dissolves. Remove from heat and place 2/3 of blackberries in the simple syrup and macerate.

4.   Strain through a fine mesh strainer and store for up to 14 days.

5.   To make the cocktail: Muddle 4 to 5 smoked blackberries in a cocktail shaker. Add vodka, Preserve Liqueur, lemon and smoked blackberry syrup. Add ice and shake vigorously. Double strain into an old fashioned glass.

6.   Garnish with a smoked blackberry and lemon twist. Enjoy!

BEEF LAMB AND GAME RECIPES

Bbq Burnt End Sandwich

Servings: 2
Cooking Time: 480 Minutes

Ingredients:

- 1 point cut brisket
- Beef Rub
- 1/2 Cup beef broth
- 1 Cup Texas Spicy BBQ Sauce
- 4 Slices Monterey Jack cheese
- 4 burger buns

Directions:

1. Supply your smoker with wood pellets and follow the start-up procedure. Preheat the grill, with the lid closed, to 250° F.
2. Trim excess fat off brisket point. Season brisket point liberally with Traeger Beef rub.
3. Place brisket point directly on the grill grate. Cook until it reaches an internal temperature of 170°F, approximately 4 to 5 hours. Grill: 250 °F
4. Remove brisket from grill and cut into 1-inch cubes. Add the beef broth to the pan with the cubed brisket. Cover pan with aluminum foil.
5. Place pan in grill and cook for 90 minutes. Grill: 250 °F
6. Remove the foil and add Traeger Texas Spicy BBQ sauce. Stir and put back on the grill, uncovered, for an additional 45 minutes. Remove from grill. Grill: 250 °F
7. Top each bun with the burnt ends, cheese, and additional BBQ sauce. Enjoy!

Wagyu Corned Beef Hash

Servings: 8
Cooking Time: 360 Minutes

Ingredients:

- 2 1/2 Pound Wagyu Corned Beef Roast
- 2 red bell pepper, diced
- 1 green bell pepper, diced
- 2 Pound Southern Hash Brown
- 3 Cup shredded cheddar cheese
- 2 Tablespoon kosher salt
- 2 Tablespoon black pepper
- 7 eggs
- 1/2 Cup whole milk

Directions:

1. Corned Beef: Corned beef needs to be cooked at least one day prior to making the hash.

2. Supply your smoker with wood pellets and follow the start-up procedure. Preheat the grill, with the lid closed, to 275° F.
3. Rinse the corned beef and place on grill. Cook for 4 to 4.5 hours. Wrap in a double layer of heavy duty tin foil and put back on the grill. Grill: 275 °F
4. Cook meat until it reaches an internal temperature of 204 degrees F. This should take 2-3 more hours. Let vent for 2 hours and place in fridge. Refrigerate overnight. Grill: 275 °F Probe: 204 °F
5. Corned Beef Hash: Chop and cook the peppers in cast iron for 20 minutes.
6. When ready to cook, start the Traeger and set the temperature to 350 degrees F and preheat, lid closed, for 10 minutes. Grill: 350 °F
7. Cut the corned beef into bite-sized pieces. Combine the hash browns, corned beef, bell peppers, cheese, salt and pepper. Mix well and place in a 9x13 baking dish.
8. Mix eggs and milk in a separate bowl. Pour over the top of the hash brown mixture.
9. Cover with foil and set on the grill for a 1.5 hours. The internal temperature should reach 165 degrees F. Serve and enjoy! Grill: 350 °F Probe: 165 °F

Breakfast Brisket Hash Recipe

Servings: 4
Cooking Time: 20 Minutes

Ingredients:

- 3 Tablespoon canola oil
- 1/2 Cup yellow onion, diced
- 1/2 Cup green bell pepper, diced
- 1/2 Cup red bell pepper, diced
- 1 Clove garlic, minced
- 2 Cup Hashbrown Potatoes, Cooked
- 2 Cup brisket, cooked and shredded
- 3 Whole eggs
- salt and pepper

Directions:

1. Supply your smoker with wood pellets and follow the start-up procedure. Preheat the grill, with the lid closed, to 450° F.
2. Place oil, peppers, and onion in the skillet; sauté until they are translucent. Grill: 450 °F
3. Add garlic and cook 3 more minutes. Add cooked potatoes, brisket, and eggs. Cook until the brisket is heated through, about 10 minutes. Sprinkle salt and pepper and stir. Enjoy!

Brined Smoked Brisket

Servings: 4
Cooking Time: 420 Minutes

Ingredients:
- 1 (5-7 lb) flat cut brisket
- 1 Cup brown sugar
- 1/2 Cup kosher salt
- 1/4 Cup Beef Rub

Directions:

1. Dissolve salt and sugar in 6 quarts boiling water. Add 6 cups ice then let it cool. Place the brisket in the brine and cover. Leave brine in the refrigerator overnight.

2. Remove the brisket from the brine and pat it dry with a paper towel. Sprinkle evenly with Traeger Beef Rub.

3. Supply your smoker with wood pellets and follow the start-up procedure. Preheat the grill, with the lid closed, to 250° F.

4. Place the brisket on the Traeger, fat cap down and smoke for 3 hours. Grill: 250 ˚F

5. After 3 hours, double wrap the brisket in foil and turn the temperature up to 275˚F. Cook meat until internal temperature reaches 204˚F, about 3 to 4 hours. Grill: 275 ˚F Probe: 204 ˚F

6. Unwrap the brisket and place it unwrapped on the grill for 30 more minutes. Grill: 275 ˚F

7. Remove the brisket from the grill and let it rest for 15 minutes before slicing against the grain. Enjoy!

Bbq Brisket Tacos

Servings: 6
Cooking Time: 45 Minutes

Ingredients:
- 5 Pound leftover beef brisket
- 1/2 Cup beef broth
- 5 avocados
- 4 diced Roma tomatoes
- 1 jalapeño, minced
- 1/2 Cup sour cream
- 1 lime juice
- salt and pepper
- 20 flour tortillas

Directions:

1. Supply your smoker with wood pellets and follow the start-up procedure. Preheat the grill, with the lid closed, to 300° F.

2. If not already sliced, slice brisket against the grain to 1/4 inch slices. Place sliced brisket in a double layer of foil and add beef broth. Seal foil and place on grill for 45 to 60 minutes until warm. Grill: 300 ˚F

3. If not using leftover brisket, see here for our favorite brisket recipe.

4. While brisket is warming up, make the guacamole. Mash the avocados and mix with tomatoes, jalapeño, onion, sour cream, lime juice and salt and pepper. Set aside.

5. Wrap the tortillas in foil and place in grill for 15 minutes or until warm. Grill: 300 ˚F

6. Remove brisket and tortillas from grill and assemble. Top with guacamole and your favorite toppings. Enjoy!

Duck Fat Fries (confit)

Servings: 6
Cooking Time: 180 Minutes

Ingredients:
- 1/4 Cup sea salt
- 12 Whole black peppercorn
- 2 Sprig thyme sprigs
- 2 Clove garlic, crushed
- 1 Whole bay leaves
- 6 Whole Duck Leg Quarters, (leg with thigh attached), preferallb moulard
- olive oil

Directions:

1. Combine the salt and the water in a large resealable plastic bag (or a large bowl) and stir until the salt crystals dissolve.

2. Add the peppercorns, thyme, garlic, bay leaf, coriander, if using, and duck leg quarters. Seal the bag, put in a pan or bowl (to contain any potential leaks) and refrigerate for 24 hours.

3. Drain the duck leg quarters (discard the brine) and rinse under cold running water. Pat dry with paper towels. Prick the skin all over with a darning needle or sharp fork, being careful not to nick the meat. (It helps if you go in at an angle.) This creates channels for the fat to escape, making for crispier skin.

4. Supply your smoker with wood pellets and follow the start-up procedure. Preheat the grill, with the lid closed, to 400° F.

5. Meanwhile add enough olive oil to a large cast iron skillet or roasting pan to film the bottom. Arrange the duck leg quarters in the skillet or roasting pan in a single layer, skin-side down.

6. Put the skillet or roasting pan on the grill grate. Roast the duck for 30 minutes, or until the duck fat begins to render. Reduce the temperature to 300F (150C). Turn the duck legs so they are skin-side up. Cover the skillet or roasting pan tightly with foil. Grill: 300 ˚F

7. Continue to roast the duck for 2 hours. Uncover the duck and roast for an additional hour, or until the skin is crisp and golden brown. Remove the duck, shred, and serve immediately. (Alternatively, you can refrigerate the duck for up to a week. Re-crisp the skin by grilling the duck, skin-side down, in a hot cast iron skillet or on your Traeger.) Serve with brown butter french fries.

8.   Strain the remaining duck fat through cheesecloth or a fine-mesh kitchen strainer and transfer to a covered container; refrigerate for up to 6 months. Use the flavorful fat to saut potatoes or sturdy greens.

Citrus Grilled Lamb Chops

Servings: 4 - 6
Cooking Time: 15 Minutes

Ingredients:
- 2 Tablespoons Chophouse Steak Seasoning
- 4 Finely Garlic Clove, Minced
- 2 Pounds Thick Cut Rib Chops Or Lamb Loin
- Juice From 1/2 Lemon
- Juice From 1/2 Lime
- ¼ Cup Olive Oil
- 3 Tablespoons Orange Juice
- ¼ Cup Red Wine Vinegar

Directions:
1.   In a mixing bowl, whisk together all the ingredients and 2 tbsp Chophouse Steak. Place the lamb chops in a glass baking pan and pour the marinade over the top. Flip the chops over a few times to make sure that they are completely coated.
2.   Cover the glass pan in aluminum foil and allow the lamb chops to marinade for 4-12 hours. Once the meat has finished marinating, drain off the excess marinade and discard.
3.   Supply your smoker with wood pellets and follow the start-up procedure. Preheat the grill, with the lid closed, to 400° F. If you're using a gas or charcoal grill, set it up for medium high heat. Grill the chops for 5-7 minutes per side, then lower the temperature to 350°F or medium heat, and flip and grill for another 5-7 minutes.
4.   Remove the lamb chops from the grill, cover in foil, and allow to rest for 5 minutes before serving.

Rosemary Prime Rib

Servings: 8
Cooking Time: 60 Minutes

Ingredients:
- 1 (8 Lb) Prime Rib Roast
- 4 Tablespoon olive oil
- 4 Tablespoon tri-color peppercorns
- 3 Whole rosemary sprigs
- 3 Whole thyme sprigs
- 1/2 Cup garlic, minced
- 1/2 Cup Jacobsen Salt Co. Cherrywood Smoked Salt
- 4 Tablespoon Olive Oil

Directions:

1.   Supply your smoker with wood pellets and follow the start-up procedure. Preheat the grill, with the lid closed, to 450° F.
2.   Cut rib loin in half (roast halves separately for more controlled/even cooking.) Sear both halves in olive oil over very high heat until nice dark golden color.
3.   Place tricolor peppercorns into a bag, crush pepper corns with a rolling pin.
4.   Strip the leaves from the rosemary and thyme springs. Mix salt, crushed peppercorns, rosemary leaves, thyme leaves and garlic.
5.   Pour olive oil over the rib loin and pour on the rub mix. Pat slightly to get it to stick to the meat.
6.   Roast for 20-30 minutes on HIGH setting, then reduce heat to 300°F and roast for another 30 to 40 minutes or until a meat thermometer registers 125 degrees F for rare/medium rare (roast will continue to cook slightly after removing from the grill). Grill: 300 °F
7.   Remove from the Traeger and let rest at least 20 minutes before slicing. Enjoy!

Savory Chili Mac And Cheese

Servings: 4
Cooking Time: 25 Minutes

Ingredients:
- 4 Cups Beef Stock
- 2 Teaspoons Chili Powder
- 2 Tbsp Chopped Fresh Parsley Leaves
- 2 Cloves Garlic, Minced
- 1 1/2 Teaspoon Cumin
- 10 Oz. Elbow Macaroni / Noodles
- 8 Oz Ground Beef
- 3/4 Cup Kidney Beans, Drained And Rinsed
- And Freshly Ground Black Pepper Kosher Salt
- 1 Tbs Olive Oil
- 1 Onion, Diced
- 1 Tbs Sweet Heat Rub
- 3/4 Cup Shredded Cheddar Cheese
- 1 (14.5-Ounce) Tomatoes, Canned And Diced

Directions:
1.   Supply your smoker with wood pellets and follow the start-up procedure. Preheat the grill, with the lid open, to 350° F. If you're using a gas or charcoal grill, set it up for medium heat.
2.   Heat olive oil in a Dutch oven or cast iron pan over medium-high heat. Add garlic, onion and ground beef, and cook until browned, about 3-5 minutes. Break up the beef as it cooks with a large wooden spoon or fork.
3.   Stir in beef broth, tomatoes, beans, Sweet Heat, chili powder and cumin. Add salt and pepper to taste. Bring to a simmer and stir in pasta.

4.   Transfer pot to the preheated grill and cover. Cook until pasta is cooked through, about 15-20 minutes. Remove from heat and top generously with shredded cheese, replace the cover to allow cheese to melt, about 2 minutes. Garnish with fresh parsley and serve immediately!

Herb Grilled Venison Stew

Servings: 4 - 6
Cooking Time: 210 Minutes

Ingredients:

- 2 Bay Leaves
- 2 Cups Beef Stock
- 3 Carrots, Chopped
- 2 Cups Cauliflower Florets
- ¼ Tsp Cayenne Pepper
- 2 Celery Stalks, Chopped
- 4 Garlic Cloves, Minced
- 1 Tbsp Italian Parsley
- ¼ Tsp Marjoram, Dried
- 2 Tbsp Olive Oil
- 1 Onion, Chopped
- 1 Tsp Pulled Pork Rub
- 1 Cup Red Wine
- 1 Tsp Chopped Rosemary, Fresh
- (To Taste) Salt And Pepper
- 2 Cups Chopped Spinach
- 2 Sweet Potatoes, Diced
- 2 Tbs Tomato Paste
- ½ Cup Tomatoes, Canned And Diced
- 2 Lbs. Venison Stew Meat, Cut Into 1" Cubes
- 1 Cup Zucchini, Largely Diced

Directions:

1.   Supply your smoker with wood pellets and follow the start-up procedure. Preheat the grill, with the lid open, to 400° F. If using a gas or charcoal grill, set heat to medium-high heat.

2.   Place cast iron Dutch oven directly on grill grates and heat olive oil until shimmering. Add onion, celery, carrot, and garlic and cook, stirring constantly, for about 5-10 minutes or until onion is translucent.

3.   Increase heat on the grill to 500° F. Add venison to the pot and cook until browned on all sides. Add the red wine and allow to simmer for 2 minutes.

4.   Add tomato paste, beef stock, mushrooms, sweet potato, tomatoes, rosemary, Pulled Pork Rub, sage, marjoram, cayenne, salt, pepper and bay leaves and mix well to combine. Cover pot, reduce temperature to 300° F and let the stew simmer for at least 2.5 to 3 hours.

5.   Remove lid and stir in the cauliflower, spinach, and zucchini. Return cover to pot and simmer an additional 15 minutes. Stir in parsley and serve hot.

Lime Carne Asada Tacos

Servings: 4
Cooking Time: 10 Minutes

Ingredients:

- 1/2 Tsp Black Pepper
- 1 Tsp Garlic Powder
- 2 Lime, Juiced
- 1 Tsp Salt
- 1 1/2 Lbs Steak, Skirt
- 8 Tortilla

Directions:

1.   Supply your smoker with wood pellets and follow the start-up procedure. Preheat the grill, with the lid closed, to 400° F. Place the steaks on the grill, and grill them for 4-8 minutes, then flip the steaks and grill for an additional 4-8 minutes.

2.   Remove steaks from the grill, loosely cover them with foil, and let them sit for 5-10 minutes. Next chop the steaks into pieces and serve with tortillas and any desired toppings.

Smoked Pheasant

Servings: 4-6
Cooking Time: 240 Minutes

Ingredients:

- 1 gallon hot water
- 1 cup salt
- 1 cup packed brown sugar
- 2 (2- to 3-pound) whole pheasants, cleaned and plucked
- ¼ cup extra-virgin olive oil
- 2 tablespoons onion powder
- 2 tablespoons freshly ground black pepper
- 2 tablespoons cayenne pepper
- 1 tablespoon minced garlic
- 2 teaspoons smoked paprika
- 1 cup molasses

Directions:

1.   In a large container with a lid, combine the hot water, salt, and brown sugar, stirring to dissolve the salt and sugar. Let cool to room temperature, then submerge the pheasants in the brine, cover, and refrigerate for 8 to 12 hours.

2.   Remove the pheasants from the brine, then rinse them and pat dry. Discard the brine.

3.   Supply your smoker with wood pellets and follow the start-up procedure. Preheat, with the lid closed, to 250°F.

4. In a small bowl, combine the olive oil, black pepper, cayenne pepper, onion powder, garlic, and paprika to form a paste.

5. Rub the pheasants with the paste and place breast-side up on the grill grate. Close the lid and smoke for 1 hour.

6. Open the smoker and baste the pheasants with some of the molasses. Close the lid and continue smoking for 2 to 3 hours, basting with the molasses every 30 minutes, until a meat thermometer inserted into the thigh reads 160°F.

7. Remove the pheasants from the grill and let rest for 20 minutes before serving warm or cold.

Savory Teriyaki Smoked Steak Bites

Servings: 2

Cooking Time: 90 Minutes

Ingredients:
- Sirloin steak
- Teriyaki sauce
- Light brown sugar
- Garlic powder
- Garlic salt
- Soy sauce
- Apple cider vinegar
- Pepper

Directions:
1. Mix all ingredients for the marinade.
2. Trim steak and cut into 2 inches pieces.
3. Place in a zip lock bag and pour marinade over the steak. Squeeze as much air out as possible and tightly seal the bag.
4. Freeze the steak for at least 8 hours or overnight.
5. Supply your smoker with wood pellets and follow the start-up procedure. Preheat the grill, with the lid closed, to 225 °F.
6. Place the steak bites directly on the rack. Discard remaining marinade.
7. Smoke for 1 hour and 30 minutes or until the internal temp is 135-140 degrees F.

Bacon Burger

Servings: 8

Cooking Time: 180 Minutes

Ingredients:
- 1 Pack Bacon
- 2 Lbs Beef, Ground
- 1 Fresh Bread, French Loaf
- Condiments (Ketchup, Mustard, Relish, Etc.)
- 2 Egg
- Lettuce
- 2 1/2 Cups Mac And Cheese, Prepared
- 2 Tbsp   Mandarin Habanero Spice
- 1/2 Cup   Original BBQ Sauce
- 1 Lb Pork, Ground
- Red Onion, Chopped
- Tomato, Sliced

Directions:
1. Place plastic wrap on a clean surface and lay the mac cheese in the middle. Wrap the plastic wrap around the mac cheese so that it becomes a tube. Freeze for 30 minutes or until you're ready to put the burger together.

2. Supply your smoker with wood pellets and follow the start-up procedure. Preheat the grill, with the lid closed, to 250° F.

3. In a large pan or a clean working surface, combine the ground beef, pork, eggs, barbecue sauce, and seasoning. Mix with your hands until everything is combined.

4. Next, you're going to make a bacon weave. There are many strategies for making a bacon weave, so use whatever method you're most comfortable with. Take half of the pack of bacon and lay each strip vertically next to each other. Starting at the top left corner, lay a piece of bacon horizontally on top of the first strip of bacon. Place it under the second piece of bacon and over the third piece. Repeat this pattern until you finish the row. Now, flip the first, third, fifth, and seventh vertical strip of bacon from the end closest to you over the entire bacon weave. Lay another piece of bacon horizontally over the pieces that are still lying flat (the second, fourth, sixth, and eighth piece). Return the odd pieces of bacon back to their original vertical placement. Flip the second, fourth, sixth, and eighth vertical strip of bacon from the end closest to you over the entire bacon weave. Lay another piece of bacon horizontally over the pieces that are still lying flat (the first, third, fifth, and seventh pieceReturn the even pieces of bacon back to their original vertical placement. Continue this pattern until the bacon weave is complete.

5. On top of your bacon weave, spread out the ground beef mixture so that it completely covers the bacon. Remove the mac cheese from the plastic wrap and lay in the middle of the meat spread. Roll the bacon weave and ground beef mixture around the mac cheese tube to form a log. Ensure that the mac cheese is completely surrounded and place on the grill. Smoke for 2 1/2 to 3 hours or until the internal temperature of the meat is 145°F. If you're using a meat probe, make sure that the meat probe is in the center of the MEAT, not in the mac cheese center.

6. Prepare the French loaf by slicing it in half, topping the bottom with lettuce, red onion, tomato and any condiments you prefer. Place the burger directly on to your toppings. Top with the second half of the loaf, cut into slices and enjoy!

Italian Beef Pinwheels

Servings: 6
Cooking Time: 45 Minutes

Ingredients:

- 3 Pound skirt steak
- Prime Rib Rub
- 2 Cup spinach
- 4 Slices havarti cheese
- 4 Slices provolone cheese
- 1 Cup sun-dried tomatoes

Directions:

1. Supply your smoker with wood pellets and follow the start-up procedure. Preheat the grill, with the lid closed, to 375° F.
2. Season skirt steak generously with Traeger Prime Rib Rub. Lay your skirt steak flat and add a layer of spinach. Depending on the size of the steak, add up to the full 2 cups. Then add a layer of cheese and lastly the sun-dried tomatoes.
3. Tightly roll the meat up and insert toothpicks to hold it together.
4. Place meat roll directly on the grill grate and cook for 45 minutes. After 45 minutes, remove from the grill and let rest for 10 minutes before slicing. Grill: 375 °F
5. Serve with a large helping of mashed potatoes or your favorite side dish. Enjoy!

Philly Cheese Onion Steaks

Servings: 6
Cooking Time: 45 Minutes

Ingredients:

- 2 Green Bell Pepper, Sliced
- 6 Hot Dog Bun(S)
- 2 Cups Mozzarella Cheese, Shredded
- 1 Quart Mushroom
- 1 Onion, Sliced
- Pepper
- Salt
- 2 Thick Steak, Flank

Directions:

1. Supply your smoker with wood pellets and follow the start-up procedure. Preheat the grill, with the lid closed, to 250° F.
2. Season both sides of your steaks with salt and pepper to your liking. We're going to reverse sear these steaks, so place on the grates of your preheated Grill. You'll want to cook the steaks until the internal temperature reaches 130°F (for medium-rare). Follow these internal temperatures if you'd like to cook your steak more/less done:
3. Rare: 125°F
4. Medium Rare: 130°F
5. Medium: 140°F
6. Well Done: 160°F
7. If you're cooking your steaks medium rare, it will take around 45 minutes depending on how thick the steaks are.
8. While the steaks are cooking, slice up the onion, mushrooms, and peppers thinly and sauté until soft.
9. When the steaks have reached your desired internal temperature, remove steaks from the grill and let them rest for 15 minutes. In the meantime, open up your flame broiler and crank up the grill to HIGH. Sear each side of the steak for about 1 minutes each.
10. Rest steaks again for 10 minutes.
11. Slice steak thinly, combine with the sautéed vegetables and fill a hot dog bun generously with the mixture.

Baked Venison Tater Tot Casserole

Servings: 4
Cooking Time: 40 Minutes

Ingredients:

- 2 Pound Venison, ground
- 2 Can Peas, canned
- 2 Can cream of mushroom soup
- 28 Ounce frozen tater tots

Directions:

1. Cook ground venison in a medium sauté pan over medium high until browned. Drain off excess fat and set venison aside.
2. In a 13x9 pan, combine venison, peas and soup. Top with tater tots.
3. Supply your smoker with wood pellets and follow the start-up procedure. Preheat the grill, with the lid closed, to 350° F.
4. Place casserole dish directly on grill grate and cook for 30 minutes. Serve hot, enjoy!

Flavour Bbq Brisket Burnt Ends

Servings: 6-8
Cooking Time: 420 Minutes

Ingredients:

- 1 Brisket Point
- Georgia Style BBQ Sauce (Mustard Base)
- As Needed Chop House Steak Rub

Directions:

1. Supply your smoker with wood pellets and follow the start-up procedure. Preheat the grill, with the lid closed, to 250° F.
2. Place your brisket on the grates, cook for 6 to 7 hours or until the internal temperature reaches 190°F
3. Remove from the grill and cut into 1-inch cubes. Toss brisket cubes with seasoning and your favorite BBQ sauce into a pan.
4. Place the pan in the grill for 2 hours, stirring half-way through.

Sirloin Steak

Servings: 2
Cooking Time: 45 Minutes

Ingredients:

- 2 Tablespoons Chili Pepper Flakes
- 1/2 Cup Extra-Virgin Olive Oil
- 1 Garlic, Cloves
- 2 Tbsp Oregano, Leaves
- 1/4 Teaspoon Paprika, Powder
- 2 Cups Lightly Packed Parsley, Leaves
- 1 Teaspoon   Smoked Infused Classic Sea Salt
- 1/4 Cup Red Onion, Chopped
- 1 1/2 Lbs Steak, Sirloin
- 6 Tablespoon Vinegar, Red Wine

Directions:

1.   Supply your smoker with wood pellets and follow the start-up procedure. Preheat the grill, with the lid closed, to 250° F.

2.   Season both sides of your steaks with salt and pepper to your liking. Place on the grates of your preheated grill. You'll want to cook the steaks until the internal temperature reaches 130°F (for medium-rare). Follow these internal temperatures if you'd like to cook your steak more/less done:

3.   Rare: 125°F

4.   Medium Rare: 130°F

5.   Medium: 140°F

6.   Well Done: 160°F

7.   If you're cooking your steaks medium rare, it will take around 45 minutes.

8.   While the steaks are cooking, combine parsley, garlic, red onion, oregano, paprika, and chili pepper flakes in a food processor and pulse to combine. Add salt, vinegar, and oil and continue to pulse for another 20 seconds, or until mixture is chunky but combined.

9.   When the steaks have reached your desired internal temperature, remove steaks from the grill and let them rest for 15 minutes. In the meantime, open your flame broiler and crank up the grill to HIGH. Sear each side of the steak for about 1 minutes each. Slice steak thinly and drizzle with chimichurri sauce.

Smoked Black Pepper Beef Ribs

Servings: 4-6
Cooking Time: 330 Minutes

Ingredients:

- 1/4 Cup Hot Sauce
- Kosher Salt
- Coarse Black Pepper
- Your Favorite Beef Rib Rub Or Sweet Heat Rub
- 4 Pound Rib(S)

Directions:

1.   Supply your smoker with wood pellets and follow the start-up procedure. Preheat the grill, with the lid closed, to 250° F.

2.   Peel the membrane off the bone side and remove excess fat.

3.   Rub the ribs down with hot sauce and season generously with Sweet Heat, salt, and pepper.

4.   Place the ribs on the grill. Then, insert your meat probe before closing the lid to cook.

5.   Check on your ribs after 3-4 hours. If one side is cooking faster than the other, rotate them.

6.   Once the beef reaches 195°F, start probe testing the ribs for doneness. Because the finished temperature can vary, do a check with each time the temperature increases by 3°F.

7.   To probe test: insert the meat probe vertically in between the bones to push through the second membrane on the bottom. The meat should have a consistent butter like tenderness throughout the rack with a final internal temp ranging from 200°F – 205°F.

8.   Once the ribs finish cooking, remove from the grill to let them rest.

9.   To let the ribs rest: wrap them tightly in foil. Then, wrap in a towel and place in a dry, empty cooler for 1 hour.

10.   Slice between the bones to serve and enjoy!

Smoked Brisket

Servings: 8
Cooking Time: 720 Minutes

Ingredients:

- 2 Tablespoon garlic powder
- 2 Tablespoon onion powder
- 2 Tablespoon paprika
- 2 Teaspoon chile powder
- 1/3 Cup Jacobsen Salt or kosher salt
- 1/3 Cup coarse ground black pepper, divided
- 1 (12-14 lb) whole packer brisket, trimmed
- 1 1/2 Cup beef broth

Directions:

1.   Supply your smoker with wood pellets and follow the start-up procedure. Preheat the grill, with the lid closed, to 225° F.

2.   For the Rub: Mix together garlic powder, onion powder, paprika, chili pepper, kosher salt and pepper in a small bowl.

3.   Season the brisket on all sides with the rub.

4.   Place brisket, fat side down on grill grate. Cook brisket until it reaches an internal temperature of 160°F, about 5 to 6 hours. When brisket reaches internal temperature of 160°F, remove from grill. Probe: 160 °F

5.   Double wrap meat in aluminum foil and add the beef broth to the foil packet. Return brisket to grill and cook until it reaches an internal temperature of 204°F, about 3 hours more. Probe: 204 °F

6.   Once finished, remove from grill, unwrap from foil and let rest for 15 minutes. Slice against the grain and serve.

Naked Juicy Lucy Burgers With Special Sauce

Servings: 4
Cooking Time: 40 Minutes

Ingredients:

- 2lb (1kg) ground beef (80/20), preferably chuck, well chilled
- 1 tbsp Worcestershire sauce or liquid aminos
- 6oz (170g) grated Cheddar, pepper Jack, or another melting cheese
- coarse salt
- freshly ground black pepper
- for the sauce
- ¼ cup reduced-fat mayo
- ¼ cup yellow mustard
- ¼ cup ketchup
- ¼ cup Heinz 57 sauce
- 2 tbsp sweet pickle relish
- for serving
- sliced tomatoes
- sliced sweet onions
- lettuce leaves
- cooked bacon strips
- Pickles

Directions:

1. Supply your smoker with wood pellets and follow the start-up procedure. Preheat the grill, with the lid closed, to 225° F.
2. In a small bowl, make the sauce by combining the ingredients. Transfer the sauce to a serving bowl. Cover and refrigerate until ready to use. (Leftover sauce will keep for several weeks.)
3. Place the ground beef in a large bowl and add the Worcestershire sauce. Wet your hands with cold water and lightly mix. Divide the mixture into 8 equal-sized balls. Flatten each ball into a round patty.
4. Place 4 patties on a rimmed sheet pan. Mound an equal amount of cheese in the middle of each patty, leaving a meat border. Place a patty on top of each cheese mound. Rewet your hands with cold water and press and pinch the edges of patties together to form a tight seal. (You don't want the cheese to leak out.) Season on both sides with salt and pepper.
5. Place the patties on the grate and smoke for 30 minutes. Transfer the burgers to a clean plate.
6. Raise the temperature to 450°F (232°C). Return the burgers to the grate and sear them until the burgers reach an internal temperature of 160°F (71°C), about 3 to 4 minutes per side, turning once.
7. Transfer the burgers to a platter and let rest for 3 minutes. Serve with the special sauce and the suggested accompaniments.

Smoked Moink Burger By Scott Thomas

Servings: 4
Cooking Time: 60 Minutes

Ingredients:

- 1 Pound Ground Sirloin
- 1/2 Pound ground pork
- 1/4 Cup Worcestershire sauce
- 1 Teaspoon garlic, minced
- salt
- black pepper

Directions:

1. Combine all the ingredients in a bowl and mix together. Form into six patties.
2. Supply your smoker with wood pellets and follow the start-up procedure. Preheat the grill, with the lid closed, to 350° F.
3. Cook until the burgers reach an internal temperature of 160 degrees F (about an hour depending on the size of the patties and the heat of the grill).
4. Top with your favorite cheese to melt a few minutes before burgers are done and serve with your favorite toppings.

The Perfect T-bones

Servings: 4
Cooking Time: 30 Minutes

Ingredients:

- 4 (1½- to 2-inch-thick) T-bone steaks
- 2 tablespoons olive oil
- 1 batch Espresso Brisket Rub or Chili-Coffee Rub

Directions:

1. Supply your smoker with wood pellets and follow the start-up procedure. Preheat the grill, with the lid closed, to 500°F.
2. Coat the steaks all over with olive oil and season both sides with the rub. Using your hands, work the rub into the meat.
3. Place the steaks directly on a grill grate and smoke until their internal temperature reaches 135°F for rare, 145°F for medium-rare, and 155°F for well-done. Remove the steaks from the grill and serve hot.

Santa Maria Tri-tip With Pico De Gallo

Servings: 4
Cooking Time: 68 Minutes

Ingredients:

- 1 tri-tip roast, about 2 to 2½lb (1 to 1.2kg)
- coarse salt

- freshly ground black pepper
- granulated garlic or garlic powder
- for the pico de gallo
- 8 Roma tomatoes, decored, deseeded, and diced
- 1 white onion, peeled and diced
- 1 serrano pepper, destemmed, deseeded, and minced, plus more
- 1 garlic clove, peeled and minced
- juice of 1 lime
- ½ cup loosely packed cilantro leaves, chopped
- 1 tsp coarse salt

Directions:

1. In a medium bowl, make the pico de gallo by combining the tomatoes, onion, serrano, garlic, lime juice, and cilantro. Stir gently with a rubber spatula and season with salt to taste. Cover and refrigerate for 2 hours.

2. Approximately 45 minutes before you're ready to cook, season the roast on all sides with salt and pepper and granulated garlic.

3. Supply your smoker with wood pellets and follow the start-up procedure. Preheat the grill, with the lid closed, to 180° F.

4. Place the roast on the grate and smoke until the internal temperature in the thickest part of the roast reaches 115°F (46°C), about 45 minutes to 1 hour. Transfer the roast to a plate.

5. Raise the temperature to 450°F (232°C). Place the roast on the grate and sear until the internal temperature in the thickest part of the roast reaches 130 to 135°F (54 to 57°C), about 3 to 4 minutes per side. For best results, don't cook beyond medium rare. (The thinner tail should satisfy any diner who prefers beef to be more well done.)

6. Remove the roast from the grill and thinly slice on a sharp diagonal against the grain. Serve with the pico de gallo.

Cheese Onion Steak Sandwiches

Servings: 4

Cooking Time: 10 Minutes

Ingredients:

- 2 tbsp, divided butter
- 4 hoagie rolls, sliced lengthwise
- 2 tbsp olive oil
- 1-2 tbsp chop house steak rub
- 8 slices provolone cheese, sliced
- 2 lbs, sliced thinly rib-eye steaks
- 1 yellow onion, sliced

Directions:

1. Supply your smoker with wood pellets and follow the start-up procedure. Preheat the grill, with the lid closed, to 375° F. If using a gas or charcoal grill, set heat to medium heat. For all other grills, preheat cast iron skillet on grill grates.

2. Melt 1 tablespoon of butter and 1 tablespoon of olive oil on griddle. With a serrated knife, slice rolls 3/4 of the way through, then place facedown onto griddle and cook until toasted. Set aside.

3. Melt remaining tablespoon of butter and olive oil on the griddle. Add sliced onions and cook for 2 minutes, or until lightly caramelized. Move to the lower-right corner of griddle to keep warm.

4. Season steak generously with Chop House Steak Rub, then place on griddle and cook for 3 minutes, stirring to brown all sides. Mix in caramelized onions.

5. Divide steak and onions into 4 portions on the griddle, then top each with 2 slices of provolone cheese. Let cheese melt slightly and transfer to a toasted hoagie roll using a bench scraper or metal spatula. Serve hot and enjoy!

Smoked Garlic Meatloaf

Servings: 8

Cooking Time: 180 Minutes

Ingredients:

- 2 Tsp Apple Cider Vinegar
- 2 Lbs Beef, Ground
- 1/2 Tsp Chipotle Pepper Flakes
- 3 Cups Crushed Chips Corn Tortillas
- 2 Grated Garlic, Cloves
- 2/3 Cup Ketchup
- 1 Small Grated Onion, Chopped
- 4 Oz Into Sticks Pepper Jack Cheese, Sliced
- 2 Tbsp Competition Smoked Rub
- 1 Lbs Pork, Ground
- 1/4 Cup Tomato Paste
- 1 Tsp Worcestershire Sauce

Directions:

1. Supply your smoker with wood pellets and follow the start-up procedure. Preheat the grill, with the lid closed, to 250° F.

2. First make the glaze: in a bowl, combine the ketchup, tomato paste, vinegar, Worcestershire, chipotle flakes and Competition Smoked Seasoning. Whisk well to combine and set aside.

3. In a large bowl, mix together the crushed corn chips, eggs, onion and garlic. Add 2/3rds of the glaze to this mixture, reserving the rest for glazing the meatloaf. Mix well to combine and allow to sit until the corn chips have hydrated.

4. Add the ground beef and pork to the corn chip mixture and mix until everything is well distributed.

5. Form the meatloaf into a log and push the sticks of pepper jack cheese into the center of the meatloaf and cover with the meat mixture. Loosely wrap in tin foil and poke holes in the foil with a knife to allow smoke to penetrate.

6.   Grill for 1 ½ hours covered, then remove the top half of the tin foil, glaze with reserved glaze, and grill for another 1 ½ hours or until the internal temperature is 165F.

Cheddar Bacon Beef Burgers

Servings: 12
Cooking Time: 30 Minutes

Ingredients:
- Bacon Cheddar Burger Seasoning
- 3/4 Cup Bacon, Chopped
- 3 Lbs Beef, Ground
- 1 Jalapeno, Chopped
- Pepper
- 1/2 Cup Ranch Dressing
- Salt
- 1 1/2 Cups Shredded Cheddar Cheese

Directions:
1.   Supply your smoker with wood pellets and follow the start-up procedure. Preheat the grill, with the lid closed, to 350° F.
2.   In a small bowl, combine cheese, bacon, jalapeno and ranch dressing.
3.   In a clean, large bowl, combine ground beef with enough salt and pepper to taste.
4.   Form meat into patties and place on a pan. A good rule of thumb is for each patty to be about the size of the palm of your hand.
5.   Using a clean glass, press into each patty, leaving the imprint of the bottom of the glass in the patty. Stuff the filling into the indent. Grill for 25 minutes or until the ground beef reaches an internal temperature of 160°F. Serve hot.

Braised Onion Chuck Roast Beef Sandwiches

Servings: 4
Cooking Time: 540 Minutes

Ingredients:
- 3 cups beef stock, divided
- 2 lbs chuck roast
- 4 hoagie rolls, sliced lengthwise
- to taste, lone star brisket rub
- 1 yellow onion

Directions:
1.   Place chuck roast in a glass baking dish. Season with Lone Star Brisket Rub, then cover with plastic wrap and refrigerate overnight.
2.   The next day, remove chuck roast from the refrigerator. Supply your smoker with wood pellets and follow the start-up procedure. Preheat the grill, with the lid closed, to 225° F. If using a gas or charcoal grill, set it up for low, indirect heat.
3.   Place chuck roast directly on the grill grate, then close the lid and smoke for 3 hours, spraying with 1 cup of beef stock every hour.
4.   Slice the onion and place in a cast iron skillet, then pour the remaining cup of stock over the onions and set roast on top of onions.
5.   Increase temperature to 275° F and cook an additional 2 ½ to 3 hours, or until internal temperature reaches 165° F.
6.   Cover the roast with a cast iron lid or aluminum foil, and cook for another 2 ½ to 3 hours, or until the internal temperature reaches 200° F.
7.   Remove chuck roast from the grill. Allow the roast to rest for 10 minutes, then remove from the skillet and shred.
8.   Serve pulled roast beef in a hoagie roll with braised onions and pan jus.

Flavour Memphis Bbq Beef Brisket

Servings: 10
Cooking Time: 600 Minutes

Ingredients:
- 1 Cup Beef Broth
- 1, 10-12 Pound Brisket
- 1 Bottle Sweet Rib Rub

Directions:
1.   Cut away any silver skin or excess fat from the flat muscle and discard. Next, there will be a large, crescent shaped fat section on the flat of the meat.
2.   Trim that fat until it is smooth against the meat so that it looks like a seamless transition between the point and flat. Flip the brisket over and trim the fat cap to ¼ inch thick. Slice between the point and the flat and save the flat for later.
3.   Generously season the trimmed brisket point on all sides with the Sweet Rib Rub. Allow the brisket to sit for 30 minutes to marinate.
4.   Pour the beef broth in the spray bottle and set aside.
5.   Supply your smoker with wood pellets and follow the start-up procedure. Preheat the grill, with the lid closed, to 225° F. Place the brisket in the smoker, insert the smoker's attached temperature probe, if you have one, and set the brisket to cook for about 6-8 hours or until the internal temperature reaches 165°F. Spray the brisket with the beef broth every 2 hours to keep it moist.
6.   Once the brisket reaches 165°F, remove from the smoker, wrap in peach butcher paper, folding the edges over to form a leakproof seal, and return to the smoker seam-side down for another 3-4 hours, or until the brisket reaches 200°F.
7.   Remove the brisket from the smoker and allow it to rest for at least one hour before serving.

Teriyaki Deer Jerky

Servings: 4
Cooking Time: 240 Minutes

Ingredients:

- 1/2 Cup soy sauce
- 1/4 Cup mirin
- 2 Tablespoon sugar
- 3 coins fresh ginger, each ¼ inch thick
- 1 Clove garlic, crushed
- 1/2 Teaspoon onion powder
- 1/2 Teaspoon black pepper
- 2 Pound venison, trimmed

Directions:

1. In a mixing bowl, combine the soy sauce, mirin, sugar, ginger, garlic, onion powder and pepper.
2. With a sharp knife, slice the venison into 1/4 inch thick slices. Trim any fat or connective tissue.
3. Put the meat slices in a large resealable plastic bag. Pour the marinade mixture over the venison and massage the bag so that all the slices get coated with the marinade. Seal the bag and refrigerate for several hours, or overnight.
4. Supply your smoker with wood pellets and follow the start-up procedure. Preheat the grill, with the lid closed, to 180° F. Remove the venison from the marinade; discard marinade. Dry the meat slices between paper towels.
5. Arrange the meat in a single layer directly on the grill grate. Smoke for 3 hours or until the jerky is dry but still chewy and somewhat pliant when you bend a piece. Grill: 180 °F
6. Transfer to a resealable plastic bag while the jerky is still warm leaving the top open. Let the jerky rest for an hour at room temperature.
7. Squeeze any air from the bag and refrigerate the jerky. It will keep for several weeks. Enjoy!

Bbq Brisket Breakfast Tacos

Servings: 6
Cooking Time: 30 Minutes

Ingredients:

- 4 Pound leftover beef brisket
- 1/2 Teaspoon extra-virgin olive oil
- 1 green bell pepper, diced
- 1 Yellow Bell Pepper, diced
- 10 eggs
- 1/2 Cup milk
- salt and pepper
- 2 Cup shredded cheddar cheese
- flour tortillas

Directions:

1. Supply your smoker with wood pellets and follow the start-up procedure. Preheat the grill, with the lid closed, to 375° F.
2. Place leftover brisket in a double layer of foil and warm in grill. Grill: 375 °F
3. Coat the inside of a cast iron skillet with oil and preheat the skillet in the grill for 10 minutes. When skillet is hot, sauté diced peppers, stirring every few minutes until desired doneness.
4. While peppers are cooking, whisk together the eggs, milk, salt and pepper to taste. Add the beaten eggs to the skillet and scramble. Add cheese to the skillet when the eggs are almost done.
5. Remove eggs and heated brisket from grill. Serve eggs in a tortilla topped with brisket. Top with salsa or guacamole if desired. Enjoy!

Reverse-seared Tri-tip

Servings: 4
Cooking Time: 180 Minutes

Ingredients:

- 1½ pounds tri-tip roast
- 1 batch Espresso Brisket Rub

Directions:

1. Supply your smoker with wood pellets and follow the start-up procedure. Preheat the grill, with the lid closed, to 180°F.
2. Season the tri-tip roast with the rub. Using your hands, work the rub into the meat.
3. Place the roast directly on the grill grate and smoke until its internal temperature reaches 140°F.
4. Increase the grill's temperature to 450°F and continue to cook until the roast's internal temperature reaches 145°F. This same technique can be done over an open flame or in a cast-iron skillet with some butter.
5. Remove the tri-tip roast from the grill and let it rest 10 to 15 minutes, before slicing and serving.

Smoked Prime Rib

Servings: 8
Cooking Time: 180 Minutes

Ingredients:

- 1 (8-10 lb) boneless rib-eye roast, choice grade or higher
- kosher salt
- Meat Church Holy Cow BBQ Rub
- Meat Church Gourmet Garlic and Herb Seasoning
- Worcestershire sauce
- beef stock or water, optional
- 3 Tablespoon butter

Directions:

1. Supply your smoker with wood pellets and follow the start-up procedure. Preheat the grill, with the lid closed, to 275° F.

2.   Truss your prime rib, since using the boneless option. This will help keep its shape and cook evenly.

3.   Apply a very heavy coat of salt to the entire roast. Let the salt sit for one hour, then wash it off and pat it dry. Apply Meat Church Holy Cow BBQ Rub liberally on all sides of the meat. It's hard to put too much on as we want to form a great bark. Remember, this cut is so big that there will not be much crust in many bites.

4.   Next, come back over the entire rib roast with a heavy coat of Meat Church Gourmet Garlic and Herb seasoning. Let these two rubs sit and adhere for 15 to 20 minutes.

5.   Place your rib roast on the Traeger. Grill: 275 °F

6.   If you'd like, you can baste it every 45 minutes with Worcestershire sauce, beef stock or even water.

7.   We are targeting a medium-rare cook in the middle which is 130°F to 135°F. Therefore, continue to cook your rib roast until you reach an internal temperature of 125°F in the middle. Keep in mind the outer edges will be further along. The ends will be closer to medium. Remove the meat from the grill when that temperature is obtained. Grill: 275 °F Probe: 125 °F

8.   Tent the meat with aluminum foil and allow it to rest for at least 10 to 15 minutes. I prefer to top the rib roast with a high-quality butter. Let this butter melt down over your prime rib as it rests. The meat will continue to rise another 5°F to a final temperature of 130°F.

Smoked Peppered Beef Tenderloin

Servings: 4
Cooking Time: 60 Minutes

Ingredients:
- 1 (2 to 2-1/2 lb) Snake River Farms Beef Tenderloin Roast, trimmed
- 1/2 Cup Dijon mustard
- 2 Clove garlic, minced to a paste
- 2 Tablespoon bourbon or strong cold coffee
- Jacobsen Salt Co. Pure Kosher Sea Salt
- coarse ground black and green peppercorns

Directions:
1.   Lay the tenderloin on a large piece of plastic wrap.

2.   Combine the mustard, garlic and bourbon in a small bowl. Slather the mixture evenly all over the tenderloin. Wrap in plastic and allow to sit at room temperature for 1 hour.

3.   Unwrap the plastic wrap and generously season the tenderloin on all sides with the salt and ground black and green peppercorns.

4.   Supply your smoker with wood pellets and follow the start-up procedure. Preheat the grill, with the lid closed, to 180° F.

5.   Place the tenderloin directly on the grill grate and smoke for 60 minutes. Grill: 180 °F

6.   Remove the tenderloin from the grill and set aside. Increase the grill temperature to 400°F. Once the grill is hot, place the tenderloin back on the grill. Roast until the internal temperature reaches 130°F, about 20 to 30 minutes depending on the thickness of the tenderloin. Do not overcook. Grill: 400 °F Probe: 130 °F

7.   Let rest for 10 minutes before slicing. Enjoy!

Smoked Spiced Beef Pot Roast

Servings: 8
Cooking Time: 30 Minutes

Ingredients:
- roast
- 2 tbsp sugar
- 1 tbsp kosher salt
- 1 tbsp ground black pepper
- 1 tbsp garlic powder
- 1 tbsp smoked paprika
- 1 tsp cayenne pepper

Directions:
1.   Drizzle roast with maple syrup and apply rub.

2.   Randomly insert garlic chunks into roast approximately 1-2" deep.

3.   Supply your smoker with wood pellets and follow the start-up procedure. Preheat the grill, with the lid closed, to 450 °F.

4.   Set roast on grate in roast pan and fill bottom 1/2" with beef broth and red wine.

5.   Roast at 450 °F for about 30 minutes.

6.   Remove roast.

7.   Drop cooking temp to 225°F.

8.   Replace the roast and cook your desired temp. 130°F for med rare.

9.   Tent for 5-10 minutes and slice away.

Savory Reverse Seared Ny Steak

Servings: 4
Cooking Time: 68 Minutes

Ingredients:
- 4 Tbsp Butter
- Steak Seasoning
- 4 - 1 1/2" Steak, New York Strip

Directions:
1.   Supply your smoker with wood pellets and follow the start-up procedure. Preheat the grill, with the lid closed, to 250° F.

2.   As the grill is preheating to the perfect temperature, spice the steaks with the Chop House steak rub.

3.   Lay the steaks on the grill for roughly 60 minutes or until the steaks reach an internal temperature of 105 to 110 degrees F. Remove the steaks and set aside.

4. Crank up the heat to 500°F, open the Flame Broiler plate and let the grill preheat.

5. Place the steaks back on the grill and sear for 4 minutes. Don't forget to add 1 TBSP of butter for flavor to each steak. You know when your steak is done once the internal temperature reaches 130 to 135°F (for medium-rare). Follow the below internal temperature for your cooking preference:

6. Rare: 125°F

7. Medium Rare: 130°F

8. Medium: 140°F

9. Well Done: 160°F

10. Once reached for personal preference, take the steaks off the grill and let them rest for 5 to 10 minutes before eating. ENJOY!

Grilled Bell Pepper Flank Steak Fajitas

Servings: 1
Cooking Time: 30 Minutes

Ingredients:
- 1 Green Bell Pepper, Sliced
- 3 Tbsp Olive Oil
- 1 Onion, Diced
- Sweet Heat Rub
- 1 Red Bell Peppers, Sliced
- 1 -16Oz Steak, Flank
- 8 Tortilla, Corn
- 1 Yellow Bell Pepper, Sliced

Directions:
1. Rub flank steak with 1 tbsp olive oil and Sweet Heat Rub Grill seasoning. Cover and marinate in the refrigerator for 1 hour.
2. Lightly brush peppers and onion with olive oil.
3. Supply your smoker with wood pellets and follow the start-up procedure. Preheat the grill, with the lid closed, to 400° F. Place pepper and onion on grill and cook 5 minutes per side. Watch carefully to ensure the peppers and onion do not burn.
4. Remove peppers and onion from grill and toss lightly with remaining olive oil in a medium sized bowl. Transfer peppers and onions to a cutting board and slice into strips. Set aside.
5. Place flank steak directly on grill. Cook until medium rare (an internal temperature of 165°F).
6. Remove flank steak from the grill and transfer to cutting board. Let meat rest for 5 minutes, then slice against the grain into strips.
7. Place flank steak, peppers, and onions in a platter and serve immediately with warm tortillas, salsa, guacamole, sour cream, shredded cheese, thinly sliced iceberg lettuce, or your favorite fajita toppings.

Flavour Texas Twinkies

Servings: 7-14
Cooking Time: 40 Minutes

Ingredients:
- 14, slices bacon
- ½ cup BBQ sauce
- 1 lb. brisket
- 8 oz. cream cheese
- 1 tsp cumin
- 14 large jalapeños
- ½ tsp pepper
- 1 cup pepper jack cheese, grated
- 2 tsp hickory bacon rub
- ½ tsp salt

Directions:
1. Supply your smoker with wood pellets and follow the start-up procedure. Preheat the grill, with the lid closed, to 400° F. If using a gas or charcoal grill, set it for medium-high heat.
2. In a food processor, combine the brisket, Hickory Bacon, cumin, salt, pepper, pepper jack and cream cheese. Pulse several times until well combined. Transfer to a bowl and place into refrigerator to chill while preparing jalapeños.
3. Place jalapeños on a sheet tray. Cut each in half lengthwise and remove the seeds and rib with a spoon or by hand, then discard. Note: we recommend using gloves when handling jalapenos, as the seeds can be very hot.
4. Fill each jalapeño half with cream cheese mixture until full, then place other jalapeño half on top. Wrap each jalapeño with a slice of bacon, then skewer crosswise with toothpicks.
5. Place a mesh, metal pan on grill grate and transfer jalapeños to pan. Cover grill and cook for 35 minutes.
6. Open grill and baste jalapeños generously with BBQ sauce, close grill and continue to cook another 5 minutes.
7. Remove from grill and serve hot.

Delicious Reverse Seared Picanha Steak

Servings: 4
Cooking Time: 120 Minutes

Ingredients:
- olive oil
- 3 lbs picanha steak, top sirloin cap, fat cap removed
- chop house steak rub

Directions:
1. Supply your smoker with wood pellets and follow the start-up procedure. Preheat the grill, with the lid closed, to 225° F. If using a gas or charcoal grill, set it up for low, indirect heat.

2. Generously season both sides of steak with Chop House, insert temperature probe, and place steak directly on the grill grate.
3. Cover grill and cook 1 ½ to 2 hours, or until internal temperature reads 125°F to 130°F.
4. Remove steak from grill, then preheat KC Combo griddle to medium-high flame. Heat olive oil on the griddle, then sear steak 2 minutes per side on all sides.
5. Remove steak from the griddle, and allow to rest on a cutting board for 10 minutes. Slice steak, against the grain, and serve warm.

Beginner's Smoked Beef Brisket

Servings: 4
Cooking Time: 720 Minutes

Ingredients:
- 1 (6 lb) flat cut brisket, trimmed
- Beef Rub
- 2 Cup beef broth, beer or cola
- 1/4 Cup apple cider vinegar, apple cider or apple juice
- 2 Tablespoon Worcestershire sauce
- Texas Spicy BBQ Sauce

Directions:
1. Supply your smoker with wood pellets and follow the start-up procedure. Preheat the grill, with the lid closed, to 180° F.
2. Season on both sides with the Traeger Beef Rub.
3. Make the Mop Sauce: In a clean spray bottle combine the beef broth, beer or cola with apple cider vinegar and Worcestershire sauce.
4. Arrange the brisket fat-side down on the grill grate and smoke for 3 to 4 hours, spraying with the mop sauce every hour. Grill: 180 °F
5. Increase the grill temperature to 225°F and continue to cook, spraying occasionally with mop sauce, until an instant-read thermometer inserted in the thickest part of the meat reaches 204°F, this should take about 6 to 8 hours. Grill: 225 °F Probe: 204 °F
6. Foil the meat and let it rest for 30 minutes. Slice with a sharp knife across the grain into pencil-width slices. Serve with BBQ sauce. Enjoy!

Roasted Prime Rib

Servings: 8
Cooking Time: 105 Minutes

Ingredients:
- 1 four-bone prime rib roast, about 8lb (3.6kg), trimmed
- extra virgin olive oil
- 1 cup beef stock or broth
- fresh coarsely ground black pepper

- Horseradish Sauce
- for the seasoned salt
- ¼ cup coarsely chopped fresh rosemary leaves
- 5 fresh sage leaves, coarsely chopped
- 1 tbsp granulated garlic or 2 tsp garlic powder
- 2 tsp whole black peppercorns or fresh coarsely ground black pepper
- 1¼ cups coarse salt, divided

Directions:
1. Supply your smoker with wood pellets and follow the start-up procedure. Preheat the grill, with the lid closed, to 450° F.
2. In a coffee grinder, make the seasoned salt by combining the rosemary, sage, granulated garlic, peppercorns, and ½ cup of salt. Pulse until the herbs and peppercorns are finely ground and the coarse salt resembles table salt. (The mixture will be damp from the moisture in the herbs.)
3. Transfer the mixture to a bowl and stir in the remaining ¾ cup of salt. Reserve 3 to 4 teaspoons of the seasoned salt for the prime rib. Spread the remaining mixture on a rimmed sheet pan and let dry completely, stirring occasionally, before storing at room temperature in a covered jar. Set aside. (Place the mixture in a dehydrator or low-temperature oven or your smoker to hasten the drying time.)
4. Carve the bones off the roast in a single slab. Set aside. Use butcher's twine to tie the roast at 1½-inch (3.75cm) intervals. Lightly coat on all sides with olive oil and season with the reserved seasoned salt.
5. Place the bones convex (rounded) side up in an aluminum foil roasting pan. Place the prime rib atop the bones. Add the beef stock to the bottom of the pan.
6. Place the pan on the grate and roast until the exterior is nicely browned, about 30 minutes. Lower the temperature to 350°F (177°C) and continue to roast the meat until the internal temperature reaches 125°F (52°C) to 130°F (54°C), about 60 to 75 minutes, basting with the drippings every 20 minutes. (To avoid overcooking, check the internal temperature of the roast every 20 minutes.)
7. Transfer the roast to a cutting board and loosely tent with aluminum foil. Let rest for 15 minutes. Carve the prime rib into ¾-inch (2cm) slices and serve with the horseradish sauce.

Flank Steak Breakfast Potato Burrito

Servings: 4
Cooking Time: 30 Minutes

Ingredients:
- 2 avocado
- 1 cup bacon slices, diced
- 2 tbsp butter
- 1 cup cheddar cheese, shredded

- 2 lbs flank steak
- 4 large flour tortillas
- tt hot sauce
- 2 tsp olive oil
- 1/2 cup onion, chopped
- chop house steak rub
- 2 cups potatoes, diced

Directions:

1. Supply your smoker with wood pellets and follow the start-up procedure. Preheat the grill, with the lid closed, to 425° F. If using a gas or charcoal grill, set it up for medium-high heat. Preheat griddle to medium-low flame.

2. Drizzle olive oil over steak, then generously season steak with the Chop House Steak Rub. Grill steak 3 minutes [depending on thickness of steak] per side for medium-rare. Remove steak from grill and allow the steak to rest for 10 minutes, then thinly slice against the grain. Set aside.

3. Turn off the grill, then place tortillas inside to warm.

4. Add bacon to the griddle and cook for 2 minutes, then add potatoes to bacon and cook for 2 minutes. Add onions, then cook mixture until bacon is crisp, potatoes have browned, and onions are translucent. Set mixture aside.

5. Melt butter on griddle and then cook scrambled eggs. Set aside.

6. To assemble breakfast burritos, sprinkle cheddar cheese on tortillas. Add scrambled egg, sliced steak, potatoes, and sprinkle with more cheese. Wrap tortillas, by folding sides in, then rolling from the bottom up.

7. Serve hot with fresh avocado and hot sauce.

Garlic Pigs In A Blanket

Servings: 10

Cooking Time: 15 Minutes

Ingredients:

- 1 Crescent Dough, Can
- 1 Egg
- 1 Tsp Garlic, Minced
- 20 Hot Dog, Mini
- 1/4 Cup Mustard, Dijon
- 1 Tbsp Onion, Diced
- 2 Tbsp Poppy Seeds
- 1 Tsp Salt, Coarse

Directions:

1. Supply your smoker with wood pellets and follow the start-up procedure. Preheat the grill, with the lid closed, to 350° F. Combine the poppy seeds, dried minced onion, minced garlic, and salt in a bowl.

2. Unroll the crescent roll dough, pull apart the triangles and slice each segment into three little triangle pieces. Try to get 3 strips for each roll for the mini hot dogs.

3. After the strips are cut, spread some Dijon mustard on each piece of dough. Roll the dough around mini hot dogs. Lay the pigs in a blanket on a greased cookie sheet. Brush with egg wash and sprinkle with the prepared seasoning.

4. Bake for 15 minutes, serve hot and enjoy!

Delicious Barbecue Beef Brisket

Servings: 12

Cooking Time: 480 Minutes

Ingredients:

- 1 Beef Soup, Campbells Can
- 1 - 12 To 14 Lb Packer Beef, Brisket

Directions:

1. The night before you plan on cooking the brisket, trim the surface fat off the brisket with your sharp boning knife. Trim to leave about 1/8 to ¼ in fat.

2. Place the brisket in an unscented trash bag or on a sheet pan fat side up and season the meat side liberally with your favorite Rub. Let rest on the counter for 30 minutes until the rub is all soaked up. Flip the brisket over and season the fat side liberally. Cover or wrap up the brisket and put in the fridge overnight.

3. Prep your Grill by cleaning the grates, grease tray and firepot is clean. Supply your smoker with wood pellets and follow the start-up procedure. Preheat the grill, with the lid closed, to 250° F.

4. When grill has settled to 250°F place brisket in center of grill fat side down and cook for 4 hours.

5. After 4 hours, insert the meat probe into the fat seam between the point and flat so the end of the meat probe is in the center of the fat seam and continue to cook for about 2 more hours.

6. Prep aluminum foil to wrap the brisket in by tearing off 4 sheets of foil at least twice as large as the brisket. Plus one more piece about the same size as the brisket.

7. When the meat thermometer reads 150°F to 160°F wrap the brisket in foil by placing the brisket fat side down on 2 sheets of foil. The cover with the other 2 sheets of foil and tightly roll/fold 3 sides up to seal – leaving one side open. Leave the meat probe in place in the brisket and lay the probe wire between the bottom and top foil sheets. Roll/fold the meat probe wire between the foil sheets as you are closing the foil. Dump the can of Campbell's Beef Consume into the foil through the open end and roll/fold that end closed.

8. Place the small foil sheet on the grill grate and place the foil-wrapped brisket on the small foil sheet on the grate. The small foil sheet will prevent the foil from sticking to the grate to prevent the foil from ripping and losing the foil juice that you can use later.

9. Continue to cook until the meat thermometer reads 200°F. Then unwrap one or two sides of the foil being careful not to lose any of the liquid in the foil. Insert a dinner fork into the flat portion of the brisket – if it goes in and out like a hot knife through butter it is done, if it has very much resistance, seal the sides of the foil and place back in grill and cook until the meat thermometer reads 205°F and test for tenderness again.

10. When the brisket is done, remove from grill, wrap in a clean towel and place in a small clean cooler to rest for at least 2 hours.

11. When ready to slice, remove brisket from foil. Separate the point end from the flat end by running your slicing knife down the fat seam. Slice the brisket across the grain into slices just thick enough to hold together.

12. Cube the point section into ½ in sq cubes by slicing ½ in slices across the grain first and then ½ in slices with the grain.

13. Place all slices and cubes into a pan and pour some of the liquid from the foil over the brisket.

14. Serve with your favorite BBQ Sauce on the side.

Reverse-seared Steaks

Servings: 4
Cooking Time: 120 Minutes

Ingredients:
- 4 (4-ounce) sirloin steaks
- 2 tablespoons olive oil
- Salt
- Freshly ground black pepper
- 4 tablespoons butter

Directions:
1. Supply your smoker with wood pellets and follow the start-up procedure. Preheat the grill, with the lid closed, to 180°F.
2. Rub the steaks all over with olive oil and season both sides with salt and pepper.
3. Place the steaks directly on the grill grate and smoke until their internal temperature reaches 135°F. Remove the steaks from the grill.
4. Place a cast-iron skillet on the grill grate and increase the grill's temperature to 450°F.
5. Place the steaks in the skillet and top each with 1 tablespoon of butter. Cook the steaks until their internal temperature reaches 145°F, flipping once after 2 or 3 minutes. (I recommend reverse-searing over an open flame rather than in the cast-iron skillet, if your grill has that option.) Remove the steaks and serve immediately.

Kansas City Cheese Brisket Burger

Servings: 4
Cooking Time: 30 Minutes

Ingredients:
- 1/2 Cup Barbecue Sauce
- 4 Brioche Burger Buns
- 4 Slices Brisket
- 1 Lbs Ground Beef
- 8 Onion Rings
- 4 Tablespoons Sweet Rib Rub
- 4 Slices Smoked Guoda Cheese, Sliced

Directions:
1. In a large bowl, sprinkle the Sweet Rib Rub over the ground beef and mix well to combine. Shape the ground beef into 4 patties and set aside.
2. Supply your smoker with wood pellets and follow the start-up procedure. Preheat the grill, with the lid closed, to 350° F. Grill your burgers for 8-10 minutes, or until desired degree of doneness.
3. Halfway through cooking, top each burger patty with a slice of smoked Guoda cheese.
4. Remove the burgers from the grill and assemble the burgers. Place each burger on a bun and top with 2 tablespoons of barbecue sauce, 2 onion rings and a slice of brisket, then serve and enjoy!

Easy Breakfast Cheeseburger

Servings: 2
Cooking Time: 10 Minutes

Ingredients:
- 4 Bacon, Strip
- 6 Ounce Lean Beef, Ground
- 2 Burger Buns
- 2 Cheese, Sliced
- 2 Egg
- Pepper
- Salt

Directions:
1. Supply your smoker with wood pellets and follow the start-up procedure. Preheat the grill, with the lid closed, to 400° F.
2. Take the ground beef and divide it into two thin patties. Brush the grate with oil, then add the patties and grill them on about 2-5 minutes on each side, or until the desired doneness, pressing down to get a good sear.
3. Remove the burgers from the grill, then build your burger. Starting with the bottom bun or bread slice, add the patty, then a slice of American cheese, top with bacon, hash browns, an egg over easy, and finish with the top bun or bread slice. Now it's ready to serve!

Salt & Pepper Dinosaur Bones

Servings: 3-4
Cooking Time: 480 Minutes

Ingredients:

- 1 rack of beef plate short ribs, about 4 to 5lb (1.8 to 2.3kg) total, or 3 bones
- coarse kosher salt
- freshly ground black pepper
- granulated garlic
- crushed red pepper flakes (optional)
- 1½ cups sugar-free dark-colored soda, sugar-free root beer, beef broth, or brewed coffee

Directions:

1. Supply your smoker with wood pellets and follow the start-up procedure. Preheat the grill, with the lid closed, to 250° F.
2. Place the ribs in an aluminum foil roasting pan. If the rack has a thick cap of fat on the meaty side, trim most of it off because that will impede the formation of a nice bark on the ribs.
3. Generously season the ribs on all sides with salt, pepper, garlic, and red pepper flakes (if using). Place the ribs bone side down on the grate and smoke for 3 hours.
4. Add the soda to a spray bottle and spritz the ribs. Continue to smoke the ribs until the internal temperature reaches 203°F (95°C), about 4 to 5 hours more, spritzing once an hour. (Insert the probe next to the middle rib, being careful not to touch the bone.) When the ribs are tender, the meat will feel gelatinous and springy and will have shrunk back from the ends of the bones by up to 2 inches (5cm).
5. Transfer the ribs to a clean sheet pan and wrap with heavy-duty aluminum foil. Let rest for 1 hour, preferably in an insulated cooler.
6. Slice the ribs apart or remove the meat from the bones and thinly slice before serving with additional salt and pepper.

Spiced Smoked Kielbasa Dogs

Servings: 12
Cooking Time: 300 Minutes

Ingredients:

- 1 tsp all spice, ground
- 2 tsp black peppercorns, ground
- 3 tbsp brown sugar
- 1 cup distilled ice water, divided
- 1 1/2 tsp garlic powder
- 1 1/2 lbs ground beef
- 5 lbs ground pork
- 32 - 35 hog casings
- 2 tbsp kosher salt
- 2 tsp marjoram, dried
- 1 1/2 tsp paprika
- 1 1/4 tsp speed cure, pink salt curing

Directions:

1. In a glass bowl or measuring cup, cover hog casings in warm water and let soak for 1 hour.

2. In a small bowl, whisk together brown sugar, salt, black pepper, marjoram, garlic powder, paprika, allspice, and speed cure.
3. In a large tub, combine ground pork and ground beef. Mix together by hand, then add seasoning and distilled ice water. Mix mixture by hand for 1 minute, until seasoning is incorporated throughout.
4. Prepare the sausage stuffer, and fit one hog casing over a 1 to 1 ¼ inch horn. Place a sheet tray, with a bit of water on it, underneath the nozzle of the stuffer and start filling the casings.
5. Once the casings are filled, twist off into desired lengths, and refrigerate overnight.
6. Hang the links with S-hooks from the top rack of your Grill or Smoker. Smoke on SMOKE mode for 3 hours. Supply your smoker with wood pellets and follow the start-up procedure. Preheat the grill, with the lid closed, to 300° F, which will raise the temperature of the smoking cabinet to 170°F. If using a vertical smoker, keep smoking on SMOKE mode. Continue smoking the sausage for another 1 to 2 hours, until the internal temperature of the sausage reaches 155° F.
7. Remove sausage from the smoking cabinet and either enjoy hot with your favorite toppings, or place in an ice water bath for 15 minutes, dry at room temperature and refrigerate or freeze for future use.

Savory Bacon Wrapped Hot Dogs

Servings: 6
Cooking Time: 10 Minutes

Ingredients:

- 1 - 2 Green Bell Pepper, Diced
- 1 Per Hot Dog Bacon, Strip
- 6 - 8 Hot Dog Bun(S)
- 6 - 8 Hot Dog(S)
- Smoke Infused Applewood Bacon Rub
- 2 Tbsp Vegetable Oil

Directions:

1. Supply your smoker with wood pellets and follow the start-up procedure. Preheat the grill, with the lid closed, to 400° F. Before placing anything on the grill, generously oil the cooking grids, using a cloth and vegetable oil.
2. Heat your grill to medium-high heat.
3. Lay a slice of bacon on a cutting board.
4. Roll the bacon and hot dog around until the bacon covers the whole hot dog. Secure with a toothpick on each end.
5. Repeat steps 3 and 4 again, by wrapping each hot dog with one strip of bacon, and secure with a toothpick on each end.
6. Cook the bacon wrapped hot dogs on the grill. When the bacon is lightly crisp, remove from the heat. This takes about 4-6 minutes.
7. Toast the buns by turning the grill up to high. Open the flame broiler. Place bun face down on cooking grids. Toast until desired done.

8.   As soon as the hot dogs are done, place them on a toasted bun, pile on the chopped green peppers, and serve.

Pastrami

Servings: 6-8
Cooking Time: 960 Minutes

Ingredients:
- 1 (8-pound) corned beef brisket
- 2 tablespoons yellow mustard
- 1 batch Espresso Brisket Rub
- Worcestershire Mop and Spritz, for spritzing

Directions:
1.   Supply your smoker with wood pellets and follow the start-up procedure. Preheat the grill, with the lid closed, to 225°F.
2.   Coat the brisket all over with mustard and season it with the rub. Using your hands, work the rub into the meat. Pour the mop into a spray bottle.
3.   Place the brisket directly on the grill grate and smoke until its internal temperature reaches 195°F, spritzing it every hour with the mop.
4.   Pull the corned beef brisket from the grill and wrap it completely in aluminum foil or butcher paper. Place the wrapped brisket in a cooler, cover the cooler, and let it rest for 1 or 2 hours.
5.   Remove the corned beef from the cooler and unwrap it. Slice the corned beef and serve.

Smoked Chicken Steak Sandwiches

Servings: 6
Cooking Time: 270 Minutes

Ingredients:
- 1 1/2 tsp black pepper, ground
- 3 lbs brisket flat
- 1 tbsp butter
- 1 1/2 cups chicken stock
- 1/4 cup chop house steak rub
- for topping, dill pickles
- 2 tsp garlic powder
- 8 oz maple cure
- 2 tsp mustard powder
- 1 onion, sliced
- 1 1/2 tbsp pickling spice
- pumpernickel rye, sliced
- to taste, sauerkraut
- to taste, spicy brown mustard
- 6 swiss cheese, sliced
- 2 qts water, cold

Directions:
1.   Set the brisket flat on a cutting board, then trim off excess fat and silver skin.
2.   Whisk together water and maple cure, until dissolved.
3.   Lay brisket in a large container, season with pickling spice, then cover with brine/cure. The meat must be completely immersed. Cover and place in the refrigerator for 3 to 4 days.
4.   Remove brisket flat from brine/cure. It will be pale grey in color, which is normal. Discard the cure and replace with plain water. Allow brisket to soak 1-2 hours.
5.   Combine all ingredients for the rub in a bowl. Remove the brisket from the water and blot dry with paper towel.
6.   Season the brisket well with the rub, pushing and massaging it into the surface. Place the brisket back into the refrigerator, uncovered, overnight.
7.   Supply your smoker with wood pellets and follow the start-up procedure. Preheat the grill, with the lid closed, to 250° F. If using a gas or charcoal grill, set it up for low, indirect heat.
8.   Transfer the brisket flat directly on the grill grate, fat side down, over indirect heat. Smoke for 2 hours, flipping after 1 hour.
9.   Remove the brisket from the grill and place it in a cast iron skillet, or foil-lined aluminum pan with chicken stock and onions. Cover with a lid, or foil and return to the grill.
10. Increase temperature to 275° F, and cook an additional 1 hour, then check the brisket to see if enough liquid remains. If reducing too quickly, add 1 cup of water. Cook the brisket for another 1 hour, or until the brisket is probe tender
11. Remove from the grill and rest for at least 30 minutes, prior to slicing thin.
12. Preheat the griddle over low flame.
13. Grease griddle with 1 tablespoon of butter, then spread mustard on 4 slices of rye, then set on griddle. Add 2 portions of sliced pastrami. Warm pastrami 1 to 2 minutes, then flip. Top pastrami with sauerkraut and cheese, then close the griddle lid for 1 minute to crisp up the underside of the pastrami and melt the cheese.
14. Brush rye with mustard then set pastrami on every other slice. Set remaining toasted rye on top complete the smoked pastrami sandwich.
15. Remove from the griddle, then repeat. Slice each sandwich on the bias and serve warm with dill pickles.

Beer Chili Bratwurst

Servings: 4
Cooking Time: 45 Minutes

Ingredients:
- 1 Chopped Chipotle In Adobo
- 3 - 4 Cans Of Beer, Any Brand
- 4 Bratwursts, Raw
- 4 Bratwurst Buns

- ½ Cup Prepared Nacho Cheese Sauce
- 1 Cup Chili, Prepared
- Caramelized Onions
- Sweet Rib Rub

Directions:

1. Supply your smoker with wood pellets and follow the start-up procedure. Preheat the grill, with the lid closed, to 350° F. If you're using charcoal or gas, set the temperature to medium high.

2. Place a pot filled with beer, Sweet Rib Rub, caramelized onions and raw brats. Place on grill and par-boil for 20 minutes.

3. Grill the brats for 7-10 minutes, or until internal temperature of the brats is 160°F. Remove the brats from the grill and allow them to rest for 5 minutes.

4. While the brats rest, place the chili in a sauce pan, and place the sauce pan on the grill. Heat the chili all the way through.

5. In a separate sauce pan, add the nacho cheese to the pan, add adobo chili peppers and a shake of Sweet Rib Rub. Place the saucepan on the grill and heat until warm all the way through.

6. Assemble the brats: place a brat in a bun, then top with a spoonful of chili and a spoonful of nacho cheese. Serve immediately.

Chuck Roast Burnt Ends

Servings: 4
Cooking Time: 480 Minutes

Ingredients:

- 1 chuck roast, about 3 to 4lb (1.4 to 1.8kg)
- 2 tbsp Worcestershire sauce, plus more
- coarse salt, plus more
- freshly ground black pepper, plus more
- granulated garlic, plus more
- 1 cup low-carb barbecue sauce
- ¼ cup sugar-free dark-colored soda, plus more

Directions:

1. Supply your smoker with wood pellets and follow the start-up procedure. Preheat the grill, with the lid closed, to 250° F.

2. Place the roast on a rimmed sheet pan and brush with the Worcestershire sauce. Lightly season with salt, pepper, and granulated garlic. Place the roast on the grate and smoke until the internal temperature reaches 170°F (77°C), about 5 to 6 hours.

3. Transfer the roast to a cutting board and let rest for 10 minutes. (Leave the grill going.) Use a sharp knife to slice the meat into bite-size cubes, trimming any excess fat if necessary. Place the meat in an aluminum foil roasting pan. Lightly season with more salt, pepper, and granulated garlic and toss the cubes with your hands to distribute the seasonings. Add the barbecue sauce and soda. Toss again to coat.

4. Place the pan on the grate and smoke until the meat is tender and somewhat sticky with sauce, about 1 to 2 hours, stirring occasionally. (Don't let the sauce scorch.) Add another splash of soda if needed.

5. Remove the pan from the grill and stir the meat again before serving.

Spiced Cowboy Steak

Servings: x
Cooking Time: 53 Minutes

Ingredients:

- 2 cowboy steaks about 1 3/4 inches to 2 inches thick
- Rub:
- 1 1/2 tablespoon olive oil
- 2 cloves garlic minced
- 1 tablespoon coarse salt kosher or sea salt
- 1 teaspoon black pepper
- 1 teaspoon dried thyme
- 1/2 teaspoon onion powder
- 1/2 teaspoon marjoram
- 1/4 teaspoon smoked paprika

Directions:

1. Combine all the rub ingredients and slather onto both sides of the cowboy steaks.

2. Supply your smoker with wood pellets and follow the start-up procedure. Preheat the grill, with the lid closed, to 225 °F.

3. Place steaks on the cooking grate and cook until the internal temperature reaches 120 degrees F (about 45 minutes).

4. Remove steaks from grill, cover it and set aside. Turn pellet grill to the HIGH setting.

5. Place steaks back on the hot grill. After 4 minutes, rotate 45 degrees to create a diamond pattern of sear marks. After 4 minutes turn it over and repeat on the other side.

6. Once seared to perfection, remove steaks from grill and place onto a clean cutting board. Let rest for 5-7 minutes and serve with a dollop of flavored butter on top, or carve and share.

Bbq Sweet Pepper Meatloaf

Servings: 8
Cooking Time: 180 Minutes

Ingredients:

- 5 Pound ground beef, 80% lean
- 2 eggs
- 1 Cup plain panko breadcrumbs
- 1 Tablespoon kosher salt
- 1 Tablespoon black pepper
- 2 Tablespoon Rub
- 1 Cup diced sweet red peppers
- 1 Cup green onion, finely chopped
- 1 Cup ketchup

Directions:

1. Thoroughly mix together the ground beef, eggs, plain panko bread crumbs, kosher salt, black pepper, Traeger Rub, red sweet peppers and green onion.
2. Supply your smoker with wood pellets and follow the start-up procedure. Preheat the grill, with the lid closed, to 225° F.
3. Mold the meat mixture into a loaf and season exterior with the Traeger Rub.
4. Place meatloaf directly on the grill grate and cook for 2 hours and 15 minutes. Grill: 225 °F
5. Increase the grill temperature to 375°F and cook until an internal temperature of 155°F. Grill: 375 °F Probe: 155 °F
6. Glaze the meatloaf with ketchup and cook an additional 15 minutes. Grill: 375 °F
7. Allow to rest for 15 minutes before slicing. Enjoy!

Grilled Brisket Burger

Servings: 2
Cooking Time: 15 Minutes

Ingredients:

- 2 Pound ground beef brisket
- 2/3 Medium Red Onion, Sliced 1/4" Thick
- 4 Slices cheddar cheese
- 8 Slices cooked bacon
- 2 Whole Burger Buns, Halved
- 6 Ounce Sweet & Heat BBQ Sauce

Directions:

1. Supply your smoker with wood pellets and follow the start-up procedure. Preheat the grill, with the lid closed, to 375° F. Form meat into 6 patties and season with Traeger Beef Rub.
2. Place them directly on the grill grate and cook for 4 minutes, flip patties and cook for 2 more minutes. Grill: 375 °F
3. Place the red onions on the grill next to the burger and cook for 8 minutes total, flipping halfway through. Grill: 375 °F

4. Top burgers with cheese and cook until cheese is melted, about 1–2 minutes. Remove burgers from grill and keep warm.
5. If desired, toast burger buns face side down on the grill for 2 minutes. Assemble as double burgers with the grilled onions, bacon, and Traeger Sweet & Heat BBQ sauce. Enjoy! *Cook times will vary depending on set and ambient temperatures.

Garlic Cheese Bacon Burger

Servings: 7
Cooking Time: 16 Minutes

Ingredients:

- 14 Bacon, Strip
- 3 Lbs Chuck Beef, Ground
- 7 Burger Buns
- 4 Cloves Garlic, Minced
- 1 Onion, Chopped
- 1 Tsp Pepper
- 8 Oz Pepper Jack Cheese, Sliced
- 2 Tomato, Sliced

Directions:

1. Supply your smoker with wood pellets and follow the start-up procedure. Preheat the grill, with the lid closed, to 400° F.
2. In a bowl, mix together the ground chuck, garlic, onion, and pepper. Separate the beef mixtures into about 7 equal bundles and form hamburger patties.
3. Brush the grate with oil, then add the patties and grill them on about 5-8 minutes on each side, or until desired doneness.
4. Remove the burgers from the grill. On the bottom half of the burger bun, add two tomato slices, top with a slice of pepper jack cheese, add the patty,
5. Place another slice of cheese on top, add two slices of bacon and top it off with the other half of the burger bun and serve.

Bistro Steaks With Avocado Relish

Servings: 4
Cooking Time: 34 Minutes

Ingredients:

- 2lb (1kg) bistro steaks
- extra virgin olive oil
- liquid aminos
- for the rub
- 2 tsp coarse salt
- 2 tsp fresh coarsely ground black pepper
- 2 tsp light brown sugar or low-carb substitute
- 2 tsp chili powder
- 2 tsp ground cumin
- 2 tsp granulated garlic
- 2 tsp sweet or smoked paprika

- for the relish
- 2 avocados
- 1½ tbsp freshly squeezed lime juice, plus more
- 2 garlic cloves, peeled and finely minced
- 1 Roma tomato, decored, deseeded, and diced
- 1 jalapeño, destemmed, deseeded, and finely diced
- ¼ cup coarsely chopped fresh cilantro leaves
- 2 tbsp diced red onion
- 1 tbsp mayo
- 1 tsp hot sauce
- coarse salt

Directions:

1. Supply your smoker with wood pellets and follow the start-up procedure. Preheat the grill, with the lid closed, to 180° F.

2. In a small bowl, make the rub by combining the ingredients.

3. Trim any silver skin from the steaks and place them on a rimmed sheet pan. Coat with olive oil. Dust with the rub, patting it on with your fingertips.

4. Place the steaks on the grate and grill until the internal temperature reaches 110 to 115°F (43 to 46°C), about 30 minutes. Pour some liquid aminos into a small spray bottle and spritz the steaks before wrapping them in heavy-duty aluminum foil. Let the steaks rest.

5. Cut the avocados in half and then pit, peel, and dice them. In a medium bowl, make the relish by combining the avocado and lime juice. Add the remaining ingredients and season with salt to taste. Use a rubber spatula to gently mix. Transfer to an attractive serving bowl. Cover and refrigerate. (The relish is best if not made more than 1 hour ahead.)

6. Raise the temperature to 450°F (232°C). Remove the steaks from the foil and place them on the grate. Sear until they're browned and the internal temperature reaches 130 to 135°F (54 to 57°C), about 2 minutes per side, turning with tongs.

7. Transfer the steaks to a cutting board and let rest for 3 minutes. Slice them crosswise on a diagonal into 3/8-inch (1cm) slices. Shingle the slices on a platter and pour any juices remaining on the cutting board over the meat. Serve with the avocado relish.

Sweetheart Steak

Servings: 2
Cooking Time: 12 Minutes

Ingredients:

- 1 (20 Oz) Boneless Strip Steak Or Rib Steak, Butterflied Into Heart Shape
- 2 Teaspoon Jacobsen Salt Co. Pure Kosher Sea Salt
- 2 Teaspoon black pepper
- 2 Tablespoon Raw Dark Chocolate, finely chopped
- 1/2 Tablespoon extra-virgin olive oil

Directions:

1. Draw a large heart on a piece of cardboard, shape to size of meat selected. Cut out cardboard heart shape, then trim meat into heart shape.

2. Combine all ingredients on the cut steak.

3. Supply your smoker with wood pellets and follow the start-up procedure. Preheat the grill, with the lid closed, to 450° F.

4. Grill steak for 5 to 7 minutes per side, or until you've reached desired doneness. Remove from grill. Let rest for 5 minutes. Enjoy!

Savory Smoked Brisket

Servings: 10
Cooking Time: 600 Minutes

Ingredients:

- 4 Tbsp Apple Cider Vinegar
- 10Lb Trimmed Brisket
- 2 Cups Broth, Beef
- Sweet Heat Rub
- 2 Tbsp Worcestershire Sauce

Directions:

1. Trim the fat cap from your brisket, leaving enough fat to baste the meat during the smoke process.

2. Generously coat the brisket with   Sweet Heat rub, and massage into the brisket.

3. In a bowl, whisk together the apple cider vinegar, Worcestershire sauce and beef broth, then pour into a clean spray bottle.

4. Supply your smoker with wood pellets and follow the start-up procedure. Preheat the grill, with the lid closed, to 225° F. Once the smoker is up to temperature, place the brisket inside and insert the temperature probe. Smoke for 10 to 12 hours, or until the internal temperature of the brisket reaches 200°F at the thickest part. Once an hour, spray the brisket with the mop sauce to baste it.

5. Once the brisket is done, remove from the smoker, allow to rest for 30 minutes under tin foil, then slice and enjoy!

Bistecca Alla Fiorentina With Mushroom Ragout

Servings: 3
Cooking Time: 25 Minutes

Ingredients:

- 2 sprigs of fresh sage
- 2 sprigs of fresh rosemary
- 2 sprigs of fresh thyme
- 1 porterhouse steak, about 2½lb (1.25kg)
- extra virgin olive oil
- coarse salt
- fresh coarsely ground black pepper

- for the ragout
- 3 tbsp unsalted butter
- 3 shallots or 1 white onion, peeled and chopped
- 2 garlic cloves, peeled and minced
- 2lb (1kg) wild mushrooms, cleaned, destemmed, and sliced or chopped
- coarse salt
- freshly ground black pepper
- 2 tbsp Cognac or brandy
- ½ cup low-salt beef broth, plus more
- 2 tsp light soy sauce
- 2 tsp chopped fresh thyme or 1 tsp dried thyme
- ½ cup heavy whipping cream, plus more
- freshly squeezed lemon juice
- freshly chopped chives

Directions:

1. Place a cast iron skillet or cast iron griddle on the grate. Supply your smoker with wood pellets and follow the start-up procedure. Preheat the grill, with the lid closed, to 450° F.

2. In a large skillet on the stovetop over medium heat, begin making the ragout by melting the butter. Add the shallots and sauté until they soften, about 2 to 3 minutes, stirring often. Add the garlic and mushrooms. Season with salt and pepper. Cook until the mushrooms give up their liquid and begin to brown, about 5 minutes. Add the Cognac and cook for 1 minute. Stir in the broth, soy sauce, and thyme. Cook until the liquid reduces slightly, about 5 minutes. Remove the skillet from the stovetop and set aside.

3. Tie the sprigs of sage, rosemary, and thyme together with butcher's twine. Place the steak on a rimmed sheet pan and use the herb brush to generously brush both sides with olive oil. Season with salt and pepper.

4. Place the steak on the skillet and grill until the internal temperature reaches 125°F (52°C), about 8 to 10 minutes per side, occasionally using the herb brush to brush the steak with olive oil. If your grill has enough clearance, stand the porterhouse upright, resting on the bone, and continue to cook for a few minutes more.

5. Transfer the meat to a cutting board and brush it one final time with olive oil. Let rest for 5 minutes.

6. Add the cream to the ragout and reheat over medium-high heat until the mixture boils. Taste for seasoning, adding salt and pepper. If the ragout seems dry, add more cream or broth. If the flavors need brightening, stir in 1 or 2 teaspoons of lemon juice. Transfer the ragout to an attractive serving bowl and top with chives.

7. Carve off the strip steak and filet mignon. Slice them on a diagonal, keeping the slices in order. Place the bone on a platter and then place the slices around the bone. Serve immediately with the mushroom ragout.

Smoked Garlic Prime Rib Roast

Servings: 12
Cooking Time: 60 Minutes

Ingredients:

- 1 10 pounds Prime Rib Roast (the bones cut off and tied back on)
- 1/2 cup horseradish mustard
- 2 tablespoons Worcestershire sauce
- 4 cloves garlic (minced)
- Coarse ground salt and black pepper (to taste)

Directions:

1. Supply your smoker with wood pellets and follow the start-up procedure. Preheat the grill, with the lid closed, to 225 °F.

2. Prepare your roast while the grill is heating. Trim any excess fat from the top of the roast down to 1/4 inch thick.

3. In a small bowl, combine the mustard, Worcestershire sauce,and garlic. Slather the entire roast with the mustard mixture and season liberally with salt and pepper.

4. Place the roast on the grill grate and close the lid. Smoke until the internal temperature of the roast reaches 120 °F for Rare or 130 °F for Medium. For a rare, bone-in roast, plan on 35 minutes per pound of prime rib.

5. Remove the roast to a cutting board, cover the roast with foil, and allow it to rest for 20 minutes.

6. While the roast is resting, increase the temperature of your grill to 400 °F.

7. Once the grill temperature reaches 400 °F, return the roast to the grill and sear until it reaches your desired internal temperature. Pull the roast off at 130 °F for rare, 135 °F for medium rare, 140 °F for medium. This process should go quickly, so keep an eye on your temperature.

8. Remove your roast to the cutting board and let the meat rest for at least 15 minutes.

9. Slice and serve.

Smoked Bourbon Jerky

Servings: 6
Cooking Time: 360 Minutes

Ingredients:

- 3 Pound flank steak
- 1 Cup bourbon
- 1/2 Cup brown sugar
- 1/4 Cup Jerky Rub
- 1 Can chipotle peppers in adobo sauce
- 3 Tablespoon Worcestershire sauce
- 1/2 Cup apple cider vinegar

Directions:

1. Roll flank steak up parallel to the grain. Slice, with the grain, into 1/4 inch thick slices.

2. Combine all ingredients for marinade in a medium bowl and mix well. Place sliced flank steak in a large zip top bag and pour marinade over steak.

3. Place in refrigerator and marinate overnight.

4. Supply your smoker with wood pellets and follow the start-up procedure. Preheat the grill, with the lid closed, to 180° F.

5. Remove flank from the marinade, discard marinade and lay slices on a jerky rack or directly on the grill grate. Grill: 180 °F

6. Smoke for about 6 hours or until jerky has dried out but is still pliable. Grill: 180 °F

7. Remove from grill and let cool at room temperature, lightly covered for 1 hour.

8. Store in an airtight container or zip top bag in the refrigerator. Enjoy!

Green Bell Pepper Cheese Steak Burger

Servings: 4
Cooking Time: 30 Minutes

Ingredients:
- 4 Burger Buns
- 1 Green Bell Pepper, Sliced
- 1 Pound Ground Beef
- 1 Tablespoon Olive Oil
- 1 Tablespoon Chop House Steak Seasoning
- 4 Provolone Cheese, Sliced

Directions:
1. In a large bowl, mix the ground beef and Chop House Steak seasoning together until well combined. Form into patties. Supply your smoker with wood pellets and follow the start-up procedure. Preheat the grill, with the lid closed, to 350° F and grill for 5-7 minutes, flipping halfway through. Once you flip the burgers, top with a slice of provolone cheese.

2. Once the burgers have cooked to your desired degree of doneness, remove from the grill and set aside.

3. For the pepper and onion: in a sauté pan over medium heat, heat the olive oil until it shimmers, then add the onion and pepper. Cook until the pepper and onion are soft and start to caramelize and develop a little char, about 15 minutes.

Roasted Venison Steaks By The Bowmars

Servings: 4
Cooking Time: 25 Minutes

Ingredients:

- 10 Whole Venison Steaks, 6oz
- 1 L Diet Sprite
- 6 Ounce Big Game Rub
- 2 Pound asparagus
- 3 Tablespoon Rub

Directions:
1. The night before, marinade the steaks with sprite and big game rub.

2. Supply your smoker with wood pellets and follow the start-up procedure. Preheat the grill, with the lid closed, to 350° F.

3. Remove steaks from marinade and pat dry. Place steaks directly on the grill grate and cook 10-15 minutes flipping once until the internal temperature reaches 125 degrees for medium rare. Grill: 350 °F

4. Sprinkle asparagus with Traeger Rub and add to Traeger. Cook for 10 minutes turning once.

5. Let steaks rest ten minutes before serving. Enjoy!

Diva Q's Herb-crusted Prime Rib

Servings: 4
Cooking Time: 300 Minutes

Ingredients:
- 1/4 Cup fresh rosemary leaves
- 1/4 Cup fresh flat-leaf parsley leaves
- 1/4 Cup minced garlic
- 1/4 Cup canola oil
- 3 Tablespoon Dijon mustard
- 2 Tablespoon finely ground black pepper
- 2 Tablespoon kosher salt
- 1 (5-7 lb) bone-in prime rib roast

Directions:
1. Combine rosemary, parsley, garlic, canola oil, mustard, salt and pepper in a food processor. Pulse until the herbs are finely chopped and the ingredients are combined.

2. Coat the entire prime rib with the herb mixture. Refrigerate prime rib uncovered, for 4 hours.

3. Supply your smoker with wood pellets and follow the start-up procedure. Preheat the grill, with the lid closed, to 250° F.

4. Place the prime rib bone side down on the grill. Roast meat (allowing 12 to 15 minutes per pound) until the internal temperature in the thickest part of the prime rib reaches 120°F-130°F for rare to medium-rare, about 5 hours. Begin taking the internal temperature every 45 minutes after the 2 hour mark. Grill: 250 °F Probe: 120 °F

5. Remove the prime rib from the grill, tent loosely with foil and let rest for 15 minutes before slicing. Enjoy!

Spicy Smoked Chili Beef Jerky

Servings: 6
Cooking Time: 240 Minutes

Ingredients:
- 1 Cup chili sauce
- 1/3 Cup beer
- 2 Tablespoon soy sauce
- 1 Tablespoon Worcestershire sauce
- 2 Tablespoon Morton Tender Quick Home Meat Cure
- 1 Tablespoon minced pickled jalapeño peppers
- 2 Pound flank steak, cut into 1/4 inch thick slices

Directions:
1. In a mixing bowl, combine the chili sauce, beer, soy sauce, Worcestershire sauce, curing salt and pickled jalapeño peppers.
2. Put the beef slices in a large resealable bag. Pour the marinade mixture over the beef, and massage the bag so that all the slices get coated with the marinade. Seal the bag and refrigerate for several hours, or overnight.
3. Supply your smoker with wood pellets and follow the start-up procedure. Preheat the grill, with the lid closed, to 165° F.
4. Remove the beef from the marinade, discarding the marinade. Dry beef slices between paper towels.
5. Arrange the meat in a single layer directly on the grill grate or smoke shelf.
6. Smoke for 4 to 5 hours, or until the jerky is dry but still chewy and somewhat pliant when bending a piece. Grill: 165 °F
7. Transfer to a resealable bag while the jerky is still warm.
8. Let the jerky rest for an hour at room temperature. Squeeze any air from the bag, and refrigerate the jerky.
9. Pro Tip: you can use this recipe for any cut of beef or wild game. Enjoy!

Smoked Beer Brisket

Servings: 16
Cooking Time: 420 Minutes

Ingredients:
- 1 15 lb brisket
- Brisket Baste:
- 1 cup beer
- 1/4 cup apple cider vinegar
- 1/4 cup beef stock
- 5 tbsp butter, melted
- Brisket Rub:
- 2 tbsp garlic powder
- 2 tbsp onion powder
- 2 tbsp paprika
- 2 tbsp chili powder
- 2 tbsp kosher salt
- 2 tbsp coarse ground black pepper
- 1 tbsp brown sugar

Directions:
1. Supply your smoker with wood pellets and follow the start-up procedure. Preheat the grill, with the lid closed, to 225 °F.
2. In a small bowl, mix together garlic powder, onion powder, paprika, chili pepper, kosher salt, and pepper.
3. Rub the seasonings on all sides of the brisket.
4. Place the brisket on the grill grate, fat side down.
5. Cook the brisket until it reaches an internal temperature of 160 °F(about 3 to 4 hours).
6. When brisket reaches an internal temperature of 160 °F, remove it from the grill.
7. Double wrap the meat in aluminum foil and add the beef broth to the foil packet.
8. Return brisket to the grill grate and cook until it reaches an internal temperature of 204 °F(about 3 hours more).
9. Once finished, remove the brisket from the grill, unwrap from foil and let it rest for 15 minutes.
10. Cut against the grain and serve. Enjoy!

Succulent Lamb Chops

Servings: 4-6
Cooking Time: 20 Minutes

Ingredients:
- ½ cup rice wine vinegar
- 1 teaspoon liquid smoke
- 2 tablespoons extra-virgin olive oil
- 2 tablespoons dried minced onion
- 1 tablespoon chopped fresh mint
- 8 (4-ounce) lamb chops
- ½ cup hot pepper jelly
- 1 tablespoon Sriracha
- 1 teaspoon salt
- 1 teaspoon freshly ground black pepper

Directions:
1. In a small bowl, whisk together the rice wine vinegar, liquid smoke, olive oil, minced onion, and mint. Place the lamb chops in an aluminum roasting pan. Pour the marinade over the meat, turning to coat thoroughly. Cover with plastic wrap and marinate in the refrigerator for 2 hours.
2. Supply your smoker with wood pellets and follow the start-up procedure. Preheat, with the lid closed, to 165°F, or the "Smoke" setting.
3. On the stove top, in a small saucepan over low heat, combine the hot pepper jelly and Sriracha and keep warm.
4. When ready to cook the chops, remove them from the marinade and pat dry. Discard the marinade.

5. Season the chops with the salt and pepper, then place them directly on the grill grate, close the lid, and smoke for 5 minutes to "breathe" some smoke into them.

6. Remove the chops from the grill. Increase the pellet cooker temperature to 450°F, or the "High" setting. Once the grill is up to temperature, place the chops on the grill and sear, cooking for 2 minutes per side to achieve medium-rare chops. A meat thermometer inserted in the thickest part of the meat should read 145°F. Continue grilling, if necessary, to your desired doneness.

7. Serve the chops with the warm Sriracha pepper jelly on the side.

Cheesy French Dip Sliders

Servings: 8 - 12
Cooking Time: 60 Minutes

Ingredients:

- 1 ¾ cup beef stock
- 3 lbs. beef top round roast, boneless
- 1 tbsp olive oil
- 2 tbsp chop house steak rub
- 1 8 oz. block of provolone cheese
- 1 red onion, sliced thinly
- ¼ cup sherry
- 1 dozen slider rolls, sliced

Directions:

1. Supply your smoker with wood pellets and follow the start-up procedure. Preheat the grill, with the lid closed, to 400° F.If using a gas or charcoal grill, set it up for medium-high heat.

2. Rub roast with olive oil, then season with Chop House Steak Rub.

3. Place red onion in the bottom of a cast iron skillet and set roast on top. Transfer to grill and roast for 15 minutes. Reduce grill temperature to 325°F then add beef stock and sherry, and continue to cook another 30 minutes, or until 125 to 130°F internal temperature is reached.

4. Remove from grill and allow the roast to rest for 10 minutes, then slice thinly.

5. Assemble sliders on sheet tray by placing sliced beef on the bottom half of each roll. Top with onion and provolone cheese, then place top half of roll on top of cheese. Transfer jus into a metal gravy boat or porcelain ramekin and reserve for serving.

6. Transfer rolls back into cast iron skillet and return to grill for 5 minutes, until cheese melts. Serve hot with jus for dipping

Slow Smoked And Roasted Prime Rib

Servings: 8
Cooking Time: 240 Minutes

Ingredients:

- 1 (8-10 lb) 4-bone prime rib roast
- 5 Tablespoon kosher salt
- 5 Tablespoon ground black pepper
- 3 Tablespoon fresh chopped thyme
- 3 Tablespoon fresh chopped rosemary

Directions:

1. Supply your smoker with wood pellets and follow the start-up procedure. Preheat the grill, with the lid closed, to 250° F.

2. While grill preheats, trim excess fat off roast. Combine remainder of ingredients and coat the entire roast with the mixture.

3. Place roast on grill and cook until the internal temperature reaches 120°F, about 4 hours. Begin checking the internal temperature every hour or so until it reaches 120°F. Pull roast off the grill and allow to rest for 20 minutes. Grill: 250 °F Probe: 120 °F

4. While roast rests, increase grill temperature to 450°F and preheat. Once the grill is hot, place the roast back on for 15 minutes, flipping halfway through or until the internal temperature registers 130°F for medium rare. Grill: 450 °F Probe: 130 °F

5. Remove roast from grill and allow to rest for 30 minutes before slicing. Enjoy!

Garlic Prime Rib Roast

Servings: 8
Cooking Time: 30 Minutes

Ingredients:

- 2 tsps black pepper
- 10 cloves garlic, minced
- steak seasoning
- 2 lbs prime rib roast
- 2 tsps salt

Directions:

1. Supply your smoker with wood pellets and follow the start-up procedure. Preheat the grill, with the lid closed, to 400° F.

2. Rub roast garlic, salt, pepper and some Chop House Steak Rub.

3. Insert meat thermometer sideways into the center of the roast so that the shaft is not visible, avoiding fat and bone.

4. Cook in a closed grill, maintaining constant heat, until the thermometer reads 145°F(63°C) for medium-rare for about 50 minutes, or cook until desired doneness.

5. Remove roast to cutting board; tent with foil for 5 to 10 minutes. Serve with mashed potatoes and asparagus on the side.

Cheesy Nachos

Servings: 8
Cooking Time: 20 Minutes

Ingredients:

- Cilantro
- Olive Oil
- Pepper
- 1 Red Bell Peppers, Sliced
- 2 Rib-Eye Steaks
- Salsa
- Salt
- 1 Cup Shredded Cheddar Cheese
- Sour Cream
- 1 Yellow Bell Pepper, Sliced
- 1 Zucchini, Sliced

Directions:

1. Supply your smoker with wood pellets and follow the start-up procedure. Preheat the grill, with the lid closed, to 400° F.
2. Coat both sides of the steak with olive oil and season with sea salt and pepper. Place the steak on the grates and grill for about 4 to 5 minutes per side.
3. Remove the steak off the grill and let rest for about 10 minutes before cutting into bite-sized strips.
4. Brush with barbecue sauce if desired.
5. Empty a large bag of nacho chips evenly into a cast iron pan. Start loading up with toppings - steak, cheddar cheese, sautéed vegetables.
6. These are just suggested toppings, so feel free to add anything you like!
7. Place your loaded nachos on the grill and let the hot smoke melt your toppings into one hearty creation.
8. Cook for about 10 minutes, or until the cheese has fully melted.
9. Remove and serve with sour cream and salsa.

Smoked Tomato Brisket Chili

Servings: 6-8
Cooking Time: 120 Minutes

Ingredients:

- 4 Tablespoon Chipotles In Adobo, Diced
- 1 Cup Cooked Bacon, Chopped
- 1 (12 Oz) Beer, Any Brand
- 1 (Drained And Rinsed) Black Beans, Can
- 3 Cups Diced Cooked, Fat Trimmed Brisket
- 2 Tablespoon Chili Powder
- 1/2 Can Corn Kernels, Drained
- 1/2 (Drained) Corn, Can
- 1 Tablespoon Cumin
- 1 Green Hatch Chilies, Can
- 1 Can Kidney Beans, Drained And Rinsed
- 1 Red Onion, Diced
- 1 Tablespoon Beef And Brisket Seasoning
- 1 (15 Oz) Tomato Sauce

Directions:

1. In a sauce pan, sauté the red onion, bacon, and 2 tablespoons of the beer in oil or butter on medium heat until the onions are caramelized, and the bacon is cooked.
2. Supply your smoker with wood pellets and follow the start-up procedure. Preheat the grill, with the lid closed, to 250° F. Grill for 2 hours, or until the chili is bubbling and brisket is tender.
3. Remove from the grill and serve.

Zucchini Onion Meatloaf

Servings: 8
Cooking Time: 180 Minutes

Ingredients:

- 3 Pounds Ground Beef
- 1 Pound Italian Sausage
- 1/2 Cup Diced Onion
- 1/2 Cup Diced Green Pepper
- 1 Cup Shredded Fresh Zucchini
- 1 Egg
- 3/4 Cup Ketchup
- 1 Sleeve Crackers, Crushed (Buttery Or Saltine)
- 4 Slices Bread, Cubed
- 1/3 Cup Grated Parmesan Cheese
- 1/4 Teaspoon Each Salt and Pepper to Taste
- Garnish:
- Onion Slices, For Eyes
- 1 Pound Thick Sliced Bacon, for Bandages
- Green Pepper Slices, Nose and Teeth
- Sweet Ketchup Sauce:
- 2 Cups Ketchup
- 1/3 Cup Brown Sugar
- 1 Tablespoon Worcestershire Sauce
- 1/2 Teaspoon Onion Powder
- 1/2 Teaspoon Garlic Powder

Directions:

1. Supply your smoker with wood pellets and follow the start-up procedure. Preheat the grill, with the lid closed, to 350 °F.
2. In a large bowl mix together all ingredients.
3. Place mixture into a 13 x 9 inch baking dish and shape into a skull.
4. Place onion slices on meatloaf where the eyes should beand green pepper slices for teeth.
5. Randomly place bacon slices on meatloaf skull to look like bandages.

6. Bake meatloaf in your grill, covered with foil for 2 hours (drain excess grease if necessary).

7. Remove foil, and continue baking for another hour (drain excess grease if necessary).

8. Meanwhile, in a small saucepan, stir together ketchup, brown sugar, Worcestershire sauce, onion powder,and garlic powder. Put in the grill grate and simmer on low until warm. Baste meatloaf with sauce every 15 minutes during last hour of baking.

9. Serve with remaining sauce.

Slow Smoked Rib-eye Roast

Servings: 6
Cooking Time: 240 Minutes

Ingredients:
- 1 (4-6 lb) rib-eye roast
- 4 Tablespoon yellow mustard
- 1 Tablespoon Worcestershire sauce
- 1 Clove garlic, minced
- Prime Rib Rub
- 4 Sprig fresh thyme

Directions:
1. Supply your smoker with wood pellets and follow the start-up procedure. Preheat the grill, with the lid closed, to 250° F.

2. While the Traeger is warming up, prepare roast. Trim excess fat from the top of the roast down to 1/4 inch thick.

3. In a small bowl, combine the mustard, Worcestershire sauce and garlic. Cover entire roast with the mustard mixture and season liberally with Traeger Prime Rib rub.

4. Lay the sprigs of fresh thyme on the top of the roast.

5. Place the roast directly on the grill grate and smoke until the internal temperature of the roast reaches 135°F for rare or 145°F for medium, about 3 to 4 hours. Grill: 250 °F Probe: 135 °F

6. Remove roast from grill. Tent with foil and rest for 20 minutes before carving. Enjoy!

Smoked Sirloin Roast Beef

Servings: 2
Cooking Time: 10 Minutes

Ingredients:
- 1 top sirloin beef roast (5-6 pounds)
- 3 tbsp sea salt
- 1/4 cup Montreal steak spice

Directions:
1. Trim the roast of any excess fat. Tie the roast up with kitchen twine if desired.

2. Rub the roast down with the sea salt and then rub the roast with the Montreal steak spice.

3. Supply your smoker with wood pellets and follow the start-up procedure. Preheat the grill, with the lid closed, to 250 °F.

4. Lay the roast on the grill grate and smoke until 135 degrees F, or until the desired doneness.

5. Remove the roast from the pellet smoker and let rest for 10 minutes. Slice and serve.

Burnt Beer Beef Brisket

Servings: 10-12
Cooking Time: 1440 Minutes

Ingredients:
- 1 Cup Apple Cider Vinegar
- 1 Jar Barbecue Sauce
- 1/2 (Any Brand) Beer, Can
- Beef And Brisket Rub
- 10 - 12 Pound Whole Beef Brisket
- 2 Tablespoons Worcestershire Sauce

Directions:
1. Remove the brisket from the refrigerator. Trimming a cold brisket is easier than trimming a room temperature brisket. Flip the brisket over so that the pointed end of the meat is facing under. Cut away any silver skin or excess fat from the flat muscle and discard. Next, there will be a large, crescent shaped fat section on the flat of the meat. Trim that fat until it is smooth against the meat so that it looks like a seamless transition between the point and flat. Flip the brisket over and trim the fat cap to ¼ inch thick.

2. Generously season the trimmed brisket on all sides with the Beef and Brisket Seasoning.

3. In a bowl, mix together the beer (for a gluten free brisket, be sure to use GF beer), apple cider vinegar and Worcestershire sauce to make mop sauce.

4. Supply your smoker with wood pellets and follow the start-up procedure. Preheat the grill, with the lid closed, to 225° F. Place the brisket in the smoker, insert a temperature probe, and smoke until the internal temperature reads 165°F, about 8 hours. Baste the brisket with the mop sauce every 2 hours to keep it moist. Once the brisket reaches 165°F, remove from the smoker, wrap in butcher paper, folding the edges over to form a leak proof seal, and return to the smoker seam-side down for another 5-8 hours, or until the brisket reaches 202°F.

5. Remove from the smoker, place in an insulated cooler, and allow to rest for 3 hours. Once the brisket has finished resting, heat your smoker to 275°F. Unwrap the brisket and cut the flat from the point. Re wrap the flat and save for another recipe. Cut the point into chunks, coat in barbecue sauce, and sprinkle with Beef and Brisket seasoning.

6. Smoke the burnt ends for 1 hour, or until deeply burnished and glazed. Serve and enjoy!

Smoked Bacon Brisket Flat

Servings: 4
Cooking Time: 480 Minutes

Ingredients:
- 1/2 lbs bacon
- 4 lbs brisket flat, trimmed
- tt lonestar brisket rub

Directions:
1. Supply your smoker with wood pellets and follow the start-up procedure. Preheat the grill, with the lid open, to 250° F. If using a gas or charcoal grill, set it up for low, indirect heat.
2. Place the brisket in a foil-lined aluminum pan. Season the fat side of the brisket with Lonestar Brisket Rub, then flip and season the meat side with additional rub.
3. Transfer the brisket to the grill and smoke for 1 hour.
4. Use tongs to flip the brisket over, so the fat side is up, then drape half the bacon slices over the brisket. Smoke for 2 hours, then remove the browned bacon, and set aside.
5. Lay the remaining raw bacon strips over the brisket, and continue cooking until these new bacon strips are browned and the internal temperature of the brisket reads 202°F, which will likely take an additional 3 to 4 hours cook time.
6. Remove the brisket from the grill, and rest for 1 hour, then slice thin. Serve warm.

Pulled Beef

Servings: 5-8
Cooking Time: 840 Minutes

Ingredients:
- 1 (4-pound) top round roast
- 2 tablespoons yellow mustard
- 1 batch Espresso Brisket Rub
- ½ cup beef broth

Directions:
1. Supply your smoker with wood pellets and follow the start-up procedure. Preheat the grill, with the lid closed, to 225°F.
2. Coat the top round roast all over with mustard and season it with the rub. Using your hands, work the rub into the meat.
3. Place the roast directly on the grill grate and smoke until its internal temperature reaches 160°F and a dark bark has formed.
4. Pull the roast from the grill and place it on enough aluminum foil to wrap it completely.
5. Increase the grill's temperature to 350°F.
6. Fold in three sides of the foil around the roast and add the beef broth. Fold in the last side, completely enclosing the roast and liquid. Return the wrapped roast to the grill and cook until its internal temperature reaches 195°F.
7. Pull the roast from the grill and place it in a cooler. Cover the cooler and let the roast rest for 1 or 2 hours.
8. Remove the roast from the cooler and unwrap it. Pull apart the beef using just your fingers. Serve immediately.

Texas Style Smoked Beer Brisket

Servings: 10-12
Cooking Time: 480 Minutes

Ingredients:
- 1 cup apple cider vinegar
- 1/2 (any brand) beer, can
- beef and brisket rub
- 10-12 pound whole beef brisket
- 2 tablespoons Worcestershire Sauce

Directions:
1. Remove the brisket from the refrigerator. Trimming a cold brisket is easier than trimming a room temperature brisket.
2. Flip the brisket over so that the pointed end of the meat is facing under. Cut away any silver skin or excess fat from the flat muscle and discard.
3. Next, there will be a large, crescent shaped fat section on the flat of the meat. Trim that fat until it is smooth against the meat so that it looks like a seamless transition between the point and flat.
4. Flip the brisket over and trim the fat cap to ¼ inch thick.
5. Generously season the trimmed brisket on all sides with the Beef and Brisket Seasoning.
6. In a bowl, mix together the beer, apple cider vinegar and Worcestershire sauce to make mop sauce.
7. Supply your smoker with wood pellets and follow the start-up procedure. Preheat the grill, with the lid closed, to 225° F.
8. Place the brisket in the smoker, insert a temperature probe, and smoke until the internal temperature reads 165°F, about 8 hours.
9. Baste the brisket with the mop sauce every 2 hours to keep it moist.
10. Once the brisket reaches 165F, remove from the smoker, wrap in butcher paper, folding the edges over to form a leakproof seal, and return to the smoker seam-side down for another 5-8 hours, or until the brisket is tender enough to slide in a probe with little to no effort (around 203°F).
11. Remove the brisket from the smoker and allow to rest for 1 hour before slicing.

RECIPE INDEX

3-2-1 Bbq Baby Back Ribs 54
3-2-1 Spare Ribs 62

A

A Smoking Classic Cocktail 173
Alder Smoked Scallops With Citrus & Garlic Butter Sauce 78
Amazing Bacon Cheese Fries 75
Anzac Coconut Biscuits 20
Apple Cider Maple Glazed Ham 73
Applewood-smoked Whole Turkey 117
Apricot Glazed Ham 122
Asian Bbq Chicken 128
Asian Chicken Sliders 127

B

Baby Back Ribs With Mustard Slather 72
Bacon Burger 185
Bacon Old-fashioned Cocktail 172
Bacon Pork Pinwheels (kansas Lollipops) 159
Bacon Stuffed Smoked Pork Loin 63
Bacon Weave Smoked Country Sausage 67
Bacon Wrapped Corn On The Cob 135
Bacon Wrapped Pickles 55
Bacon Wrapped Scallops 87
Bacon Wrapped Shrimp 87
Bacon Wrapped Turkey Legs 113
Bacon-wrapped Jalapeño Poppers 159
Baked Artichoke Parmesan Mushrooms 153
Baked Bacon Green Bean Casserole 144
Baked Bourbon Maple Pumpkin Pie 17
Baked Bourbon Monkey Bread 15
Baked Breakfast Mini Quiches 138
Baked Buttermilk Biscuits 40
Baked Cast Iron Berry Cobbler 38
Baked Cheesy Parmesan Grits 27
Baked Chocolate Brownie Cookies With Egg Nog 19
Baked Chocolate Coconut Brownies 23
Baked Garlic Duchess Potatoes 152
Baked Green Chile Mac & Cheese By Doug Scheiding 42

Baked Heirloom Tomato Tart 140
Baked Honey Glazed Ham 61
Baked Kale Chips 157
Baked Loaded Tater Tots 143
Baked Maple And Brown Sugar Bacon 71
Baked Molten Chocolate Cake 39
Baked Peach Cobbler Cupcakes 38
Baked Pear Tarte Tatin 31
Baked Potatoes & Celery Root Au Gratin 16
Baked Pumpkin Pie 15
Baked Steelhead 81
Baked Stuffed Avocados 154
Baked Sweet And Savory Yams By Bennie Kendrick 153
Baked Sweet Potato Casserole With Marshmallow Fluff 149
Baked Sweet Potatoes 145
Baked Venison Tater Tot Casserole 186
Baked Whole Fish In Sea Salt 79
Baked Winter Squash Au Gratin 139
Barbecued Scallops 79
Barbecued Shrimp 91
Barbecued Tenderloin 71
Basil Margherita Pizza 31
Batter Up Cocktail 171
Bayou Wings With Cajun Rémoulade 160
Bbq 3-2-1 St. Louis Ribs 56
Bbq Brisket Breakfast Tacos 191
Bbq Brisket Tacos 182
Bbq Burnt End Sandwich 181
Bbq Cheese Chicken Stuffed Bell Peppers 115
Bbq Chicken Breasts 119
Bbq Chicken Drumsticks 131
Bbq Chicken Tostada 128
Bbq Game Day Chicken Wings And Thighs 119
Bbq Oysters 93
Bbq Pork Belly 65
Bbq Pork Belly Burnt Ends 50
Bbq Pork Short Ribs 59
Bbq Pork Shoulder Roast With Sugar Lips Glaze 60
Bbq Pulled Pork Grilled Cheese Sandwich 53

Bbq Pulled Pork Hash 71
Bbq Pulled Pork With Sweet & Heat Bbq Sauce 64
Bbq Pulled Turkey Sandwiches 124
Bbq Smoked Turkey Jerky 126
Bbq Sweet Pepper Meatloaf 200
Bbq Turkey Drumsticks 131
Beer Braised Garlic Bbq Pork Butt 48
Beer Bread 18
Beer Chili Bratwurst 198
Beer-braised Cabbage With Bacon 46
Beginner's Smoked Beef Brisket 194
Bell Pepper Chicken Sliders 114
Big Game Roast Chicken 116
Bistecca Alla Fiorentina With Mushroom Ragout 201
Bistro Steaks With Avocado Relish 200
Blt Pasta Salad 151
Blueberry Bread Pudding 25
Blueberry Pancakes 35
Blueberry Sour Cream Muffins 29
Bourbon Chile Glazed Ham 53
Braised Creamed Green Beans 150
Braised Onion Chuck Roast Beef Sandwiches 190
Breakfast Brisket Hash Recipe 181
Brined Smoked Brisket 182
Broccoli-cauliflower Salad 133
Buffalo Wings 121
Burnt Beer Beef Brisket 207
Butter Braised Green Beans 148
Butternut Squash 139
Butternut Squash Macaroni And Cheese 42

C

Cajun Catfish 87
Cajun Double-smoked Ham 74
Cajun-blackened Shrimp 103
Cake With Smoked Berry Sauce 35
Caramel Bourbon Bacon Brownies 19
Caramelized Bourbon Baked Pears 29
Carolina Baked Beans 152
Carrot Cake 28
Cast Iron Pineapple Upside Down Cake 36
Cast Iron Potatoes 157
Cedar Smoked Garlic Salmon 92

Championship Ribs With Kansas City Style 72
Charleston Crab Cakes With Remoulade 95
Cheddar Bacon Beef Burgers 190
Cheese Buffalo Chicken Wings 116
Cheese Onion Steak Sandwiches 189
Cheesy Buffalo Chicken Pinwheels 122
Cheesy French Dip Sliders 205
Cheesy Nachos 206
Chef Curtis' Famous Chimichurri Sauce 141
Cherry Ice Cream Cobbler 24
Chicken Cordon Bleu Rollups 118
Chicken Egg Rolls With Buffalo Sauce 114
Chicken Pizza On The Grill 24
Chicken Pot Pie 20
Chicken Tenders 107
Chicken Wings With Teriyaki Glaze 159
Chili Cheese Fries 21
Chinese Alcoholic Bbq Pork Tenderloin 65
Chocolate Lava Cake With Smoked Whipped Cream 30
Chocolate Peanut Cookies 37
Chorizo Queso Fundido 161
Christmas Brussel Sprouts 156
Chuck Roast Burnt Ends 199
Chuckwagon Beef Jerky 163
Cider Glazed Baked Holiday Ham 50
Cider Hot-smoked Salmon 85
Cider-brined Turkey 123
Cinnamon Pull-aparts 15
Citrus Grilled Lamb Chops 183
Citrus-infused Marinated Olives 161
Citrus-smoked Trout 97
Classic Pulled Pork 70
Coconut Shrimp Jalapeño Poppers 97
Cold-smoked Cheese 166
Cornbread Chicken Stuffing 22
Cornish Game Hens 131
County Fair Turkey Legs 129
Cran-apple Tequila Punch With Smoked Oranges 174
Cranberry Turkey Breast 130
Crème Brûlée 37
Crescent Rolls 34
Crispy Spiced Chicken Wings 106
Crown Roast Of Pork 64

Cuban Onion Pork Sandwich 65

D

Dark Chocolate Brownies With Bacon-salted Caramel 43
Delicious Barbecue Beef Brisket 195
Delicious Deviled Crab Appetizer 165
Delicious Pulled Pork Poutine 66
Delicious Reverse Seared Picanha Steak 193
Delicious Smoked Bone-in Pork Chops 51
Delicious Smoked Trout 85
Deviled Eggs With Smoked Paprika 162
Diva Q's Herb-crusted Prime Rib 203
Donut Bread Pudding 16
Double Smoked Apple Spiral Ham 51
Double Vanilla Chocolate Cake 24
Double-smoked Cheese Potatoes 146
Dry Rub Grilled Ribs 68
Dublin Delight Cocktail 176
Duck Fat Fries (confit) 182

E

Easy Bbq Chicken Wings 116
Easy Breakfast Cheeseburger 196
Easy Grilled Chicken Shawarma 125
Easy Rapid-fire Roast Chicken 107
Egg Sausage Casserole 49
Eggs Ham Benedict 33
Everything Pigs In A Blanket 48
Eyeball Cookies 15

F

Fast Bbq Spare Ribs 57
Fig Slider Cocktail 172
Flank Steak Breakfast Potato Burrito 194
Flavour Bbq Brisket Burnt Ends 186
Flavour Fire Spiced Shrimp 86
Flavour Memphis Bbq Beef Brisket 190
Flavour Texas Twinkies 193
Florentine Shrimp Al Cartoccio 89
Focaccia 20
Fried Chicken Sliders 125

G

Garden Gimlet Cocktail 170

Garlic Bacon Wrapped Shrimp 95
Garlic Blackened Catfish 78
Garlic Blackened Salmon 99
Garlic Cheese Bacon Burger 200
Garlic Cheese Pull Apart Bread 31
Garlic Grilled Shrimp Skewers 83
Garlic Lemon Pepper Chicken Wings 36
Garlic Pigs In A Blanket 195
Garlic Prime Rib Roast 205
Garlic Sriracha Buffalo Chicken Wings 127
Gen's Old-fashioned Barbecued Chicken 119
Glazed Bbq Half Chicken 106
Green Bean Casserole 155
Green Bean Casserole Circa 1955 39
Green Bell Pepper Cheese Steak Burger 203
Green Chile Chicken Enchiladas 113
Green Goddess Chicken Legs 124
Grilled Albacore Tuna With Potato-tomato Casserole 77
Grilled Apple Pie 30
Grilled Artichoke Cheese Salmon 99
Grilled Asparagus & Honey-glazed Carrots 144
Grilled Asparagus And Hollandaise Sauce 135
Grilled Asparagus And Spinach Salad 138
Grilled Bacon Dog 71
Grilled Beantown Chicken Wings 119
Grilled Beer Cabbage 154
Grilled Bell Pepper Flank Steak Fajitas 193
Grilled Blackened Saskatchewan Salmon 104
Grilled Blood Orange Mimosa 168
Grilled Bourbon Pecan Pie 31
Grilled Brisket Burger 200
Grilled Broccoli Rabe 153
Grilled Cabbage Steaks With Warm Bacon Vinaigrette 156
Grilled Chili-lime Corn 151
Grilled Corn On The Cob With Parmesan And Garlic 136
Grilled Crab Legs With Herb Butter 84
Grilled Dr. Pepper Ribs 63
Grilled Fingerling Potato Salad 148
Grilled Fresh Fish 97
Grilled Frozen Strawberry Lemonade 171

Grilled Garlic Shrimp With Cajun Dip 77

Grilled German Sausage With A Smoky Traeger Twist 73

Grilled Guacamole 161

Grilled Hand Pulled Chicken 105

Grilled Hawaiian Sour 170

Grilled Honey Chicken Kabobs 127

Grilled Lemon Lobster Tails 98

Grilled Lemon Salmon 99

Grilled Lemon Shrimp Scampi 101

Grilled Lobster Tails With Smoked Paprika Butter 88

Grilled Maple Syrup Salmon 96

Grilled Mussels With Lemon Butter 80

Grilled Oysters With Mignonette 100

Grilled Parmesan Chicken Wings 121

Grilled Peach Mint Julep 176

Grilled Peach Smash Cocktail 179

Grilled Peach Sour Cocktail 169

Grilled Pepper Lobster Tails 91

Grilled Pork Belly 55

Grilled Pork Loin 56

Grilled Pork Tacos Al Pastor 59

Grilled Rabbit Tail Cocktail 177

Grilled Raspberry Chipotle Pork Ribs 56

Grilled Ratatouille Salad 140

Grilled Salmon 78

Grilled Salmon Gravlax 103

Grilled Salmon Steaks With Dill Sauce 102

Grilled Shrimp Brochette 88

Grilled Street Corn 134

Grilled Whole Steelhead Fillet 83

Grilled Zucchini Squash Spears 141

H

Hanging St. Louis-style Grilled Ribs 53

Herb Grilled Venison Stew 184

Hickory Smoked Pork Shoulder 47

Holiday Smoked Cheese Log 60

Home-cured Hickory-smoked Bacon 67

Honey Balsamic Salmon 97

Honey Glazed Grapefruit Shandy Cocktail 178

Honey Glazed Pork Chops 60

Honey-soy Garlic Salmon 77

I

In Traeger Fashion Cocktail 167

Injected Drunken Smoked Turkey Legs 129

Irish Soda Bread 16

Italian Beef Pinwheels 186

Italian Herb & Parmesan Scones 26

J

Jalapeño- & Cheese-stuffed Chicken 112

Jalapeno Cheddar Smoked Sausages 62

Jalapeno Chicken Sliders 109

Jalapeño Poppers With Chipotle Sour Cream 165

Jalapeño-bacon Pork Tenderloin 62

Jamaican Jerk Chicken Quarters 111

Juicy Jerk Chicken Kebabs 117

K

Kansas City Cheese Brisket Burger 196

Kansas City Hot Fried Chicken 114

Kimi's Simple Grilled Fresh Fish 87

Korean Pulled Pork Lettuce Wraps 61

L

Leftover Pulled Pork With Eggs 66

Lemon Cajun Chicken Carbonara 111

Lemon Chicken Breast 120

Lemon Chicken, Broccoli, String Beans Foil Packs 35

Lemon Herb Grilled Salmon 88

Lemon Lobster Rolls 90

Lemon Parmesan Chicken Wings 126

Lemon Scallops Wrapped In Bacon 98

Lemon Shrimp Scampi 82

Lemon Strawberry Rhubarb Pie 32

Lime Carne Asada Tacos 184

Lip-smackin' Pork Loin 63

Loaded Chicken Fries 112

Lobster Tail 91

Lynchburg Bacon 70

M

Mango Rice Wine Thai Shrimp 104

Maple Baked Ham 57

Maple Syrup Pancake Casserole 34

Maple-smoked Pork Chops 64

Marbled Brownies With Amaretto & Ricotta 44

Marinated Grilled Honey Chicken Wings 121
Mashed Red Potatoes 145
Mexican Mahi Mahi With Baja Cabbage Slaw 92
Mezcal Shrimp With Salsa De Molcajete 81
Mint Butter Chocolate Chip Cookies 17
Moules Marinières With Garlic Butter Sauce 80

N
Naked Juicy Lucy Burgers With Special Sauce 188

O
Old Fashioned Cornbread 28
Onion Cheese Nachos 42
Onion Pork Shoulder 52
Onion Turkey Burger Sliders 117
Orange & Maple Baked Ham 75
Oysters In The Shell 95
Oysters Margarita 79

P
Pacific Northwest Salmon 78
Parmesan Roasted Cauliflower 139
Pastrami 198
Peanut Butter Chicken Wings 109
Peper Fish Tacos 101
Philly Cheese Onion Steaks 186
Pickle Brined Grilled Pork Chops 71
Pig On A Stick With Buffalo Glaze 68
Pig Pops (sweet-hot Bacon On A Stick) 163
Pigs In A Blanket 162
Pineapple Cake 41
Pizza Bites 44
Planked Trout With Fennel, Bacon & Orange 94
Pork & Pepperoni Burgers 75
Pork Loin Porchetta 61
Portobello Marinated Mushroom 146
Potluck Salad With Smoked Cornbread 142
Pretzel Rolls 45
Prosciutto-wrapped Scallops 89
Pull-apart Dinner Rolls 37
Pulled Beef 208
Pulled Pork Corn Tortillas 66
Pulled Pork Loaded Nachos 160
Pulled Pork Shoulder And Chicken 73
Pumpkin Bread 26

Q
Quick Baked Dinner Rolls 33

R
Red Potato Grilled Lollipops 138
Reverse-seared Steaks 196
Reverse-seared Tri-tip 191
Roasted Artichokes With Garlic Butter 141
Roasted Asparagus 134
Roasted Beer Can Chicken 118
Roasted Beet & Bacon Salad 148
Roasted Christmas Goose 115
Roasted Do-ahead Mashed Potatoes 157
Roasted Fall Vegetables 152
Roasted Garlic Herb Fries 141
Roasted Green Beans With Bacon 146
Roasted Halibut With Spring Vegetables 95
Roasted Hasselback Potatoes By Doug Scheiding 133
Roasted Honey Bourbon Glazed Turkey 111
Roasted Jalapeno Cheddar Deviled Eggs 147
Roasted Jalapeño Poppers 146
Roasted Mashed Potatoes 133
Roasted New Potatoes 144
Roasted New Potatoes With Compound Butter 154
Roasted Olives 138
Roasted Pickled Beets 148
Roasted Potato Poutine 133
Roasted Prime Rib 194
Roasted Prosciutto Stuffed Chicken 124
Roasted Pumpkin Seeds 137
Roasted Red Pepper Dip 164
Roasted Red Pepper White Bean Dip 157
Roasted Sheet Pan Vegetables 143
Roasted Sweet Potato Steak Fries 143
Roasted Tomatoes 150
Roasted Tomatoes With Hot Pepper Sauce 155
Roasted Vegetable Napoleon 145
Roasted Venison Steaks By The Bowmars 203
Rosemary Cranberry Apple Sage Stuffing 24
Rosemary Prime Rib 183
Rub-injected Pork Shoulder 48
Ryes And Shine Cocktail 168

S

S'mores Dip Skillet 41
Salmon Cakes With Homemade Tartar Sauce 83
Salt & Pepper Dinosaur Bones 196
Salt Crusted Baked Potatoes 134
Santa Maria Tri-tip With Pico De Gallo 188
Savory Bacon Wrapped Hot Dogs 197
Savory Cheesecake With Bourbon Pecan Topping 43
Savory Chili Mac And Cheese 183
Savory Pork Belly Banh Mi 74
Savory Reverse Seared Ny Steak 192
Savory Smoked Brisket 201
Savory Smoked Turkey Legs 115
Savory Teriyaki Smoked Steak Bites 185
Savory-sweet Turkey Legs 112
Seared Ahi Tuna Steak With Soy Sauce 102
Seared Bluefin Tuna Steaks 86
Shrimp Cabbage Tacos With Lime Cream 85
Sicilian Stuffed Mushrooms 155
Simple Cream Cheese Sausage Balls 162
Simple Glazed Salmon Fillets 77
Simple Smoked Ribs 47
Sirloin Steak 187
Skillet Buttermilk Cornbread 43
Skillet Potato Cake 153
Slow Smoked And Roasted Prime Rib 205
Slow Smoked Rib-eye Roast 207
Smo-fried Chicken 108
Smoke And Bubz Cocktail 180
Smoked & Loaded Baked Potato 150
Smoked Airline Chicken 107
Smoked Apple Cider 168
Smoked Apple Pork Belly 57
Smoked Asparagus Soup 136
Smoked Avocado Turkey Tamale Pie 108
Smoked Baby Back Ribs 57
Smoked Bacon Brisket Flat 208
Smoked Barnburner Cocktail 175
Smoked Bbq Onion Brussels Sprout 156
Smoked Beer Brisket 204
Smoked Beet-pickled Eggs 151
Smoked Berry Cocktail 167
Smoked Black Pepper Beef Ribs 187
Smoked Blackberry Pie 39

Smoked Blt Sandwich 74
Smoked Bologna 58
Smoked Boneless Chicken Thighs 106
Smoked Bourbon & Orange Brined Turkey 126
Smoked Bourbon Jerky 202
Smoked Brisket 187
Smoked Cashews 163
Smoked Cheese 164
Smoked Cheesy Alfredo Sauce 23
Smoked Cheesy Chicken Quesadilla 118
Smoked Chicken Fajita Quesadillas 125
Smoked Chicken Leg & Thigh Quarters 109
Smoked Chicken Steak Sandwiches 198
Smoked Chicken With Apricot Bbq Glaze 132
Smoked Chili Con Queso By Doug Scheiding 51
Smoked Cold Brew Coffee 174
Smoked Crab Legs 91
Smoked Deviled Eggs 105
Smoked Ditch Chicken 130
Smoked Drumsticks 107
Smoked Eggnog 179
Smoked Garlic Meatloaf 189
Smoked Garlic Prime Rib Roast 202
Smoked Grape Lime Rickey 178
Smoked Hibiscus Sparkler 174
Smoked Honey Salmon 80
Smoked Hot Buttered Rum 169
Smoked Ice Mojito Slurpee 171
Smoked Irish Coffee 176
Smoked Jacobsen Salt Margarita 175
Smoked Jalapeño Poppers 145
Smoked Lemon Cheesecake 40
Smoked Lobster Scampi 93
Smoked Macaroni Salad 137
Smoked Mango Shrimp 84
Smoked Mashed Potatoes 151
Smoked Moink Burger By Scott Thomas 188
Smoked Mulled Wine 171
Smoked Mushrooms 144
Smoked Parmesan Herb Popcorn 140
Smoked Peppered Beef Tenderloin 192
Smoked Pheasant 184
Smoked Pickled Green Beans 142

Smoked Pico De Gallo 136
Smoked Pineapple Hotel Nacional Cocktail 175
Smoked Plum And Thyme Fizz Cocktail 178
Smoked Pomegranate Lemonade Cocktail 170
Smoked Porchetta 54
Smoked Pork Tomato Tamales 46
Smoked Prime Rib 191
Smoked Pumpkin Spice Latte 172
Smoked Quarters 120
Smoked Rack Of Pork 49
Smoked Raspberry Bubbler Cocktail 180
Smoked Salt Cured Lox 94
Smoked Salted Caramel White Russian 173
Smoked Sangria 172
Smoked Sirloin Roast Beef 207
Smoked Spatchcocked Cornish Game Hens 110
Smoked Spiced Beef Pot Roast 192
Smoked Stuffed Avocado Recipe 69
Smoked Sugar Halibut 96
Smoked Sweet Beer Bread 22
Smoked Texas Ranch Water 176
Smoked Thanksgiving Turkey 123
Smoked Tomato Brisket Chili 206
Smoked Turkey 121
Smoked Turkey Breast 111
Smoked Turkey Legs 114
Smoked Turkey Sandwich 165
Smoked Turkey Wings 116
Smoked Vanilla Apple Pie 26
Smoked Whiskey Peach Pulled Chicken 131
Smoked Whole Chicken 129
Smoked, Salted Caramel Apple Pie 19
Smoker Wheat Bread 32
Smoke-roasted Beer-braised Brats 58
Smoke-roasted Halibut With Mixed Herb Vinaigrette 99
Smokin' Lemon Bars 38
Smoking Gun Cocktail 167
Smoky Apple Crepes 22
Smoky Crab Dip 93
Smoky Mountain Bramble Cocktail 180
Smoky Pimento Cheese Cornbread 30
Smoky Pork Tenderloin 69

Smoky Scotch & Ginger Cocktail 173
Sopapilla Cheesecake By Doug Scheiding 33
Sourdough Pizza 29
Spatchcocked Chicken With White Barbecue Sauce 110
Spatchcocked Turkey 128
Spiced Bbq Turkey 123
Spiced Carrot Cake 21
Spiced Cowboy Steak 199
Spiced Grilled Pork Chops 46
Spiced Lemon Cherry Pie 25
Spiced Orange Ribs 47
Spiced Smoked Chicken Quarters 105
Spiced Smoked Kielbasa Dogs 197
Spiced Smoked Swordfish 103
Spicy Asian Brussels Sprouts 154
Spicy Bacon Wrapped Grilled Chicken Skewers 49
Spicy Crab Poppers 86
Spicy Lime Shrimp 102
Spicy Ribs 59
Spicy Shrimp Skewers 93
Spicy Smoked Chili Beef Jerky 204
Sriracha & Maple Cashews 165
St. Louis–style Pork Steaks 55
Steak Fries With Horseradish Creme 139
Strawberry Basil Daiquiri 18
Strawberry Mule Cocktail 169
Stuffed Jalapenos 137
Succulent Lamb Chops 204
Summer Paella 101
Sunset Margarita 168
Sweet And Spicy Baked Pork Beans 40
Sweet And Spicy Pork Roast 75
Sweet And Spicy Smoked Wings 113
Sweet Bacon 72
Sweet Cheese Muffins 21
Sweet Potato Marshmallow Casserole 142
Sweet Smoked Salmon Jerky 82
Sweetheart Steak 201
Swordfish With Sicilian Olive Oil Sauce 90

T

Tater Tot Bake 149

Tequila & Lime Shrimp With Smoked Tomato Sauce 82

Teriyaki Deer Jerky 191

Teriyaki Smoked Honey Tilapia 84

Texas Style Smoked Beer Brisket 208

Thai-style Swordfish Steaks With Peanut Sauce 98

The Dan Patrick Show Chorizo Armadillo Eggs 68

The Dan Patrick Show Pull-apart Pesto Bread 34

The Grilled Chicken Challenge 108

The Perfect T-bones 188

Traeger Baked Focaccia 28

Traeger Baked Potato Torte 136

Traeger Baked Protein Bars 44

Traeger Baked Rainbow Trout 90

Traeger Boulevardier Cocktail 177

Traeger Crab Legs 81

Traeger Gin & Tonic 179

Traeger Grilled Whole Corn 149

Traeger Mandarin Wings 127

Traeger Old Fashioned 177

Traeger Paloma Cocktail 178

Traeger Pulled Pork Sandwiches 52

Traeger Smoked Coleslaw 135

Traeger Smoked Daiquiri 167

Traeger Smoked Salmon 89

Triple Threat Pork Fattywith Stuffed Jalapeños 69

Twice-smoked Potatoes 134

U

Ultimate Baked Garlic Bread 35

V

Vanilla Cheesecake Skillet Brownie 41

Vanilla Chocolate Bacon Cupcakes 34

Vanilla Chocolate Chip Cookies 27

Vodka Brined Smoked Wild Salmon 91

W

Wagyu Corned Beef Hash 181

Wet-rubbed St. Louis Ribs 58

Whole Hog 70

Whole Roasted Cauliflower With Garlic Parmesan Butter 147

Whole Smoked Honey Chicken 122

Whole Vermillion Red Snapper 83

Wild West Wings 110

Wood-fired Chicken Breasts 132

Wood-fired Halibut 96

Y

Yucatán-spiced Chicken Thighs 120

Z

Zombie Cocktail Recipe 169

Zucchini Bread 27

Zucchini Onion Meatloaf 206